K. J. POWERS

MANAGEMENT COMMUNICATION
A Case-Analysis Approach

James S. O'Rourke, IV

Director, The Eugene D. Fanning Center for Business Communication
Mendoza College of Business
University of Notre Dame

Upper Saddle River, New Jersey 07458

Library of Congress Cataloging-in-Publication Data

O'Rourke, James S., IV
    Management communication: a case-analysis approach / James S. O'Rourke IV.—1st ed.
      p. cm.
    Includes bibliographical references and index.
    ISBN 0-13-010996-7
      1. Communication in management. 2. Communication in management—Case studies.
I. Title.

HD30.3.O766 2001
658.4′5—dc21   00-034700

Vice President/Editorial Director: James Boyd
Senior Editor: Linda Schreiber
Editorial Assistant: Virginia Sheridan
Assistant Editor: Jennifer Surich
Media Project Manager: Michele Faranda
Senior Marketing Manager: Debbie Clare
Production/Manufacturing Manager: Gail Steier de Acevedo
Production Coordinator: Maureen Wilson
Senior Prepress/Manufacturing Manager: Vincent Scelta
Manufacturing Buyer: Natacha St. Hill Moore
Cover Design: Bruce Kenselaar
Composition: Carlisle Communications Ltd.

10 9 8 7 6 5 4 3 2 1
ISBN 0-13-010996-7

To those who matter most in my life: Pam, Colleen, Molly, and Kathleen. My success in life would have been impossible without you and meaningless had it happened by chance. You are the reason I write.

To my colleagues: Carolyn, Sandra, Renee, and Cynthia. You are among many who have inspired me, corrected me, kept me honest, and held me accountable for my ideas. And to my friends in MCA and the Arthur Page Society: Thank you for the encouragement, counsel, and good ideas. My life has been richer for having shared your company.

CONTENTS

❧

PREFACE

Many years ago, as an Air Force officer assigned to a flight test group in the American Southwest, I had the opportunity to speak with an older (and obviously wiser) man who had been in the flying business for many years. Our conversation focused on what it would take for a young officer to succeed—to become a leader, a recognized influence among talented, trained, and well-educated peers. His words were prophetic: "I can think of no skill more essential to the survival of a young officer," he said, "than effective self-expression." That was it. Not physical courage or well-honed flying skills. Not advanced degrees or specialized training, but "effective self-expression."

In the years since that conversation, I have personally been witness to what young managers call "career moments." Those are moments in time when a carefully crafted proposal, a thorough report, or a deft response to criticism have saved a career. I've seen young men and women offered a job as a result of an especially skillful speech introduction. I've seen others sputter and stall when they couldn't answer a direct question—one that fell well within their area of expertise—during a briefing. I've watched in horror as others simply talked their way into disfavor, trouble, or oblivion.

Communication is, without question, the central skill any manager can possess. It is the link between ideas and action. It is the process that generates profit. It is the emotional glue that binds humans together in relationships, personal and professional. It is, as the poet William Blake put it, "the chariot of genius." To be without the ability to communicate is to be isolated from others in an organization, an industry, or a society. To be skilled at it is to be at the heart of what makes enterprise, private and public, function successfully.

The fundamental premise on which this book is based is simple: communication is a skill which can be learned, taught, and improved. You have the potential to be better at communicating with other people than you now are. It won't be easy, but this book can certainly help. The very fact that you've gotten this far is evidence that you're determined to succeed, and what follows is a systematic yet readable review of those things you'll need to pay closer attention to in order to experience success as a manager.

What This Book Is About. This book will focus on the processes involved in management communication and concentrate on ways in which business students and entry-level managers can become more effective by becoming more knowledgeable and skilled as communicators.

The second premise on which this book is based is also simple: writing, speaking, listening, and other communication behaviors are the end-products of a process that begins with critical thinking. It is this process that managers are called on to employ every day in the workplace to earn a living. The basic task of a manager, day in and day out, is to solve managerial problems. The basic tools at a manager's disposal are mostly rhetorical.

Management Communication supports learning objectives that are strategic in nature, evolving as the workplace changes to meet the demands of a global economy that is changing at a ferocious pace. What you will find in these pages assumes certain basic competencies in communication, but encourages growth and development as you encounter the responsibilities and opportunities of mid-level and higher management, whether in your own business or in large and complex, publicly-traded organizations.

What's Different About This Book.   This book is aimed directly at the way most professors of management communication teach, yet in a number of important ways is different from other books in this field.

First, the process is entirely strategic. We begin with the somewhat non-traditional view that all communication processes in successful businesses in this century will be fully integrated. What happens in one part of the business affects all others. What is said to one audience has outcomes which influence others. Without an integrated, strategic perspective, managers in the New Economy will find themselves working at cross-purposes, often to the detriment of their businesses.

Second, the approach offered in *Management Communication* integrates ethics and the process of ethical decision-making into each aspect of the discipline. Many instructors feel either helpless or slightly uncomfortable teaching ethics in a business classroom. Yet, day after day, business managers find themselves confronted with ethical dilemmas and decisions that have moral consequences for their employees, customers, shareholders, and other important stakeholders.

This text doesn't moralize or preach. Instead, it offers a relatively simple framework for ethical decision-making that students and faculty alike will find easy to grasp. Throughout the book, especially in case studies and role-playing exercises, you will learn to ask questions that focus on the issues that matter most to your classmates and colleagues. The answers won't come easily, but the process of confronting the issues will make you a better manager.

Third, this text includes separate chapters on Listening and Feedback, as well as Communicating Nonverbally, Communicating in Intercultural and International Contexts, and Managing Conflict. These are topics that are often either ignored or shortchanged in other texts. Interpersonal communication skills such as these are clearly central to the relationship-building and personal influence all managers tell us they find indispensable to their careers.

Finally, *Management Communication* examines the often tenuous but unavoidable relationship that business organizations and their managers have with the news media. A step-by-step approach is presented to help you develop strategies and manage relationships—in both good news and bad news situations. Surviving a close encounter with a reporter while telling your company's story—fairly, accurately, and completely—may mean the difference between a career that advances and one that does not.

The Added Value of a Case Study Approach.   You will observe that each chapter of this book contains at least two original, classroom-tested case studies that will challenge you to discuss and apply the principles outlined in the chapter. Some chapters include role-playing exercises. You'll find an appendix entitled "Analyzing a Case Study" that will introduce you to the reasons business students find such value in cases and show you how to get the most from those included in this book. A rich, interesting case study is always an opportunity—to show what you know about business and communication, to learn from your professors and classmates, and to examine the intricate processes at work when humans go into business together. Reading and analyzing a case are always useful, but the more profound insights inevitably come from listening carefully as others discuss and defend their views.

The Rest Is Up to You.   What you take from this book and how you use it to become shrewder and more adept at the skills a manager needs most is really up to you. Simply reading the principles, looking through the examples, or talking about the case studies with your friends and classmates won't be enough. You'll need to look for ways to apply what you have learned, to put into practice the precepts articulated by successful executives and discussed at length in this book. The joy of developing and using those skills, however, comes in the relationships you will develop and the success you will experience throughout your business career and beyond. These aren't simply essential skills for learning how to earn a living. They're strategies for learning how to live.

1

MANAGEMENT COMMUNICATION IN TRANSITION

This book will argue that Management Communication is the central skill in the global workplace of the twenty-first century. An understanding of language and its inherent powers, combined with the skill to speak, write, listen, and form interpersonal relationships, will determine whether or not you will succeed as a manager.

At the mid-point of the twentieth century, management philosopher Peter Drucker wrote, "Managers have to learn to know language, to understand what words are and what they mean. Perhaps most important, they have to acquire respect for language as [our] most precious gift and heritage. The manager must understand the meaning of the old definition of rhetoric as 'the art which draws men's hearts to the love of true knowledge.' "[1]

Later in the twentieth century, Harvard Business School professors Robert Eccles and Nitin Nohria re-framed Drucker's view to offer a view of management that few others have seen. "To see management in its proper light," they write, "managers need first to take language seriously."[2] In particular, they argue, a coherent view of management must focus on three issues: the use of rhetoric to achieve a manager's goals, the shaping of a managerial identity, and taking action to achieve the goals of the organizations that employ us. Above all, they say, "the essence of what management is all about [is] the effective use of language to *get things done.*"[3]

The job of becoming a competent, effective manager thus becomes one of understanding language and action. It also involves finding ways to shape how others see and think of you in your role as a manager. A number of noted researchers have examined the important relationship between communication and action within large and complex organizations and conclude that the two are inseparable. Without the right words, used in the right way, it is unlikely that the right actions will ever occur. "Words *do* matter," write Eccles and Nohria, "they matter very much. Without words we have no way of expressing strategic concepts, structural forms, or designs for performance measurement systems." Language, they conclude, "is too important to managers to be taken for granted or, even worse, abused."[4]

So, if language is a manager's key to effective action, the next question is obvious: How good are *you* at using your language? Your ability to take action—to hire people, to restructure an organization, to launch a new product line—depends entirely on how effectively you use rhetoric, both as a speaker *and* as a listener. Your effectiveness as a speaker and writer will determine how well you are able to get others to do what you want. And your effectiveness as a listener will determine how well you understand others and can do things for them.

This book will examine the role language plays in the life of a manager and the central position occupied by rhetoric in the life of business organizations. In particular, though, this book will help you examine your own skills, abilities, and competencies as you use language, attempt to influence others, and respond to the requirements of your superiors and the organization where you work.

Management Communication is about the movement of information and the skills which facilitate it—speaking, writing, listening, and processes of critical thinking—but it's more than just skill, really. It's also about understanding who you are, who others think you are, and the contributions you as an individual can make to the success of your business. It's about confidence—the knowledge that you *can* speak and write well, that you *can* listen with great skill as others speak, and that you *can* both seek out and provide the feedback essential to your survival as a manager and a leader.

This chapter will first look at the nature of managerial work, examining both the roles managers play and the characteristics of the jobs they hold. We'll also look at what varies in a manager's position, what is different from one manager's job to another. And we'll look at the management skills you will need to succeed in the years ahead. At the heart of this chapter, though, is the notion that communication, in many ways *is* the work of managers, day in and day out. This book will go on to examine the roles of writing and speaking in your life as a manager, as well as other specific applications and challenges you will face as you grow and advance on the job.

WHAT DO MANAGERS DO ALL DAY?

If you were to consult a number of management textbooks for advice on the nature of managerial work, many—if not most—would say that managers spend their time engaged in planning, organizing, staffing, directing, coordinating, reporting, and controlling. These activities, as Jane Hannaway found in her study of managers at work, "do not, in fact, describe what managers do."[5] At best they seem to describe vague objectives for managers which they are continually trying to accomplish. The real world, however, is far from being that simple. The world in which most managers work is a "messy and hectic stream of ongoing activity."[6]

Managers are in constant action. Virtually every study of managers in action has found that they "switch frequently from task to task, changing their focus of attention to respond to issues as they arise, and engaging in a large volume of tasks of short duration."[7] Professor Harvey Mintzberg of McGill University observed CEOs on the job to get some idea of what they do and how they spend their time. He found, for instance, that they averaged 36 written and 16 verbal contacts per day, almost every one of them dealing with a distinct or different issue. Most of these activities were brief, lasting less than nine minutes.[8]

More recently, managers studied by Lee Sproull showed similar patterns. During the course of a day, they engaged in 58 different activities with an average duration of just nine minutes.[9] Interruptions also appear to be a natural part of the job. Rosemary Stewart found that the managers she studied could work uninterrupted for half an hour only nine times during the four weeks she studied them.[10] Managers, in fact, spend very little time by themselves. Contrary to the image offered by management textbooks, they are rarely alone drawing up plans or worrying about important decisions. Instead, they spend most of their time interacting with others—both inside and outside the organization. If you include casual interactions in hallways, phone conversations, one-on-one meetings, and larger group meetings, managers spend about two-thirds of their time with other people.[11] As Mintzberg has pointed out, "Unlike other workers, the manager does not leave the telephone or the meeting to get back to work. Rather, these contacts *are* his work."[12]

The interactive nature of management means that most management work is conversational.[13] When managers are in action, they are talking and listening. Studies on the nature of managerial work indicate that managers spend about two-thirds to three-quarters of their time in verbal activity.[14] These verbal conversations, according to Eccles and Nohria, are the means by which managers gather information, stay on top of things, identify problems, negotiate shared meanings, develop plans, put things in motion, give orders, assert authority, develop relationships, and spread gossip. In short, they are what the manager's daily practice is all about. "Through other forms of talk, such as speeches and presentations," they write, "managers establish definitions and meanings for their own actions and give others a sense of what the organization is about, where it is at, and what it is up to."[15]

THE ROLES MANAGERS PLAY

In Professor Mintzberg's seminal study of managers and their jobs, he found the majority of them clustered around three core management roles.

Interpersonal Roles   Managers are required to interact with a substantial number of people in the course of a workweek. They host receptions; take clients and customers to dinner; meet with business prospects and partners; conduct hiring and performance interviews; and form alliances, friendships, and personal relationships with many others. Numerous studies have shown that such relationships are the richest source of information for managers because of their immediate and personal nature.[16]

Three of a manager's roles arise directly from formal authority and involve basic interpersonal relationships. First is the *figurehead* role. As the head of an organizational unit, every manager must perform some ceremonial duties. In Mintzberg's study, chief executives spent 12 percent of their contact time on ceremonial duties; 17 percent of their incoming mail dealt with acknowledgments and requests related to their status. One example is a company president who requested free merchandise for a crippled schoolchild.[17]

Managers are also responsible for the work of the people in their unit, and their actions in this regard are directly related to their role as a *leader.* The influence of managers is most clearly seen, according to Mintzberg, in the leader role. Formal authority vests them with great potential power. Leadership determines, in large part, how much power they will realize.[18]

Does the leader's role matter? Ask the employees of Chrysler Corporation. When Lee Iacocca took over the company in the 1980s, the once-great auto manufacturer was in bankruptcy, teetering on the verge of extinction. He formed new relationships with the United Auto Workers, reorganized the senior management of the company, and—perhaps, most importantly—convinced the U.S. Federal Government to guarantee a series of bank loans that would make the company solvent again. The loan guarantees, the union response, and the reaction of the marketplace were due in large measure to Iacocca's leadership style and personal charisma.

Popular management literature has had little to say about the *liaison* role until recently. But this role, in which managers establish and maintain contacts outside of the vertical chain of command, becomes especially important in view of the finding of virtually every study of managerial work that managers spend as much time with peers and other people outside of their units as they do with their own subordinates. Surprisingly, they spend very little time with their own superiors. In Rosemary Stewart's study, 160 British middle and top managers spent 47 percent of their time with peers, 41 percent of their time with people inside their unit, and only 12 percent of their time with superiors.[19] Robert H. Guest's study of U.S. manufacturing foremen revealed similar findings.[20]

Informational Roles   Managers are required to gather, collate, analyze, store, and disseminate many kinds of information. In doing so, they become information resource centers, often storing huge amounts of information in their own heads, moving quickly from the role of gatherer to the role of disseminator in minutes. Although large, expensive management information systems have been installed in most business organizations to perform many of those functions, nothing can match the speed and intuitive power of a well-trained manager's brain for information processing. Not surprisingly, most managers prefer it that way.[21]

As *monitors,* managers are constantly scanning the environment for information, talking with liaison contacts and subordinates, and receiving unsolicited information, much of it as a result of their network of personal contacts. A good portion of this information arrives in verbal form, often as gossip, hearsay, and speculation.[22]

In the *disseminator* role, managers pass privileged information directly to subordinates, who might otherwise have no access to it. Managers must also decide not only who should receive such information, but how much of it, how often, and in what form. Increasingly, managers are being asked to decide whether subordinates, peers, customers, business partners, and others should have direct access to information 24 hours a day without having to contact the manager directly.

In the *spokesperson* role, managers send information to people outside of their organizations: An executive makes a speech to lobby for an organizational cause, or a foreman suggests a product modification to a supplier. Increasingly, managers are also being asked to deal with representatives of the news media, providing both factual and opinion-based responses that will be printed or broadcast to vast unseen audiences, often directly or with very little editing. The risks in such circumstances are enormous, but so too are the potential rewards in terms of brand recognition, public image, and organizational visibility.

Decisional Roles   Ultimately, managers are charged with the responsibility of making decisions on behalf of both the organization and the stakeholders with an interest in it. Such decisions are often made under circumstances of high ambiguity and with inadequate information. Often, the other two managerial roles—interpersonal and informational—will assist a manager in making difficult decisions in which outcomes are not clear and interests are often conflicting.

In the role of *entrepreneur,* managers seek to improve their businesses, adapt to changing market conditions, and react to opportunities as they present themselves. Managers who take a longer-term view of their responsibilities are among the first to realize that they will need to reinvent themselves, their product/service lines, their marketing strategies, and their ways of doing business as older methods become obsolete and competitors gain advantage.

While the entrepreneur role describes managers who initiate change, the *disturbance or crisis handler* role depicts managers who must involuntarily react to conditions. Crises can arise because bad managers let circumstances deteriorate or spin out of control, but just as often good managers find themselves in the midst of a crisis that they could not have anticipated but must react to just the same.

The third decisional role of *resource allocator* involves managers making decisions about who gets what, how much, when, and why. Resources, including funding, equipment, human labor, office or production space, and even the boss' time are all limited, and demand inevitably outstrips supply. Managers must make sensible decisions about such matters while still retaining, motivating, and developing the best of their employees.

The final decisional role is that of *negotiator.* Managers spend considerable amounts of time in negotiations: over budget allocations, labor and collective bargaining agreements, and other formal dispute resolutions. Often, though, managers will make dozens of decisions in the course of a week which are the result of brief but important negotiations between and among employees, customers and clients, suppliers, and others with whom managers must deal.[23]

MAJOR CHARACTERISTICS OF THE MANAGER'S JOB

Time Is Fragmented   Managers have acknowledged from antiquity that there never seems to be enough time to get all those things done that need to be done. In the latter years of the twentieth century, however, a new phenomenon arose: Demand for time from those in leadership roles increased, while the number of hours in a day remained constant. Increased work hours was one reaction to such demand, but managers quickly discovered that the day had just 24 hours and that working more of them produced diminishing marginal returns. According to one researcher, "Managers are overburdened with obligations yet cannot easily delegate their tasks. As a result, they are driven to overwork and forced to do many tasks superficially. Brevity, fragmentation, and verbal communication characterize their work."[24]

Values Compete and the Various Roles Are in Tension   Managers clearly cannot satisfy everyone. Employees want more time to do their jobs; customers want products and services delivered quickly and at high-quality levels. Supervisors want more money to spend on equipment, training, and product development; shareholders want returns on investment maximized. A manager caught in the middle cannot deliver to each of these people what each most wants; decisions are often based on the urgency of the need and the proximity of the problem.

The Job Is Overloaded   During the 1980s and 1990s, many North American and transnational organizations were reorganized to make them more efficient, nimble, and competitive. For the most part, this meant decentralization of many processes along with the wholesale elimination of middle management layers. Many managers who survived such downsizing found that their number of direct reports had doubled. Classical management theory suggests that seven is the maximum number of direct reports a manager can reasonably handle. Today, high-speed data processing and remarkably efficient telecommunication systems mean that many managers have as many as 20 or 30 people reporting to them directly.

Efficiency Is a Core Skill   With less time than they need, with time fragmented into increasingly smaller units during the workday, with the workplace following many managers out the door and even on vacation, and with many more responsibilities loaded onto managers in downsized, flatter organizations, efficiency may well have become *the* core management skill of the twenty-first century.

WHAT VARIES IN A MANAGER'S JOB? THE EMPHASIS

The Entrepreneur Role Is Gaining Importance   Managers must increasingly be aware of threats and opportunities in their environment. Threats include technological breakthroughs on the part of competitors, obsolescence in a manager's organization, and dramatically shortened product cycles. Opportunities might include product or service niches that are underserved, out-of-cycle hiring opportunities, mergers, purchases, or upgrades in equipment, space, or other assets. Managers who are carefully attuned to the marketplace and competitive environment will look for opportunities to gain an advantage.

So Is the Leader Role   Managers must be more sophisticated as strategists and mentors. A manager's job involves much more than simple *caretaking* in a division of a large organization. Unless you are able to attract, train, motivate, retain, and promote good people, your organization cannot possibly hope to gain advantage over the competition. Thus, as leaders, managers must constantly act as mentors to those in the organization with promise and potential. When you lose a highly capable worker, all else in your world will come to a halt until you can replace that worker. Even if you should find someone ideally suited and superbly qualified for a vacant position, you must still train, motivate, and inspire that new recruit, and you must live with the knowledge that productivity levels will be lower for a while than they were with your previous employee.

Managers Must Create a Local Vision as They Help People Grow   The company's annual report and those slick-paper brochures your sales force hands to customers may articulate the vision, values, and beliefs of the company. But what do those concepts *really* mean to workers at your location? What does a competitive global strategy mean to your staff at 8:00 A.M. on Monday morning? Somehow, you must create a local version of that strategy, explaining in practical and understandable terms what your organization or unit is all about and how the work of your employees fits into the larger picture.

MANAGEMENT SKILLS REQUIRED FOR THE TWENTY-FIRST CENTURY

The twenty-first century workplace will require three types of skills, each of which will be useful at different points in your career.

Technical Skills These are most valuable at the entry level, but less valuable at more senior levels. Organizations hire people for their technical expertise: Can you assess the market value of a commercial office building? Can you calculate a set of net present values? Are you experienced in the use of C++ or SAP/R3 software? These skill sets, however, constantly change and can become quickly outdated. What gets you in the door of a large organization won't necessarily get you promoted.

Relating Skills These are valuable across the managerial career span and are more likely to help you progress and be promoted to higher levels of responsibility. These skills, which help you to form relationships, are at the heart of what management communication is about: reading, writing, speaking, listening, and thinking about how you can help others and how they can help you as the demands of your job shift and increase at the same time.

Conceptual Skills These are least valuable at the entry level, but more valuable at senior levels in the organization. These are the skills that permit you to look past the details of today's work assignment and see the bigger picture. Successful managers who hope to become executives in the highest levels of a business must begin, at a relatively early age, to develop the ability to see beyond the horizon and ask long-term questions. If you haven't formed the relationships that will help you get promoted, however, you may not be around long enough to have an opportunity to use your conceptual skills.

TALK IS THE WORK

Managers across industries, according to Deirdre Borden, spend about 75 percent of their time in verbal interaction.[25] Those daily interactions include the following.

One-on-One Conversations Increasingly, managers find that information is passed orally, often face-to-face in offices, hallways, conference rooms, cafeterias, rest rooms, athletic facilities, parking lots, and literally dozens of other venues. An enormous amount of information is exchanged, validated, confirmed, and passed back and forth under highly informal circumstances.

Telephone Conversations Managers spend an astounding amount of time on the telephone these days. Curiously, the amount of time per telephone call is decreasing, but the number of calls per day is increasing. With the nearly universal availability of cellular and satellite telephone service, very few people are out of reach of the office for very long. The decision to switch off your cellular telephone, in fact, is now considered a decision in favor of work-life balance.

Video Teleconferencing Bridging time zones as well as cultures, videoconferencing facilities make direct conversations with employees, colleagues, customers, and business partners across the nation or around the world a simple matter. Carrier Corporation, the air-conditioning manufacturer, is now typical of firms using desktop videoconferencing to conduct everything from staff meetings to technical training. Engineers at Carrier's Syracuse, New York, headquarters can hook up with service managers in branch offices thousands of miles away to explain new product developments, demonstrate repair techniques, and update field staff on matters that would, just recently, have required extensive travel or expensive, broadcast-quality television programming. Their exchanges are informal, conversational, and not much different than they would have been if both people were in the same room.[26]

Presentations to Small Groups   Managers frequently find themselves making presentations, formal and informal, to groups of three to eight people for many different reasons: they pass along information given to them by executives; they review the status of projects in process; they explain changes in everything from working schedules to organizational goals. Such presentations are sometimes supported by overhead transparencies or printed outlines, but they are oral in nature and retain much of the conversational character of one-to-one conversations.

Public Speaking to Larger Audiences   Most managers are unable to escape the periodic requirement to speak to larger audiences of several dozen or, perhaps, several hundred people. Such presentations are usually more formal in structure and are often supported by *PowerPoint* or *Harvard Graphics* software that can deliver data from text files, graphics, and photos, and even motion clips from televised video. Despite the more formal atmosphere and sophisticated audio-visual support systems, such presentations still involve one manager talking to others, framing, shaping, and passing information to an audience.

THE MAJOR CHANNELS OF MANAGEMENT COMMUNICATION ARE TALKING AND LISTENING

A series of scientific studies, beginning with Rankin in 1926,[27] and later with Nichols and Stevens (1957)[28] and Wolvin and Coakley (1982)[29], have served to confirm what each of us knows intuitively: most managers spend the largest portion of their day talking and listening. E. K. Werner's thesis at the University of Maryland, in fact, found that North American adults spend more than 78 percent of their communication time either talking or listening to others who are talking.[30]

According to Werner and others who have studied the communication habits of postmodern business organizations, managers are involved in more than just speeches and presentations from the dais or teleconference podium. They spend their days in meetings, on the telephone, conducting interviews, giving tours, supervising informal visits to their facilities, and at a wide variety of social events.

Each of these activities may look to some managers like an obligation imposed by the job. Shrewd managers see them as opportunities: to hear what others are thinking, to gather information informally from the grapevine, to listen in on office gossip, to pass along viewpoints that haven't yet made their way to the more formal channels of communication, or to catch up with a colleague or friend in a more relaxed setting. No matter what the intention of each manager who engages in these activities, the information they produce and the insight that follows from it, can be put to work the same day to achieve organizational and personal objectives.

THE ROLE OF WRITING

Writing plays an important role in the life of any organization—in some organizations, it becomes more important than in others. At Procter & Gamble, for example, brand managers cannot raise a work-related issue in a team meeting unless the ideas are first circulated in writing. For P&G managers, that means explaining their ideas in explicit detail in a standard one-to-three-page memo, complete with background, financial discussion, implementation details, and justification for the ideas proposed.

Other organizations are more oral in their traditions—3M Canada comes to mind as a very "spoken" organization—but the fact remains: The most important projects, decisions, and ideas end up in writing. Writing also provides analysis, justification, documentation, and analytic discipline, particularly as managers approach important decisions that will affect the profitability and strategic direction of the company.

Writing Is a Career Sifter   If you demonstrate your inability to put ideas on paper in a clear, unambiguous fashion, you're not likely to last. Stories of bad writers who've been shown the door early in their careers are legion. Your principal objective, at least during the first few years of your own career, is to keep your name out of such stories. Remember, those who are most likely to notice the quality and skill in your written documents are the very managers most likely to matter to your future.

Managers Do Most of Their Own Writing and Editing   The days when managers could lean back and thoughtfully dictate a letter or memo to a skilled secretarial assistant are mostly gone. Some senior executives know how efficient dictation can be, especially with a top-notch administrative assistant taking shorthand, but how many managers have that advantage today? Very few, mostly because buying a computer and printer are substantially cheaper than hiring another employee. Managers at all levels of most organizations draft, review, edit, and dispatch their own correspondence, reports, and proposals.

Documents Take On Lives of Their Own   Once it's gone from your desk, it isn't yours anymore. When you sign a letter and put it in the mail, it's no longer your letter—it's the property of the person or organization you sent it to. As a result, the recipient is free to do as he or she sees fit with your writing, including using it against you. If your ideas are ill-considered or not well expressed, others in the organization who are not especially sympathetic to your views may head for the copy machine with your work in hand. The advice for you is simple: Don't mail your first draft, and don't ever sign your name to a document you're not proud of.

COMMUNICATION IS INVENTION

Without question, communication is a process of invention. Managers literally *create* meaning through communication. A company, for example, is not in default until a team of auditors sits down to examine the books and review the matter. Only after extended discussion do the accountants come to the conclusion that the company is, in fact, in default. It is their discussion that creates the outcome. Until that point, default was simply one of many possibilities.

The fact is, managers create meaning through communication. It is largely through discussion and verbal exchange—often heated and passionate—that managers decide who they wish to be: market leaders, takeover artists, innovators, or defenders of the economy. It is only through communication that meaning—for shareholders, for employees, for customers, and others—is created. Those long, detailed, and very intense discussions determine how much the company will declare in dividends this year, whether the company is willing to risk a strike or labor action, and how soon to roll out the new product line customers have been asking for.

Additionally, it is important to note that managers usually figure things out by talking about them as much as they talk about the things they have already figured out. Talk serves as a wonderful palliative: justifying, analyzing, dissecting, reassuring, and analyzing the events that confront managers each day.

INFORMATION IS SOCIALLY CONSTRUCTED

If we are to understand just how important human discourse is in the life of a business, several points seem especially important.

Information Is Created, Shared, and Interpreted by People   Meaning is a truly human phenomenon. An issue is only important if people think it is. Facts are facts only if we can agree upon their definition. Perceptions and assumptions are as important as truth itself in a discussion about what a manager should do next.[31]

Information Never Speaks for Itself   It is not uncommon for a manager to rise to address a group of his colleagues and say, "Gentlemen, the numbers speak for themselves." Frankly, the numbers *never* speak for themselves. They almost always require some sort of interpretation, some sort of explanation or context. Don't assume that others see the facts in the same way you do and never assume that what you see is the truth. Others may see the same set of facts or evidence, but may not reach the same conclusions. Very little in life is self-explanatory.

Context Always Drives Meaning   The backdrop to a message is always of paramount importance to the listener, viewer, or reader in reaching a reasonable, rational conclusion about what she sees and hears. What's in the news these days as we take up this particular subject? What moment in history do we occupy? What related or relevant information is under consideration as this new message arrives? We cannot possibly derive meaning from one message without considering everything else that surrounds it.

A Messenger Always Accompanies a Message   It is difficult to separate a message from its messenger. We often want to react more to the source of the information than we do to the information itself. That's natural and entirely normal. People speak for a reason and we often judge their reasons for speaking before analyzing what they have to say. Keep in mind that, in every organization, message recipients will judge the value, power, purpose, intent, and outcomes of the messages they receive by the source of those messages as much as by the content and intent of the messages themselves. If the messages you send as a manager are to have the impact you hope they will, they must come from a source the receiver knows, respects, and understands.

YOUR GREATEST CHALLENGE

Every manager knows communication is vital. But every manager also seems to "know" that he or she is great at it. Your greatest challenge is to admit to flaws in your skill set and work tirelessly to improve them. But first, you must admit to the flaws.

T. J. Larkin and Sandard Larkin in a book entitled, *Communicating Change: Winning Support for New Business Goals,* write: "Deep down, managers believe they are communicating effectively. In ten years of management consulting, we have never had a manager say to us that he or she was a poor communicator. They admit to the occasional screw-up, but overall, everyone, without exception, believes he or she is basically a good communicator."[32]

YOUR TASK AS A PROFESSIONAL

As a professional manager, your first task is to recognize and understand your strengths and weaknesses as a communicator. Until you identify those communication tasks at which you are most and least skilled, you'll have little opportunity for improvement and advancement.

Foremost among your goals should be to improve existing skills. Improve your ability to do what you do best. Be alert to opportunities, however, to develop new skills. Add to your inventory of abilities to keep yourself employable and promotable.

Two other suggestions come to mind for improving your professional standing as a manager. First, acquire a knowledge base that will work for the twenty-first century. That means speaking with and listening to other professionals in your company, your industry, and your community. Be alert to trends which could affect your products and services, as well as your own future.

This also means reading. You should read at least one national newspaper each day, including either *The Wall Street Journal* or the *New York Times,* as well as a local newspaper. Your reading should include weekly news magazines, such as *U.S. News & World Report, Business Week,* and *The Economist.* Subscribe to monthly magazines such as *Fast Company* and *Fortune.* And you should read at least one new hardcover title a month. A dozen books each year is the bare minimum on which you should depend for new ideas, insights, and managerial guidance.

Your final challenge is to develop the confidence you will need to succeed as a manager, particularly under conditions of uncertainty, change, and challenge.

Endnotes

1. Drucker, P. F. *The Practice of Management.* New York, NY: Harper & Row, 1954.
2. Eccles, R. G. and N. Nohria. *Beyond the Hype: Rediscovering the Essence of Management.* Boston, MA: The Harvard Business School Press, 1992, p. 205.
3. Eccles, R. G. and N. Nohria, p. 211.
4. Eccles, R. G. and N. Nohria, p. 209.

5. Hannaway, J. *Managers Managing: The Workings of an Administrative System.* New York, NY: Oxford University Press, 1989, p. 39.

6. Eccles, R. G. and N. Nohria, p. 47.

7. Hannaway, J., p. 37. See also J. P. Kotter. *The General Managers.* New York, NY: The Free Press, 1982.

8. Mintzberg, H. *The Nature of Managerial Work.* New York, NY: Harper & Row, 1973, p. 31.

9. Sproull, L. S. "The Nature of Managerial Attention," in L. S. Sproull (ed.), *Advances in Information Processing in Organizations.* Greenwich, CT: JAI Press, 1984, p. 15.

10. Stewart, R. *Managers and Their Jobs.* London, UK: Macmillan, 1967.

11. Eccles, R. G. and N. Nohria, p. 47.

12. Mintzberg, H. *The Nature of Managerial Work,* p. 44 (emphasis mine).

13. Pondy. "Leadership Is a Language Game," in M. W. McCall, Jr. and M. M. Lombardo (eds.), *Leadership: Where Else Can We Go?* Durham, NC: Duke University Press, 1978.

14. Mintzberg, H. *The Nature of Managerial Work,* p. 38.

15. Eccles, R. G. and N. Nohria, pp. 47–48.

16. Mintzberg, H. "The Manager's Job: Folklore and Fact." *Harvard Business Review,* March–April 1990, pp. 166–167.

17. Mintzberg, H. "The Manager's Job: Folklore and Fact," p. 167.

18. Mintzberg, H. "The Manager's Job: Folklore and Fact," p. 168.

19. Stewart, R. *Managers and Their Jobs.* London, UK: Macmillan, 1967.

20. Guest, R. H. "Of Time and the Foreman." *Personnel,* May 1956, p. 478.

21. Mintzberg, H. "The Manager's Job: Folklore and Fact," p. 166–167.

22. Mintzberg, H. "The Manager's Job: Folklore and Fact," p. 168, 170.

23. Mintzberg, H. "The Manager's Job: Folklore and Fact," p. 167–171.

24. Mintzberg, H. "The Manager's Job: Folklore and Fact," p. 167.

25. Borden, D. *The Business of Talk: Organizations in Action.* New York, NY: Blackwell, 1995.

26. Ziegler, B. "Video Conference Calls Change Business." *Wall Street Journal,* October 13, 1994, pp. B1, B12.

27. Rankin, P. T. "The Measurement of the Ability to Understand Spoken Language" (unpublished Ph.D. dissertation, University of Michigan, 1926). *Dissertation Abstracts* 12, No. 6 (1952), 847–848.

28. Nichols, R. G. and L. Stevens. *Are You Listening?* New York, NY: McGraw-Hill, 1957.

29. Wolvin, A. D. and C. G. Coakley. *Listening.* Dubuque, IA: Wm. C. Brown and Co., 1982.

30. Werner, E. K. "A Study of Communication Time" (M.S. thesis, University of Maryland, College Park, 1975), p. 26.

31. Searle, J. R. *The Construction of Social Reality.* New York, NY: The Free Press, 1995. See also Berger, P. L. and T. Luckmann. *The Social Construction of Reality.* New York, NY: Doubleday, 1967.

32. Larkin, T. J. and S. Larkin. *Communicating Change: Winning Employee Support for New Business Goals.* New York, NY: McGraw-Hill, 1994.

For Further Reading

Axley, S. R. *Communication at Work: Management and the Communication-Intensive Organization.* Westport, CT: Quorum Books, 1996.

Clampitt, P. G. *Communicating for Managerial Effectiveness.* Newbury Park, CA: Sage Publications, 1991.

Kotter, J. P. "What Effective General Managers Really Do." *Harvard Business Review,* March–April 1999, 145–159.

Case 1–1   ODWALLA, INC. (A)

Greg Steltenpohl's worst nightmares were about to come true. As chairman and chief executive officer of Odwalla Incorporated, he was at the helm of a company worth nearly $60 million whose products in the premium juice market were widely regarded by customers and competitors alike for quality and freshness. The company's reputation was solid throughout the Pacific Northwest, but the press release on his desk was filled with nothing but bad news.

Steltenpohl had just met with his corporate communications director, reviewed the crisis communication plan, and was now applying the last few corrections to a press release before faxing it to *PR Newswire*. The date was Wednesday, October 30, 1996, and less than an hour ago, the Seattle-King County Department of Public Health and the Washington State Department of Health had reported an outbreak of *E.coli* (0157-H7) infections that were "epidemiologically" associated with drinking Odwalla apple juices and mixes. More specifically, the public health physicians had uncovered a direct link between people who had the infection and those who had consumed Odwalla's product.

E. COLI BACTERIA

Escherichia coli are a species of microscopic bacteria named for the German biologist who discovered them during the early 1900s. Virtually all large animals, including humans, benignly host some form of the bacterium in their large intestinal tracts. But a particularly virulent form of the organism, known specifically as 0157-H7, can sicken and kill those whose immune systems may be compromised. The elderly and young children are especially at risk.

E. *coli* 0157-H7 can grow quickly in uncooked food products, including meat, cheeses, fruit, dairy products, and juices. The bacteria may be completely destroyed, however, by heat or radiation. If meats are cooked to a temperature of 160°F, or if juices and other potable liquids are pasteurized, the danger posed by such organisms is dramatically reduced or eliminated completely.

Odwalla's juice products, however, were *not* pasteurized. *E. coli* and other harmful bacteria were kept at bay with a multistep production process that selected only the finest fresh fruit, washed each piece twice, and then refrigerated the squeezings to slow the growth of microorganisms. Deliveries were made to retailers each day in refrigerated trucks, and products were displayed and sold from special Odwalla coolers. The process was repeated each business day, with the previous day's unsold products gathered up by Odwalla's drivers and returned to the plant for disposal. Thus, the product customers bought from Odwalla retailers each day was guaranteed to be fresh-squeezed that very day—a feature that loyal customers willingly paid premium prices to obtain.

The question remained: How could the lethal strain of *E. coli* bacteria get into Odwalla juice? How could the careful, meticulous production process have failed? Over the past 16 years, Steltenpohl and the team at Odwalla had worked hard to establish a stellar reputation for the company and their premium, trendy products. Yet, all of their hard work was at this moment on the line. The future of his growing company would depend on how he and his senior team reacted to events over the next few hours. Gathering the papers on his desk, Steltenpohl took a deep breath and began dialing fax numbers.

ODWALLA, INCORPORATED

Greg Steltenpohl, his wife Bonnie Bassett, and a friend named Gerry Percy founded Odwalla in September 1980. A backyard shed served as the manufacturing facility for three longtime friends who used a $200 hand juicer (purchased with borrowed funds) and one box of oranges to make freshly squeezed orange juice. They distributed the juice to local restaurants in a Volkswagen microbus, earning just enough profits from their first day of business to purchase two more boxes of oranges for the next day's run. Thus began this fruit juice empire.

Over the years, the Santa Cruz–based company has grown to become the leading western United States supplier of freshly squeezed fruit juices. Currently, it markets more than 20 flavors of juice, smoothies, and vitamin-packed drinks. "If it's not fresh squeezed, then it's not part of Odwalla. . . ." said Steltenpohl. In 1993, Odwalla went public and sales skyrocketed from $9 million in 1991 to $59 million in 1996. Odwalla had experienced approximately 40 percent annual sales growth during those five years.

Steltenpohl, Bassett, and Percy's entrepreneurial inspiration was a suggestion drawn from a paperback tradebook entitled *100 Businesses You Can Start for Under $100.* Based on their concerns about social trends and environmental issues, the founders decided to create a company with a social conscience. The name *Odwalla* came from a musical piece by The Art Ensemble of Chicago, in which the hero Odwalla guides his followers from the gray haze. Similarly, during a hazy gray time in the processed foods business, this company could guide their customers, friends, and neighbors by providing fresh citrus alternatives.

The vision of Odwalla encompasses the idea of "nourishing the whole body." The foundation of the company has been maintained through Odwalla's dedication to providing superior fresh fruit juices, preserving the environment, and fostering community relationships. This people-centered approach is focused both internally on employees and shareholders as well as externally on customers and the broader community.

A DIVERSE PRODUCT LINE

The diverse product offerings of fruit juices, smoothies, all natural meal replacements, quenchers, and geothermal natural spring water comprise what Odwalla terms, *Nourishing Beverages.* (See Exhibit A, Nourishment Ensemble Attachment.) The core competencies of the organization involve the use of minimal production processes to deliver superior taste and nutritional value as compared to concentrate and artificially flavored substitutes. This is accomplished through strict quality production systems, selective agreements with suppliers and vendors, and the continued adaptation to changing consumer tastes and preferences. Moreover, the nutritional value and flavor qualities are complimented by artful packaging.

The product line is distributed throughout California, Oregon, Colorado, Washington, New Mexico, Texas, and Nevada. Despite this large seven-state territory, a company goal remains to deliver "day of juicing quality." Such stringent standards preserve both the nutritional and flavor integrity. Thus, the shelf life of the fruit and vegetable products is limited to between 8 and 17 days after retail purchase.

The fruity flavors, outrageous names, and all-natural ingredients have allowed the company to achieve tremendous success based on the health benefits derived from consumption of the product. Their products have attracted a loyal customer base of health-conscious adults seeking nutritious vitamin supplements, but also they are extremely popular among young children. Parents, aware of the nutritional goodness of Odwalla juices, see them as a healthy alternative to other commercially prepared fruit drinks.

ODWALLA'S "ALL NATURAL" PRODUCTION PROCESS

Odwalla has strategically differentiated itself based on the "all-natural" composite of their

ESSENTIALS
Pure Squeezed Orange Juice
Pure Squeezed Grapefruit Juice
Pure Squeezed Tangerine Juice(seasonal)
Pure Pressed Apple Juice
Pure Pressed Carrot Juice
Rooty Fruity®
Carrotonic™

QUENCHERS
Lemonade
Summertime Lime®(seasonal)
Strawberry Lemonade

FUTURE SHAKES®
Vanilla Al'Mondo®
Dutch Chocolate,
Inner Chai™
Café Latté

NUTRITIONALS
C Monster®
Strawberry C Monster®
Super Protein
Mo' Beta®
Superfood
Serious Energy®
Wellness
Femme Vitale®
Think Drink™

SMOOTHIES
Mango Tango®
Strawberry Banana
Blackberry Fruitshake
Orange Piña

NATURAL SPRING WATER
Water

NOURISHING THE BODY WHOLE™

products. The company uses strictly pure fruit extracts in the creation of their juices, smoothies, and vitamin supplements. However, the all-natural base of Odwalla's products holds implications for virtually every aspect of the procurement and production processes. For example, the majority of their fruit is grown in the state of Washington. The seasonal nature of the fruit industry, however, necessitates a switch at some point in the season to less-expensive California fruit. As part of their purchasing agreement, Odwalla mandates that all of the fruit they pur-

chase be hand-picked. This reduces the number of bruised and rotten pieces received in the shipments.

Aside from the actual procurement of basic ingredients, the company also maintains both a production and quality-control division. The production division is responsible for overseeing the creation of the product. This division employs people not only to run the presses, mix the ingredients, and bottle the juices, but also employs sorters, whose main function is to determine which pieces of fruit are acceptable

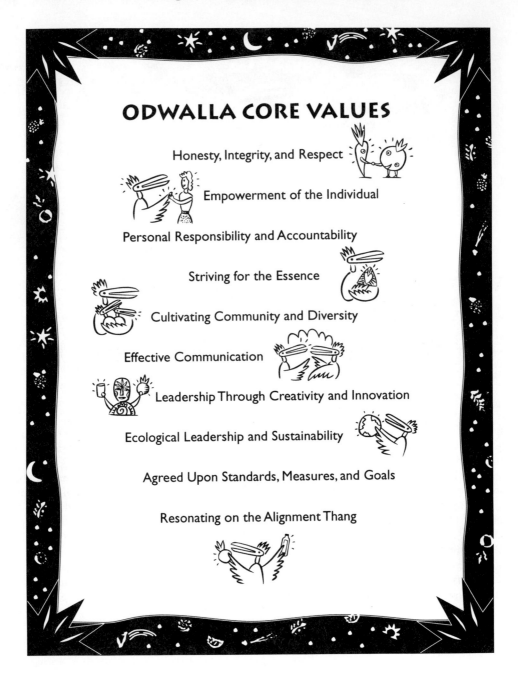

ODWALLA CORE VALUES

Honesty, Integrity, and Respect

Empowerment of the Individual

Personal Responsibility and Accountability

Striving for the Essence

Cultivating Community and Diversity

Effective Communication

Leadership Through Creativity and Innovation

Ecological Leadership and Sustainability

Agreed Upon Standards, Measures, and Goals

Resonating on the Alignment Thang

ODWALLAVISION

ODWALLA

A BREATH OF FRESH

INTOXICATING RHYTHM

LIVING FLAVOR

SOIL TO SOUL

PEOPLE TO PLANET

NOURISHING THE BODY WHOLE

for production. The company uses a quality-control division to monitor all processes and uphold strict safety guidelines.

Though 98 percent of the nation's fruit juice went through a pasteurization process, Odwalla's products were unpasteurized. Steltenpohl feared that the use of a pasteurization process and other cleaning agents would kill important nutrients and detract from the taste of the final product. "Absolute freshness," he observed, is a key component of Odwalla's product offering.

PRODUCTION VERSUS QUALITY

In mid-1995, juice makers in Florida were hit by an outbreak of salmonella in orange juice served at Walt Disney World. This outbreak sickened more than 60 children and adults. Consequently, the state of Florida drafted strict rules that required larger juice companies to take additional measures to ensure the safety of their production processes. As a California-based company, Odwalla was under no obligation to adhere to these standards and very few juice companies outside of Florida actually did.

In early 1996, Odwalla hired two managers from the Florida juice industry. One of them, Dave Stevenson, who oversaw quality assurance, suggested that Odwalla add a chlorine-based rinse for precautionary measures. However, the other executive, Chip Beetle, feared chlorine would leave an after-taste and was simply not necessary. Steltenpohl agreed and Odwalla continued with their previous procurement, production, and distribution processes. By the summer of 1996, business was booming. In fact, sales were so strong that Odwalla was struggling to keep up with the demand for their product. Some former company officials say that production demands became more important than safety concerns.

WILL AN APPLE A DAY KEEP THE DOCTOR AWAY?

As Greg Steltenpohl returned to his office, he picked up the phone and dialed the director of corporate communication's extension. When she answered, he simply said, "I sent the press release. What do we do now?"

This case was prepared from personal interviews and public sources by research assistants Suzanne Halverson and Kristan L. Rake under the direction of James S. O'Rourke, concurrent associate professor of management, as the basis for class discussion rather than to illustrate either effective or ineffective handling of an administrative situation.

Case 1–2   F. W. WOOLWORTH COMPANY
A new image and a new workforce

When Roger N. Farah became chief executive officer of the F. W. Woolworth Company in 1994, the company was nearly insolvent. Its inventory systems were so antiquated that Halloween candy sat melting in a storeroom in the middle of July. Its stores were not equipped to tally daily sales, a

shortcoming unheard of in modern retailing, and its namesake dime stores were bleeding cash, as were many of its other divisions.

In a few short years, however, Roger Farah reduced the company's overall debt to $440 million from $1.2 billion, winnowed its 41 widely disparate divisions down to 21 store formats by unloading most of the underperforming mall specialty stores, and sold its elegant headquarters building in Manhattan. And, in perhaps his most dramatic move, Roger Farah closed the company's fabled dime stores.

Now in his sixth year as CEO, Farah has changed not only the company's name to The Venator group, but also its century-old strategy. The company that virtually invented the five-and-dime format is now running a sporting goods specialty company. Venator Group's crown jewels now include Foot Locker (as well as Lady Foot Locker and Kid's Foot Locker), Sports Authority, Champs, Colorado, the Kinney footwear chain, Northern Reflections, and the San Francisco Music Box Company.

The venerable F. W. Woolworth Company, founded in 1879 and for a hundred years the staple of main street shopping in America, had transformed itself into a footwear and sporting goods retailing powerhouse. That transformation, under the direction of Mr. Farah, however, came at a price.

In the last few years of its existence, F. W. Woolworth illegally dismissed as many as 400 older employees and often replaced them with younger ones, according to Federal officials. The dismissals were apparently part of an effort to give the failing company a more youthful image. In a Federal lawsuit filed in 1999, the United States Equal Employment Opportunity Commission said that the older employees, many of whom had worked for Woolworth for decades, were let go between 1995 and 1997, before the chain finally closed its 400 stores in the United States.

Along with its trademark lunch counters, Woolworth was known for its genial, dedicated workforce. But lawyers for the USEEOC have said that in the mid-1990s, Woolworth store managers around the country submitted lists of employees being proposed for termination, along with their ages, to Woolworth's headquarters in New York, where officials approved the dismissals of longtime workers.

Some of those dismissed were in their 40s, the commission said, but many more were in their 60s, 70s, and 80s. "The company analyzed each store," said Elizabeth Grossman, a senior lawyer with the commission, "and in the overwhelming majority of cases selected a grossly disproportionate number of older employees for termination. It's a very clear pattern of age discrimination," she said.

A spokesman for Woolworth, which changed its name to The Venator Group in 1998, said the company's policy was not to comment on pending litigation, saying only that the company denied the charges. The federal suit sought an injunction against future age discrimination by the company as well as back pay and damages for the employees, which could total in the millions of dollars.

The commission did not say explicitly what it suspected Woolworth's motives to be for the large-scale dismissals of older employees, who in most cases were replaced by teenagers. Apparently, without realizing it, many older employees had actually helped to recruit their replacements. While working at the cash register, they were told to stuff fliers into shoppers' bags. On one side of the flier was a Woolworth job application, while the other side announced: "Join our team! We're changing! How about you?" The flier also included the statement that Woolworth was an "equal opportunity employer." When dismissed employees asked about the part-time employment advertised on the fliers, they were told they could not apply.

DISCUSSION QUESTIONS

1. Assuming Mr. Farah's strategy is one of rejuvenation, or renovation of the aging, stodgy Woolworth image—what's wrong with his approach?
2. Is a failing company obligated to employ everyone currently on their payroll, even if it means financial peril for shareholders?
3. If Mr. Farah were to ask you for advice regarding his turn-around strategy, what would you tell him? What cautions would you offer? What bold, innovative strokes would you suggest?
4. In communicating change to the marketplace, which audiences would you be *most* concerned about? What would you say to shareholders? To your core customers? To your suppliers and business partners? To your employees? To the communities in which you do business?
5. Assuming you could choose the ideal workforce, what would the demographic composition of your employee base look like? What advice would you give to Mr. Farah to recruit and retain such employees?

SOURCES

Bongiorno, Lori. "Lost in the Aisles at Woolworth's." *Business Week,* October 30, 1995; and Ono, Yumiko. "Woolworth Seeks to Shed Stodgy Image." *Wall Street Journal,* March 20, 1998, p. B8; Ono, Yumiko. "At Woolworth, a New Moniker Flags a New Era." *Wall Street Journal,* April 2, 1998, pp. B1, B4; Steinhauer, Jennifer. "A Highflier in an Uphill Battle: A Retail Star Has Yet to Win Respect for Woolworth's Successor." *New York Times,* July 12, 1998, Section 3, pp. 1, 11; and Weiser, Benjamin. "Woolworth Fired Old Workers to Change Its Image, Suit Says." *New York Times,* July 2, 1999, p. A-15.

2
COMMUNICATION AND STRATEGY

༝

In Chapter 1, we looked at the role communication plays in the life of a manager—we examined *why* managers communicate. In this chapter, we will look much more closely at *how* managers communicate—we'll examine the process itself. Elsewhere in this book we'll examine the products of that process: writing, speaking, listening, conflict management, and group interaction.

DEFINING COMMUNICATION

First, though, a definition may be helpful. If you read enough books on this subject, you'll find more definitions than you can understand or remember. Here's one that is both easy to understand and easy to remember: *Communication is the transfer of meaning.*[1]

"I sent you an e-mail," your manager asserts. "Didn't you get it?" You got forty e-mails that day. What did his say?

"We put out a memo on that subject just last month," a junior VP claims. "Why aren't the employees complying?" They get dozens—literally dozens of pieces of paper in their in-boxes each day. Are you surprised no one read it? For those of you who remember the memo, did you understand it? For those who think they understood what the vice president meant, what was your reaction? Wasn't that just a *backgrounder?* An update of some sort, meant to provide you with information about the development and implementation of some policy that won't really affect you?

For those who received, read, understood, and remembered the memo: What was your incentive for complying with the vice president's request? How does this affect you and—more importantly—what's your motivation for getting involved?

"That memo is crucial to the future of this company," your boss thunders. "It's about the vision our senior team wants to see throughout the entire organization." Gee, all that in one memo, and you just glanced through it and tossed it aside. Maybe it's still around somewhere. When you get a few minutes, you really should read it. For now, though, there's a lot more on your plate that seems much more urgent, and "vision memos" will have to wait.

Sound familiar? It's all too familiar in many organizations because people, particularly managers, confuse the act of communicating with the process of communication. They honestly believe that a message sent is a message received. And a message received would certainly be understood and complied with, right? For them, communication is mostly, if not entirely, about sending messages.

For managers who truly understand the process, however, communication is about much more than sending messages. It's about *the transfer of meaning.*

When I understand a subject the way you understand it—with all of the intricacies, complexities, context, and detail—then you have communicated with me. If I am not only aware of what you *know* about a subject, but how you *feel* about it, then you have communicated with me. When I comprehend just how important a subject is to you and why you think it's important to take action now, you have communicated with me. All of this may be possible in a memo to the staff, but it's certainly not easy. Because communication is a very complex, ongoing process that involves the whole substance of ourselves, it would be an unusual memo that could capture all of that. The transfer of meaning may take more than just a phone call or an e-mail message.

ELEMENTS OF COMMUNICATION

To successfully transfer meaning you must understand that every *message* you receive comes from a *sender* who *encodes* the details of its content and selects a *medium* through which to *transmit* what she *knows* or *feels.* That message may be impeded by *noise,* primarily because of the *cultural context* against which it will be delivered as well as the *field of experience* of the receiver. And, of course, the *effect* the message has will depend on the *frame of mind* or *attitudinal set* which you bring to the situation, along with the *system of ethics* that governs communication in your organization, your industry, and your society.

If all of that looks complex, congratulations. You now have a firm grasp on the obvious: Human communication is intricate, delicate, difficult, and above all, complex. The remarkable fact is, however, we do it every day, and, more often than not, we achieve some degree of success. Orders get placed, deliveries are made, customers are satisfied, people do what you ask of them, and the business you work for runs—more or less—the way it's supposed to.

The real question here isn't whether you can communicate. You showed that you can do that when you filled out a business school admissions application. The real question is whether you can get better at it. Can you impress your clients enough to keep them? Can you encourage a reluctant employee to give the best he's got? Can you convince the boss that you are the one to take on those new responsibilities? We each have basic skills. What we need is a set of higher-level competencies that will serve the world-class organizations we will work for in the century ahead.

PRINCIPLES OF COMMUNICATION

Communication is a process that involves half a dozen basic principles. These are things we know to be true about human communication across time and cultures, across organizations and professions, and across nations and economies. Above all, we know that communication is:

Dynamic   Human communication is constantly undergoing change. One message builds on another; one experience adds to another.

Continuous   Communication never stops. Even when you hang up the telephone, you're communicating the message that you have nothing more to say. Silence, in fact, can be among the more powerful forms of communication. Simply said: You cannot *not* communicate.

Circular   Communication is rarely ever entirely one-way. We each take in information from the outside world, determine what it means, and respond. The cycle we refer to as *feedback* is nothing more than receivers becoming senders, and vice versa. When we stop speaking to listen, we join the feedback loop.

Unrepeatable   Some processes are repeatable—we can freeze water into ice and then thaw it back into water again—but not communication. Even if we say something again in precisely the same way, our listeners have heard it before. The same message delivered to two different listeners amounts to two different communications, just as does the same message delivered twice to the same listeners. Once we have heard or seen a message, we have some notion of what to expect. Thus, it's not the same experience as when we heard it or saw it for the first time.

Irreversible   Heraclitus, a Greek philosopher-mathematician, once wrote that "No man can step in the same river twice." What he meant was that if you attempt to repeat an experience, the experience will be different—circumstances change and so will you. So it is with communication. We may wish we could *unsay* something, but we can't. All we can do is explain, apologize, and say more—but we can't ever get it back.

Complex   Communication is complex, not only because of the various elements and principles at work in the process, but also because it involves human beings. Each of us is different in a number of important and meaningful ways. And because of that, each of us will assign slightly different meaning to words, react in slightly different ways because of our background, education, and experience, and behave in slightly different ways around other people. Nothing is simple or entirely straightforward about the ways in which people communicate.[2]

LEVELS OF COMMUNICATION

Human communication also occurs at various levels. The complexities of the process, particularly audience analysis and message construction, elevate as the level of communication elevates.

Intrapersonal   When we communicate *within* ourselves, sending messages to various parts of our bodies, thinking things over, or working silently on a problem, we are communicating intrapersonally.

Interpersonal   When we communicate *between* or *among* ourselves, sending messages from one person to another—verbally and nonverbally—we are communicating interpersonally.

Organizational When we communicate with one another *in the context of an organization,* sending and receiving messages through various layers of authority, using various message systems, discussing various topics of interest to the group we belong to or the company we work for, we are communicating organizationally.

Mass or Public Occasionally, when we send messages from just one person or source to *many people simultaneously,* as in a newspaper advertisement or television commercial, we are communicating *publicly.*[3]

BARRIERS TO COMMUNICATION

If we each understand the principles of communication and the levels at which it can take place, and if we each use and understand the same language, why don't we succeed more often than we do? What's holding back the transfer of meaning? Broadly speaking, two barriers keep us from communicating successfully.

Physiological Barriers Because all the information we receive about the world must come through one or more of our five senses (sight, sound, touch, smell, and taste), we depend on those senses to report accurately on what's going on around us. It is possible, though, for our senses to be impaired or for the source of the message to provide inadequate information (insufficient light to read a message, an announcement not loud enough to be audible, and so on). In sending messages to others, we must be sensitive to the fact that they may not see, hear, touch, smell, or taste in the same way we do.

Psychological Barriers Communication is much more than simply sending and receiving messages. It's about understanding them, as well. Remember, communication is the transfer of meaning, and if I don't know what you mean—even though I may see and hear you well enough—no communication has taken place. Everything from the culture in which we live to the norms or standards of the groups we belong to can influence how we perceive and react to the messages, events, and experiences of everyday life. Even individual mind-sets, including prejudice and stereotypes, can affect what we understand and how we react to others. We'll examine each of these barriers in greater detail in Chapter 4, *Speaking.*

COMMUNICATING STRATEGICALLY

To communicate strategically means several things. First, it means that your plans for communication, your proposed messages, the medium (or media) you select, the code you employ, the context and experience you bring to situations, and the ethics you adopt will all have a direct effect on the outcome. Remember the elements of communication we discussed earlier? Those are the keys to successful strategic communication.

You should know, however, that those are all just tools; they are means to an end. You should first ask what end you hope to reach. What are your communication goals? If you are communicating strategically, those goals will be aligned with and will directly support the goals of the organization you work for. And, at each level of your organization, the ways in which you communicate will be consistent and aimed at the same objectives.

To develop a communication strategy that will help you and your organization achieve the goals you have set for yourselves, you first must ask yourself a few questions related to the elements of communication listed above.

Sender   Who should communicate this message? Will your signature compel people to action? Should you ask your manager or vice president to sign this? Should someone closer to the intended audience send the message?

Receiver   Who *is* the intended audience for this message? What do you know about them? More important, what do they know about you and your subject? What feelings do they have about it and you? What's their previous experience with this subject and this sender? What's their likely reaction?

Message   What should your message contain? How should your message say what you intend for your audience to know? Should your message contain the bare minimum to evoke a reaction, or should you provide greater detail? Should the message focus on just one topic or should you include many issues for them to consider?

Medium   What's the best way to send this message? Is one medium quicker than another? Will one medium offer your audience better opportunities for feedback? Will one medium carry more detail than another? Does one medium carry a greater sense of urgency than another? Will one medium cost more than another?

Code   Encoding your message simply means selecting the right words and images. Style and tone matter very much as you approach readers and listeners with new information. Will they understand the words you plan to use? Will they understand the concepts you offer them? For your audience, decoding is a more complex matter of assigning meaning to the words and images you have selected. Will they mean the same thing to your receiver as they mean to you? Do these words and images have multiple meanings for you and your audience?

Feedback   What's the reaction of your audience? How will you know if you've communicated successfully? What measure will you use to determine whether they understand this subject the same way you understand it? Will the audience response be delayed? Will it be filtered through another source? How much feedback will you need before you decide to communicate again?

Noise   How many other senders and messages are out there? Whose message traffic are you competing with? Will others try to deflect, distort, or disable your communication attempts? How can you get the attention of your intended audience with all that they have to read, see, hear, and think about each day?

Effect   To achieve the goals you've set for yourself and your organization, you must know how to motivate them. You must show them how the information or ideas you have shown them are useful and worth acting upon.

SUCCESSFUL STRATEGIC COMMUNICATION

Getting people to listen to what you say, read what you write, or look at what you show them isn't easy. More often than not, people up and down the line have other interests that seem more immediate and other concerns to focus on. How, then, do you persuade them that paying attention to your message and cooperating with you is in their best interest?

Successful strategic communication usually involves the following six steps.

Link Your Message to the Strategy and Goals of the Organization   What are the strategic objectives of your business? Chances are good that your organization has published a document listing its vision, values, and beliefs. And, of course, the corporate annual report to shareholders is a good place to look for business strategy. If you can't find what you're looking for, call corporate communication and explain what you want and why you want it.

Every division within a business should have a set of simple, easy-to-understand business objectives (for example, "Increase cash flow by 10 percent during this fiscal year," or "Increase market share by 15 percent within the next three years.") All of your communication—no matter what the audience, no matter what the medium, no matter what the purpose for communicating—should be consistent with and directly supportive of those business objectives. If your writing and speaking don't fit that description, either you don't understand the company's objectives or you don't agree with them. If that is the case, you should make an effort to learn and understand them or look for work elsewhere.

Attract the Attention of Your Intended Audience   Appeal to basic needs or to the fundamentals of physiology to attract the attention of your intended audience. Basic needs would include the bottom rungs of Abraham Mazlow's Hierarchy of Human Needs. This explains the frequent focus on issues related to survival, food, water, sex appeal, and other needs.[4] The fundamentals of physiology are simply activities designed to appeal to the sight, hearing, taste, touch, or smell capacities of the audience. Loud noises, bright lights, and similar devices can attract attention; the more important issue is whether you can hold that attention once the audience knows who you are and what you want.

Explain Your Position in Terms They Will Understand and Accept   If your audience is willing to spend time and effort attending to your message but cannot understand what you intend, you'll raise nothing other than their frustration level. As you will see in Chapter 5, using language they are likely to understand and accept will make comprehension and compliance that much easier. This implies knowing your audience: knowing who they are, how much they know about this subject, how they feel about it, and their level of sophistication.

Motivate Your Audience to Accept and Act on Your Message   Several motivational appeals are available for you to reach and move your audience. First, consider an *appeal to authority*. If you are either in a position of organizational authority or are an acknowledged expert on the matter, you may legitimately ask your audience to respond to those forms of authority. It is the equivalent, to some, of hearing ". . . because I'm you're mother," but it works more often than not. And, in some instances, you may have neither the time nor the motivation to explain in detail why the audience should comply. Successful appeals to authority usually involve a follow-up stage in which the authority figure provides justification for the request.

Second, you might consider *social conformity* to move your audience. This is equivalent to the "celebrity endorsement" or "millions of satisfied customers can't be wrong" approach. The vast majority of people don't like to be out of step with other members of the society in which they live; they appreciate and value conformity and what it does for society. An endorsement to your intended audience from a person they respect (it doesn't matter if *you* respect him or her) may prove helpful. If not, you can always resort to opinion polls ("Four out of five dentists who chew gum recommend our product.")

Finally, you might use *rationality and consistency* theory to motivate your audience. Just as the majority of people wish to conform to what others think is proper, so too do they want rational, consistent behavior in their lives. If they see what you are advocating as irrational or inconsistent with their existing beliefs, they won't buy it. You must show them that it is consistent with what they already believe and—for those who admire logic—entirely rational.[5]

Innoculate Them Against Contrary Messages and Positions   Persuasion theorists have shown that beliefs persist in the face of contrary evidence if the holder of those beliefs has been inoculated against counter-persuasion at some point. Several means exist to make those actions you advocate resistant to the appeals of your competitors. First, you can ask for a *tangible commitment* from your audience. If that commitment is public, or at least known to other members of the target audience, so much the better. Everything from signing a pledge card to wearing a campaign button will bolster the beliefs of your audience.[6] A Los Angeles restauranteur dramatically cut the number of reservation "no-shows" by asking diners a simple question as they called for reservations: "Do you promise to call us if your dinner plans change?" The act of saying "yes" on the telephone committed them to a course of behavior that benefitted the restaurant substantially.[7]

Manage Audience Expectations   People are disappointed in the service or the products you deliver only if their expectations exceed the quality of what they receive. The same is true of communication. Always deliver what you promise, never less. Always meet or exceed your audience's expectations. Manage those expectations by cueing your audience about what to expect from your communications with them. If you deliver what you say you will, your audience will reward you with its attention and consideration for your message.

WHY COMMUNICATING AS A MANAGER IS DIFFERENT

Communication is a fundamental skill central to the human experience. We each know how to do it; we've done it since birth and receive additional practice each day. So, why is it so difficult to communicate on the job? What does the workplace do to change the nature of communication? Several factors in business life alter the way we look at communication. These factors influence the way we write and speak with others, right down to word selection and format. They influence our willingness to listen or to devote time to the concerns of others. And they influence the way we think about our daily problems, responsibilities, and challenges.

Levels of Responsibility and Accountability   The higher your level of responsibility in an organization, the more you have to think about. If you spend the majority of your day focused on just one or a few fairly well-defined issues, your communication will tend to be much more keenly focused. If you have many problems, many challenges to address during the day, your communication style will be more fragmented and broadly focused. As you read in Chapter 1, time management and communication efficiency become core skills.

Additionally, as you become more accountable, you tend to keep better records. If you know you'll be asked about particular issues, it's to your advantage to update and maintain what you know about those subjects. A phone call from your boss, posing questions you can't answer, is always a difficult experience.

Organizational Culture   Some organizations have a very written culture. Procter & Gamble, for example, requires that every issue be written in memo form and circulated to team members before it can be raised as an agenda issue in a team meeting. Other organizations, such as 3M Canada, are very "oral" in nature, offering employees an opportunity to talk things through before writing anything down. Many companies rely on a particular culture to move day-to-day information through the organization and, to succeed in such a business, you must adapt to the existing culture rather than try to change it or ask it to adapt to you.

Organizational Dynamics   Organizations, like the humans who populate and animate them, are in constant flux. Businesses change with the conditions of the marketplace and the lives of the managers who run them. Your communication will have to adapt to the conditions in which you find yourself.

That does not mean signing your name to a document that is false or passing along information that you know isn't true, even if the organization presses you for time or will not give you access to information you really need to do your job. It does mean adapting your style to the standards and norms of the industry. It may mean greater concision or more detail than you might personally prefer. It may mean shorter turn-around times on requests than you think is reasonable. Or it may mean sharing or withholding information from those you work with each day. Each organization has its own style which is conditionally and temporally affected by a range of issues from market share to target-status in a takeover.

Personality Preferences   Finally, it's important to acknowledge that each of us has his or her own preference for gathering, organizing, and disseminating information. And each of us has a style for making decisions. You'll have to accommodate those you work with and for in order to succeed in business.

If the boss wants plenty of detail and plenty of time to think it over before making a decision, accommodate that. Provide an executive summary, but give her the detail in tabular or annex form, if that is what she wants. Meet or beat submission deadlines. And provide the information in the form your reader or listener most wants. If your client likes e-mail, learn to live with brief, typewritten messages and attached text files.

If your client likes personal briefings, schedule the time it will take to go over the information in detail. It is counter-intuitive, but if you put the information-gathering and decision-making needs of others—particularly your boss and your clients—ahead of your own preferences, you'll get what you want faster and with much less pain.

THE TACTICS OF COMMUNICATION

Having decided on a strategy that will best convey what you intend your audience to know, you'll want to pay some attention to the tactics of communication. That, in fact, is what the rest of this book is about: fact-finding, analysis, methods, timing, media, cost, and the dozens of assumptions you must make about your audience, your reasons for communicating, and the context within which it all takes place.

Endnotes

1. Fabun, D. *Communication: The Human Experience.* New York, NY: Wm. Morrow, 1968.
2. See DeVito, J. A. *The Interpersonal Communication Book,* 5th ed. New York, NY: HarperCollins Publishers, 1989, pp. 23–36. See also Watzlawick, P., Beavin, J. H., and Jackson, J. D., *Pragmatics of Human Communication: A Study of Interactional Patterns, Pathologies, and Paradoxes.* New York, NY: Norton, 1967.
3. DeVito, J. A. *Human Communication: The Basic Course,* 5th ed. New York, NY: HarperCollins Publishers, 1991, p. 5.
4. Maslow, A. "A Theory of Human Motivation." *Psychological Review,* Vol. 50 (1943): 370–396.
5. Bem, D. J. *Beliefs, Attitudes, and Human Affairs.* Belmont, CA: Brooks/Cole Publishing Company, 1970, pp. 24–38.
6. Cialdini, R. B. *Influence: The Psychology of Persuasion.* New York, NY: Quill Books, 1993.
7. William Grimes. "In War Against No-Shows, Restaurants Get Tougher." *New York Times,* October 15, 1997, pp. B1–B6.

For Further Reading

O'Hair, D., Friedrich, G. W., and Shaver, L. D. *Strategic Communication in Business and the Professions,* 2nd ed. Boston, MA: Houghton Mifflin Company, 1995.

Quirke, B. *Communicating Corporate Change: A Practical Guide to Communication and Corporate Strategy.* London, UK: McGraw-Hill Publishing Company, 1996.

Spaeth, M. *Marketplace Communication.* New York, NY: MasterMedia Limited, 1996.

⨎

Case 2–1 GREAT WEST CASUALTY VS. ESTATE OF G. WITHERSPOON (A)

A. C. Zucaro, chairman and CEO of Old Republic International Corporation, arrived at work on January 15, 1999, and picked up that morning's edition of The *Wall Street Journal,* as usual. As he worked deliberately through his first cup of coffee, his well-honed business instincts told him this would be a good day: Interest rates were down, the market was up, and the many subsidiaries of Old Republic were performing well. For the moment, Mr. Zucaro was a happy man.

As he moved to section two of the *Journal,* his optimism sank. There, on the front page of the Marketplace section, was an article discussing a lawsuit involving a subsidiary of Old Republic, Great West Casualty Company. Nothing new for a company with $2 billion in revenues and nine operating subsidiaries. But Zucaro knew from the headline that this Friday morning would be less pleasant than most: "An Old Woman Crossed the Road, and Litigiousness Sank to New Low."

THE EVENTS OF JULY 1, 1998

On her way to work at 4:30 A.M. on July 1, 1998, 81-year old Gertie Witherspoon blew out a tire and careened into a roadside ditch. With her automobile disabled, Mrs. Witherspoon left her car and began walking along U.S. Route 71 near Adrian, Missouri. Still dazed from the accident, she attempted to cross the highway to reach help. At just that moment, two semitrucks traveling almost side by side spotted the small figure in the road as they passed under a bridge. Traveling nearly 70 miles per hour, the truckers were unable to avoid hitting her. According to the police report, the driver of the rig slammed on his brakes and skidded more than 100 feet. Mrs. Witherspoon was pronounced dead at the scene.

Friends and relatives were stunned and saddened, particularly at Dave's Wagon Wheel Restaurant, where Ms. Witherspoon worked 50 hours a week as a waitress. No one took the news harder than Joyce Lang, Mrs. Witherspoon's only daughter. "The family was crushed," she said, "and I was determined to find out more about what happened that morning."

A RELATIVE CONTACTS THE INSURANCE COMPANY

In the days and weeks following the accident, Ms. Lang sought more information about the accident. She received only indifferent statements from the Missouri Highway Patrol and the truck owner, Rex Williams, of Vernon County Grain & Supply. Frustrated in her attempts to learn more about her mother's death, Ms. Lang telephoned a claims adjuster at Great West Casualty Company to ask a few questions.

The adjuster at Great West Casualty explained that the police report and witness' statements showed no fault on the part of the truck driver. "Is that all you can tell me?" she asked.

"The case is closed," the adjuster responded.

"Well," said Ms. Lang, "I can open it."

Believing the family was preparing legal action against Great West Casualty Company, the claims representative moved to file suit on behalf of his company against Gertie Witherspoon's estate. "It was never my intention to sue the company." Ms. Lang said later. "I did contact an attorney, but it was only to find out what our rights were. We filed no claims or lawsuits."

About five months later—just a few days before Christmas—on December 18, 1998, Joyce Lang received notice of a legal claim filed against the Witherspoon estate for damages to the truck that struck her mother. Specifically, the claim sought $2,886 "on account of property damage caused to a vehicle due to the negligent actions of Gertie Witherspoon on July 1, 1998."

The local news media first reported this incident on September 4, 1998, when Barbara

Shelly, a reporter for the *Kansas City Star* and an acquaintance of Ms. Lang, wrote a brief article elaborating on the life of Gertie Witherspoon. By coincidence, Ms. Shelly happened to be speaking with Ms. Lang on the day the claims notice arrived. "Seeing my mother's name in print like she was a criminal," said Ms. Lang, "I was devasted." Ms. Lang received the notice because she was serving as executor of her mother's estate. "I'm not paying them for killing my mom," she said. "I'll sit in jail first."

Amazed by the insurance company's actions, Ms. Shelly wrote a second article discussing the accident and the insurance company's response. Details in the second article appeared in the January 8, 1998, edition of the *Kansas City Star*. The story was then picked up by the *Wall Street Journal* and reported on January 15, 1998 (Attachment 1). It was at that moment that A. C. Zucaro sensed trouble. Covering the claim filed by Rex Williams was a fairly small matter. The more immediate problem for him would be the company's response to the storm of media criticism.

OLD REPUBLIC INTERNATIONAL CORPORATION

In January 1999, Old Republic International Corporation was a financially strong and efficient insurance enterprise with substantial interests in each segment of the insurance and reinsurance industry. Old Republic International was primarily a commercial line underwriter, serving many of America's leading industrial and financial services companies as valued customers. For the year ended 1997, the company's net income was $298 million on revenues of $1.962 billion.

Old Republic International had grown steadily as a specialty insurance business since 1923. The company was regarded as independent and innovative, which was reflected in its growth. Most Wall Street insurance analysts thought the company's performance reflected an entrepreneurial spirit, sound forward planning, and an effective corporate structure that promoted and encouraged the assumption of prudent business risks. At the time, Old Republic International had nine subsidiaries across four general business lines, including General Insurance Group, Mortgage Guaranty Group, Title Insurance Group, and Life Insurance Group.

Old Republic International's corporate communication department consists of one individual who handled investor relations. All other forms of communication were outsourced to a large public relations firm in Chicago, Illinois, that reported directly to the company's president. The work performed by the public relations firm was financially oriented and included such tasks as preparing annual reports and earnings announcements.

GREAT WEST CASUALTY COMPANY

Great West Casualty Company was an independent subsidiary of Old Republic. Founded in 1956, Great West Casualty served the special needs of the trucking industry. By 1999, the company served 29 states and had regional offices in Boise, Idaho (Western Region); Bloomington, Indiana (Eastern Region); Arlington, Texas (Southern Region); and Knoxville, Tennessee (Southeastern Region). The corporate headquarters in South Sioux City, Nebraska, served the central and northern regions. Great West Casualty employed more than 600 professionals companywide. Their policies included automobile liability, cargo coverage, general liability, inland marine floaters, physical damage, property coverage, umbrellas, and workers' compensation.

The Great West Casualty communication department also had just one employee, Ms. Leslie Bartholomew. As corporate information director, she handled all communications for the firm. Aside from an operational manual provided by Old Republic International, consisting mostly of general guidelines for handling corporate communication, Great West Casualty made virtually all communication decisions independently.

For Zucaro and his senior team at Old Republic International, the questions were direct and fairly simple: What should they do, how soon should they do it, and how should their actions be communicated? Would they need professional help from a public relations firm? And, more to the point, what did this series of events say to the company about its corporate communication strategy?

AN OLD WOMAN CROSSED THE ROAD, AND LITIGIOUSNESS SANK TO NEW LOW

By Carl Quintanilla

Staff Reporter of THE WALL STREET JOURNAL

Anybody in the insurance industry could answer this one: An 81-year-old woman steps in front of a big truck on a highway and gets killed. What happens next?

A claim for damages, of course. But in this case, it isn't the woman's family that is seeking compensation. Instead, the trucker's insurance company is charging the elderly dead woman with negligence—and seeking damages from her estate.

"I'm not paying them for killing my mom," says Joyce Lang, the dead woman's daughter. "I'll sit in jail first."

The accident happened before dawn one morning last July when Gertie Witherspoon of Adrian, Mo., was on her way to work. At 81, she was vibrant and active, working 50 hours a week at a restaurant called Dave's Wagon Wheel, where regulars called her "Sammy."

Suddenly she had a blowout. Her car careened into a roadside ditch. Dazed, she climbed out and walked in front of an oncoming grain truck. According to the police report, the driver of the rig slammed on his brakes and skidded more than 100 feet. But Mrs. Witherspoon was pronounced dead at the scene.

About five months later, just before Christmas, Ms. Lang received notice of a claim from the grain truck's insurer, Great West Casualty Co., for damage incurred by the truck. The amount Great Western is seeking: $2,800.

"Seeing my mother's name in print like she was a criminal, I was devastated," says Ms. Lang, the executor of her mother's estate.

Ms. Lang, who first told her story to the Kansas City Star, has hired an attorney to fight the bill. "How much damage can a 5-foot, 105-pound woman do to a big truck like that?" she asks.

Great West, a unit of Chicago-based Old Republic International Corp., won't say. Citing company policy, it refuses to discuss the specifics of the case. But the company does claim that the way in which Mrs. Witherspoon crossed the road was "negligent."

Rex Williams, owner of Vernon County Grain & Supply, the company whose truck was involved in the accident, says he has no comment on the matter.

Still, Scott Rager, Great West's executive vice president, concedes that the insurance company's pursuit of $2,800 is risky from a public-relations standpoint. "It doesn't do anything to help people's impressions of us," he says.

_____

The Wall Street Journal, Friday, January 15, 1999, p. B1.

Case 2–2   GREAT LAKES GARMENTS, INC.

BACKGROUND NOTE

As managers are called on to communicate with various audiences, they must keep in mind that some documents are written with more than one purpose or one audience in mind.

Writing direct correspondence from one person to another is relatively easy if the sender understands his or her purpose for writing, the occasion on which the message is sent, and the audience (of just one) to whom the letter is addressed. With just one intended recipient, it is usually easier to know the receiver's background, vocabulary, knowledge of the subject, and likely reaction to the message.

Writing messages intended for a very large audience, or more than one audience, is more complex. The writer must take into account varying ages, educational backgrounds, reading abilities, vocabulary, knowledge of the subject, and literally dozens of other, possibly relevant factors.

Composing an "all hands" memorandum in which one message is sent to a large number of people simultaneously is difficult. It is doubly so, if you have been asked to speak in someone else's voice. The accompanying memorandum explains a difficult situation in a company you work for. You are being asked to draft a letter for the company president explaining some impending layoffs.

Keep in mind that letters of this sort have lives of their own. Once written, they are no longer your property. They belong to those people to whom they're addressed and they, in turn, may choose to share them with others, including the press.

Great Lakes Garments, Inc. is a mid-sized, publicly held manufacturing firm located in the midwestern United States. The current collective bargaining agreement with the ILGWU is in the second year of a four-year term. This case requires two documents in response: a one- or two-page communication strategy memorandum and a letter. The memo should be directed to the president of the company; the letter should be directed to the firm's employees. Both documents must be in finished form and ready to transmit.

InterOffice Memorandum
GREAT LAKES GARMENTS, INC.
2800 North Sheridan Road
Lake Bluff, Illinois 60691

DATE: [Today's Date]
FROM: Richard J. Gidley
          President
TO: Vice President, Corporate Communication
SUBJECT: **COMMUNICATION PLAN FOR PROPOSED GLG LAYOFFS**

Background

The board of directors has just met in executive session and has voted to implement our plan of structured layoffs in order to avoid a near-term cash flow problem. As you know, interest payments on a large series of long-term bonds are coming due, as are pension payments and tax payments, and we simply don't have the cash to handle them.

I have directed that all management employees will be subject to an immediate pay freeze. All senior management at the level of assistant vice president and above have agreed to an immediate 10% pay cut. These are important symbolic measures, but they will not generate sufficient cash to meet our immediate needs. Rather than borrow additional funds to meet this shortfall, the directors have agreed that some layoffs will be necessary—particularly in light of rising inventories and a slowdown in demand from our wholesalers.

The layoffs will involve only recent hires, though some people who have been with the firm as long as five years may be among those we lay off. Out of some 1,500 employees, we plan to name about 200 for short-term unemployment. They will be principally third-shift production employees, including assemblers, finishers, sorters, cutters, and other lower wage-scale employees.

How long will these layoffs last? I don't think anyone here knows for sure, but my guess is that most of these folks will be out for a minimum of 90 days, perhaps as long as six months. The unspoken assumption about all of this is that we'll get back on our feet in sales and cash flow and can resume our third shift in a few months.

I pass this next piece of information on to you, but it's not for public dissemination: We may well learn to live without some of these people permanently, but I just can't say which ones and how many of them just now. A few, perhaps 25 to 50, just won't come back at all. We will do what we can to help them find new work. We'll help everyone to fill out the proper paperwork to receive unemployment benefits and we will keep in touch with the unions once every 30 days or so to let them know how we're doing. They, in turn, can contact their membership.

Your Task

We need to draft a plan of some sort to let our people know what's happening. Obviously, those who will be laid off should be approached directly. But how should we do it? Who should deliver the message? Should I be involved personally in this, or can we handle this in some other way? In your strategy memo, give me some idea of timing as well as methods for delivering this news to them.

Communication Plan for Proposed GLG Layoffs
[Today's Date]
Page Two

Our contract with the ILGWU calls for a minimum of two-weeks' notice prior to layoffs. It also calls for notification in writing. I need a letter for my signature to those people being laid off. It should be direct and in plain English, but sensitive to the difficulty that both we and they are going to experience. Be warm, be responsive, but be firm and don't promise them anything that's not going to happen. Let me see your first draft today.

###

3
COMMUNICATION ETHICS
∂℧

Pick up *The Wall Street Journal* any given morning and look through sections one and three. Frequently, you'll find stories such as this:

> NASD FINES FIRM, 2 EXECUTIVES IN CASE OF MISLEADING ADS. More than three years after the alleged violations took place, the National Association of Securities Dealers' regulatory arm assessed its largest-ever fine for misleading mutual-fund advertising.
>
> NASD announced late yesterday that it levied a fine totaling $125,000 against Fundamental Service Corporation, its vice president . . . , and its marketing chief, . . . [The vice president] was fined $100,000 jointly with the firm, while the NASD fined [the marketing director] $25,000. The company neither admitted nor denied wrongdoing in reaching the settlement.
>
> Most NASD advertising-case settlements are less than $50,000. In addition to the fines, the NASD suspended the executives for 30 days each, and [the vice president] agreed not to apply for registration as a general securities principal for three years.
>
> At issue: charges that the firm distributed more than a million copies of "false and misleading" no-load mutual-fund advertisements, according to the NASD.[1]

On other days, it's likely to be a story like this:

> AN EMPLOYEE ON WALL ST. IS ARRESTED. Said to Profit from Her Position of Trust. Prosecutors said yesterday that they had arrested a brokerage firm employee responsible for protecting market-sensitive information and charged her with using the information to profit from insider trading.
>
> The employee, . . . , an analyst in the legal department at Morgan Stanley, Dean Witter, Discover & Company, was arrested on Monday at work and charged on Tuesday with grand larceny, possession of stolen property, scheming to defraud, commercial bribe receiving and securities fraud, the office of District Attorney Robert M. Morgenthau of Manhattan said. Investigators indicated at a news conference yesterday that they expected to make more arrests. . . .
>
> [She] is said to have sold to other unnamed parties her advance knowledge of a revamping of Georgia Pacific, and—just last week—sold proprietary information about a Morgan Stanley analyst's forthcoming downgrade of Einstein Bagels stock. "Whenever you have a market as heated as this market is, there's a temptation for someone with inside information to trade on it," Mr. Morgenthau said.

[The employee] is a law school graduate who, according to one investigator, earned a little more than $70,000 a year at Morgan Stanley. She lives on Manhattan's Upper East Side. . . .[2]

Unless it is an unusual day, you'll find at least one news item dealing with allegations of misstatement, misappropriation, equivocation, or fraud. They're often printed alongside stories of people who have lied to their employers, to their customers and clients, to regulatory agencies, and to the courts. In other instances, they have simply deceived themselves.

What's going on here? Does this behavior represent a sudden outbreak of unethical conduct or confusion over appropriate uses of proprietary information in North American businesses? Or, are investigative and prosecution techniques improving? While the latter may be true in part, it's hard to believe that management information processing and communication techniques have only recently begun to display illegal or unethical tendencies.

Many experts on this subject report that a surprisingly large percentage of businesspeople seem to believe they can handle information in any way they see fit, and can communicate (or fail to do so) with shareholders, clients, customers, competitors, regulatory agencies, legislative bodies, and other branches of government without regard to truth, fairness, equity, justice, and ethics.

According to Gary Edwards, president of the Ethics Resource Center, a consulting firm in Washington, D.C., "The message out there is, reaching objectives is what matters and how you get there isn't important." The result, in his view, has been a steady stream of questionable and sometimes plainly criminal behavior throughout corporate America.[3]

Michael Josephson, a prominent Los Angeles ethicist who consults for some of the nation's largest public corporations, says his polls reveal that between 20 and 30 percent of middle managers have written deceptive internal reports. At least part of this, in his view, is relatively harmless—managers inflating budget proposals in the hope of ultimately getting what they really need, for example. "But a good share of it will almost surely hurt the people and the companies involved, in some cases grievously."[4]

THE ETHICAL CONDUCT OF EMPLOYERS

A recent National Business Ethics Survey discovered that employees care about the ethical conduct of their employers. But what should be of serious concern is that employees are questioning the ethics of many of their managers today. The Hudson Institute and Walker Information, both located in Indianapolis, surveyed more than 3,000 workers from business and not-for-profit organizations across the United States about their experiences and attitudes. The most worrisome finding? Less than half of working Americans believe that their senior leaders are people of high integrity.[5]

Other findings in the Hudson-Walker survey may be cause for concern, as well. Only a third of employees feel comfortable reporting misconduct, in part because less than half feel that ethical or compliance problems are dealt with fairly and completely. Case in point: 30 percent of employees know of or suspect ethical violations in their organizations in the past two years. However, the majority of these employees—six in ten—who have seen or know about a violation have *not* reported it. Why not? Three primary reasons were given for not reporting actual observed misconduct.

- Employees did not feel the organization would respond.
- There was a perceived lack of anonymous and confidential means of reporting.
- Fear of retaliation from management prevented workers from reporting the misconduct they had witnessed.[6]

Do any of these findings—these attitudes about ethical behavior—have any effect on you? Virtually all business leaders say they do. Business—even in a free market-place—is governed by rules. Those rules range from complex tax laws and restrictions on exports to broad, general notions of truth in advertising and reliance on a person's word. If competitors either break the rules or behave as though there were no rules, the free marketplace is undermined, expectations are destroyed, and trust is eliminated.

If you behave in unethical ways, people will quickly realize that you cannot be trusted. Your performance will be seen as unreliable and self-centered. Aside from running afoul of the law, unethical behavior will eventually isolate you from the community of business practitioners who play by the rules and for whom trust is an important part of doing business.

DEFINING BUSINESS ETHICS

Raymond Baumhart, a college professor and ethicist, once asked a number of business managers what the word *ethical* meant to them. Fifty percent of the managers in his interviews defined *ethical* as "what my feelings tell me is right." Yet feelings are often an inadequate basis on which to make decisions. Twenty-five percent of his respondents defined *ethical* in terms of what is "in accord with my religious beliefs" and 18 percent defined the term as what "conforms to the golden rule." Religious authority has been devastatingly criticized, along with the "golden rule," as an inadequate foundation for ethical claims.[7]

For one thing, religion often requires an act of faith to accept guidelines, norms, dogma, or precepts. And the golden rule (Do unto others, as you would have others do unto you) assumes that we each would wish for the same form of treatment. Our interests and preferences, in fact, may be substantially different. A supervisor's inquiry on behalf of an employee may be seen as a thoughtful, caring gesture by some and as intrusive snooping or prying by others. If such guides are helpful, but hardly definitive, how should we make ethical judgments? What does *ethical* mean to a business communicator?

Ethics most often refers to a field of inquiry, or discipline, in which matters of right and wrong, good and evil, virtue and vice, are systematically examined. *Morality,* by contrast, is most often used to refer not to a discipline but to patterns of behavior that are actually common in everyday life. In this sense, morality is what the discipline of ethics is about. And so business morality is what business ethics is about.[8]

The phrases "corporate social responsibility" and "the social responsibility of business" are sometimes used as though they were synonymous with business ethics. Oil companies frequently advertise about how careful they are with the environment, and chemical companies proclaim their "good citizen" role of providing jobs, opportunity, and the chance to "do good things." But these can be misleading if they imply that business ethics deals exclusively with the relationships between business organizations and what have come to be called their *external constituencies,* such as consumers, suppliers, government agencies, community groups, and host countries.

While these relationships define a large and very important part of business ethics, they do not encompass the entire field. Important *internal constituencies,* such as employees, stockholders, boards of directors, and managers, are also involved, as well as ethical issues that do not lend themselves to constituency or stakeholder analysis. Thus, business ethics is a much larger notion than corporate social responsibility, even though it includes that concept.[9]

THREE LEVELS OF INQUIRY

The three most common concerns in the moral responsibilities, obligations, and virtues of business decision making have been the choices and characters of persons, the policies and cultures of organizations, and the arrangements and beliefs of entire social and economic systems, such as capitalism. Business ethics, then, is multileveled.

The Individual   For the individual businessperson, business ethics concerns the values by which self-interest and other motives are balanced with concern for fairness and the common good, both inside and outside of a company. The project leader who unfairly claims credit for a proposal that many of his subordinates worked on is clearly putting his own self-interest ahead of that of the organization and his fellow employees. It may not be illegal, but it's certainly unfair.

The Organization   At the level of the organization, business ethics concerns the group conscience that every company has (even though it may be unspoken) as it pursues its economic objectives. This conscience is a reflection of both organizational culture and conduct. A real estate development firm that buys an entire city block filled with low-income housing may see only the benefits to be derived from demolishing the apartments and constructing offices, shops, and a parking garage. The people occupying the low-income apartments to be demolished may have great difficulty finding another place to live that they can afford. A failure to see them as an important part of the purchase and development plans, again, would not likely be against the law, but it would certainly be unjust.

The Economy   Finally, at the level of the entire economic system, business ethics concerns the pattern of social, political, and economic forces that drives individuals and businesses–the values that define capitalism, for example. But even capitalism works within a system of ethical rules. For the government of one nation to decide that it will not enforce copyright laws or extend patent protection to products or intellectual property produced overseas is to invite chaos within the free-market system.[10]

THREE VIEWS OF DECISION MAKING

For business communicators and others who make business decisions, three points of view are available to assist in making those decisions. These include a *moral point of view,* an *economic point of view,* and a *legal point of view.*

Moral Point of View From this perspective, businesspeople ask, "Morally, what is the best thing to do?" Such questions would be separate from inquiries about economic decisions that seek to maximize shareholder wealth, or legal decisions that ask what the law permits and forbids. According to many business ethicists, a moral point of view has two important features. The first is a willingness to seek out and act on reasons.

Second, a moral point of view requires the decision maker to be impartial. This means that decision makers will demonstrate a commitment to use reason in deliberating about what to do, constructing moral arguments that are persuasive to themselves and to others. They will also give all interests equal weight in deciding what to do. The problem with this point of view is that most ethical business issues aren't especially clear and, in many instances, decision makers don't have adequate information at the time they need it most.[11]

Economic Point of View An economic point of view, by contrast, employs a free market model of capitalism in which scarce resources or factors of production are used to produce goods and services. The forces of supply and demand are used to allocate resources and the structure of the marketplace determines what is in the best interests of the organization. Economic theory, however, is not entirely value-neutral. Certain assumptions about a free market underlie all business activities, including basic notions about honesty, theft, fraud, and the like.

In addition, it is important for business communicators to understand that companies are not merely abstract economic entities, but large-scale organizations that involve flesh-and-blood human beings. Those same firms, further, must operate in a complex environment with many constituencies to please, some of which are often in conflict with others.[12]

Legal Point of View A third point of view for ethical decision making in business is the legal viewpoint. Most business activity takes place within an extensive system of laws, so that all business decisions—especially those involving communication—must be made from a legal as well as an economic standpoint. Many businesspeople assume that "If it's legal, then it's morally okay." This ignores a number of realities involving the law and decision making.

First, the law is inappropriate for regulating certain aspects of business activity. Not everything that is immoral is, in fact, illegal. Hiring a relative for a position that other, better qualified, applicants have applied for will certainly raise conflict-of-interest questions, but it may not be illegal. Second, the law is often slow to develop in new areas of concern. Technology, for example, not only presents new opportunities for unethical behavior, but often outpaces legal restrictions.[13]

The law often employs moral concepts which are not precisely defined, so that it is often difficult to use the law to make decisions without also considering issues of morality. In addition, the law itself is often unsettled or in a state of evolution on many issues. Frequently, the notion of whether an action was legal or illegal must be decided case-by-case in the courts, with key issues often being decided higher within the appellate court system. The law does not provide specific guidance for behavior in all possible instances. For example, the issue of whether a conversation among a few friends constitutes protected speech or is sexual harassment is one that courts must decide on the merits of the specific incident. Finally, the law is generally seen as an inefficient instrument, inviting expensive legislation and litigation where more efficient systems of decision making might do just as well in producing workable answers.[14]

AN INTEGRATED APPROACH

Many business ethicists advocate a decision-making process that integrates these three viewpoints, considering the demands of morality, economics, and the law together. Decisions, they say, can be made on the basis of morality, profit, and legality together to arrive at workable solutions which will take into account the best interests of all concerned, protect the investment of shareholders, and obey the law.

A company that elects voluntarily to remove a tainted or defective product from supermarket shelves considers the safety and welfare of its customers while, at the same time, avoiding lawsuits and protecting the company's good name and market share. Such decisions, though costly in the short run, almost always prove to be beneficial in the long run.

What about those cases in which neither the issue at hand nor the outcome of the decision is entirely clear? Some ethicists focus on the value of dialogue in arriving at an ethical answer. Michael G. Bowen and F. Clark Power write, "In this regard, our definition of the moral manager is a person willing to engage in a fair and open dialogue with interested stakeholders or their representatives."[15]

Making choices based on the input and ideas of those who are most affected by the outcome of your decisions can help to produce better decisions. Becoming an ethical business communicator may involve more than a simple willingness to talk about the issues with stakeholders, though. It might also include some knowledge of moral judgments and how they are made.

THE NATURE OF MORAL JUDGMENTS

Two basic types of judgments are *normative judgments* and *moral judgments*. Normative judgments are claims that state or imply that something is good or bad, right or wrong, better or worse, ought to be or ought not to be. Normative judgments, then, express our values. They indicate our attitudes toward some object, person, circumstance, or event. Nonnormative judgments, on the other hand, are value neutral. They describe, name, define, report, or make predictions.[16]

If I were to say, "These figures are mistaken," that would be normative. To say, "These figures do not match the auditor's," would be nonnormative. Normative judgments are prescriptive, while nonnormative judgments are descriptive. Moral judgments, then, are a special subset or category of normative judgments.

Ethics does not study all normative judgments, only those that are concerned with what is morally right and wrong or morally good and bad. When decisions are judged to be morally right or wrong, or morally good or bad, the underlying standards on which the judgment is based are moral standards. It would be immoral by such standards to short-weight a shipment of goods, for example, or to identify the contents of a package as containing "all natural ingredients," when, in fact, they are not.

Businesspeople use two types of moral standards to make decisions. *Moral norms,* on the one hand, are standards of behavior that require, prohibit, or allow certain kinds of behavior. *Moral principles,* on the other hand, are much more general concepts used to evaluate both group and individual behavior. A norm, for example, might permit rounding of figures to the nearest hundred or thousand in standard accounting procedure, while principles might deal with the general notion of full disclosure to interested stakeholders.

DISTINGUISHING CHARACTERISTICS OF MORAL PRINCIPLES

Moral standards, in many respects, are like other standards. They provide direction, guidance, and counsel. They are guideposts or compass headings when decisions have to be made. They are different from other standards in several important respects, though.

They Have Serious Consequences to Human Well-Being　This means distinguishing between things that matter and things that don't. Omitting small details about packaging or manufacturing from a product insert may be an important legal matter, but is probably not a moral issue. Failing to reveal potential hazards of product use is certainly a moral issue.

Their Validity Rests on the Adequacy of the Reasons Which Are Used to Support and Justify Them　If the reasons you employ to support your decisions are not accepted by the society at large, or at least by a thoughtful group of people who have given the matter careful consideration, then you may wish to reassess just how adequate your standards are.

They Override Self-Interest　Genuine moral standards transcend the interests of just one or a few people. They involve doing things for the greater good of society or people at large. Rather than asking, "How will this affect me?" you might wish to ask, "How will this decision affect the entire firm or the whole community?"

They Are Based on Impartial Considerations　Moral standards are devised from a universal standpoint and are clearly more objective than subjective. They don't bring harm or disruption to many simply to benefit a few.[17]

FOUR RESOURCES FOR DECISION MAKING

Four simple but powerful resources are available to every business communicator who is trying to make ethical decisions. They are proposals, observations, value judgments, and assumptions. Let's examine each of them independently.

Proposals　These are *prescriptive* statements, suggesting actions. "We should develop a child care center for our company," would be an example of a proposal. It is a statement that relies on observations, value judgments, and assumptions, but goes further. It suggests actions that people should take and that can be evaluated by examining supporting reasons. Proposals often reveal what people have been paying attention to (observations) and can frequently serve as a clue to their values and assumptions.

Proposals are often answers to questions. Good questions can generate good proposals. "Should we revise our performance review system?" The best questions are specific and action-oriented, while the best proposals are specific responses to such questions. For example: "We should revise our performance review system to include semi-annual peer feedback." The only missing element of this proposal is the underlying reasoning or values which prompted it.

Observations   These are *descriptive* statements, describing situations. "Not all of the information about pending litigation against the company is revealed in the annual report to shareholders." Such statements rely on a correct presentation of the facts and can usually be verified through more research. The usefulness of observations can also be evaluated by the degree of objectivity they contain. The more objective the statement, the more likely it is to be an observation.

A statement qualifies as an observation if contrary evidence can disprove it. If I observe, for example, that "an increasing number of product liability suits is jeopardizing our industry," I could verify or refute that statement with specific evidence.

Observations sometimes look like assumptions, since they both appear to describe. An important difference is that observations are usually specific and empirical in nature. "Our product package insert does not reveal all of the potential hazards associated with this product's use." This is an example of an observation; a related assumption might be that revealing all potential hazards would be useful or instructive to our customers. An opposing assumption might be that revealing all potential hazards would only serve to frighten our customers, since many of the hazards are extremely rare.

Value Judgments   These are *normative* statements, guiding the actions of others. "Information that significantly affects a worker's schedule or position should be delivered in person by the supervisor." Such statements rely on assumptions, and make the connection between a proposal and an observation. These are statements, however, that cannot be verified by empirical research. They can be evaluated by different ethical traditions.

Value judgments can also be asserted as *should statements*. Unlike proposals, which are usually specific, value judgments are general statements. "We should be fair in our dealings with customers." This is not a statement of what we should do specifically in each instance with a customer. It is, rather, a general guideline for action.

Assumptions   These are *reflective* statements, expressing world views and attitudes. "Our employees are honest." Statements such as this one rely on culture, religion, social, and personal history. They're usually taken for granted in day-to-day conversation and business correspondence, but they each have theoretical roots in our attitudinal system. They can be evaluated by such criteria as relevance, consistency, and inclusiveness.

Table 3–1 summarizes the key differences among these resources. Proposals and value judgments, for example, are action-oriented, telling the listener or reader what to do. Observations and assumptions, on the other hand, merely serve to describe. Proposals and observations tend to be very specific in nature, focused on the action or situation at hand. Value judgments and assumptions, though, are more general in nature and provide very broad guidance to a decision maker.[18]

Table 3–1	Four resources for decision making.	
	Action-Orientation	*Descriptive-Orientation*
Specific	Proposals	Observations
General	Value Judgments	Assumptions

Source: Adapted from Marvin T. Brown, *The Ethical Process: A Strategy for Making Good Decisions.* Upper Saddle River, NJ: Prentice Hall, Inc., 1996, p. 7.

MAKING MORAL JUDGMENTS

Moral judgments seem to depend on decision makers having and using four separate capacities: ethical sensibility, ethical reasoning, ethical conduct, and ethical leadership.[19]

Ethical Sensibility   This is reflected in your capacity to impose ethical order on a situation—to identify aspects of the situation that have ethical importance. A person lacking in ethical sensibility will be insensitive to the ethically important features of a situation and, thus, vulnerable to acting in ways that are improper.

Suppose you are working as a computer software consultant, and a local charitable group asks you to serve as a member of its volunteer advisory board. Sounds noble and worthwhile, right? Well, suppose further that the charitable group decides to accept bids on a data processing system that will assist in fund-raising. You're in a position to provide expert advice. Now what happens if your employer decides to bid on that data processing system? Can you remain a member of that advisory board? Not if you recognize the *conflict of interest* which faces you. Your interests as a commercial software consultant conflict with your interests as an advisor to the charitable group. Ethical sensibility would make you aware of that conflict.

Ethical Reasoning   Recognizing the ethically important features of a situation is the first step toward dealing with them appropriately. The next step is to reason carefully about the situation to determine what kind of ethical problem you face: Is it bribery, an unfair labor practice, or consumer deception? Ethical reasoning then offers opportunities for solution: What would be fairest for all concerned? Is this problem similar to one we've seen in the past? Is there a rule or policy determining our conduct in this case? If not, should we consider writing one? What's the basis for the argument I'm faced with?

Sometimes simple recognition of an ethical problem will point toward a solution. Let's say your job is to review advertising copy for your company's products. As you do so, you recognize a series of misleading claims in the proposed ad copy. Your solution is easy enough: Return the copy to the writing team with specific instructions to remove or correct the misleading claims. More often, however, the solution to an ethical problem involves conflicting values.

Let's say you are a manager who discovers that the production line presents potential hazards to the reproductive health of female workers. You also recognize that removing women from the line would be unfair. Two competing values in this instance—equal employment opportunity and keeping workers from harm—require some careful ethical reasoning in order to make an appropriate moral judgment.

Ethical Conduct   Recognizing ethical dilemmas and reasoning your way to an appropriate solution are simply the first two steps in living an ethical life in business. It's one thing to know what you should do, and quite another to do it. Lynn Sharp Paine of the Harvard Business School says, "Hypocrisy and cowardice, both reflected in discrepancies between professed beliefs and actual conduct, are the enemies of integrity."[20]

Recognizing that it would be wrong to file an inflated travel voucher following a business trip, you remind your colleagues that the company will gladly reimburse all necessary expenses, but only for the amounts actually spent. While you encourage and expect others to comply with that reasoning, you claim expenses in excess of what you actually spent, and ask for reimbursement for expenditures that were not legitimate business expenses. In such a case, hypocrisy would best describe your behavior.

If you were witness to a fellow employee stealing supplies from your company but failed to speak with either him or your supervisor, you might well be guilty of cowardice. You recognized the problem and knew what the appropriate response would be, but failed to act. Such situations require a certain amount of *moral courage*. That's the ability to stand up and do what is right, even though it won't be easy, popular, or profitable.

Ethical Leadership   The capacity for ethical leadership, according to Professor Paine, "is associated with the highest levels of integrity." She quotes Confucius, saying "The superior person seeks to perfect the admirable qualities of others and does not seek to perfect their bad qualities. The lesser person does the opposite of this." She goes on to note that most business students will work in organizations in which they will have the power and responsibility not only to exercise their own ethical capacities, but to influence the exercise of those capacities in others.[21]

Numerous researchers and commentators have attributed critical importance to the ethical example provided by an organization's top officials. It seems unlikely that great integrity would emerge in an organization led by men and women lacking in basic integrity. Yet, without question, leadership is not confined to the chairman or chief executive officer of an organization.

Ethical leadership begins with front-line supervisors setting examples for and assisting those who work for them. Others in an organization will watch what you do and, if you're in a position of leadership or responsibility, an ethical obligation accompanies your management duties. If you let your employees know, directly or indirectly, that you condone industrial spying or the theft of competitive marketing data, they will assume that the company approves and that such acts are probably alright. The plain fact is, the moral education of those beneath you in an organization depends on your willingness to engage in and reward ethical behavior.[22]

APPLYING ETHICAL STANDARDS TO MANAGEMENT COMMUNICATION

Ethical business practice is a noble goal to which virtually all firms aspire. Many companies, however, fail to achieve this lofty ideal for a number of reasons. Increased levels of global competition, financial pressures, lack of communication throughout organizations, and the absence of moral leadership at the top levels are but a few of the most prevalent reasons.[23]

STATEMENTS OF ETHICAL PRINCIPLES

Perhaps the most important means of establishing moral leadership in a business organization—and demonstrating that leadership to employees, customers, clients, competitors, and the world at large—is through a formal statement of ethical principles.

Developing and publishing a corporate statement of ethics certainly will not, by itself, make a company ethical. But it is certainly a good first step. To the question of why a company should have such a statement, Professor Patrick Murphy offers this response:

> First, and most important, ethics statements denote the seriousness with which the organization takes its ethical commitments. Words are empty without some documentation. The written statement then serves as a foundation from which ethical behavior can be built. Corporate culture is often viewed as being more important than policies in setting the ethical climate for any organization. However, written ethical principles send a strong signal that ethics matters to the firm.[24]

Once an organization's size, according to Murphy, goes beyond a handful of employees who interact regularly face to face, it becomes difficult to convey a sense of an organization's principles and values. An ethics statement makes expectations more concrete. Furthermore, developing such a document forces those engaged in the process, whether they be the founder or current management, to articulate their beliefs in a cohesive fashion and then set them down in writing for possible challenge by others.[25]

Types of Ethical Statements   Although ethics statements can be classified into several types, three appear to predominate. They include values statements, corporate credos (or set of basic beliefs), and corporate codes of ethics.

The most prevalent form in which ethical principles are stated in U.S.–based corporations is a *code of ethics.* Over 90 percent of large organizations have one. More than half of those same companies also have a *values statement.* A *corporate credo* appears to exist in about one-third of all large U.S.–based firms. Interestingly, while fewer firms seem to have a corporate credo, many that do have such documents have had them in place for a long time.[26] A recent Conference Board survey of 124 companies in 22 countries found that more than three-quarters of all boards of directors are now setting ethical standards in those companies, up from just 41 percent in 1991 and 21 percent in 1987. Executives at those companies see the self-regulation as a way to avoid legislative or judicial intrusions in their business operations. The study also found that ethics codes help promote tolerance of diverse practices and customers while doing business overseas.[27]

Jacques Polet, in reviewing corporate ethical statements in both the United States and Europe, has found that the most recurring principles are: clarity, transparency, honesty, truth or objectivity (negative and unpleasant information must be communicated, as well as positive information), credibility, coherence, loyalty, and respect for human beings.[28]

In examining corporate ethical statements, the importance of communication, as well as many other behaviors, receives considerable attention. "In the same spirit," writes Polet, "communication must serve the company (its shareholders, staff, and customers) without prejudicing third parties nor hurting respectable feelings. Basically, it should reflect the company project, expressing its goals, its strategy, and the corporate culture. . . ."[29] Thus, effective management communication is not only a means to an end (a way to convey the principles), but an end in itself (ethical communication is a fundamental principle guiding management behavior).

Tension and Ethical Values   Many values, along with the roles and objectives that managers must follow, are in competition with one another, and—inevitably—a certain tension pulls first in one direction, and then another. The value of *transparency,* or of not hiding from public view what the company really does and how it does it, may be in competition with the value of *confidentiality.* Employees expect a certain measure of privacy in the workplace, yet the demand for disclosure is ever-present. Managers must respond to these conflicts and to the tension that arises from them with caution, sensitivity, and a sense of fairness to everyone concerned.[30]

Every communication activity, from annual reports to general shareholder meetings, becomes a balancing act for executives and managers. To be honest with our employees and our shareholders, what and how much must we disclose? To preserve our competitive edge, what and how much shall we hold back? Ethical philosopher Gilles Lipovetsky, in *The Dawn of Duty,* captures the dialectical debate in this way:

> It is obvious: an ethics of company communication does not present itself in terms of a choice between Good and Evil (a question of Morality). In real life, there is a balance between "various more or less contradictory imperatives."[31]

How Ethical Statements Can Help   While the presence of an ethical statement will not automatically ensure ethical behavior on the part of corporate employees, such documents certainly can raise ethical awareness, create an atmosphere in which ethical behavior is expected and rewarded, and promote a companywide dialogue about the value of ethical behavior.

In 1982, seven people died in the United States after taking Tylenol capsules which had been poisoned with cyanide. Investigators eventually determined that some unknown person had tampered with the capsules after they had been placed on store shelves for sale. Even before Johnson & Johnson, which manufactures the product, had obtained all the information on the cause of the tragedy, and even before legal liability had been evaluated, the company assumed moral liability for it, immediately recalling 31 million bottles of Tylenol with a market value of $100 million. The company set up a toll-free help line to answer questions from the general public.[32]

Johnson & Johnson chairman and CEO James Burke opened up the company's meetings to the news media, and offered a reward of $100,000 to anyone able to supply information leading to the arrest of the culprit. According to Lipovetsky, "There is no doubt as to the ethical orientation of the operation. It was nonetheless a triumph of communication which managed to dramatize the firm's responsible action."[33]

The Tylenol crisis highlights the importance of personal ethical commitment of top management in a special way. In these periods of extreme tension, while managers may wish to do the right thing, it's not always immediately clear what the right thing to do is. Johnson & Johnson employees had worked with their *Credo,* a broadly phrased statement of company ethics, since 1947. In the words of one Johnson & Johnson official during the crisis, "What we are doing here is not specifically *mentioned* in the Credo, but it is definitely *generated* by the Credo."[34]

Johnson & Johnson's Jim Burke had no hesitation in assuming direct responsibility for and control over the true spirit of the Credo.[35] As Laura Nash reports, "Jim Burke has often stated that the guidance of the Credo played the most important role in management's decision making during the crisis."[36] And, if anyone doubted that Burke and his president, David Collins, had done the right thing, the proof is that eleven weeks after the start of the crisis, the Tylenol brand had recovered 80 percent of its initial market share and, by 1984, had recovered all of it.[37]

How to Make Ethical Statements Work Murphy offers a series of seven imperatives to follow when writing and living out the principles of a corporate code of ethics.

- *Write it.* Writing down the guiding philosophy or values of the firm makes it possible for management to communicate those ideas to all stakeholders, especially to the employees. A written document also signals to everyone concerned that the company is serious about its ethical views.
- *Tailor it.* Tailoring a statement of ethics to an organization's industry or line of business offers managers an opportunity to place special emphasis on those issues most likely to arise in the course of ordinary business, and to address those matters which it regards as especially important.
- *Communicate it.* This may be the most important step in ensuring that all stakeholders, external as well as internal, are aware of and understand the behavior that the company expects of them. Many authors note that this must be a continuing process for every company.
- *Promote it.* It is not enough to simply communicate the ethics document. It should be actively promoted at every opportunity through as many publications, events, and channels as possible.
- *Revise it.* Revising the document every few years will help to keep it current, reflecting changing worldwide conditions, community standards, and evolving organizational practices.
- *Live it.* The litmus test for any type of ethics document, according to Murphy and others, is whether members of the organization follow it on a daily basis. Top management must make a concerted effort to reward employees who follow the principles listed in the statement.
- *Enforce/Reinforce it.* And, for those who refuse to live by the principles, management must exact punishment. Sanctions and penalties must be enforced in a fair and even-handed manner so that all stakeholders understand how they will be treated and exactly what the consequences of their behavior will be.[38]

THE "FRONT PAGE" TEST

In judging whether its policies or its actions are fundamentally sound, managers might simply apply what's come to be known as the *Front Page* test. Would you be pleased if the policies in your organization, or the behavior of your employees, were to appear in a story on the front page of The *Wall Street Journal* or, perhaps, your hometown newspaper? If not, then you might ask yourself, "Why not?" What are we doing wrong that I wouldn't want others to know about?

Do the methods and means of communication in your organization hold up to that test? Does your company deal honestly with its customers and clients, treating each of them fairly and with respect? Do you honestly and accurately disclose to regulatory agencies and governmental organizations all that they are entitled to know? Are your relations with the press and news media based on openness, honesty, and candor? If not, what can you do to improve them?

Are the rituals, ceremonies, and formal activities of your organization planned and conducted with a sense of inclusion, honesty, and equality? Do people in your organization know *how* they will be evaluated, *by whom,* and against *which set of standards* in their hopes for promotion or advancement?

Day in and day out, do you and others in your company speak, write, listen, and act with a sense that others will appreciate and respect? Do you treat people not simply as they might treat you, but in a way they prefer to be treated? In many ways, ethics and communication are not simply inseparable, but are essential to the success of any business and at the heart of how human beings interact with one another. Striving for ethical perfection, both as you communicate and as you manage your business, is probably pointless. But striving each day to observe the best of ethical principles, to demonstrate a level of conduct that others can aspire to, and to lead by example is not only possible but unquestionably worthwhile.

Endnotes

1. Gasparino, Charles. "NASD Fines Firm, 2 Executives in Case of Misleading Ads." The *Wall Street Journal,* February 11, 1998, p. C3.
2. Truell, Peter. "An Employee on Wall St. Is Arrested." The *Wall Street Journal,* November 7, 1997, p. C8.
3. Labich, K. "The New Crisis in Business Ethics." *Fortune,* April 20, 1992, p. 167.
4. Ibid., p. 167.
5. *The 1999 National Business Ethics Survey.* Indianapolis, IN: Walker Information, September, 1999. A summary is available on-line at *http://www.walkerinfo.com/.*
6. Ibid.
7. Baumhart, R. *An Honest Profit: What Businessmen Say About Ethics in Business.* New York: Holt, Rinehart, Winston, 1968, pp. 11–12.
8. Goodpaster, Kenneth E. "Business Ethics," in L. C. Becker (ed.), *Encyclopedia of Ethics.* New York, NY: Garland Publishing, Inc., 1992, p. 111.
9. Ibid., pp. 111–112.
10. Boatright, J. R. *Ethics and the Conduct of Business.* Englewood Cliffs, NJ: Prentice-Hall, Inc., 1993, pp. 4–8.
11. Bowen, Michael G. and F. Clark Power, "The Moral Manager: Communicative Ethics and the Exxon Valdez Disaster." *Business Ethics Quarterly,* February 1993, p. 10.
12. Ibid., pp. 10–12.
13. Boatright, J. R., *Ethics and the Conduct of Business,* pp. 13–16.
14. Ibid., pp. 15–16.
15. Bowen and Power, "The Moral Manager," p. 14.
16. Velasquez, Manuel G. *Business Ethics: Concepts and Cases,* 3rd ed. Englewood Cliffs, NJ: Prentice Hall Publishing, Inc., 1992, pp. 9–12.
17. Ibid., pp. 11–13.
18. Brown, Marvin T. *The Ethical Process: A Strategy for Making Good Decisions,* Upper Saddle River, NJ: Prentice Hall, Inc., 1996, pp. 5–7.

19. Paine, Lynn Sharp. "Ethics as Character Development: Reflections on the Objective of Ethics Education," in R. Edward Freeman (ed.), *Business Ethics: The State of the Art.* New York, NY: Oxford University Press, 1991, pp. 67–86.
20. Ibid., p. 81.
21. Ibid., p. 82.
22. Ibid., pp. 82–83.
23. Murphy, Patrick E. *Eighty Exemplary Ethics Statements.* Notre Dame, IN: University of Notre Dame Press, 1998, p. xiii.
24. Ibid., p. 1.
25. Ibid., p. 1.
26. Ibid., p. 2.
27. "Global Ethics Codes Gain Importance as a Tool to Avoid Litigation and Fines." *Wall Street Journal,* August 19, 1999, p. A-1.
28. Polet, Jacques. "Company Communication: From the Ethics of Communication to the Communication of Ethics," in Georges Enderle (ed.), *International Business Ethics: Challenges and Approaches.* Notre Dame, IN and Hong Kong, China: The University of Notre Dame Press and the University of Hong Kong Press, 1998.
29. Ibid., p. 6.
30. Ibid., p. 7.
31. Lipovetsky, Gilles. *Le crepuscule du devoir. L'ethique indolore des noveaux temps democratiques.* Paris: Gallimard, 1992, p. 248.
32. Barton, Lawrence. *Crisis in Organizations: Managing and Communicating in the Heat of Chaos.* Cincinnati, OH: Southwestern Publishing Company, 1993, pp. 84–85.
33. Lipovetsky, *Le crepuscule du devoir,* pp. 269–270.
34. Nash, Laura L. "Johnson & Johnson's Credo," in *Corporate Ethics: A Prime Business Asset.* New York, NY: The Business Roundtable, 1988, p. 100.
35. Ibid., p. 80.
36. Ibid., p. 97.
37. Lipovetsky, *Le crepuscule du devoir,* p. 270.
38. Murphy, *Eighty Exemplary Ethics Statements,* pp. 5–9.

For Further Reading

Brown, Marvin T. *The Ethical Process: A Strategy for Making Good Decisions.* Upper Saddle River, NJ: Prentice Hall, Inc., 1966.

Cadbury, Sir Adrian, "Ethical Managers Make Their Own Rules." *Harvard Business Review,* September–October 1987, pp. 69–73.

Ferrell, O. C. and John Fraedrich, *Business Ethics: Ethical Decision Making and Cases,* 3rd ed. Boston, MA: Houghton Mifflin Company, 1997.

Fritzsche, David J. *Business Ethics: A Global and Managerial Perspective.* New York, NY: The McGraw-Hill Companies, Inc., 1997.

Labich, Kenneth. "How to Fire People and Still Sleep at Night." *Fortune,* June 10, 1996, pp. 65–72.

Laczniak, Gene R. and Patrick E. Murphy. *Ethical Marketing Decisions: The Higher Road.* Upper Saddle River, NJ: Prentice Hall, 1993.

Lancaster, Hal. "You Have Your Values: How Do You Identify Your Employer's?" *The Wall Street Journal,* April 8, 1997, p. B1.

McCarthy, Michael J. "Virtual Morality: A New Workplace Quandry." *The Wall Street Journal,* October 21, 1999, pp. B1, B4.

Murphy, Patrick E. "Creating Ethical Corporate Structures." *Sloan Management Review,* Winter 1989, pp. 81–87.

Paine, Lynn Sharp. "Managing for Organizational Integrity." *Harvard Business Review,* March–April 1994, pp. 106–117.

Seglin, Jeffrey L. "In Ethics, It's the Thought That Counts." *The New York Times,* December 19, 1999, p. BU-4.

🐾

Case 3–1   EXCEL INDUSTRIES (A)

BACKGROUND NOTE

The workforce in North America, particularly in the United States and Canada, is becoming increasingly female, reflecting a general trend toward two-paycheck families.

According to a recent study from The Hudson Institute, an increasing number of women are entering the North American job market. Since 1990, approximately two-thirds of all new entrants to the workforce have been women. And, by early in the next century, nearly two-thirds of all working-age women in the United States will be employed.

Other studies indicate that women in the United States are entering the job market more for economic than for professional reasons. While the number of women with college degrees and professional credentials is rising, so is the number of single-parent families headed by women. These families are, for the most part, well below average in income and education and are more likely than two-parent households to require public assistance.

Employers are coming to realize that what had formerly been seen as "women's issues"—including flexible scheduling, maternity and family leave, and daycare—are really "family issues," deserving serious attention from both the public and private sectors. Some of these matters have become the object of protracted and heated negotiation during collective bargaining. And, what once was regarded as a luxury or fringe benefit in many organizations, is more frequently viewed by employees as an entitlement.

In North America, and especially in the United States, daycare for the children of working mothers is not seen as an entitlement to be provided by government. The U.S. federal government views itself as constitutionally excluded from issues related to management of education and child care, and state and local governments cite a lack of funding. Corporate America has increasingly come to see a social responsibility

for the children of their employees, and employees have come to expect and depend on such corporate responsiveness to their needs.

This case deals with several aspects of these recently emerging family issues. While each employee has both a cost and a value to a business organization, each employer has concomitant obligations and responsibilities to those employees. This case is about balance among those obligations and management decision making when obligations are in conflict or when responsibilities pull in opposite directions.

This is also a case involving corporate communication. The executives and management of every business enterprise operate in an environment that is information-rich, yet rife with rumor, misunderstanding, and misinformation. Business leaders must understand that every action, whether intended for public discussion or not, will have an effect on the public's perception of their business.

Business leaders should also understand that, as they draft their corporate strategy and implement tactical moves in the marketplace, they will interact and communicate with a very diverse and complex audience. Those who will see and hear of management's actions will have varying backgrounds, reading abilities, knowledge of the subject, political views, prejudices, and interests.

In many ways, the mass audience reached by radio, television, newspapers, and magazines is many smaller audiences. It may be helpful to think of the larger audience as comprised of shareholders, customers, suppliers, competitors, politicians, local, regional, and national government officials, potential investors, prospective employees, neighbors, community members, and others.

In some cases, business leaders might well consider separate messages for separate audiences, designing their content for the backgrounds, needs, interests, inclinations, and potential reactions of each. Shareholders, for instance, might have a greater interest in knowing how an event or announcement will affect their investment than do members of the surrounding community. Employees might have a much keener interest in how an event will affect their jobs and their lives in the organization than would others.

A MANUFACTURER MOVES INTO CHILD CARE

In 1988, Excel Industries, Inc., a supplier of window systems to the automotive industry, purchased Nyloncraft, Inc., a $40 million injection molding company. Both firms are headquartered in Northern, Indiana, in the heart of the domestic automobile supply region. At the time of the acquisition, Nyloncraft was a highly regarded firm with great promise for growth and had exactly the sort of manufacturing capacity, equipment, and labor force that Excel Industries was looking for.

At the time of the corporate takeover, Nyloncraft, Inc., operated a daycare facility that was regarded as among the most innovative in the nation. *Money* magazine, *U.S. News & World Report,* and other business publications featured the facility, describing it as "one of the best-equipped 24-hour-a-day learning centers in the Midwest that is operated by a corporation for the benefit of its employees."

James J. Lohman is chairman, president, and chief executive officer of Excel Industries. "When the Learning Center was opened," he said, "it suited the needs of Nyloncraft very nicely. It was expensive, but it helped us to attract and retain a reliable workforce that would help the company grow. We had a number of female workers who were of child-bearing age and it made good sense for us to assist them with their child care needs. We knew from experience," he added, "that a first-class, on-site learning center would reduce turnover, absenteeism, and tardiness. It was good for business, it was good for our employees, and it was good for the kids."

When he said expensive, Lohman wasn't exaggerating. "When Excel acquired Nyloncraft, we immediately invested $200,000 in the Learning Center, improving it so that it met or exceeded all recommended standards for facili-

ties of that type." The center's annual budget was in excess of $400,000 to provide round-the-clock care and instruction for 162 children.

THE COST OF PROVIDING ON-SITE CHILD CARE

"Within a few years," Lohman said, "we discovered that fewer and fewer of our employees had children enrolled in the Nyloncraft Learning Center, so we expanded enrollment to the community at large." By July 1988, employees' children accounted for about 45 percent of the enrollment at the Center. "By 1990," he said, "less than seven percent of those enrolled were children of Nyloncraft employees." And by then, he added, the annual subsidy had grown to nearly $300,000. All parents with children enrolled in the Learning Center, regardless of who their employer might be, received a substantial tuition discount, each paying just a fraction of what such care and instruction would be worth on the retail market.

"We weren't just looking after these children, as a baby-sitting service might," he added. "We provided state-certified instruction, professional pre-school development programs, and we fed them. Our insurance, reporting, and oversight problems were growing by the day. It was becoming increasingly difficult to justify a subsidy that was well in excess of a quarter-of-a-million dollars for the children of only 10 Excel employees. The financial pressure was simply too great for us to continue the operation."

Excel tried unsuccessfully for nearly a year to find a buyer for the Learning Center. Failing that, they tried to find a management firm that would agree to take over the day-to-day operations of the facility. "No one would step forward to help us," he said, "We didn't want to close the Nyloncraft Learning Center. But, increasingly, I saw fewer alternatives open to us."

Lohman began to think carefully about the decision alternatives available to him and the audiences that would be most affected by his choice. Looking after the children of those few employees who still used the Learning Center would be neither difficult nor expensive. But how would others react to a management decision to close the facility? What

NYLONCRAFT
Summary Balance Sheet
December 1990

Cash 97
Accounts Receivable 3,207
Inventory 7,308
Prepaid Expense 93

Total Current Assets 10,705
Fixed Assets, Net 8,585
Goodwill and Other Assets 3,691

Total Assets 22,981

Accounts Payable 1,897
Accrued Liabilities 1,232
Current Portion Ltd 413

Long Term Debt, Banks 1,800
Due to Parent/Equity 17,639

Total Liabilities & Equity 22,981

NYLONCRAFT
Income Statement
Year Ended December 1990

Sales 36,730
Cost of Goods Sold 35,332

Gross Profit 1,398

Selling and Administrative Expense 2,697

Operating Income . . . .(1,299)

Other Expenses . . . .(522)

Loss before Tax and Corp. Allocation . . . .(1,821)

Note: Figures are given in thousands of dollars (U.S.).

other choice did the company have? What other choice did the parents have? Quality daycare was in short supply in the local area, and time was running out on Jim Lohman. The board of directors wanted an answer from him soon.

The two most troubling questions were deceptively simple: What should I do about the Learning Center and how should we communicate our decision?

DISCUSSION QUESTIONS

1. What ethical obligations, if any, did Excel Industries have to the women who were employed there?
2. Is an employer obligated to provide day care for its employees' children?
3. What obligations does the firm in this case have to the community? Having once opened its doors to the children of nonemployees, was the firm obligated in any way to continue caring for them?
4. Could a firm such as Excel Industries side-step ethical issues associated with day care altogether by recruiting either male employees or women past child-bearing age?
5. What responsibilities does Mr. Lohman have as chief executive officer to the shareholders and debtholders of Excel Industries, Inc.? Does his obligation to maximize shareholder wealth and minimize debtholder risk conflict with an obligation to provide a safe, comfortable working environment for female employees who may be concerned about child care?
6. Since it became apparent to Mr. Lohman that the Nyloncraft Learning Center could

no longer be economically justified, what ethical obligations did he have to the women whose children were enrolled there? Do Mr. Lohman's responsibilities to employees of the firm exceed those to women who are not employed by Excel Industries?
7. What role should corporate public relations and the public news media play in communicating this decision to Excel Industries employees? What role should they play in communicating the decision to the community at large?
8. What vested interest do you suppose the community has in the continued operation of the Nyloncraft Learning Center? Do any reciprocal obligations exist between the community and the employers for the proper care, feeding, and education of preschool children whose parents are employed in the community? Has Excel Industries violated any "unspoken pact" between management and its workers, or between the company and the community?

Case 3–2 A COLLECTION SCANDAL AT SEARS ROEBUCK & COMPANY

It's just 8:30 A.M. on a Sunday morning. While most of Chicago was either still asleep or out retrieving the morning paper, Arthur C. Martinez was meeting with a dozen of his company's top executives at their headquarters building in suburban Hoffman Estates. For a few moments, the room grew quiet as Martinez tried to digest what he had just been told. Lawyers for Sears Roebuck & Company were explaining how employees had secretly violated federal law for nearly a decade.

Martinez couldn't believe what he was hearing: Sears attorneys and credit employees, according to a bankruptcy judge in Boston, had for years been dunning delinquent credit card holders who had filed for—and had been granted—bankruptcy protection. The newspapers and cable television news channels didn't have the story yet, but it would only be a matter of hours before they would. The company that Martinez, a former Saks Fifth Avenue executive, had struggled to turn around would quickly be mired in the worst legal and ethics scandal in its 111-year history.

The United States Department of Justice was already considering not only civil penalties, but criminal prosecution. Worse, this wasn't simply a rogue operation or an honest misinterpretation of the law: Sears appeared to have been violating the rights of many of its customers systematically and intentionally. The company, the lawyers were suggesting, may even have put the illegal practice into its procedures manual.

How could such wrongdoing have gone unchecked for years? Martinez wanted to know. "Not one phone call about this? Ever?" he demanded. According to at least one participant in the meeting, it was a "sickening moment."

A "HALF-MILLION DOLLAR" HANDWRITTEN LETTER

As an extensive investigation would later reveal, Sears struggled—first to understand and then to deal with criminal charges and an ethical lapse that would cost the company nearly $500 million

dollars. According to Sears senior vice president Ron Culp, the collection scheme began to unravel in November 1996, when Francis Latanowich, a disabled security guard, hand wrote a letter on a yellow legal pad, begging the Boston Bankruptcy Court to reopen his case. Although Judge Carol Kenner had wiped out his debts, Sears later asked Latanowich to repay the $1,161 he owed for a TV, an auto battery, and some other merchandise. But the monthly payment, he wrote, "is keeping food off the table for my kids."

Sears, it turned out, had mailed Latanowich an offer. In return for $28 a month on his account, the company wouldn't repossess the goods he had bought with a Sears charge card before he went bankrupt. The practice of urging debtors to sign such deals, called reaffirmations, is legal and relatively widespread in the retail credit business, but many judges view them as unethical practices that keep people from getting a fresh start. Moreover, every signed reaffirmation *must* be filed with the court so a judge can review whether the debtor can handle the new payment. Sears Roebuck & Company hadn't filed this one with the court and Judge Kenner wanted to know why not.

At a January 29, 1997, hearing, a Boston attorney working for Sears offered a convoluted technical excuse for not filing. Kenner's response: "Baloney." According to *Newsweek* magazine, there were hints from prior cases that Sears, both praised and feared nationwide as the most aggressive pursuer of reaffirmations, wasn't filing many of them with the court. If true, the company was using unenforceable agreements to collect debts that legally no longer existed. Judge Kenner pushed Sears for a list of such cases. Sears' response, delivered reluctantly in mid-March by a credit manager, was shocking: The company had apparently ignored the law nearly 2,800 times in Massachusetts alone. Martinez and his senior team could only imagine what the company was up to in the other 49 states.

SOARING PERSONAL BANKRUPTCIES

Between 1994 and 1998, personal bankruptcies in the United States rose from 780,000 to more than 1.3 million, leaving many retailers and credit card issuers awash in bad debt. Sears, as the nation's second-largest retailer, was in a particularly vulnerable position. That year, the company earned 50 percent of its operating income from credit, including charge cards held by more than 63 million households with Sears credit cards.

The problem, as Martinez would come to discover, is that too many of those new cardholders barely qualified for credit. In its zeal to attract new business, Sears became a lender to its riskiest customers. As the number of bankruptcies rose nationwide, so did the number of unpaid accounts at Sears. By 1997, more than one-third of all personal bankruptcies in the United States included Sears as a creditor. Companies heavily dependent on income from their credit cards chose to aggressively pursue bad debts, and Sears was just one of many to do so. The list included such prominent creditors as Federated Department Stores, the May Company, G.E. Capital, Discover Card, and AT&T.

As Martinez would also come to discover, the problem was neither isolated nor small. During the previous five years, some 512,000 customers had signed reaffirmation agreements with Sears, pledging to repay debts that totaled $412 million dollars. Martinez suspected that his company's transformation from an exhausted, defeatist bureaucracy into "an aggressive, can-do company" had an unanticipated consequence: Managers simply wouldn't send bad news up the chain of command.

A culture of aggressively pursuing bad debts while filtering out bad news from top management had become part of the company's culture and official policy. Michael Levin, chief of Sears' law department, explained to his CEO that at least one outside law firm had told someone in the company that Sears' policy was questionable. But word of the alert, which might have triggered a broader investigation within the company, somehow never worked its way up through the bureaucracy.

Martinez leaned back and motioned to his executive assistant, "Call a meeting of the Phoenix Team," he said. "Eight o'clock tomorrow." That would mean 200 of Sears Roebuck & Company's top executives would get the bad news directly from their CEO. It would also signal the start of Sears' response to the charges.

Martinez then turned to Ron Culp, Sears' senior vice president for public relations and government affairs, and Bill Giffen, vice president for ethics and business policy. "Give me your best thinking," he said. "Tell me what you think we should do."

DISCUSSION QUESTIONS

1. What is Sears' best strategy at this point? What would you advise Arthur Martinez to do?
2. As Ron Culp thinks about corporate communications and the events that have just unfolded in the board room, which audiences would you advise him to focus on first?
3. What do you suppose the interests will be for each of these audiences? Are they similar interests or are some of them in conflict with one another? What do they want to hear from Mr. Martinez?
4. As Bill Giffen examines Sears' credit collection policies and practices, what advice would you offer? How can Martinez keep a sense of enthusiasm and excitement in his company and still encourage people to report and disclose bad news?
5. Even though the reaffirmation agreements are perfectly legal and enforceable, if properly filed with the courts, is it ethical to try to extract money from people who have legally declared bankruptcy? What ethical obligations do those people in bankruptcy have toward companies who lent them credit, such as Sears?
6. Has the reward structure at Sears somehow affected the communication structure? What would you change if you could advise Mr. Martinez on restructuring either of those systems?

SOURCES

Cahill, Joseph B. "Sears's Credit Business May Have Helped Hide Larger Retailing Woes." *The Wall Street Journal,* July 6, 1999, pp. A1, A8.

Culp, E. Ronald. Personal communication, November 1999–January 2000.

"Final Accord in G.E. Debt Collection." *The New York Times,* January 23, 1999, p. B1.

McCormick, John. "The Sorry Side of Sears." *Newsweek,* February 22, 1999.

"Sears to Pay Fine of $60 Million in Bankruptcy Fraud Lawsuit." *The New York Times,* February 10, 1999, p. C1.

Sparks, Debra. "Got an AT&T Credit Card? Don't Go Bankrupt." *Business Week,* September 15, 1997.

Weimer, De'Ann. "Is Sears Putting the Comeback on Its Card?" *Business Week,* November 10, 1997.

This case was prepared from personal interviews and public sources by James S. O'Rourke, concurrent associate professor of management, as the basis for class discussion rather than to illustrate either effective or ineffective handling of an administrative situation.

4

SPEAKING

✍

Your stomach is in a knot, you're sweating, turning, tossing, anxious. The room seems hot. How can it be? You got up ten minutes ago to turn down the thermostat. A glance at the clock reveals that it's 2:00 A.M. At this rate, you'll never get to sleep.

What's going on here? Is a bad meal keeping you up? Has a lumpy hotel mattress worked its magic on your back once again? Has a case of jet-lag thrown your circadian rhythms off? While any of these maladies is possible, it's much more likely that your sleeplessness and anxiety are caused by the greatest among mankind's fears: The knowledge that you have a speech to give.

CBS News journalist Charles Osgood posed the question this way: "Have you ever been driving at night and come upon a deer frozen in the beam of your headlights? Here's my theory," says Osgood. "The deer thinks the lights are spotlights, and what has it paralyzed is stage fright. It imagines the worst: It has to give a speech."[1]

According to an often-cited study by market researchers, speaking before a group came in first among "worst human fears." Death was number six, elevators number twelve.[2] The reason, according to Osgood, is that we're all afraid of making fools of ourselves. The more important the speech, the more frightened we become.[3] The advice for people—including you and me—is simple: preparation will help you overcome that fear. Really thorough preparation can set you up for success, help you achieve the goals you've set for yourself, and get the audience you fear so much to do exactly what you want them to do.

WHY SPEAK?

Often, we don't have a choice. As a manager, you'll find yourself preparing to speak to an audience you'd rather not meet on a topic you'd rather not talk about. Addressing the corporate executive committee on the subject of a quarterly budget shortfall is no one's idea of a good time. But you will do it because it's part of your management responsibility. Many speaking assignments are directive in nature. You do it because you're told to, or you do it because you must. These occasions are not easy, but they are certainly nothing to be afraid of.

Many speaking opportunities, however, are voluntary in nature. You give the talk because you choose to do so. You drop in on a group of employees to share the good news that the company has just landed a big contract they had worked very hard to secure. You could have shared that information in a memo, but you'd rather see their faces, hear them cheer, and watch "high fives" around the room.

It might be another occasion, explaining to your daughter's elementary school class what you do for a living (come to think of it, that might be tougher than the employee meeting). Or, you might accept the invitation of a local Kiwanis Club to speak at their weekly luncheon. Each speaking opportunity that you accept, each speech that you give will increase your self-assurance and reinforce the idea that you are competent, confident, and capable of speaking in public (and speaking well).

Two keys to success present themselves time and again in public speaking: taking control of the situation and preparing yourself to succeed.

HOW TO PREPARE A SUCCESSFUL MANAGEMENT SPEECH

Here are fifteen ideas to prepare yourself for any speech, large or small, important or impromptu. Focus on these, one at time, and you're unlikely ever to develop sweaty palms on the podium again.

- Develop a strategy.
- Get to know your audience.
- Determine your reason for speaking.
- Learn what you can about the occasion for your talk.
- Know what makes people listen.
- Understand the questions listeners bring to any listening situation.
- Recognize common obstacles to successful communication.
- Support your ideas with credible evidence.
- Organize your thoughts.
- Keep your audience interested.
- Select a delivery approach.
- Develop your visual support.
- Rehearse your speech.
- Develop confidence in your message and in yourself.
- Deliver your message.

DEVELOP A STRATEGY

If you have no strategy, you probably shouldn't give a speech. But what exactly is a *strategy* for public speaking? Simply put, it's a reason for speaking, a knowledge of who will hear your speech, and some sense of the context in which it will occur.

Twenty-three-hundred years ago, Aristotle told his students they would have a greater chance for success as they prepared to deliver a speech if they would first consider three basic elements: audience, purpose, and occasion.[4]

GET TO KNOW YOUR AUDIENCE

Who are these people? What do you know about them? What do they know about you or your subject? Before you go any further in your preparation, perform a simple audience analysis. This involves just two steps: knowing something about the people you'll speak to and knowing why people listen.

What should you know about your audience? Here are a few categories of information that might prove useful as you prepare your remarks.

Age   How old are they? Will they be familiar with the concepts you plan to speak about? What's their vocabulary range? What sort of life experiences have they had? Remember, if you're speaking to a group of 18-year-old college freshmen, you should know that they were born in the latter years of the first Reagan administration. They have no direct memory of American hostages in Tehran. The Challenger blew up while these folks were being potty-trained. Make certain your references to events and ideas are both known to them and relevant to their concerns. Similarly, an older audience might have been around for certain events, but references to a SONY Game Boy or an episode of "Saved by the Bell" may well be lost on them.

Education   Knowing the age of the audience will tell you something about how much education they have had, but perhaps not as much as you would like to know. Speech content, including central themes and vocabulary, will certainly be influenced by the level and type of education of your audience.

Personal Beliefs   What this group believes may well be more important than how old or how well educated they are. The reason is simple: What you believe defines who you are. Are these folks liberal or conservative? What's their political affiliation? Are they committed to a particular religious or social point of view? Do they have certain biases favoring or opposing such issues as red meat, cigar smoking, gun ownership, or parallel parking?

Occupation   What do these people do for a living? Are they students? As such, many of them may not do anything for a living, but might hope to have occupations someday soon. Are they managers, professionals, or colleagues of yours? Knowing how people earn their living will tell you something about their educational background and their daily routines, as well as their motivations and interests.

Income   Knowing how much money an audience makes may be of some help as you formulate your remarks. By knowing their income levels, you will have some idea of what their concerns are: the less they make, the more fundamental and basic are their concerns. Abraham Maslow nicely documented the Hierarchy of Human Needs, noting that it's difficult to sell people on self-actualization if they haven't enough to eat.

Socio-Economic Status   This term describes where in the social/economic spectrum your audience is located. And it is, of course, a direct function of such other factors as income, education, occupation, neighborhood, friends, family, and more. Think of this as a single descriptor which explains just how much prestige your audience has in the eyes of others in society.[5]

Ethnic Origin   This may be of some value to know, but its worth is limited. The value may lie in knowing which issues and positions are of greatest concern to members of a particular ethnic group. The limitation lies in knowing that you cannot reasonably stereotype the views of all members of such a group. Sensitivity to ethnic causes and issues, as well as language, should be sufficient as you prepare a speech.

Sex/Gender   Sex refers to the biological differences between males and females. Gender refers to the social and psychological expectations, roles, and views of men and women. Considerable evidence now indicates that this may be among the least useful pieces of information you might want to know about your audience. Why? Because study after study has shown no statistically significant difference in the responses of professional men and women to a wide range of stimuli. Clearly, knowing that your audience might be composed exclusively of one sex or another might alter your approach somewhat, but you would be unwise to assume that you would write one speech for men and another for women. Treat them as intelligent humans and you will get the response you're seeking.

Knowledge of the Subject   This may be the one category of information (along with the next) for which you would be willing to pay in order to know more. A thorough knowledge of what your audience already knows about your speaking subject is useful in a number of ways. First, this would tell you where to begin. Don't speak down to them by explaining fundamentals they already understand. Similarly, don't start above their heads. Begin at a point they're comfortable with and move on from there.

Attitude Toward the Subject   Even more important than what they know about your subject is how they feel about it. What I know about the Federal Tax Code is far less relevant than how I feel about it when I listen to a talk about tax reform. My emotions are not irrelevant as I approach a subject. Neither are yours. And you certainly should know what the emotional response of your audience will be to the content and direction of your talk. The greater the degree of ego involvement (or emotional response) in a given topic, the narrower will be the range of acceptable positions. In other words, people are much more open-minded on topics they are indifferent about than they are on topics they care about passionately. What you don't know in this regard can hurt you.

DETERMINE YOUR REASON FOR SPEAKING

Knowing why you are speaking is almost as important as knowing to whom you will speak. Aristotle told his pupils that people rise to speak for three basic reasons: to inform, to persuade, or to inspire.[6]

Some authors have argued that all speaking is persuasive: You have chosen this topic as opposed to any other; you've selected this evidence, excluding all else. I'll accept that. But it's especially important to know whether or not your audience expects you to take a position regarding the subject of your speech.

Let's say, for example, that your boss is thinking about purchasing a new color photocopying system for the office and she has asked you to gather information about equipment available for sale or lease. She would also like you to present that information to members of the Executive Committee. You can find and organize such data easily. But should you take a position regarding which system to lease or buy? Should you become an advocate on behalf of one system or another? If the audience (your boss, in particular) expects information that will help her or the committee make such a decision, your views may be unwelcome. On the other hand, if you have been specifically asked to make your recommendations known, your speech would be seriously incomplete without them.

All public speaking should inform (without telling people what they already know). It should also inspire when appropriate to the occasion. But managers—young managers, in particular—should be careful to make certain they know the role that is expected of them as they rise to speak. Too often, young managers get into trouble with senior members of their organization by offering opinions on the topic at hand when the demand for such opinions is not especially brisk.

LEARN WHAT YOU CAN ABOUT THE OCCASION

In addition to knowing who will hear your talk and the reasons for which you will speak, it may also be useful for you to know something about the occasion. Many occasions simply call for a polite, informative presentation. Others, however, will ask that you incorporate some theme into your speech that arises from the moment. Certain holidays lend a clear and useful tone to your talk, such as Christmas ("Peace on Earth, goodwill toward mankind."), Thanksgiving ("We are grateful for what we have been given, and mindful of those who have less."), or Independence Day ("The price of freedom is eternal vigilance").

Other occasions call for different themes. Graduations, commencements, or rites-of-passage events call for a focus on the future and the responsibilities and opportunities that lie ahead. As a manager, you know you will have the opportunity to welcome new employees into the organization, or the sad task of saying farewell to them. Your audience will pay close attention to your words, to the tone of your speech, and to your approach to the subject. You are in charge and they expect you to say the right thing. It won't always be immediately clear what the right thing is to say, but your audience will know it when they hear it.

WHAT MAKES PEOPLE LISTEN?

Consultant and speech critic Sonya Hamlin says that people listen to speeches for three basic reasons: their own self-interests, who is telling the story, and how it is told.[7] If you know your audience, you will know what their interests are. You can't have much effect on their views about you, at least before you speak, but you certainly can have some influence on how the speech is delivered. In terms of control, two of the three reasons people listen are well within your grasp.

Positive Speaking Styles   Numerous studies of public speaking have shown that people react positively to speaking styles they regard as positive. Read the list of words below and see if you can think of a public speaker whose style fits many, if not most of them.

- Warm
- Friendly
- Interesting
- Organized
- Confident
- Open

- Honest
- Exciting
- Knowledgeable
- Creative
- Inspiring
- Authentic

Negative Speaking Styles   Not surprisingly, audiences react negatively to speakers whose style is the opposite of those words you've just read. Consider now this list of words and think of your reaction to certain speakers you have heard (or been forced to listen to). What was your reaction?

- Pompous
- Unenergized
- Patronizing
- Formal
- Stuffy
- Closed

- Vague
- Complex
- Unsure
- Irrelevant
- Monotonous
- Nervous

The advice in response to these research findings is simple: Make your speaking style positive, embracing all those attributes described as positive. And, do what you can to eliminate or avoid those speaking styles described as negative.[8]

UNDERSTAND THE QUESTIONS LISTENERS BRING TO ANY LISTENING SITUATION

As the members of your audience take a seat in the auditorium or conference room, each has questions about you, your message, the situation, and the consequences of this speech for them. Here are seven basic questions you should be prepared to answer, either directly or in the course of your talk to them.

Do You Know Something I Need to Know?   No matter who you are, people will listen if you know something they need to know. Obviously, the more you know about them, the better prepared you will be to answer this question. The more you can do for them, personally and professionally, the more they will reward you with their attention.

Can I Trust You?   Trust is not simply given or demanded. It's earned. You must show your audience that you are trustworthy by providing accurate information, useful points of view, and reliable evidence. This may well prove to be the most important question any audience has about a speaker.

Am I Comfortable with You?   Audiences feel more comfortable with people who are like them, or who have experiences which are similar to their own, or whose values and beliefs parallel their own. What can you do to show them who you are, to raise their comfort level?

How Can You Affect Me?   More sophisticated audiences think about outcomes. How can you influence my decisions, my career, my life? What can you do for me? If you can show them, in concrete or tangible terms, what you can do for them, they will tune in directly to what you say.

What's My Experience with You?   If your audience has no experience with you, they may not trust you. Similarly, if they have had an unfortunate experience with you, they may not trust you. What you can do is to put them at ease, assure them that you are here to speak for their benefit.

Are You Reasonable?   The question of how you *affect* people deals with their feelings. This question deals with *reason* or *logic*. Does the content of your speech reveal that you are a reasonable person? Does your argument make sense? Are you open-minded at all, particularly to viewpoints that may be shared by members of the audience?

Who Do You Represent?   This is a tricky and often difficult question, especially when you are speaking on behalf of an organization or other people. If the audience knows that you represent a particular cause or point of view, it may be difficult for them to see you as open-minded, reasonable, or unbiased. Declaring your interests early in a speech may be one way to assure them of your purpose. Acknowledging their interests may be another.[9]

RECOGNIZE COMMON OBSTACLES TO SUCCESSFUL COMMUNICATION

Every manager faces barriers to success as a speaking occasion arises. Some barriers are fairly mundane: Am I available that evening? Can I reschedule another obligation? Will I be able to gather the information I need to answer their questions? Other barriers, though, are more serious and can present great difficulty for a speaker. Obstacles to success appear to fall broadly into these five categories.

Stereotypes   Stereotyping is to ascribe to all members of a group or class those characteristics or behaviors observed in just one or a few. The word was coined by social scientist Walter Lippmann in 1921 when he wrote about why people so readily imagine how other people are, or why they behave as they do, even in the face of ready evidence to the contrary.[10]

The fact is people are comfortable with stereotypes. They help to explain the world around us, don't require much effort to construct, and give us ready categories into which we can insert new experiences, new people, and new ideas. Treating each one as unique or different is much more difficult and requires a great deal more reasoning and work on our part. Stereotypes may be useful as a starting point from which to understand groups and their members, but they can be very damaging when we fail to acknowledge differences within those groups or when we fail to admit that not all people act or think in the same ways.

To succeed as a speaker, you must put aside whatever stereotypical views you may hold of your audience and try with an open mind to treat them as individuals. If you are both successful and fortunate, they may do the same for you.

Prejudice   This is a word derived from Latin, meaning "to judge before knowing." We do it all the time. In fact, it's not necessarily bad. We have little prejudices that serve us well: the food we eat, the stores we shop in, our taste in clothing. Often, as managers, we are forced to judge before we have all the facts. We simply don't have the time or the resources to gather more information. We must act now.

As we speak to others, though, it's best that we acknowledge we are working with incomplete data. It's useful to admit that we don't know as much as we might like, or, perhaps, that we simply didn't have time to gather information that might have been easily available to us. We don't want others making judgments about us too quickly. The best way to encourage that sort of careful thinking in others is to lead by example and admit to our prejudicial thinking whenever possible.[11]

Feelings   Keep your emotions in check. Control your anger. Don't display your contempt for others and their ideas in public. Good advice, but it's all easier said than done. Our emotions and those of our audience can easily get in the way of an objective look at the facts. They can blur the important distinctions that exist between factual data and our affective interpretation of what they mean.

The best advice is simply to acknowledge that we have feelings and then use them to advance our cause. We must also recognize, however, that the people in our audience will have feelings—about us, our subject, and our evidence—and those feelings may be at odds with our own. Acknowledge that, and then move on to make your case as best you can.[12]

Language   You probably know from a basic communication course that words don't have meaning; people do. People assign meaning to the words they hear and read, and you should know that people with different backgrounds, different education, and different life experiences will assign much different meanings to the words you speak. This will happen during the course of a single speech. Various audience members will hear the same words at precisely the same moment, spoken by the same person, yet they will assign different meaning to those words and leave the speech with very different impressions of what the speaker meant.

Work around the difficulties inherent in language by offering multiple examples to illustrate your key points. Often a graph, table, or visual display can convey more meaning than whole paragraphs. Give your audience several ways to understand what you mean: Repeat yourself, re-phrase your intentions, tell stories, give examples.[13]

Culture   No two of us are the same, not only because of genetic individual differences, but also because we each have been enculturated in different ways. We tend to think of culture as an expression of entire nations or civilizations, but it's really much more specific than that. If culture is everything we have, say, think, or do as a people, then folks who live in the country are different in important ways from those who live in the city. Those who live in one state are culturally different from those who live in another.

We have other experiences as we grow up, become educated, find our life's work, and live out our lives. The experiences of one generation are not the same as those of another. The customs, habits, preferences in food and music, are different from one ethnic group to another. And, if you look carefully, you can see the cultural differences that exist among various corporations and business organizations. Some have a preference for informality while others prefer more structure. Various habits from the use of titles to the use of time distinguish us from one another. Your response to the cultural habits and preferences of others is a mark of your respect for them and an acknowledgment that they are not only different, but that those differences are important to them.[14]

Communication Obstacles Can Provoke Negative Reactions   When people feel threatened, intimidated, lost, or confused, a number of things can happen. During a speech, people may very well stop listening. They may discover how much they don't know, which can lead to frustration, anger, and hostility toward the speaker and the ideas being discussed. If the speaker has made them feel sufficiently dumb, they may withdraw entirely.

Begin with the familiar and move to the unfamiliar. Start with what the audience already knows and then move on to ideas which are a logical extension or outcome of those they are familiar with. Don't intimidate or confuse your audience; do everything you can to make them feel that they are just as smart as you are. The reward, once again, is their attention and their willingness to think about your ideas.

SUPPORT YOUR IDEAS WITH CREDIBLE EVIDENCE

While your reputation or the subject you are planning to speak about *may* keep an audience with you for awhile, you have a much better chance of convincing them of the value in your ideas if you support your talk with current, believable, easy-to-understand evidence.

Where to begin? Well, it's probably best to begin with your own experience, knowledge, and interests. If you are genuinely interested in the ideas you plan to present, your audience will pick up on that and respond accordingly. You will also know where to look for the most interesting, most believable support. If you like a particular subject, chances are good that you know which publications to read, know which experts are cited most often, and know a great deal about the latest developments. The confidence that comes with all of this will not be lost on your audience.

Secondly, consider new ideas, information, and techniques. You and your audience may together know a great deal about the subject of your talk, but they may not know about the very latest information. That's where your interests can help them. Bring them up-to-date on the subject, share the latest innovations and developments.

Next, as you consider how to support your speech, think about the availability and quality of support material. You may have a special interest that you simply can't support because you will not have access to the right information by the time you must speak.

Talk to some experts. Not all credible evidence is found in books, magazines, journals, or newspapers. Some of the most interesting, compelling evidence comes in the form of direct testimony from people who are genuine experts on the subject. Where can you find them? They're all around you. A punch-press operator working on a factory shop floor may not seem especially expert, but if he's been at his job for a number of years, chances are good that he knows a great deal about the machinery, the materials, and the processes involved in the job. Ask him a few questions. You might be surprised how much you can learn if you listen carefully.

Know how much time is available. You can't include large amounts of detail if you have only a few minutes to speak. Since you know you must respect the time limits imposed on your talk, consider carefully how much information, and in what level of detail, you'll be able to include. You'll have some idea of whether you need more or less information once you rehearse the speech. As you begin, of course, it's always better to have too much than too little. You can easily edit a speech later on; it's much tougher to go back and begin your research again as the speaking date approaches.

ORGANIZE YOUR THOUGHTS

Since you have already listened to a number of public speeches, you know that a well-organized talk is easy to follow, sensible in its patterns, and has a feeling of coherence. In other words, the parts fit together and flow along nicely.

At the risk of dwelling on the obvious, you should know that each speech has an introduction, a main body, and a conclusion. If the talk is especially well written and delivered, you may not even be aware of these separate parts, but they each exist to serve a number of important purposes.

Your Introduction   A well-crafted introduction will help you to get the audience's attention and allow them to settle in and focus on your topic and your reason for speaking to them. Unless you have a very good reason for *not* doing so (several good reasons do exist), you should disclose your purpose right up front. Telling an audience what your objectives are will build both credibility and interest. When should you withhold your real purpose in speaking to them? The research in this area tells us that you may safely delay your intentions if your audience would be confused by revealing them, if you plan to ask them for money, or if you know the audience initially disagrees with your position.

A good introduction will also recognize and involve the audience in some way. A reference to the occasion or to people who are likely to be known to the audience may help.

How Should You Begin?   Many proven methods are available to you as you begin a speech. Consider these:

An anecdote   Tell a story. People have loved listening to stories since they were kids, waiting for bedtime. Ronald Reagan's success as a speaker, in part, was due to his ability to "spin a yarn." Even those who disagreed with his politics acknowledged the importance story-telling played in his political life.

Humor   People love to laugh, but be careful with this. Humor is great, unless you're not funny. Foremost among the occasions when you are likely not to be funny is when the joke is on the audience, or someone they hold in high regard. Spontaneous, contemporary humor tends to work best. Stay away from set-piece jokes and "amusing" stories you have heard recently.

A prediction   Can you offer, based on the evidence you have gathered, a prediction which is likely to interest, amuse, frighten, or arouse your audience? Make sure you can support your contentions. And, make sure the evidence on which they are based is readily available and easily understood.

A dramatic forecast   This is similar to a prediction but longer-range in nature and usually involving extended or more complex events.

A striking example   This is just one form of an illustration or very brief anecdote. If you can make your point by citing an example, do so. Just make sure you are not citing a notable exception to prove your point.

A climactic moment   Interesting speeches often base their central premise on an event or a particular moment in time. Audiences often find such examples powerful and easy to understand.

A suitable quotation   You can find quotes everywhere. Rather than look in the usual sources (Bartlett's *Familiar Quotations, The Oxford Dictionary of Quotations,* or some similar volume), why not pick up the phone and talk with someone close to the subject? Get a reaction from a friend, family member, participant, or person who knows the events you are trying to describe. Internet search engines will turn up quotes for you by topic or by source. *Conner's Unfamiliar Quotations* is available on the Internet by typing http://www.h2net.net/p/connect2/quotes.html. Another useful source is available online at http://www.fas.harvard.edu/~liu15/quotes.html.[15]

A *reference to the occasion*   A brief explanation about why you are glad to be there or why the occasion is special might generate interest in your talk while helping to humanize you to the audience.

A *provocative question*   If you cannot predict the future with any measure of certainty, perhaps you can pose the issue in the form of a rhetorical question. If you are actually hoping for answers from the audience, remember that you must be prepared for *any* response, including no response at all.

A *description*   One effective way to introduce a topic to an audience is to describe in vivid, even lurid detail exactly what you mean. Get the audience to visualize objects or events they cannot see. Use imagery and imaginative language to involve them in the process.

A *statement of opinion*   This may work, although it is important that you reveal the source of the opinion and that the source be both well-known to and respected by the audience. An opinion from someone they hold in low repute will do little to bolster your cause; it may actually damage your own credibility.

Current or recent events   Audiences usually respond well to information that is fresh out of the newspaper or right off the Internet. An anecdote or detail taken from a breaking news story or from a conversation with a well-respected person gives an audience a feeling that they are receiving current, inside information that others don't have or won't receive.

How Should You Structure Your Speech?   Regardless of which pattern you select for your speech, research indicates that your strongest or most important point should be placed either first or last for emphasis. Don't bury your best ideas. For an overall pattern of organization, consider one (or more) of the following:

Chronological order   Time is the controlling pattern here. Start at the beginning and move to the end. Start with a particular event and move backward in time. Be consistent, giving your listeners plenty of timing cues so they will stay with you.

Topical organization   When one issue is no more important than any other, you may want to organize them by topics, one after another.

Cause-and-effect   This is a good pattern if you hope to establish a likely outcome from a particular known cause, or if you hope to trace the cause of a known event or effect.

Problem-solution   This pattern examines the nature of a problem, poses alternative solutions, and then weighs those solutions according to a set of values the speaker provides. Speeches using this pattern usually offer the listener a particular solution favored by the speaker.

Geographic Compass points are the controlling motif here. The talk moves from East-to-West, North-to-South, or in some other, readily identifiable direction.

Spatial Where compass points are inappropriate, you may wish to organize a talk from front-to-back, left-to-right, top-to-bottom, inside-to-outside, stem-to-stern, or another non-geographic pattern.

Any Advice Beyond Structure? Yes, several bits of forensic wisdom may be helpful to you.

Keep it simple After a long church service, or so the story goes, President Calvin Coolidge's wife asked him what the sermon had been about. "Sin," said Coolidge. "What did the preacher say about it?" she wanted to know. "He was against it," Coolidge replied.[16]

Your audience is going to come away with one or two of your main ideas. One or two. Not ten or fifteen. If you can't express in a sentence or two what you intend to get across, then your speech isn't focused well enough. If you don't have a clear idea of what you want to say, there is no way your audience will.

Keep it brief President Bill Clinton's State of the Union addresses were notoriously long, some of them more than 80 minutes. According to *The Wall Street Journal,* Congress was "begging for mercy" after an hour. "If you can do it in 20 minutes, you have the best shot at the minds of the people present," says Kevin R. Daley, president and CEO of Communispond, Inc. Sixty minutes is suicide. You should commit it—or they will."

At New York's Union League Club a few years ago, a prominent steel company chief ended a 90-minute presentation before 400 of his executives and managers by striding from the stage and down the middle aisle. No one applauded until he was halfway out of the room. "They didn't know he was finished," a critic recalls. "They hadn't been attentive enough to recognize that."

Offering some free advice to speakers, former New York Governor Mario Cuomo says, "When you can hear them coughing, stop whatever you are doing and get out." During his unsuccessful re-election effort in 1994, Mr. Cuomo was losing a crowd at a late-night event, but won them back when he suddenly broke into the song, "Boulevard of Broken Dreams."[17] Clever, but he'd have been better off with a shorter speech.

Talk, don't read Manuscripted speeches, particularly those written by someone other than the speaker, almost never sound authentic or convincing. I once wrote to a number of *Fortune 500* executives asking for samples of speeches they had given in the previous year. A friend who is a senior executive at PepsiCo said, "I hope you don't intend to use those speeches as teaching examples. Most chief executives," he said, "are terrible speakers simply because they won't give up the script." They bury their heads in the text, ignore the audience, and hope for the best. It rarely comes off the way they hope it will.

> *Relax* Comedian Robert Klein, in his routine about the Lamaze method of natural childbirth, points out that the husband's principal role seems to be to remind the wife to breathe.[18] That's good advice, actually. Breathing steadily and naturally will help you focus, relax, and deliver a convincing, entertaining, and interesting speech. If you fall into a pattern of rapid, shallow breathing and can't seem to finish a sentence or a paragraph, just stop for a moment. Breathe deeply, then exhale. Bring your breathing under control once more, and then continue.

How Should You Conclude?   Conclusions are among the more important (and most welcome) portions of a public speech. Why are they important? Well, to begin, they represent one more opportunity to put your best evidence or most important ideas before your audience. They represent one last chance to say what you really mean, to reinforce your purpose for speaking, and to ask for their support or compliance.

Be certain you clue people in to the fact that your speech is coming to an end. Don't leave them wondering if there's more to come. Cue them both verbally and non-verbally to the fact that you're just about done speaking. Above all else, leave them with a clear, simple, unambiguous message. Don't let them leave the room wondering what this was all about.

KEEP YOUR AUDIENCE INTERESTED

If you are worried about keeping your audience involved as you speak, think about these ideas as you prepare your remarks.

Provide Order, Structure   If your audience is forced to work in order to follow your argument, they may lose interest. Make it easy for people to follow what you are saying: Provide a structure for them to follow, an easy-to-understand structure that will carry them from one point to another.

Give Them Something They Can Use   Even the most charitable and altruistic among us is, from time to time, selfish. We ask ourselves, "What's in this for me?" Often, if we think a speech or a conversation holds nothing of interest for us, we'll excuse ourselves and go do something else. Your audience may be polite enough to stay in their seats, but they may not play close attention to your talk if they cannot see their self-interests being served. Give them something they can take to the bank, some ideas or information they can put to work as soon as they leave the room.

Make It Logical   Not everyone is influenced by logic. Many of us, in fact, can be convinced by an entirely illogical argument that contains just the right type and amount of emotion. For most of your audience members, however, logic and rationality are particularly important considerations. The more logically sound your arguments are, the greater the chance your listeners will understand and adopt your viewpoint.

Make It Reasonable   A number of important psychological studies have shown that adults will not routinely engage in behavior that they regard as unreasonable. Now, what's reasonable to one person may seem totally unreasonable to another, but the vast majority of people will remain consistent in their definitions of what is and is not reasonable. If you know your audience well, and can determine how they would characterize "reasonable behavior," you have a much better chance of convincing them to adopt your viewpoint, as long as what you ask of them falls within the limits they have established for themselves.

Make It Clear One reason many managerial speeches fail is that the audience simply has no idea what the speaker wants. The main point may be unclear, the supporting evidence may not be well understood, or the conclusion may be incomprehensible. And while ambiguity may be a deliberate communication goal in some instances, consider this statement from a Chief Executive Officer: "This firm will take all measures afforded by the law to seek the objectives we have outlined." What does that mean? Well, not only is the listener uncertain, so is the speaker. The speaker has deliberately chosen to be ambiguous, perhaps because he doesn't really know what he intends to do. Unless ambiguity is a deliberate part of your communication strategy, do what you can to make your message, your evidence, and your intentions clear to your listeners.

Use Words They Understand Plain English will go a long way toward winning friends and influencing people. U.S. Securities and Exchange Commission Chairman Arthur Levitt, in speaking to people who write financial disclosure documents, recently said:

> "The benefits of plain English abound. Investors will be more likely to understand what they are buying and to make informed judgments about whether they should hold or sell their investments. Brokers and investment advisors can make better recommendations to their clients if they can read and understand these documents quickly and easily.
>
> "Companies that communicate successfully with their investors form stronger relationships with them. These companies save the costs of explaining legalese and dealing with confused and sometimes angry investors. Lawyers reviewing plain English documents catch and correct mistakes more easily. Many companies have switched to plain English because it's a good business decision. They see the value of communicating with their investors rather than sending them impenetrable documents. And as we depend more and more on the Internet and electronic delivery of documents, plain English versions will be easier to read electronically than legalese."[19]

Chairman Levitt was speaking specifically about the language used in written documents given to potential investors. But, if plain English works for written financial disclosure documents and has the support of a large and complex governmental agency like the Securities and Exchange Commission, it will probably work for you and your employer. Frankly, unless you are writing or speaking with the hope that no one will understand you, plain English is the only sensible approach.

Keep It Moving Your audience will be patient with you for just so long. Don't try their patience and good nature by dragging the pace of your speech or dawdling on minor points for very long. If your talk moves along briskly, chances are good that you'll maintain audience interest.

Answer Their Questions Every audience has questions. Your task is to determine what they are and to answer them to their complete satisfaction. See the section earlier in this chapter, entitled "Understand the Questions Listeners Bring to Any Listening Situation." If you are unwilling to address those questions, your audience may be unwilling to pay attention to or buy into your argument.

Allay Their Fears   Everyone in your audience is afraid of something. Find out what it is. Some may be afraid that you will be asking things of them which they'll be unwilling to do. Others may be afraid that they won't understand the implications of your request. If you cannot deal with their fears, no audience will accept your point of view. Fear is a very powerful emotion and, when people feel frightened, they are usually unwilling to take risk or to try something new. Social psychologist Robert Cialdini has suggested that persuasive speakers deal with emotions by channeling fear into excitement. Rather than simply asking an audience to calm down or not to worry, he suggests redirecting the energy inherent in audience fear into excitement for the speaker's proposals.[20]

Respect Their Needs   Everyone in your audience has specific psychological needs. Each of them gathers and organizes information in slightly different ways. And each of them takes a slightly different approach to decision making. If you understand and respect their needs, they'll reward you. Some may have a need for details—show them the numbers. Others may have a need to understand where this idea fits in the larger scheme of things—show them the big picture. Still others may have a need to know who else has tried or approves of this idea—show them the celebrity endorsements. If I have a specific need—say, a strong desire to know the source of your information—and you don't deal directly with my need, I'm unlikely to adopt your viewpoint or do as you ask.

SELECT A DELIVERY APPROACH

You have four options for delivering a speech. You probably shouldn't depend on more than just one or two of them.

Memorized speeches are delivered verbatim, word-for-word just as the authors wrote them. The problem with memorized speeches is that, unless you are a trained actor, you cannot deliver them with any level of conviction. They sound wooden, contrived, and artificial. Worse yet, you may forget where you are and have to start over. Unless you're doing Shakespeare from the stage, forget about memorized talks.

Manuscripted speeches are far more common among managerial and executive speaking events. The problem with speaking from a manuscript is that it sounds *read*. The impression from the audience is almost always negative: "Why am I here? He could have mailed this to me." Reading a fully scripted speech ensures that you will include each key point and resist the temptation to ad-lib, but without a TelePrompTer, you lose eye contact with the audience and seem distant or remote to them. Unless you have no other choice, don't work with a verbatim manuscript. If you must, rehearse carefully and try looking up frequently, making regular contact with the audience.

Extemporaneous speeches are, perhaps, the best among your alternatives. These are speeches that are thoroughly researched, tightly and sensibly organized, well rehearsed, and delivered either without notes or with visual aids to prompt your memory. They are especially convincing to an audience because you make and maintain eye contact, you look at them rather than at a script, and you speak (seemingly) from the heart and not from a set of prepared notes. This is really the effect you are striving for.

Impromptu speeches are delivered without any preparation at all. Someone in charge usually asks you to stand up and "offer a few remarks." This is not the best approach to public speaking, obviously, since you have prepared no evidence and have not rehearsed. You may not even have a topic or an idea worth hearing. The good news is that audience's expectations are low. They will applaud for nearly anything as long as it's brief and not insulting to them.

GIVING AN IMPROMPTU TALK

So what do you do when someone asks you to stand up and "offer a few remarks?" Modesty usually dictates that you say very little, but protocol usually demands that you say something. Here are a few ideas that may help.

Maintain Your Poise   Just smile, thank your host for the opportunity to speak, and take advantage of the moment.

Decide on Your Topic and Approach   Speak *briefly* about something that you understand and that will be of interest to those listening. Select a pattern of organization: past, present, future; advantages, disadvantages; risks, benefits; reasons favoring an idea, reasons opposing. Once you have your pattern, stick to it. Don't get inventive as you go along.

Do Not Apologize   People know you didn't prepare a speech. Just talk to them.

Summarize Your Point and Position   In one sentence, or two at the most, underscore your key points and reiterate why they are important or worthwhile.

Be Sincere, Honest, and Direct   Nothing impresses an audience more profoundly than an honest man or woman. Convey the impression that you have nothing to hide and nothing ulterior in your motives for speaking. They will reward you by considering your ideas and applauding your delivery.

DEVELOP YOUR VISUAL SUPPORT

In preparing a speech, managers will often ask if they even need visual support. To answer this question properly, you should consider whether visual support will help to explain, reinforce, or clarify your position or your evidence. If you can't *say* it easily, you may be able to *show* it.

Graphs, charts, tables, and photographs are usually helpful, but not always. If you clutter the screen with unreadable or unnecessary detail, you may confuse your audience. On the other hand, if your graphics are clear, crisp, and uncluttered, your audience may gain insights they might otherwise miss.

Some people are visual-attenders, others are aural-attenders. Give each group an opportunity to hear and see your key points. One should reinforce the other. Don't show them something you don't plan to talk about. Similarly, if you choose to use visual support, don't talk at length about things you can't show or reinforce visually.[21]

When Do Visuals Work Best?   Visual information is often at its best when you are working with new data, complex or technical information, or a new context. Visual aids will also help you with numbers, facts, quotes, and lists. They are also frequently good for side-by-side comparisons, emphasizing similarities or differences. Geographical or spatial patterns will also frequently benefit from some form of visual illustration.[22]

Good Visuals Will . . .

- Be simple in nature.
- Explain relationships.
- Use color effectively.
- Be easy to set up, display and transport.
- Reinforce the spoken message.

REHEARSE YOUR SPEECH

Should You Practice? Absolutely! Don't even consider giving a speech you haven't rehearsed—several times. Why should you practice? Rehearsal will do at least three things for your speech. First, it will limit timing. You will know after one or two run-throughs whether you have too much, too little, or just enough to say. Second, rehearsal will improve your transitions. As you practice your speech, you will have an opportunity to identify the rough spots and work on movement from one main point to another, and from one part of the speech to another. Finally, rehearsal will polish your delivery and build confidence. When the day to deliver the speech finally comes, you will step to the podium with the knowledge that you know this stuff inside and out. A well-rehearsed speech contains no surprises.

Should You Use Notes? The best speakers seem to deliver their speeches *extemporaneously,* or "from the heart." Such speeches aren't really memorized word-for-word, but rather are thoroughly researched, well rehearsed, and professionally supported. Many extemporaneous speakers will use their visual support—acetate transparencies, 35-mm slides, *PowerPoint* or other electronic projection system—to prompt their memories, as if giant notecards had been placed on the wall for them and their audience to see.

If you do choose to use notecards, here are some suggestions. At a minimum, they should be:

- Simple.
- Compact.
- East-to-follow.
- Easy-to-handle.
- Numbered.
- Readable.

Having put your notecards together in this way, re-consider once again why you need them. Virtually all speech coaches and public speaking experts in the country are unanimous in their disapproval of notecards. Use your projected visuals instead to prompt your memory.

DEVELOP CONFIDENCE IN YOUR MESSAGE AND YOURSELF

It's one thing to know your material. It's another matter entirely to believe that you can get up on stage and speak with confidence to a group of strangers. Understanding your message and knowing that you have both quality support and a well organized speech are important to your success, but so is self-confidence.

Rehearsal will help. Simply knowing that you've been through the contents of your speech more than once is reassuring. The knowledge that you personally arranged and rehearsed the talk will give you confidence. And, as you work on your self-assurance, consider this: you're the expert. This audience asked for you to speak on this subject because they want to hear what you have to say. They are interested in your expertise and your viewpoint. Chances are good that you know more about your subject than anyone else in the room (though you can never be completely certain). Use your interest, your expertise, and your background to your advantage.

The more confident you are, the more credible you are. If you seem uncertain, the audience may be reluctant to believe you. Just approach this speech as you would any other managerial task, knowing that you have the ability, the intelligence, and the confidence to get it done. The more professional, sincere, and capable you seem, the more likely the audience is to believe you and buy into your message.

DELIVER YOUR MESSAGE

Beforehand   Before you begin your talk, make certain you've checked on all of the most important details:

Date, Time, and Location   Where are you supposed to be? When is your talk scheduled to begin? If you are unfamiliar with the location, do your best to find out all about it in advance.

Room Layout   It's never wise to walk into the room with no idea of how it will be organized. Don't depend on others to do it to your satisfaction, either. If you can arrange it, be there in advance and set things up the way you'd like them to be. It's your speech, take charge of the room.

Microphone and Acoustics   Try out the sound system in advance. If you will be wearing a wireless mike, find out exactly what you need to do to make it work. Decide in advance whether you are willing to speak without a sound system if it fails or wait for someone to repair it.

Visual-Aids   Check out the screen, the placement of your projector, and the system you plan to use to support your talk. Make sure it's focused, centered, and visible to the people in the back row.

Stage   Take a moment to find out how to get onto and off of the stage, where the sound projection limits are, and where the trap doors, cables, and high-risk footing might be.

Time Limits   Double-check with your host on the time limits for your talk and then abide by them. Don't disappoint by saying less than you had promised, and don't disappoint by speaking beyond your allotted time.

Lectern   Find out where you will speak and, if possible, whether you'll be able to move beyond a lectern and walk around the front of the room.

Notes   Don't trust anyone else with your speech. If you're working from a script or detailed notes, hang onto them personally. Review them beforehand, but don't make a point of pouring over them just as your host is about to introduce you.

Lights   Determine whether the overhead lighting will wash out a projected image on the screen. Are the lights bright enough for people to see you and whatever handouts you provide for them? Are they dim enough to allow them to see your visual aids?

Try It Out   Use the microphone, check out the projector, walk across the stage, examine the effect of your visual aids from the back of the room. See if you can be seen and heard in all parts of the room. Gain some confidence by knowing where you'll be and what it feels like before you actually begin.

As You Speak   Consider these ideas to keep your audience interested.

- Step up to the podium, breathe deeply, smile, think positively, and *speak*.
- Do your best to be one of them (unless it's obvious you are really not).
- Use humor where it may be appropriate (unless you are not funny).
- Share your own experiences, values, background, goals, and fears.
- Focus on current, local events, and other issues known to the audience.
- Begin by moving from the familiar to the unfamiliar.
- Talk process first, then detail.
- Blueprint the speech: Tell them where this talk is going.
- Visualize and demonstrate.
- Use interim summaries, transitions.
- Give examples.
- Humanize and personalize.
- Tell stories, dramatize your central theme.
- Use yourself, involve them.

As you approach the challenge of becoming a speaking professional (as opposed to a professional speaker), keep in mind a few basic ideas. No one is born with great public speaking ability. Language is the habit of a lifetime, and your ability to speak with conviction and sincerity is a function of your willingness to work at it. If you work, one speech at a time, to improve your skills, chances are quite good that others in a position of influence will notice and reward you for your effort.

Endnotes

1. Osgood, Charles. *Osgood on Speaking.* New York, NY: William Morrow and Company, Inc., 1989.
2. Suskind, Ron and Joann S. Lublin. "Critics Are Succinct: Long Speeches Tend to Get Short Interest," *The Wall Street Journal,* Thursday, January 26, 1995, pp. Al, A8.
3. Osgood, Charles. *Osgood on Speaking.* New York, NY: William Morrow and Company, Inc., 1989.
4. Cooper, Lane (ed.). *The Rhetoric of Aristotle.* Englewood Cliffs, NJ: Prentice Hall, Inc., 1960, pp. 141–142.
5. Stanton, William J., Michael J. Etzel, and Bruce J. Walker. *Fundamentals of Marketing,* 10th ed. New York, NY: McGraw-Hill, Inc., 1994, pp. 167–168.
6. Cooper, *The Rhetoric of Aristotle,* pp. 16–17.
7. Hamlin, Sonya. *How to Talk So People Will Listen.* New York, NY: Harper and Row, Publishers, 1988, p. 23.
8. Ibid., pp. 26–29.
9. Ibid., p. 30.
10. Lippmann, Walter. *Public Opinion.* New York, NY: The Free Press, 1965, pp. 53–68.
11. For an excellent discussion of the emotional foundations of prejudice and prejudicial

thinking, see Bem, Daryl J., *Beliefs, Attitudes, and Human Affairs.* Belmont, CA: Brooks/Cole Publishing Company, 1970, pp. 40–44.

12. For a thorough review of current research on human emotion and the management of human feelings, see Goleman, Daniel. *Emotional Intelligence: Why It Can Matter More Than IQ.* New York, NY: Bantam Books, 1995.

13. Borden, George A. *An Introduction to Human Communication Theory.* Dubuque, IA: William C. Brown Publishers, 1971, pp. 81–87.

14. Hoecklin, Lisa. *Managing Cultural Differences: Strategies for Competitive Advantage.* Reading, MA: Addison-Wesley Publishing Company, 1995, pp. 23–49.

15. Bilodeaux, Jean. "Use the Net to Catch Quotes," *The Toastmaster,* Vol. 64, No. 5 (May 1998), p. 15.

16. Osgood. *Osgood on Speaking.*

17. Suskind, Ron and Joann S. Lublin. "Critics Are Succinct: Long Speeches Tend to Get Short Interest." *The Wall Street Journal,* January 26, 1995, pp. Al, A8.

18. Osgood. *Osgood on Speaking.*

19. Smith, Nancy (ed.). *A Plain English Handbook: How to Create Clear SEC Disclosure Documents.* Office of Investor Education and Assistance, U.S. Securities and Exchange Commission, August 1998, p. 4.

20. Cialdini, Robert B. *Influence: The Psychology of Persuasion,* revised edition. New York, NY: Quill/William Morrow, 1993.

21. Ingersoll, G. M. *The Effects of Presentation Modalities and Modality Preferences on Learning and Recall.* Doctoral dissertation, Pennsylvania State University. Ann Arbor, MI: University Microfilms, 1970. No. 71-16615.

22. For a thorough and very useful discussion of visual support for business presentations, see Bailey, Edward P., Jr. *A Practical Guide for Business Speaking.* New York, NY: Oxford University Press, 1992, pp. 36–78 and 111–125.

For Further Reading

Arredondo, Lani. *Business Presentations: The McGraw-Hill 36 Hour Course.* New York, NY: McGraw-Hill, Inc., 1994.

Haberman, Clyde. "Forswearing Onagers and Their Ilk," *The New York Times,* April 23, 1996, p. B-15.

Hauer, Nancy and Edward Martley. *The Practical Speech Handbook.* Burr Ridge, IL: Irwin Mirror Press, 1993.

Hofmann, Therese M., Deanna F. Womack, and Janelle Shubert. *Effective Business Presentations.* Cambridge MA: Harvard Business School Publications, 1990. HBS Note 9-391-011.

Kellaway, Lucy. "Public Speaking: First, Take a Deep Breath." *The Financial Times,* December 4, 1991, p. B-1.

Lakoff, Robin Tolmach. *Talking Power: The Politics of Language.* New York, NY: Basic Books, 1990.

Mooney, William and Donald J. Noone. *Speech ASAP.* New York, NY: Barron's, 1992.

Case 4–1   A LAST MINUTE CHANGE AT OLD DOMINION TRUST

"It was a quarter to four on Friday afternoon," said Rob Leonard. "I was just closing out my accounts and trying to clear up a few more issues before the end of the business day. Then along came my division vice president. Since my desk is in the center of the mortgage banking division, I could tell long before he got to me that I was the one he was looking for. And, frankly, the folder he dropped on my desk was the last thing in the world I expected to see."

Rob Leonard is a 26-year-old assistant broker in the mortgage banking division of Old Dominion Trust, a relatively small interstate bank located in the mid-Atlantic region. Rob's branch has regional responsibility for home mortgages in Northern Virginia and the Washington D.C. area. Although he had joined Old Dominion Trust following graduation four years earlier, he was still among the more junior people in his branch.

"The boss came directly to my desk and asked if I had a minute. Of course I have a minute," said Leonard, "Who hasn't got a minute for the Branch V.P.?" Brian Lorigan was senior vice president, Mortgage Banking for Old Dominion and executive vice president for the Annandale branch office. He was not only Leonard's supervisor, but his mentor and partner in several important projects.

"Mr. Lorigan and I had been working on a new, federally funded mortgage program that would permit low-to-middle-income, first-time home buyers to obtain financing at very low rates. It was an important project that would require both thorough explanation to the community and careful screening of each of the applicants." Leonard went on to explain that the program has been more than six months in development and would require the cooperation of state and local officials if it were to work. It was an impressive attempt, Leonard thought, on the bank's part to provide mortgage financing to people who would otherwise never qualify for a home loan.

"I thought he would want to review the screening procedures we'd been working on, or perhaps talk about the software I planned to use to help set up the program," said Leonard. "What he had in mind frightened me a lot more. He said that Dick Gidley, his principal assistant, had been scheduled to speak to a Capitol Hill neighborhood group about the federally assisted home loan program. Unfortunately, Dick was in Philadelphia and had just been 'bumped' from his return flight to Washington."

"Mr. Lorigan asked if I would fill in for Dick at the neighborhood group meeting this evening and speak about the new loan program. 'The details are all in this package,' he said. I got a phone number, a set of street directions to a renovated fire station on Rhode Island Avenue, and the name of the woman who would introduce me. The rest of the information would have to come from documents I had prepared for the bank and for the select committee that had prepared the legislation."

Leonard was philosophical about the request. "It wasn't that I minded canceling dinner plans I had for that evening. It was just that I wasn't sure I was ready to stand up in public and explain a bank loan program that I wasn't in charge of. After Mr. Lorigan shook my hand and said thanks, I looked at my watch. It was five minutes to four, and this thing in Washington was scheduled for seven o'clock."

DISCUSSION QUESTIONS

1. Assuming you are in Rob Leonard's position, what would you do? Would it be a good idea to tell Mr. Lorigan you're just not ready (or willing) to give that speech?
2. What would you want to know about the audience that you don't already know? Where could you find that information?
3. What would you want to know about the occasion and speaking situation that you don't already know?
4. Is there anything you think you should know about the physical layout of the room

or the arrangements in the fire station that you'll be speaking in?
5. How would you go about preparing your notes for this speech?
6. What else would you bring with you for this event? Do you have time to get visual aids or flip charts made? Is that a good idea?
7. How should you dress for this occasion?
8. What do you think your principal message should be for these people?

This case was prepared by James S. O'Rourke, concurrent associate professor of management, as the basis for class discussion, rather than to illustrate either effective or ineffective handling of an administrative situation.

Case 4–2 PREPARING TO SPEAK AT STAPLES, INC.

As Elizabeth Allen pulled into her parking spot at Staples, Inc., headquarters in Framingham, Massachusetts, she knew the next three days would be a challenge. "This is a huge opportunity," she thought to herself. It would be visible, risky, and filled with snares. "On the other hand," she thought, "this really should be fun." Ms. Allen was thinking about a speech manuscript she had been preparing for her chairman and chief executive officer. Less than 72 hours from now, he would give one of the most important talks in his professional career across the country in California.

"Technology and the Internet are clearly the most powerful communication media available to any company today," says Elizabeth Allen. "But on some occasions, there is just no substitute for face-to-face interaction and a personal statement from a senior official of the

company." The statement Allen envisioned would be powerful, important to shareholders and the community, and seen by literally millions of people on television, both as it happened and later on news programs nationwide.

Elizabeth Heller Allen was vice president for corporate communication at Staples, Inc., and had primary responsibility—among her many other duties—for preparing members of the Staples senior team for press conferences, speeches, and public appearances. The ten most senior people in the company were known as the *Point Team,* and Allen's corporate communication staff worked very hard to prepare them for a wide range of public appearances, including the one her CEO would make the day after tomorrow.

Staples, Inc., is the number-two office supply superstore company in the United States, with market capitalization of $13.5 billion and annual revenues of $8.3 billion. They sell office products, furniture, computers, and photocopying services at more than 1,000 stores, primarily in the United States and Canada, but also in Germany, the United Kingdom, the Netherlands, and Portugal. With more than 21,500 employees, the company sells some 8,000 different office products to small- and medium-sized businesses through their retail stores, a catalogue, and an e-commerce site.

"Speaking opportunities are important at any business," says Allen, "but they are especially important at a company like Staples because the current CEO, Thomas G. Stemberg, is the company founder. Like Herb Kelleher at Southwest Airlines, Bill Gates at Microsoft, or Jim Barksdale at Netscape, the founder of a company has special visibility in the marketplace, and it's very important for shareholders, employees, and other stakeholders that we take best advantage of that."

According to Allen, speaking styles and preparation for speeches will vary greatly. "Some members of the Point Team will ask that every single word of a speech be written out in advance. They rehearse, they work from a manuscript, and—if one were available—they would ask for a TelePrompTer. Others will say, 'Send me an outline 24 hours in advance. I'll wing it.' " For each of her senior executives, Allen found a different challenge as they prepared for a public speech.

The more important the venue or the audience, the more important the text, rehearsal, and detailed preparation become. "If a lot of people are going to see and hear this speech—even fragments of it on videotape—it's all the more important that we spend time and energy in getting the speaker ready." Frequently, that means a complete manuscript, even though most executives would prefer to speak extemporaneously.

"Most of the Point Team would rather have a few key points, some supporting detail, and a couple of closing thoughts to work from," says Allen. "These are important people—supremely confident—who got to their current positions by being comfortable in front of a crowd." Her preference is to prepare such people with information about who will be in the room, the occasion on which they'll be speaking, and the business objective of the talk itself. Beyond that, delivery and rehearsal are up to the individual speaker.

"There is a value to a complete manuscript, though," she says. "We not only like to know what someone said to a particular audience on a given occasion, but my staff can get substantially greater mileage out of a speech if I can share a copy of the script with the press." Advance copies of a speech may induce a journalist to attend the talk, or inspire a reporter who couldn't attend to include direct quotes in a news story. Either way, the company and the message in the executive's speech receive greater exposure.

That morning, Elizabeth Allen had just such an opportunity as her CEO prepared for a speech on the West Coast. "Staples had an agreement to purchase the naming rights for a new basketball and hockey arena in Los Angeles," she said. "A press conference was scheduled to reveal the identity of the naming-rights company." According to Allen, the event was preceded by considerable advance media coverage and speculation throughout the L.A. basin. "Many people thought the name would be a local, California company. And, of course, we did nothing to discourage the attention given to the event." It was a closely guarded secret. And Staples was about to pay $100 million for the privilege—the highest sum ever paid for the right to name an athletic venue.

"I know several things about this event," said Allen. "First, I know that it's being covered not by the business press, but the sports press. From the news media's point of view, this isn't a business story. It's a sports story." She also knew who would be in the room. "Dave Taylor of the Los Angeles Kings and Jerry West of the LA Lakers—both general managers—will be there." Civic officials, investors, reporters, and many others would be watching and listening. "This five-minute speech of Tom Stemberg's will have huge marquee value," said Allen.

Elizabeth Allen also knew that this was more than just another corporate investment in professional sports. "This is a Boston company putting its name on a Los Angeles landmark. I know there are cultural factors at work here, and political factors as well as business factors." For Allen, this speech—brief as it would be—had to be flawless. "No faux pas," she said. "This has got to be perfect."

DISCUSSION QUESTIONS

1. If you were assisting Ms. Allen with this event, what would you want to know that you don't already know?
2. As she drafts Mr. Stemberg's remarks, what issues should Ms. Allen pay especially careful attention to?
3. Can you think of any references, issues, or remarks that Ms. Allen might want her CEO to avoid?
4. What sort of pre-event information would you want to brief Mr. Stemberg about? What sort of detail does he need about the event, the audience, and the occasion?
5. Others will certainly speak on this occasion. Would it be helpful for Ms. Allen to know who they are? Would it be important for her to know what they intend to say? Why? How can she go about obtaining that information?
6. What do you imagine Mr. Stemberg's business goals are for this speech? What specific outcomes would he and Ms. Allen want to achieve as a result of his remarks to the press and the community?
7. What shadow audiences might be watching and listening to what Mr. Stemberg has to say? How should he prepare for them?
8. Would you suggest to Mr. Stemberg that he rehearse his speech? If so, how would you go about that? What kind of advice would you give to him as he prepares for this event?

5

WRITING

B usiness writing isn't simply a way to move information from one office to another. Nor is it just another storage mechanism for business decisions. Business writing, at its best and at its worst, is an expression of the values and beliefs of the organization. A peek inside the file drawers and out-baskets of any business will reveal a great deal about what's important to an organization, as well as how the people in that organization think about their work, their customers and clients, and themselves.

Business writing is important because, as you saw in Chapter 1, the most important projects and decisions in the life of a business end up in writing. Writing is a way of thinking about business, a way of organizing. It provides analysis of and justification for our best ideas. It also provides documentation and discipline for an organization.

And, as you have learned, writing is a career sifter. Managers do most of their own writing and editing, relying on the assistance and advice of others only on occasion. If you can't write at a minimally effective level, others in positions of influence will notice and you'll be looking for work elsewhere. At the very least, an inability to express yourself effectively on paper can stop a career dead in its tracks.

Why is most business writing so bad and what makes it that way? Well, most business writing isn't terrible—some is, of course—but much of it is just badly organized, passive, not parallel in structure, littered with jargon and obscure terminology. Some business writers pay little attention to the conventions of spelling and punctuation. Others just keep writing until they've told their readers *everything* they know about the subject. Sentences run on and paragraphs take up entire pages.

Most business writing isn't bad for just one reason. It's a result of a series of reasons, and heading the list is this: Writers simply are not writing for the benefit of their readers. They don't craft a memo, a proposal, a report, or a letter with the needs and interests of their readers in mind. If they did, we would see fewer documents written like this mutual fund prospectus paragraph:

> Maturity and duration management decisions are made in the context of an intermediate maturity orientation. The maturity structure of the portfolio is adjusted in the anticipation of cyclical interest rate changes. Such adjustments are not made in an effort to capture short-term, day-to-day movements in the market, but instead are implemented in anticipation of longer term, secular shifts in the levels of interest rates (i.e., shifts transcending and/or not inherent to the business cycle). Adjustments made to shorten portfolio maturity and duration are made to limit capital losses during periods when interest rates are expected to rise. Conversely, adjustments made to lengthen maturity for the portfolio's maturity and duration strategy lie in

analysis of the U.S. and global economies, focusing on levels of real interest rates, monetary and fiscal policy actions, and cyclical indicators.[1]

Ordinary human beings who read that paragraph will recognize that it's grammatically correct and syntactically sound. Each sentence has a verb. The capital letters are used correctly. And, for the most part, people will recognize the words. But when they are put together like that, we read and feel confused. What can this mean? What's the writer trying to say here?

When Berkshire Hathaway Chairman Warren Buffett saw that paragraph, he got out a yellow legal pad, a ballpoint pen, and drafted another version:

> We will try to profit by correctly predicting future interest rates. When we have no strong opinion, we will generally hold intermediate-term bonds. But when we expect a major and sustained increase in rates, we will concentrate on short-term issues. And, conversely, if we expect a major shift to lower rates, we will buy long bonds. We will focus on the big picture and won't make moves based on short-term considerations.[2]

The first paragraph was written by a mutual fund manager with one of several ideas in mind. He may have been insecure and eager to show his boss and the customers how many big words and important business phrases he knew. Or, he may have been deliberately trying to disguise the mutual fund's lack of an investment strategy. If the prospectus isn't entirely clear, how can the fund manager be held accountable for failing to live up to the aims of his strategy?

I have another suggestion about that paragraph you just read: The fund manager who wrote it was probably modeling his writing after thousands of other mutual fund prospectus documents he's seen in his career. He's following a well-trodden path to obscurity, hoping his writing will look just like that of so many other successful managers.

Let's give him the benefit of the doubt and assume that his intentions were good but his mentors were not. Times are changing, though, and that fund manager will never again be able to write dense, impenetrable prose and get away with it. U.S Securities and Exchange Commission Chairman Arthur Levitt recently struck a blow in favor of plain English:

> Whether you work at a company, a law firm, or the U.S. Securities and Exchange Commission, the shift to plain English requires a new style of thinking and writing. We must question whether the documents we are used to writing highlight the important information investors need to make informed decisions. The legalese and jargon of the past must give way to everyday words that communicate complex information clearly.[3]

Warren Buffett responded by saying:

> Chairman Levitt's whole drive to encourage "plain English" . . . [is] good news for me. For more than forty years, I've studied the documents that public companies file. Too often, I've been unable to decipher just what is being said or, worse yet, had to conclude that nothing was being said.
>
> One unoriginal but useful tip: write with a specific person in mind. When writing Berkshire Hathaway's annual report, I pretend that I'm writing to my

sisters. I have no trouble picturing them: though highly intelligent, they are not experts in accounting or finance. They will understand plain English but jargon may puzzle them. My goal is simply to give them the information I would wish them to supply me if our positions were reversed. To succeed, I don't need to be Shakespeare; I must, though, have a sincere desire to inform.

No sisters to write to? Borrow mine: just being with "Dear Doris and Bertie."[4]

AN INTRODUCTION TO GOOD BUSINESS WRITING

Good business writing is simple, clear, and concise. It's virtually "transparent." By not calling attention to itself, good writing helps the reader focus on the idea you are trying to communicate rather than on the words that describe it.

Good writing, in business and elsewhere, is a pleasure to read. Ideas become clear, the writer's intentions are undisguised, and the evidence used to support those ideas is readily understandable.

No one I know thinks writing is easy. Good writing—that is, writing with power, grace, dignity, and impact—takes time, careful thought, and revision. Such writing is often the product of many years of training and practice. And, to be sure, the language we bring to the task is the product of a lifetime of use. Even though writing seems like hard work to many of us, I know for sure that you can learn to do it well.

No teacher of writing can lay much claim to original thinking on this subject. Instead, we each have built on the good ideas given to us by those who have written, taught, and observed organizational and business writing before us. If you can put some of this advice to work in your own writing, your reward will be the approval of your readers.

FIFTEEN WAYS TO BECOME A BETTER BUSINESS WRITER

Here are fifteen *guidelines* for better writing—a supplement, if you will, to the *rules* of grammar, syntax, and punctuation you learned in school. These were crafted by writing consultant Jean Paul Plummez and will help you bring simplicity and clarity to your writing—and power and vitality to your ideas.[5]

- *Keep in mind that your reader doesn't have much time.* Memos often travel to senior managers who have tight schedules and much to read. Your memo must be clear on first reading. The shorter it is, the better chance it has of being read and considered.
- *Know where you are going before you start writing.* Start with a list of the important points you want to cover, then put them into an outline. If you are composing a memo, write the overview section first. It should contain your purpose for writing and the keys to understanding the rest of what follows. Then, write the most important paragraphs before you get to details and supplementary material.
- *Don't make* **any** *spelling or grammatical errors.* Readers who find bad grammar and misspelled words will perceive the writer to be careless or uneducated. They will not put much stock in the writer's ideas.

- **Be responsive to the needs of the reader.** Don't be accused of missing the point. Before you write, find out what the writer expects, wants, and needs. If you must deviate from these guidelines, let the reader know why early in the memo.
- **Be clear and specific.** Use simple, down-to-earth words. Avoid needless words and wordy expressions. Avoid vague modifiers like *very* and *slightly.* Simple words and expressions are clearer and easier to understand. They show confidence and add power to your ideas.
- **Try to use the present tense.** Be careful not to slip from the present to the past tense and back again. Select one tense and stick to it. Use the present tense when possible to add immediacy to your writing.
- **Make your writing vigorous and direct.** Use active sentences and avoid the passive voice. Be more positive and definite by limiting the use of the word *not.* Avoid long strings of modifiers.
- **Use short sentences and paragraphs.** Send telegrams, not essays! Vary length to avoid monotonous-looking pages, but remember that short sentences and paragraphs are more inviting and more likely to get read.
- **Use personal pronouns.** Don't hesitate to use *I, we,* and *you,* even in formal writing. The institutional third person can be cold and sterile, while personal pronouns make your writing warm, inviting, and more natural.
- **Avoid clichés and jargon.** Tired, hackneyed words and expressions make your writing appear superficial. Find your own words and use them.
- **Separate facts from opinions.** The reader should *never* be in doubt as to what is fact and what is opinion. Determine what you *know* and what you *think* before you start writing. Be consistent about facts and opinions throughout the memo.
- **Use numbers with restraint.** A paragraph filled with numbers is difficult to read—and difficult to write. Use a few numbers selectively to make your point. Put the rest in tables and exhibits.
- **Write the way you talk.** Avoid pompous, bureaucratic, and legalistic words and expressions. Use informal, personal human language. Write to others the way you would talk to them. Read your memo out loud—if you wouldn't talk that way, change it.
- **Never be content with your first effort.** Revising and editing are critical to good writing. Putting some time between writing and editing will help you be more objective. Revise your memo with the intent to simplify, clarify and trim excess words.
- **Make it perfect!** Seek out and eliminate factual errors, typos, misspellings, bad grammar, and incorrect punctuation. Remember, if one detail in your memo is recognized as incorrect, your entire line of thinking may be suspect.

STRATEGY AND MEMO WRITING

Memos are, for the most part, *internal* documents. They are used to pass information, ideas, and recommendations to other people in the same organization. They have the advantage of not requiring an inside address, a salutation line, and perfunctory opening lines that greet the reader, inquiring about matters unrelated to the subject of the document.

Good memos get to the point, focus on just one issue, and support the writer's central ideas with coherent, relevant, convincing evidence.

The best of business memos are concise, written in plain English, and sensibly organized. That's true of business letters as well, but it's especially true of memos. They say what they must without using any more words than necessary. They present your ideas at something less than the upper reaches of bureaucratic formality, and they are organized with headings, subheadings, and parallel structure so that they are easy to read, easy to follow, and easy to understand.

Your ability to write a crisp, clean, no-nonsense memo will mark you as someone who contributes to the organization—someone worth keeping, watching, and promoting. Will a good memo get you promoted? That's unlikely. A series of bad memos—poorly crafted, disorganized, and densely expressed—however, may stop your career in its tracks. Writing, after all, is a career sifter. Good writers move up; bad writers get left behind.

The opening or overview paragraph of any memo should reveal a communication strategy for the entire document. By writing it first, you will identify your purpose and main ideas. This will give you perspective and direction that will guide the development of the memo, letter, or report.

Your reader will benefit as well. That overview paragraph provides perspective on what's coming and what's important, much like the topic sentence of a well-constructed paragraph.

An overview paragraph should simply and clearly tell the reader:

- *Purpose:* Why are you writing the memo?
- *Main idea:* What do you want to tell the reader? Or, what do you want the reader to do?
- *Opinion:* What is your point of view on the subject?

In addition, the overview should begin to establish the tone of the document for your reader.

THE SIX COMMUNICATION STRATEGIES

Before you being writing, begin thinking. Give some careful thought to your reader, to your objectives, and to the strategy you will employ to achieve your objectives. The content and pattern of organization will follow from those. When you are sure you know what you want to achieve—and what you want your reader to learn from your writing—you will need a communication strategy.

Here are six basic strategies, three designed to convey information, and three designed to promote action.[6]

Information Strategies	*Action Strategies*
• To confirm agreement	• To request assistance
• To provide facts	• To give direction
• To provide a point of view	• To seek agreement

QUALITIES OF A GOOD OVERVIEW

The Overview is the very first paragraph a reader will see and is, without question, one of the most important elements of a memo.[7] As you draft an overview paragraph, keep in mind that it should have six basic qualities.

- *Clear and simple.* Remember that the reader is trying to get oriented. The Overview provides perspective on what is coming. Keep the words simple and the sentences short. Think about your audience and what the various readers know. Anyone who receives the document should be able to understand it.
- *Brief.* The overview paragraph acts as an executive summary of the memo that follows. This is not the entire memo packed into a paragraph or two. Stick to the main ideas.
- *Deals with the* **what**—*not with the* **how.** *What* is the recommended course of action in a proposal or the main conclusion in an information memo. Avoid *how* or implementation at the early point in your memo. Readers have trouble dealing with implementation until they understand and agree with what should be done.
- *Includes and identifies the writer's opinion.* Go beyond the facts—interpret, conclude, and recommend. Then take responsibility up front for what you believe by stating your point of view in the overview. This helps convey confidence and a sense of leadership.
- *Reflects the needs of the reader.* The overview is geared to the knowledge and skill level of the reader. It takes into account what the reader needs and wants to know.
- *Thorough and complete.* Although brief, the overview should be able to stand on its own. It does not tell the reader everything in the memo; it contains key highlights. The best test of a good Overview: Can the reader say yes without reading further?

SAMPLE OVERVIEWS

From the in-baskets of Procter & Gamble Company, here are half a dozen overview paragraphs from authentic memos.

1. This recommends [this year's] Avis national television commercial pool policy of four :30 commercials replaced every 26 weeks for Avis' candid testimonial advertising. Two commercial groups will be rotated between network and spot at 13-week intervals. The agency agrees.
2. This provides a summary of Crest's shipment/share performance through January [of next year].
3. This recommends we conduct a wave of attitude research in the Boston Sales District in May [of this year] to gain additional learning about the product.
4. This recommends ending the Masters Beer premium pricing test in the Miami ADI. The purpose of the test is to determine whether a 15% price increase can improve total profitability. After six months, it is clear that the price increase has led to a substantial decrease in sales and profits. We also

believe our price increase has helped several competitive brands improve food store distribution. Accounting and Miami sales are in agreement with this recommendation.

5. This recommends we revise the quantity of package wrappers held in inventory for competitive defensive reasons.

6. This recommends we do not run a Cover Girl public relations program. The cost necessary to execute a successful plan (approx. $650M) would divert money away from current, proven business building vehicles (sampling and media). All departments concur.

THE PERSUASIVE MEMO

Writing a persuasive memo is much like constructing a winning argument. The document must provide a complete, logical argument with which the reader cannot disagree. It must anticipate all questions and responses—and deal with them.[8]

- *Consider your objective against the reader's attitudes, perceptions, and knowledge of the subject.* Be sure you know exactly what you want to accomplish with your memo. Do a careful assessment of the reader's mindset at the beginning. What will it take to get the reader to say yes?
- *Outline on paper,* focusing on the Situation Analysis and Rationale sections. This will help you construct a complete, logical argument. An outline also helps identify missing information.
- *Include a plan of action.* A well thought out implementation section adds credibility and practicality to your ideas. It gives the busy reader added incentive to consider your proposal. Even if you are awaiting approval to develop a detailed plan, include an outline of the plan to demonstrate that your concept can be accomplished.
- *Don't lose your argument in the Situation Analysis.* Your proposal should flow naturally from the problem or opportunity described in the Situation Analysis. The reader who disagrees with anything in this section of the memo cannot buy your proposal. Avoid controversial issues, opinions, and unsupported assertions in the Situation Analysis. Stick to the facts.
- *Use the direct approach.* Present your Recommendation and Rationale before you discuss other options that you have considered and rejected.
- *Always lead from strength.* Start your proposal with a strong, confident Overview paragraph. Bring the important ideas to the beginning of each section. In the Rationale section, always present your arguments in order of importance.
- *Use precedent to make your proposal appear less speculative.* Managers seek to avoid risk and error. Relevant precedent is the most effective way to reduce the perceived risk in a recommended action.
- *Gear your argument to the reader's decision criteria.* Know how your reader's mind works. Ask yourself if your argument is persuasive given the reader's interests and motivations.

OUTLINING A PROPOSAL

Many organizations require managers to put their proposed ideas into writing and circulate them to the management team responsible for action before they discuss the ideas in formal meetings. Other organizations use proposal memos to document the ideas they have been discussing in meetings. Either way, the most important ideas in virtually all businesses end up in writing. And writers are judged not only by the quality of their ideas but by the quality of the documents that capture and explain them.[9]

A proposal involves several key ingredients: the situation your reader or company is facing, your recommendations, and the reasons supporting them. Each proposal also follows a simple, basic outline:

FLOW OF THE OUTLINE

- *Situation Analysis:* Where *are* we today and why are we here?
- *Recommendation:* What should we do about it?
- *Rationale:* Why is this a good thing to do?

SEVEN-STEP OUTLINING PROCEDURE

As you draft the outline for a proposal memo, follow these steps to improve your thinking and reduce confusion for the reader.[10]

1. *Review your strategy.* Think about your reader. Know precisely what you want your memo to accomplish. Write it down.
2. *Assemble the information that will go into the memo.* Put down all facts, assumptions, and supporting arguments on paper in any order. Do not order or judge them yet.
3. *Identify and separate need to know information.* This is background information and historical perspective that will go into your Situation Analysis. Eliminate all but the minimum needed for the reader to understand the situation.
4. *Identify and separate the recommended course of action.* Make certain your reader knows precisely what you recommend and why.
5. *Develop your rationale.* Eliminate or fix invalid argument, tighten fuzzy or unclear arguments, and combine similar arguments into stronger statements.
6. *Rank your arguments from most powerful to least important.* Rank your arguments from most telling to least important. Remember, the ranking should be based mainly on what is important to the reader. Trim from the bottom up, leaving only as many arguments as you need to sell your proposal.
7. *Test your argument against the reader's decision criteria.* Look for weaknesses. Be certain you haven't missed anything the reader would consider important.

STANDARD FORMATS FOR MEMOS

Putting your ideas on paper helps you evaluate them. It forces you, the writer, to think through the issues carefully. Good ideas are invariably strengthened on paper and weak ideas are exposed for what they are.

Having a format in mind for the memo or report as you move forward with any project can eliminate one of the common stumbling blocks to sound thinking and good communication. The format becomes an organization plan for your ideas. It ensures that you think logically and that you don't overlook anything relevant to the project.

A standard format helps you organize information and concepts quickly. You don't have to think about where to put everything each time you start writing. If something is missing, it is immediately evident.

A standard format helps readers too. They don't have to figure out how your mind was working each time they get a document from you. They know immediately where to find the pieces and how they fit together. This saves time and promotes understanding.

A document can be organized or put together in a variety of ways. Always be certain your case is developed in a logical and persuasive manner. Consider using a format with which your readers are familiar, since they will be more comfortable with it. But don't compromise on clarity, simplicity, and logical flow to do this.

Here are suggested formats for the two basic business documents: The Proposal and The Information Memo. These formats are appropriate regardless of how long and complex your memo is. Many companies have adopted these (or variations on these) formats because they work particularly well when communication is moving up to senior management. Other memo and letter format samples appear at the back of this document.

If you work for an organization that has a detailed correspondence manual, you need only to follow the directions it provides. If your employer doesn't provide such guidance, your task is simple: Find a writing format that best suits your reasons for writing, the needs of your readers, and the organization(s) that you work for.

Note that the formats suggested here separate the contents of a memo into six or seven sections, each no more than a paragraph or two, and each clearly marked with an all-caps, boldface heading.

If your purpose in writing is to suggest a strategy for communicating some specific piece or body of information, you may wish to use the proposal format to recommend a course of action. *What* sort of information is to be gathered, the *format* in which it will be organized, *how* it is to be communicated, to *whom,* and *when* it is to be sent are all important aspects of business communication, and they often deserve separate treatment. A sample communication strategy memo is provided for your consideration at the end of this chapter.

THE INFORMATION MEMO FORMAT

The information memo format can be used for a wide variety of documents that seek to inform and provide points of view. These include business reviews, research summaries, competitive appraisals, test market summaries, field trip reports, and progress reports. What do these documents have in common? They all include an interpretation of data, without providing a recommended course of action. Note that this suggested format is similar to the proposal format. The logic flow of the document is essentially the same and several of the sections are identical.

⟨ **BOX 5-1** ⟩

THE PROPOSAL FORMAT

OVERVIEW

A paragraph that tells the reader the purpose of the document. It should include the main idea (the situation and recommendation) and your opinion on the subject (the reason this is a sound proposal). Include overall cost and concurrence, if possible. This opening section provides outlined information and serves as an executive summary of the complete document that follows.

SITUATION ANALYSIS

This section is the foundation on which the proposal is built. It provides background information and historical perspective that the reader must understand. Include relevant facts and key assumptions that influence your recommended course of action.

RECOMMENDATION

This is a concise statement of the recommended action and how it will be accomplished. Focus on the *what*. Provide enough to give the reader a clear overall picture, but save implementation detail (the *how*) for later.

RATIONALE

A numbered list of reasons that support the recommendation in order of importance. Try to start with the expected impact on the business and include relevant precedent. Each reason should start with a clear topic sentence followed by supporting facts.

ALTERNATIVES CONSIDERED

A brief description of other actions considered. Discuss why each was rejected in favor of your proposal. Only include serious alternatives.

IMPLEMENTATION PLAN

Present your plan for accomplishing the recommended course of action. Break your plan down into components like timing and resource requirements. Organize logically into sections with appropriate headings.

NEXT STEPS

What is the reader expected to do? Tell the reader exactly what will happen if he concurs. Be specific about dates, people, and financial commitments.

COMPETITIVE APPRAISALS

You may be called upon to analyze and evaluate what your competitors are doing. Many writers find this a demanding challenge. Using the information memo format is a food way to organize information and help you through the evaluation process. Here are some thoughts on preparing memos that evaluate the competitive activity:

- *Thinking about the competition is much like dealing with an iceberg.* The most important stuff is hidden below the surface. You will *see* what the competition is doing, i.e., execution. Often, however, you will be missing the competitive strategy that led to this plan of action.
- *Work backwards and construct a hypothetical statement of strategy based on what's happening in the marketplace.* Assess both the strategy and the execution, especially if what you are evaluating represents a strategic departure.

> BOX 5-2

THE COMPETITIVE APPRAISAL FORMAT

OVERVIEW

A paragraph that tells the reader the purpose of the document. It should include a topic synopsis and your opinion (the overall conclusion) on the subject. This opening section provides outlined information and serves as an executive summary of the complete document that follows.

BACKGROUND

Perspective on the subject with emphasis on historical aspects. What does the reader need to know to understand the sections that follow?

CONCLUSION(S)

Your interpretation of the facts. What are the implications of the data? If you have several conclusions, put them in order of importance.

FINDINGS

These are the facts that support your conclusions. This section is your rational for the conclusions you have drawn. Include only those data necessary to make your point. Organize all of this information under appropriate subheadings.

INDICATED ACTION

Given your interpretation of the data, what is being done or what should be done? Be careful: If this is a recommended course of action that requires approval, use the proposal format.

SUPPORTING DATA

Attach any exhibits relevant to the subject. Generally, these are the findings in more detail. The reader may want to review this information, but should not have to refer to this section to understand and concur with your analysis.

- *Competive appraisals are often triggered by changes.* Discuss how recent actions fit in with past efforts. Provide this historical perspective in the Background section of your report.
- *What does this mean to us?* Be sure to discuss implications to your product or the company.
- *Be objective.* If you start with the assumption that your competition is smart, you are more likely to provide a balanced and intelligent picture of what is happening and what it means.[11]

MEETING AND CONFERENCE REPORTS

The purpose of a conference or meeting report is to record decisions made at the meeting. Avoid long descriptions of what was discussed or presented, restatements of arguments, praise, or blame. Use a standard format that includes the name of the group, persons attending, and subjects covered.

Report briefly on

- What was discussed or presented
- What was decided and why

Focus your report on

- What action is required
- Who is responsible
- What the timing will be

PROJECT LISTS

Many businesses keep track of current and proposed activities with project lists. These are nothing more than simple descriptions of what the organization is doing to achieve its goals or serve its customers. Project lists usually take more time to prepare than they are worth, so try to keep them simple. This will save time and actually make them more useable documents.

Separate each project by category, then list projects in order of priority or importance. Each project on your list should include a title and brief description, status, next steps, responsible parties, and dates due.

If your project list is long, consider adding a cover page to highlight key projects that require management attention.

Projects should never just disappear. Completed or terminated projects should be shown as such the following month, with a brief notation about why the project will not appear on future project lists.

MAKE YOUR MEMOS INVITING AND ATTRACTIVE

A good document is both inviting and easy to read or easy to use as a reference.[12] Here are some ideas on how to achieve this.

- *Grab attention up front.* A strong Overview section gives the reader perspective on what's coming. This makes any memo easier to read and understand. Don't open the memo with unimportant details or information the reader already knows.
- *Vary sentence and paragraph length—but keep them short.* Short paragraphs and short sentences are inviting because they are easier to deal with. If all your sentences or paragraphs are the same length, however, the memo will seem monotonous.
- *Use headings.* The reader will understand your organization plan for the memo. Headings also make it a better reference document.
- *Use bullets and numbers to identify groupings.* This helps break up long paragraphs and is another way to indicate how the memo is organized.
- *Use parallel structure for lists* (as this one does). Keep things with things, actions with actions, do's with do's, don't's with don't's, and so on.
- *Underline or use boldface type to focus on topic sentences, key words, and phrases.* But don't overdo it; too much underlining makes a document look cluttered and busy.
- *Leave adequate margins.* Lots of white space makes any document more inviting. Use tables, charts, and exhibits. Paragraphs full of numbers are

difficult to read. Presenting the same information in a table or chart makes it easier to understand and easier to refer to.

- ***Don't settle for sloppy or illegible duplication.*** Make it a quality document.

EDITING YOUR MEMOS

Good writing requires rewriting. The overall purpose of editing is to trim, clarify, and simplify. Put the document aside for a while—overnight if possible—before revising. This helps you step back, look at the memo through the eyes of the reader, and be more objective.

Before revising your memo, quickly review the guidelines provided in the opening section. Then put yourself in the reader's place and go through the document several times, each time asking yourself one of these seven basic questions:

- ***Is it clear?*** Is the flow of the memo logical? Will the reader understand the development of your thesis? Are the words simple and concrete? Will the reader understand technical terms? Is every sentence clear, unambiguous, easy to read?
- ***Is it complete?*** Will the reader understand your purpose? Does the Situation Analysis have all the background information the reader needs to know? Are all the key numbers in the body of the memo? Have all necessary agreements been spelled out?
- ***Is it persuasive?*** Does your Rationale section lead from strength? Are your arguments in order of importance? Have you anticipated potential responses and questions—and dealt with them? Have you avoided exaggeration and provided a balanced, rational argument?
- ***Is it accurate?*** Are opinions and facts separated and clearly labeled? Is every number correct?
- ***Is it concise?*** Do you have too many arguments? Did you waste words telling readers what they already know? Do you have unnecessary words, phrases, or sentences?
- ***Is it inviting to read?*** Are there large blocks of type that can be broken up? Did you leave adequate margins? Is the memo neat, clear, legible?
- ***Is it perfect?*** Are there any typos, misspellings, or grammatical errors that could cast doubt on the quality of your thinking?

WRITING GOOD BUSINESS LETTERS

Business letters, unlike memos, are primarily *external* documents, though managers will occasionally use a letter format to correspond with subordinates and executives. Like memos, good letters are crisp, concise, spoken in tone, and organized so that readers can follow and understand with a minimum of effort. They are easy to follow and don't read like a mystery story.

More than 25 years ago, Rudolph Flesch in a small volume entitled, *On Business Communication,* offered a set of basic precepts for writing good business letters. They are just as useful today as they were back then.[13]

- ***Answer promptly.*** Answer the mail within three business days. If you don't have an answer, must speak with someone else before you can formulate a reply, or need additional information, drop your reader a note and say just that: "I'll have a more complete reply in a few days, but for now please understand that I am working on a solution to the problem."
- ***Show that you are genuinely interested.*** The person writing to you obviously thought the issue was important enough to write about; you should think so, too. The problem or matter at hand may seem trivial in your world, but in their's it is not. Show by your words and actions that you care about them and the issue they have written about.
- ***Don't be too short, brief, or curt.*** We preach brevity, but you *can* overdo it. Make sure your reader has enough information to understand the subject. Make certain you have included each issue relevant to the subject, and that you explain the process, the outcome, or the decision to the satisfaction of the reader. If you were receiving the letter, would this be enough information for you to act on? Are you satisfied that the writer (and his or her employer) have taken you seriously?
- ***If it's bad news, say you are sorry.*** With bad news, use phrases such as, "I am sorry to say that. . . ." or "I regret to say that we'll be unable to refund your money because. . . ." You can soften the blow that accompanies bad news by saying that you're sorry it happened, you regret the outcome, or some similar selection of words. If it's bad news and your reader thinks you don't care (or, worse, that you are amused by it all), you may be in for further trouble.
- ***If it's good news, say you are glad.*** With good news, use phrases such as, "I am delighted to tell you that. . . ." or "You will be pleased to learn that. . . ." Now and again, the word *congratulations* may be in order. Go ahead and share in your reader's good fortune and joy.
- ***Give everyone the benefit of the doubt.*** Don't automatically assume that the person corresponding with you is doing so for the purpose of fleecing or cheating you (or your company). If it's not clear whether product failure or customer misuse is to blame, for example, give the other person the benefit of whatever doubt may exist. In the vast majority of instances, you will have done the right thing.
- ***Never send off an angry letter.*** Venting your spleen in an angry, hostile reply to someone may feel good, but it's almost *never* a good idea to mail such a letter. One real danger with e-mail is that you may compose a vicious reply to someone and click the send button well ahead of the arrival of rational thought. Cool down before you compose a letter and, if you have written something you are not sure about, wait until tomorrow before rereading it. Chances are, you will think twice about posting that letter.
- ***Watch out for cranks.*** Occasionally, a certifiable goofball will cross your path. The advice is simple: Be police, do your job, and they will usually go away. If they persist, be firm but professional in responding. After the second letter, if you really are dealing with a whacko, you may be able to ignore their correspondence.
- ***Appreciate humor.*** If someone makes (or attempts) a joke, play along. Show that you have a sense of humor. Racist, sexist, or profane humor is

never appropriate, but ordinary self-deprecating or directionless humor can often lighten or improve a difficult situation.

- **Be careful with form letters.** A one-size-fits-all approach to writing with many recipients is a real recipe for disaster. Make sure your letter answers all (or virtually all) of the questions your audience is likely to have; respond to their fears, doubts, and concerns. Once you have written a form letter and had an opportunity to edit it, why not test market the document? Show it to several people who are (or have been) members of the audience you are writing for. Ask them to suggest improvements. Think about maps, diagrams, lists, references, and ways your readers might learn more about the subject you are writing to them about.

WHEN YOU ARE REQUIRED TO EXPLAIN SOMETHING

If you find yourself in the position of explaining something in writing to someone else, a few bits of common sense seem appropriate.[14]

- **Nothing is self-explanatory.** This may all seem self-evident to you, but that's because you've been thinking about and working on the subject for some time. Explain in simple, ordinary English what you want your reader to know. Don't assume anything.
- **Translate technical terms.** It's perfectly alright for you to use scientific or technical terminology. You just have to explain or define it first. Writing to one person you know quite well is much easier than writing to many people whom you don't know, but you cannot be sure your readers will share your vocabulary.
- **Go step-by-step.** Be sequential in your explanations, moving step by step through processes that are complex. Don't skip anything, even steps in the process that seem absolutely self-evident to you. This may be the first time many of your readers have ever read about this subject.
- **Don't say too little.** Your reader probably doesn't know as much about this subject as you do (that's why you are writing). Make certain you provide enough information to answer questions, allay fears, and quell doubts.
- **Don't say too much.** Don't overdo it. You can bury your readers in details that will eventually confuse, frighten, anger, or bore them. Provide enough detail to satisfy their curiosity, but not so much that you put them off.
- **Illustrate.** If you can't explain it, perhaps you can show it. Illustrations can take the form of examples, anecdotes, or explanations. Additionally, you may wish to include drawings, maps, schematics, or a process flow chart.
- **Answer expected questions.** Put yourself in your reader's position. What would you most want to know? What questions are likely to arise? Which areas of this subject are likely to raise the greatest doubt, confusion, or misunderstanding?
- **Warn against common mistakes.** If it's easy to misunderstand, misread, or get this subject wrong, caution your readers. Explain the pitfalls, snares, and traps they can easily fall into by not reading your words carefully.

WHEN YOU ARE REQUIRED TO APOLOGIZE

If your job requires that you apologize to someone—most likely a customer or a client—for something that you or the company has done wrong (or not done at all), here are four basic guidelines to consider:

- *Take the complaint seriously.* Once again, you may not see the issue at hand as serious or important, but it's important to the person with the complaint. The sooner you act as if it's a big deal, the sooner you will satisfy the frustration or hostility that prompted the complaint in the first place.
- *Explain what happened and why.* People with complaints often seem irrational; some really are. But, for the most part, people will calm down and adopt a more understanding attitude if you can simply explain what happened and tell them why. For one thing, they will feel that they have more control over the circumstance. When circumstances are beyond their control, they will be more likely to accept your answer.
- *Don't shift the blame.* Blaming everything on someone else is generally a bad idea. Even if someone else is at fault, your readers don't want to hear about it. Just accept responsibility for what's happened and offer a solution. Shifting the blame to "the computer," or "those geniuses over in shipping" is simply unacceptable.
- *Don't just write—do something.* All the soothing, sympathetic words you can muster will do little to make your readers feel better if you don't offer to fix the problem. "Thanks for your input" is not enough. Telling your reader that you'll share the information with higher management is a good first step, but they may want more. Most people who have taken the time and effort to write to you will expect some sort of action. Don't disappoint them.[15]

A FEW WORDS ABOUT STYLE

Your success as a business writer depends, in large measure, on your ability to convince others that what you have written is worth their attention. A considerable amount of research on this subject has shown that your writing will be better received if it meets three basic criteria: It ought to be *compact,* it should be *informal,* and it absolutely must be *organized.*

Why compact, informal, and organized writing? Three things seem to depend on writing which meets those criteria: organizational efficiency, personal productivity, and your career. Large and complex organizations have shown time and again that the less time their employees spend at the keyboard composing correspondence, the more time they have to think about and accomplish other (presumably important) things.

If you spend less time both *writing* and *reading* what's been written for all employees in your organization, you become more personally productive. And, of course, important people—those in a position to influence your career—will notice. They will notice whether you are someone who can be counted on to draft, edit, and improve written communication, or someone who struggles with the written word. In other words, they will know whether you are part of the problem or part of the solution.

MAKE YOUR WRITING EFFICIENT

You must somehow find a way to deal with a number of different problems that appear consistently in letters, memos, reports, proposals, staff studies, and other business documents. In addition to those memo-writing issues we discussed earlier, here are a dozen of the most common problems:

- **Big words.** If you want a few laughs from readers sensitive to language, use pompous substitutes for small words. Don't *start* things; *initiate* them. Don't *end* a program; *terminate* it. Readers know that *utilize* means *use* and *optimum* means *best,* but why force them to translate? You sell yourself and your ideas through your writing. Come across as a sensible person, someone who knows that good writing begins with plain English.
- **_____-*wise*.** Another no-no: words ending in *-wise*. Rather than write, "Market-wise, this firm should engage in sustained efforts to effect an improvement in our understanding of events and forces," you might consider "We need to know much more than we do about market forces."
- **Doublings.** Words which have the same or nearly the same meaning are known as *synonyms*. Select the one which most closely approximates what you really intend for your reader to know. Why write about a project's "importance and significance" when *importance* will do.
- **Noun modifiers.** Some writers insist on using one noun to modify another, when just one would do. "He is now in an important leadership position with the company" could be rewritten as "He is now a leader in this company." Look through your correspondence. You will see these noun-pairs everywhere: *management capability, market situation, habit patterns.*
- **It is.** Few words do more damage than the innocent-looking *it is.* These words stretch sentences, delay your point, encourage passives, and hide responsibility. Unless *it* refers to something definite mentioned earlier, try to write around *it is. "It is recommended* that you revise . . ." becomes "*We recommend* that you revise."
- **Legalese.** Avoid legal-sounding language like *hereto* and *aforesaid.* Such pompous and wordy language doesn't give a writer any added authority; it simply shows that his or her writing style—and perhaps his or her thinking— is outdated. Why say "Attached *herewith* is the report"? Instead, say, "Here's the report. . . ." And rather than write, *"It is incumbent upon* supervisors . . . ," just say *"Supervisors must. . . ."* If your writing reads like a fire-and-casualty policy or a mutual fund prospectus, you may want to think twice about your style.
- **Missing hyphens.** Two-word modifiers may need hyphens when the two words act as one. Don't hyphenate if the first word ends in *-ly: "Fairly* recent change." Otherwise, consider it. "Three day trips" (three trips, each for a day) differs from "three-day trips" (trips, each for three days). If you are sensitive to how hyphens work, you will see what happens when they are left out of a sentence: "We're looking for a *short term accountant.* . . ." A CPA under 5′4″, perhaps?
- **Smothered verbs.** Express ideas involving action with specific verbs. Weak writing relies on general verbs, which take extra words to complete their

meaning. When you write general verbs such as *is, give,* and *hold,* see if you can replace them by turning nearby words into specific verbs. Don't *make a choice; choose.* Don't *provide guidance; guide.* I have loaded the next two sentences with common smothered verbs: "The committee members *held a meeting (met)* to *give consideration to (consider)* the plan. They *made the decision (decided)* to *give their approval to (approve)* the product launch." Get the idea? *Make use of (use)* specific verbs!

- **Specialized terms.** Try to avoid specialized terms with outsiders and use them no more than you must with insiders. Acronyms, jargon, and verbal shorthand unique to your organization can really confuse people who don't share the vocabulary. Are technical or specialized terms forbidden? Not at all. If you must use a technical term and you are reasonably sure that some of your readers won't understand, define it—tell them what it means and how it's used. They will show their appreciation by reading (and understanding) what you have written.

- **That *and* which.** More often than not, *that* and *which* don't help the meaning or flow of a sentence so use them sparingly. Sometimes you can just leave out these words; sometimes you will have to rewrite slightly. Consider this sentence: "We think *(that)* the changes *(which)* they have asked for will cost too much." Rather than writing "A system *which* is unreliable," you could say "An unreliable system." Read the sentence aloud and ask if you need *that* or *which* for meaning or flow. If not, try a revised sentence without those words.

- **The _____ ion of** . . . Shorten this ponderous *-ion* construction whenever the context permits. Instead of saying "I recommend *the adoption of* the plan," say "I recommend *adopting* the plan." And, instead of saying "We want *the participation of* all concerned," say "We want all concerned *to participate.*" You add life to your writing by favoring the verb (action) form over the noun (static) form.

- **Wordy expressions.** Wordy expressions don't give writing impressive bulk; they litter it by getting in the way of the words that carry meaning. So simplify these sentence stretchers. The longer it takes you to say something, the weaker you come across. *In order to* means *to. For the purpose of* means *to. In the near future* could be rephrased as *soon. In the event that* can be rewritten as *if.*[16]

SPEAK WHEN YOU WRITE

To escape from outdated, excessively formal writing styles, try to make your writing more like your speaking. I'm not suggesting that you include snorts, grunts, and rambling stream-of-consciousness monologues in your correspondence. We all know people who speak no better than they can write. Still, the basic principle holds: Because people "hear" writing, the most readable writing sounds like one person talking to another. Begin by imagining your reader is in front of you, and then use these ideas to guide you.

- **Write with personal pronouns.** Use *we, us,* and *our* when speaking for the company. Use *I, me,* and *my* when speaking for yourself. And either way, be generous with *you*. Avoiding these natural references to people is false modesty. Besides, the alternatives to personal pronouns are awkwardness (*Your support is appreciated* rather than *We appreciate your support*) and hedging (*It was decided* in place of *I decided*). Stamp out "untouched by human hands" writing.

- **Use contractions (occasionally).** Write with the ones we speak with, such as *I'm, we're you'd, they've, can't, don't* and *let's*. Not all your writing has to sound like a telephone conversation, but it certainly won't hurt if some of it does. If contractions come easily to you, then you've mastered spoken writing. If contractions seem out of place, don't remove them; deflate the rest of what you say. Also, don't overlook the advantages of negative contractions for instructions; they soften direct orders and keep readers from skipping over the word *not.*

- **Reach out to your reader occasionally by asking questions.** A request gains emphasis when it ends with a question mark. In a long report, a question can be a welcome change. Do you hear how spoken this next sentence is? Rather than write "Please advise this office as to whether the conference is still scheduled for February 21st," you might simply ask "Is the conference still scheduled for February 21st?"

- **Prefer short, spoken transitions over long, bookish ones.** Use *but* more than *however, also* more than *in addition, still* more than *nevertheless, so* more than *consequently* or *therefore*. Use formal transitions only for variety. And, yes, you can start a sentence with words like *but, so, yet, and, or.*

- **A preposition is a word you can end a sentence with.** Don't rework a sentence just to shift a preposition from the end. You'll lengthen, tangle, and stiffen the sentence. These are common prepositions: *after, at, by, from, of, to, up, with.*

- **Keep sentences short, about 20 words on average.** Use some longer and shorter sentences for variety. Short ones won't guarantee clarity, but they will prevent many of the confusions common to longer ones. Try the eye test: Average about two typed lines a sentence. Or try the ear test: Read your writing aloud and break apart any sentence you can't finish in one breath.[17]

HOW TO MAKE PASSIVE VERBS ACTIVE

Passive sentences are deadly in business memos and letters for several reasons. First, they obscure responsibility by omitting a subject or human actor from the sentence. Second, they are almost always longer—one-quarter to one-third longer than active sentences. Finally, they delay discussion of the subject. The real action in a passive sentence or paragraph comes at the end.

The best advice: Use as few passives as possible. They're not grammatically wrong, but they are really overworked in most business writing. To write actively, remember this simple rule: *Put the doer before the verb.* By leading with the doer, you'll automatically avoid a passive verb. Consider these examples:

Passive: "It has been determined that more purchase decisions should be made by local managers."

Active: "The director decided that local managers should make more purchase decisions."

The passive version of that sentence (double passive, actually) contains 14 words. The active version contains just 11. Better yet, the active version tells the reader who made that decision—an important element missing from the passive sentence.
You can spot passive sentences by checking for these characteristics:

- The receiver of the verb's action comes before the verb. In the passive example above, *it* is the receiver.
- The verb has these two parts: any form of *to be,* either simple (such as *are,* or *was*) or compound (such as *is being, have been, will be,* or *must be*), plus the past participle of a main verb (most end in *-en* or *-ed*). In the passive example above, *has been decided* is the verb.
- If the doer appears at all, it follows the verb and usually has *by* just before it. But unlike active sentences, passive ones are complete without doers: *It has been determined* (by whom?).

Passive sentences may be useful in one of three circumstances:

- **When the doer is obvious:** "William Jefferson Clinton was re-elected President of the United States in 1996." No real explanation of voter lists, the Electoral College, or election rules seems appropriate here.
- **When the doer is unknown:** "My uncle was mugged in the park." Who mugged him? We don't really know—the mugger didn't leave a business card.
- **When the doer is unimportant:** "The parts were shipped on January 8th." We don't really care who shipped them; we just know that they were sent on the 8th of January.

If you use passive sentences when you might just as easily write sentences with active verbs, your writing will be wordy, roundabout, and (as the word *passive* implies), a bit sluggish. Worse, because passive sentences don't always show who is doing the action, you may forget to include important information. The result may be confusing to the reader.

- "All requests must be approved beforehand." By whom? It doesn't say because it's a passive sentence. The active version: The regional manager must approve all requests beforehand.
- "The figures were lost." Who lost them? Again, we don't know because it's cast in the passive. The active version: "We lost the figures."

The best advice: Write actively whenever you can. If you decide to cast a sentence in the passive voice, do so only after considering what the active version would look like.[18]

MAKE YOUR BOTTOM LINE YOUR TOP LINE

Open with your main point, the one sentence you'd keep if you could keep just one. You can often put that sentence in its own paragraph for added clarity, just the way I have done. Give directions *before* reasons, requests *before* justifications, answers *before* explanations, conclusions *before* details, and solutions *before* problems.

A poorly organized letter reads like a mystery story. Clue by clue, it unfolds details that make sense only toward the end. Try the approach used in newspaper articles. They start with the most important information and taper off to the least important.

You might delay the main point to soften bad news or to remind your reader of an old conversation, for example, but avoid delaying for long. Readers, like listeners, are put off by people who take forever to get to the point. They need to know the main point at the start so they can appreciate the relevance of whatever else you may say.

If no single sentence stands out, you probably need to create one to keep from drifting aimlessly. Occasionally, as in a set of instructions or a reply to a series of questions, all your points may be equally important. In this case, create a starting sentence that tells your readers what to expect: "Here's the information you asked for."

To end most letters, just stop. When writing to persuade rather than to routinely inform, you may want to end strongly—perhaps with a forecast, appeal, or implication. When feelings are involved, you may want to exit gracefully—with some expression of goodwill. When in doubt, offer your help and encourage the reader to call or write back to you.[17]

Here are three ideas that will help you to better organize your letters.

- *Use headings and subheadings.* Boldface headings or italicized subheadings can help to organize your writing. When topics vary widely in one document, they let readers follow at a glance. Use them in recurring reports, proposals, and even short business letters when you need to catch a reader's eye or break up long, complex paragraphs.
- *Keep paragraphs short.* Average roughly four or five sentences in each paragraph. For lists and instructions, try using subparagraphs. You make reading easier by adding white space.
- *Don't clutter up the first paragraph.* It's the most important paragraph in your letter; don't waste the prime space and impact of that paragraph with endless references to letters you've exchanged, previous reports, regulatory documents, or other pieces of paper. Put your reason for writing—your most important point—right up front.

HOW TO ENCOURAGE AND DEVELOP GOOD WRITERS

Every manager has a responsibility—in some respects, a moral obligation—to improve the skills of his or her subordinates. Writing skills are no exception. Too often our people get frustrated because assignments are given with careless direction, and comments on writing are vague and difficult to understand.

Working effectively with subordinates is not easy. It takes knowledge, experience, and patience. Surprisingly, it doesn't take much time. It does take a willingness to sit down and review your expectations and their performance in very specific terms. Here are some ideas to consider as you work with your people on improving communication.

- *Show your people you want clear, concise writing by example.* Give them samples of good writing and explain why it works. Sit down with new people and discuss your writing guidelines.
- *Know what you want before giving assignments.* Discuss projects with subordinates before they head off in the wrong direction. Be as specific as you can.
- *When projects are difficult or complex, break up the assignment into manageable parts.* Start with an Overview section to identify purpose and main ideas. Then have the writer prepare an outline of the document. Review this work before the writer tackles a first draft. This will save both of you time and eliminate the frustration of trying to deal with a disaster.
- *Read and review before discussing a memo.* When a memo is submitted for your review, spend some time reviewing it before meeting with the writer. Be sure you understand what's wrong and how it can be fixed.
- *Try to see the big picture first.* When you review a memo, start with big issues such as strategy, logic flow, and conclusions versus facts. Then move to smaller issues like grammar and appearance. Do not rewrite the memo, but be specific about areas that need work. And do remember to be positive.
- *Be certain the writer understands—and agrees with—your comments.* Make sure your writer can repeat, in his or her own words, what you want so that you're sure you are both on the same page.
- *Don't force writers to parrot your style and expressions.* Give your people flexibility and freedom to develop their own style.[19]

The Eugene D. Fanning Center
University of Notre Dame • Mendoza College of Business

DATE: August 21, 2000

ACTION: Management Communication Students

INFO: Interested People with a Need to Know but No Responsibility for Action

FROM: J.S. O'Rourke (234 College of Business; Phone 631-8397)
           Fanning Center for Business Communication

SUBJECT: **COMMUNICATION STRATEGY MEMO: FORMAT AND CONTENTS**

This memo format recommends a communication plan in response to a specific event or circumstance facing a company or organization. It will briefly summarize the details of the event/circumstance; discuss their implications, importance, or probable outcome; and will provide a specific list of actions taken and actions recommended.

BACKGROUND

In this portion of the memo, the writer briefly but completely reviews the *facts* of the case. This paragraph will contain historical data, information that is a matter of public record, and facts that are relevant to the recommended communication strategy.

- Crisp, tightly-expressed sentences set apart from the main paragraph by bullet points are often useful in highlighting factual information.
- This paragraph *does not* include assumptions, suppositions, or speculative information. Nor does it include gratuitous references in the first personal singular, such as "I think, . . ." "In my opinion, . . ." or "I feel . . ."
- If a specific source is available for each piece of information in this paragraph, the writer should consider embedding it directly in a sentence, i.e., "1990 Census figures reveals that . . ." Another approach is to list a source in parentheses following the information you provide, i.e., "Mead Corporation's Stevenson, Alabama mill has an annual production capacity of 400,000 tons of corrugated containerboard. (Source: *Mead Financial Fact Book,* Mead Corp., 1999, p. 5).

DISCUSSION

In this portion of the memo, the writer expands on the implications of the facts cited above. This is where the writer explains to the reader what those facts mean and why they matter. The discussion paragraph often becomes the basis for the recommendations that follow. If the discussion is extended or complex, writers often use separate paragraphs, sub-headings, and bullet-points to highlight various issues.

COMMUNICATION STRATEGY MEMO: FORMAT AND CONTENTS
August 21, 2000
Page 2 of 2

RECOMMENDATIONS

In this paragraph, the writer lays out each recommendation in specific terms. Where possible, recommendations lead with a verb, are separated from one another with white space, are underlined or printed in boldface type for emphasis, and are either numbered (if the writer recommends more than three actions) or bullet-pointed. For example:

1. **Sign the attached letter of apology to the customer.** The letter not only apologizes for the flaw discovered in our shipment of July 1st, but offers a 2% discount on the shipment and a full replacement of all defective parts. (Action: President)
2. **Forward the defective parts to Quality Control for examination.** When the QC report is complete, copies of their fundings should be shared with Sales & Marketing, Customer Service, and members of the Senior Management Team. (Action: Customer Service)
3. **Contact the retailer who sold the equipment to review return/refund procedures.** We must make certain that each retailer handling our products fully understands his/her obligation to accept customer returns and to provide full refunds, if appropriate. (Action: Sales Manager)
4. **Follow-up with the customer to make sure he is satisfied with our actions on his behalf.** This is a particularly large account and, while each customer is important to this company, some customers are more important than others. Direct, personal contact to assure customer satisfaction, followed by an after-action report for company files is essential. (Action: Customer Service)

OTHER ISSUES

On occasion, the paragraph above will be labeled "Actions Recommended," and would be preceded by a paragraph labeled "Actions Taken." The difference is a matter of authority in the organization. The memo writer clearly has authority to take certain actions on his or her own and to *backbrief* the supervisor or manager by means of this memo. That same writer might propose actions for his superiors or for other divisions/agencies in the company that the reader is asked to agree to. It's always useful for the reader to know what tasks have already been done, and what tasks he or she is being asked to approve.

Most memoranda *do not* include a signature block, nor do they feature salutation lines ("Dear . . .") or complimentary closing lines ("Sincerely yours,"). Rather than a full signature, most memos will include the initials of the writer next to the "FROM:" line above.

Please note that this two-page memo requires a "second page header" which includes the subject line (exactly as written on page one), a date line, and a page number.

To conclude, most memos will feature some distinctive typographical mark just beneath the last line of type. Some authors will use their initials, other will simply use the pound sign or other mark of their choice.

Endnotes

1. *USA Today,* October 14, 1994, p. C1.
2. Ibid.
3. Smith, N. *A Plain English Handbook: How to Create Clear SEC Disclosure Documents,* 1998, pp. 5–6.
4. Ibid., p. 4.
5. Plumez, J. P. *Leadership on Paper.* Larchmont, NY: Leadership on Paper, 1996, pp. 1–2.
6. Ibid., p. 3.
7. Ibid., pp. 4–5.
8. Ibid., p. 6.
9. Ruch, W. V. and Crawford, M. L. *Business Reports: Written and Oral.* Boston, MA: PWS-Kent Publishing Company, p. 203.
10. Plumez, J. P., *Leadership*, p. 7.
11. Plumez, J. P., *Leadership*, p. 12.
12. Plumez, J. P., *Leadership*, p. 14.
13. Flesch, R. *On Business Communication: How to Say What You Mean in Plain English.* New York: Harper & Row, 1974, pp. 100–112.
14. Ibid., pp. 113–126.
15. Ibid., pp. 139–151.
16. Murawski, T., Luckett, P., Mace, J., and Shuttleworth, J. *The United States Air Force Academy Executive Writing Course.* Colorado Springs, CO: HQ USAFA, Department of English, 1983.
17. Ibid.
18. Bailey, E. *The Plain English Approach to Business Writing.* New York, NY: Oxford University Press, 1993, pp. 93–101.
19. Plumez, J. P., *Leadership*, p. 16.

For Further Reading

Baldridge, L. "E-Etiquette: A Guide to Cyber-Manners for the Next Century." *New York Times,* December 6, 1999, p. A-29.

Brusaw, C. T., Alred, G. J., and Oliu, W. E. *The Business Writer's Companion*, 2nd ed. New York, NY: St. Martin's Press, 1999.

Brusaw, C. T., Alred, G. J., and Oliu, W. E. *Writing That Works: How to Write Effectively on the Job*, 6th ed. New York, NY: St. Martin's Press, 1997.

Hall, D. and Birkets, S. *Writing Well.* Boston, MA: Addison-Wesley-Longman Publishers, 1997.

Holcombe, M. *Writing for Decision Makers: Memos and Reports with a Competitive Edge.* New York, NY: Lifetime Learning, 1997.

Roman, K. and Raphaelson, J. *Writing That Works: How to Improve Your Memos, Letters, Reports, Speeches, Resumes, Plans, and Other Business Papers.* New York, NY: HarperCollins, 1995.

Smith, N. *A Plain English Handbook: How to Create Clear SEC Disclosure Documents.* Washington, D.C.: The U.S. Securities and Exchange Commission, 1997. You can obtain a copy of this document by calling the Office of Investor Education and Assistance toll-free information service: 1/800-SEC-0330.

Stott, B. *Write to the Point: And Feel Better about Your Writing.* New York, NY: Columbia University Press, 1991.

Strunk, W. and White, E. B. *The Elements of Style*, 3rd ed. New York, NY: Macmillan Publishing Company, Inc., 1979.

Williams, J. *Style: Ten Lessons in Clarity and Grace*, 4th ed. New York, NY: HarperCollins College Publishers, 1994.

Zinsser, W. *On Writing Well: The Classic Guide to Writing Nonfiction.* New York, NY: HarperCollins, 1998.

Case 5–1 CYPRESS SEMICONDUCTOR CORPORATION

BACKGROUND NOTE

Trusted senior managers are often called upon by executives to provide advice regarding relations with important and sensitive publics. Relations with customers, employees, suppliers, vendors, affiliates, shareholders, market analysts, and others may well depend on the quality of advice managers are able to provide to the senior leadership of their organization.

Much of the contact that a chief executive officer may have with such groups, along with others in the world outside the company, is subject to filtering by front-office staff and executive support personnel. Frequently, CEOs won't even *see* a letter of complaint or other corespondence from small-lot shareholders, minor customers, or members of public interest groups seeking donations, favors, or support of some sort. In such cases, midlevel managers are often delegated to respond on the executive's behalf.

Depending on company size and the personality of the CEO, however, some correspondence from external sources may very well land on the chief executive's desk. Some CEOs enjoy responding to selected correspondents personally; others delegate the task of preparing a reply. In both cases, the tone and style of a response is central to success of the letter or message. Trusted managers are frequently asked to review the executive's correspondence for accuracy, completeness, and appropriateness of the response.

THE CASE AT HAND

T. J. Rodgers, chairman and CEO of Cypress Semiconductor Corporation, has received a letter from a Catholic nun, suggesting he appoint qualified women and minorities to his company's board of directors. Rodgers has responded to the one-page form letter (attached) with a six-page reply (also attached), blasting Sister Doris for the "political correctness" which seemed to motivate her letter. The scathing retort which he proposes to send to Sister Doris tells her ". . . to get down from your moral high horse." "Choosing a board of directors based on race and gender is a lousy way to run a company," he writes. Adding, "Cypress will never do it." And for good measure, Rodgers suggests that "bowing to special-interest groups is an immoral way to run a company."

As vice president for investor relations, you are, frankly, not surprised at either the tone or length of Rodgers' response. Once known as the "bad boy of Silicon Valley," Rodgers, who is now 48 years old, often makes a habit of publishing provocative, editorial-style articles on everything from proposed immigration restrictions to federal support of high-tech industries—he is opposed to both. His attack on Sister Doris, however, has stirred some concern among senior managers and the executive support staff at Cypress. Mr. Rodgers has circulated a draft version of his proposed reply to the corporate senior team and asked for comment.

In addition to a response to Sister Doris in Philadelphia, Rodgers has proposed sending his letter to all Cypress shareholders and a select group of sympathetic veterans of the affirmative-action debate.

Cypress Semiconductors is an international producer and distributor of computing chips with about US$600MM in annual sales. The company's headquarters and principal production facilities are located in Palo Alto, California. Mr. Rodgers began the company when he was 35 years old, developing a gruff management style that earned him a place on *Fortune* magazine's list of the country's toughest bosses. He is not, however, an altogether unreasonable man, and you may assume that your working relationship with him is amiable, personal, and sound. He listens when you speak, though he doesn't always do as you suggest.

Your Task

Rodgers has asked for your opinion of the two letters attached to this case. He wants to send a response to Sister Doris within 48 hours, providing copies of his letter to shareholders and selected analysts. His memo to you explains that the "arrogance" of Sister Doris' letter spurred him to action. "It was Friday night and I got it and I said, 'It's time.' Then, I looked down and . . . she didn't even sign the . . . thing." Rodgers also acknowledged that he "was kind of pumped, so I really let her have it."

The CEO trusts your judgment and, in particular, your ability to advise him when he's gone too far. In response to his request, please prepare two documents: a memo responding to his appeal for your thoughts, and a draft letter to Sister Doris that you believe to be appropriate. You may take whichever position regarding Sr. Doris' request you care to—just be certain to justify your approach. Simply agreeing with the boss is insufficient. Mr. Rodgers, after all, has said repeatedly that he "can't stand 'yes men.'"

Your memo to Mr. Rodgers should be confidential and for his eyes only. The proposed reply to Sister Doris should be in final form and ready for dispatch.

The Sisters of St. Francis of Philadelphia
Our Lady of Angels Convent—Glen Riddle
Aston, Pennsylvania 19014
(610) 459-4125
Fax (610)558-1421

Dear _____

The Sisters of St. Francis of Philadelphia, a religious congregation of approximately 1000 women, is the beneficial owner of _____ shares of stock in _____ Corporation.

We believe that a company is best represented by a Board of qualified Directors reflecting the equality of the sexes, races, and ethnic groups. As women and minorities continue to move into upper level management positions of economic, educational, and cultural institutions, the number of qualified Board condidates also increases. Therefore our policy is to withhold authority to vote for nominees of a Board of Directors that do not include women and minorities.

It appears from the proxy statement which does not include pictures that _____ Company has no women or minority Directors. We have voted our proxy accordingly, and we urge you to enrich the Board by seeking qualified women and members of racial minorities as nominees.

Sincerely,

Doris Gormley OSF
Director, Corporate Social Responsibility

Cypress

May 23, 1996

Doris Gormley, OSF
Director, Corporate Social Responsibility
The Sisters of St. Francis of Philadelphia
Our Lady of Angels Convent—Glen Riddle
Aston, PA 19014

Dear Sister Gormley:

Thank you for your letter criticizing the lack of racial and gender diversity of Cypress's Board of Directors. I received the same letter from you last year. I will reiterate the management arguments opposing your position. Then I will provide the philosophical basis behind our rejection of the operating principles espoused in your letter, which we believe to be not only unsound, but even immoral, by a definition of that term I will present.

The semiconductor business is a tough one with significant competition from the Japanese, Taiwanese, and Koreans. There have been more corporate casualties than survivors. For these reason, our board of directors is not a ceremonial watchdog, but a critical management function. The essential criteria for Cypress board membership are as follows:

- Experience as a CEO of an important technology company.
- Direct expertise in the semiconductor business based on education and management experience.
- Direct experience in the management of a company that buys from the semiconductor industry.

A search based on these criteria usually yields a male who is 50-plus years old has a masters degree in an engineering science, and has moved up the managerial ladder to the top spot in one or more corporations. Unfortunately, there are currently few minorities and almost no women who chose to be engineering graduate students 30 years ago. (That picture will be dramatically different in 10 years, due to the greater diversification of graduate students in the 80s).

Bluntly stated, a "woman's view" on how to run our semiconductor company does not help us, unless that woman has an advanced technical degree and experience as a CEO. I do realize there are other industries in which the last statement does not hold true. We would quickly embrace the opportunity to include any woman or minority person who could help us as a director, because we pursue talent—and we don't care in what package that talent comes.

I believe that placing arbitrary racial or gender quotas on corporate boards is fundamentally wrong. Therefore, not only does Cypress not meet your requirements for boardroom diversification, but we are unlikely to, because it is very difficult to find qualified directors, let alone directors that also meet investors' racial and gender preferences.

I infer that your concept of corporate *morality* contains in it the requirement to appoint board of directors with, in your words, "equality of sexes, races, and ethnic group." I am unaware of any Christian requirements for corporate boards, and your views seem more accurately described as "politically correct," than "Christian."

My views aside, your requirements are—in effect—immoral. By immoral, I mean "causing harm to people," a fundamental wrong. Here's why:

- I presume you believe your organization does good work and that the people who spend their careers in its service deserve to retire with the necessities of life assured. If your investment in Cypress is intended for that purpose, I can tell you that each of the retired Sisters of St. Francis would suffer if I were forced to run Cypress on anything but a profit-making basis. The retirement plans of thousands of other people also depend on Cypress stock—$1.2 billion worth of stock—owned directly by investors or through mutual funds, pension funds, 401K programs, and insurance companies. Recently a fellow 1970 Dartmouth classmate wrote to say that his son's college fund ("Dartmouth, Class of 2014," he writes) owns Cypress stock. Any choice I would make to jeopardize retirees and other investors from achieving their lifetime goals would be fundamentally wrong.
- Consider charitable donations. When the U.S. economy shrinks, the dollars available to charity shrink faster, including those dollars earmarked for the Sisters of St. Francis. If all companies in the United States were forced to operate according to some arbitrary social agenda, rather than for profit, all American companies would operate at a disadvantage to their foreign competitors, all Americans would become less well off (some laid off), and charitable giving would decline precipitously. Making Americans poorer and reducing charitable giving in order to force companies to follow an arbitrary social agenda is fundamentally wrong.
- A final point with which you will undoubtedly disagree. Electing people to corporate boards based on racial preferences is demeaning to the very board members placed under such conditions, and unfair to people who are qualified. A prominent friend of mine hired a partner who is a brilliant, black Ph. D. from Berkeley. The woman is constantly insulted by being asked if she got her job because of preferences: The system that creates that institutionalized insult is fundamentally wrong.

Finally, you ought to get down from your moral high horse. Your form letter signed with a stamped signature does not allow for the possibility that a CEO could run a company morally and disagree with your position. You have voted against me and the other directors of the company, which is your right as a shareholder. But here is a synopsis of what you voted against.

- Employee ownership. Every employee of Cypress is a shareholder and every employee of Cypress—including the lowest-paid—receives new Cypress stock options every year, a policy that sets us apart even from other Silicon Valley companies.
- Excellent pay. Our employees in San Jose averaged $78,741 in salary and benefits in 1995. (That figure excludes my salary and that of Cypress's vice presidents; it's what "the workers" really get.)

- A significant boost to our economy. In 1995, our company paid out $150 million to its employees. That money did a lot of good: It bought a lot of houses, cars, movie tickets, eyeglasses, and college educations.
- A flexible health-care program. A Cypress-paid health care budget is granted to all employees to secure the health care options they want, including medical, dental, and eye care, as well as different life insurance policies.
- Personal computers. Cypress pays for half of home computers (up to $1,200) for all employees.
- Employee education. We pay for our employees to go back to school and we offer dozens of internal courses.
- Paid time off. In addition to vacation and holidays, each Cypress employee can schedule paid time off for personal reasons.
- Profit sharing. Cypress shares its profits with its employees. In 1995, profit sharing added up to $5,000 per employee, given in equal shares, regardless of rank or salary. That was a 22% bonus for an employee earning $22,932 per year, the taxable salary of our lowest-paid San Jose employee.
- Charitable work. Cypress supports Silicon Valley. We support the Second Harvest Food Bank (food for the poor), the largest food bank in the United States. I was chairman of the 1993 food drive, and Cypress has won the food-giving title three years running. (Last year, we were credited with 354,131 pounds of food, or 454 pounds per employee, a record.) We also give to the Valley Medical Center, our Santa Clara–based public hospital, which accepts all patients without a "VISA check."

Those are some of the policies of the board of directors you voted against. I believe you should support management teams that hold our values and have the courage to put them into practice. So, that's my reply. Choosing a board of directors based on race and gender is a lousy way to run a company. Cypress will never do it. Furthermore, we will never be pressured into it, because bowing to well-meaning, special-interest groups is an immoral way to run a company, given all the people it would hurt.

We simply cannot allow arbitrary rules to be forced on us by organizations that lack business expertise. I would rather be labeled as a person who is unkind to religious groups than as a coward who harms his employees and investors by mindlessly following high-sounding, but false, standards of right and wrong.

You may think this letter is too tough a response to a shareholder organization voting its conscience. But the political pressure to be what is euphemized as a "responsible corporation" today is so great that it literally threatens the well-being of every American. Let me explain why.
In addition to your focus on the racial and gender equality of board representation, other investors have their pet issues, for example, whether or not a company:

- is "green," or environmentally conscious.
- does or does not do business with certain countries or groups of people.
- supplies the U.S. Armed Forces.
- is involved in the community in appropriate ways.
- pays its CEO too much compared with its lowest-paid employee.
- pays its CEO too much as declared by self-appointed "industry watchdogs."
- gives to certain charities.
- is willing to consider layoffs when the company is losing money.
- is willing to consider layoffs to streamline its organization (so-called downsizing).

- has a retirement plan.
- pays for all or part of a health care plan.
- budgets a certain minimum percentage of payroll costs for employee training.
- places employees on its board of directors (you forgot this one).
- shares its profits with employees.

We believe Cypress has an excellent record on these issues. But that's because it's the way we choose to run the business for ourselves and our shareholders—not because we run the business according to the mandates of special-interest groups. Other companies, perhaps those in older industries just trying to hold on to jobs, might find the choices our company makes devastating to their businesses and, consequently, their employees. No one set of choices could be correct for all companies. Indeed, it would be impossible for any company to accede to all of the special interests because they are often in conflict with one another. For example, Cypress won a San Jose Mayor's Environmental Award for water conservation. Our waste water from the Minnesota plant is so clean we are permitted to put it directly into a lake teeming with wildlife. (A game warden station is the next-door neighbor to that plant.) Those facts might qualify us as a "green" company, but some investors would claim the opposite because we adamantly oppose wasteful, government-mandated, ride-sharing programs and believe car-pool lanes waste the time of the finest minds in Silicon Valley by creating government-inflicted traffic jams—while increasing pollution, not decreasing it, as claimed by some self-declared "environmentalists."

The May 13, 1996, issue of *Fortune* magazine analyzed the "ethical mutual funds" which invest with a social-issues agenda and currently control $639 billion in investments. Those funds produced an 18.2% return in the last 12 months, while the S&P 500 returned 27.2%. The investors in those funds thus lost 9% of $639 billion, or $57.5 billion in one year, because they invested on a social issues basis. Furthermore, their loss was not simply someone else's gain, the money literally vanished from our economy, making every American poorer. That's a lot of houses, food, and college educations that were lost to the "higher good" of various causes. What absurd logic would contend that Americans should be harmed by "good ethics?"

Despite our disagreement on the issues, the Sisters of St. Francis, the ethical funds, and their investors are merely making free choices on how to invest. What really worries me is the current election-year frenzy in Washington to institutionalize "good ethics" by making them law—a move that would mandate widespread corporate mismanagement. The "corporate responsibility" concepts promoted by Labor Secretary Reich and Senator Kennedy make great TV sound bites, but if they were put into practice, it would be a disaster for American business that would dwarf the $57 billion lost by the inept investment strategy of the "ethical funds." And that disaster would translate into lost jobs and lost wages for all Americans, a fundamental wrong.

One Senate proposal for "responsible corporations," as outlined in the February 26 issue of *Business Week,* would grant a low federal tax rate of 11% to "responsible corporations," and saddle all other companies with an 18% rate. One seemingly innocuous requirement for a "responsible corporation," as proposed by Senators Bingaman and Daschle, would limit the pay of a "responsible" CEO to no more than 50 times the company's lowest-paid, full-time employee. To mandate that a "responsible corporation" would have to limit the pay of its CEO is the perfect, no-lose, election-year issue. The rule would be viewed as the right thing to do by voters who distrust and dislike free markets, and as a don't-care issue by the rest. But the following analysis of this proposal underscores the fact that the simplistic solutions fashioned by politicians to provoke fear and anger against America's businesses often sound reasonable—while being fundamentally wrong.

Consider the folly of the CEO pay limit as it applies to Intel: the biggest semiconductor company in the world, the leader of America's return to market dominance in semiconductors, the good corporate citizen, the provider of 45,325 very high-quality jobs, the inventor of the random-access memory, the inventor of the microprocessor, and the manufacturer of the "brains" of 80% of the world's personal computers. Suppose that Intel's lowest-paid trainee earns $15,000 per year. The 50 to 1 CEO salary rule would mandate that the salary of Intel's co-founder and CEO, Andy Grove, could be no more than $750,000. Otherwise, Intel would face a federal tax rate of 18% rather than 11%. Last year, Andy Grove earned $2,756,700, well over that $750,000 limit, and Intel's pretax earnings were $5.6 billion. Seven percentage points on Intel's tax rate translates into a whopping $395 million tax penalty for Intel. Consequently, the practical meaning of this "responsible corporation" law to Intel would be this gun-to-the-head proposition. "Either cut the pay of your Chief Executive Officer by a factor of four from $2,756,700 to $750,000, or pay the federal government an extra $395 million in taxes."

The Bingaman-Daschle proposal would limit the pay of the CEO of the world's most important semiconductor company to less than that of a second-string quarterback in the NFL. That absurd result is not about "responsible corporations," but about two leftist senators, out of touch with reality, making political hay, causing harm, and labeling it "good." Their plan is particularly immoral in that it would cause the losses inherent in practicing their newly invented false moral standard to fall upon all investors in American companies, even though the government itself had not invested in those companies.

Meanwhile, my current salary multiple of 25-to-1 relative to our lowest-paid employee would qualify Cypress as a "responsible corporation," only because we are younger and not yet as successful as Intel—a fact reflected by my lower pay. If Cypress had created as much wealth and as many jobs as Intel, and if my compensation were higher for that reason, then, according to the amazingly perverse logic of the "responsible corporation," Cypress would be moved from the "responsible" to the "irresponsible" category for having been more successful and for having created more jobs! A final point: Why should either Intel or Cypress, both companies making 30% pretax profit, be offered a special tax break by the very politicians who would move on to the next press conference to complain about "corporate welfare?"

How long will it be before Senators Kennedy, Bingaman, and Daschle hold hearings on the "irresponsible corporations" that pay tens of millions of dollars to professional athletes? Or are athletes a "protected group," leaving CEOs as their sole target? If not, which Senate Subcommittee will determine the "responsible" pay level for a good CEO with 30% pretax profit, as compared to a good pitcher with a 1.05 earned run average? These questions highlight the absurdity of trying to replace free market pricing with the responsible-corporation claptrap proposed by Bingaman, Daschle, Kennedy, and Reich.

In conclusion, please consider these two points: First, Cypress is run under a set of carefully considered moral principles, which rightly include making a profit as a primary objective. Second, there is fundamental difference between your organization's right to vote its conscience and the use of coercion by the federal government to force arbitrary "corporate responsibilities" on America's businesses and shareholders.

Cypress stands for personal and economic freedom, for free minds and free markets, a position irrevocably in opposition to the immoral attempt by coercive utopians to mandate even more government control over America's economy. With regard to our shareholders who exercise their right to vote according to a social agenda, we suggest that they reconsider whether or not their strategy will do net good—after all the real costs are considered.

Sincerely,

T. J. Rodgers
President CEO

TJR/cxs

This case was prepared from public sources by James S. O'Rourke, concurrent associate professor of management, with the assistance of Ellen Jean Pollock of the *Wall Street Journal* as the basis for class discussion rather than to illustrate either effective or ineffective handling of an administrative situation.

Case 5–2 FARBERWARE PRODUCTS OF AMERICA

BACKGROUND NOTE

Managers occupying junior-to-middle level positions in large organizations are often called upon to resolve disputes. Some of these are disagreements between lower-level supervisors and employees; some are disputes with suppliers or distributors; others, like the dispute in this case, are between the organization and a customer.

Every customer has a value to an organization, and every customer has a price to that organization. Customers are, of course, the lifeblood and source of revenue to a business, but not all customers are worth saving. Some, in fact, may be more trouble and expense to maintain than they're worth.

Dealing with customers—or with anyone else who is in disagreement with your organization—requires patience, tact, and a certain measure of skill. A variety of response modes is open to the manager who faces an angry customer, along with a range of options in dealing with the case.

This case requires two documents in response: a brief (one- or two-page) communication strategy memo and a letter to the customer. The strategy memo should be directed to the president of Farberware Products of America and should describe in some detail how you plan to handle this case and why. The letter to the customer explains what you have chosen to do.

Assume that you are the director of customer service and report through the vice president for sales and marketing to the president. Your memorandum and customer letter should be in finished form, ready to transmit.

[Dated One Week Ago]
312 Bay View Road
Portland, ME 02175

Office of the President
Farberware Products of America
P.O. Box 11743
Manitowoc, WI 55617

Dear Sir,

Enclosed you will find one Farberware "GrilleMaster" indoor smokeless grill and rotisserie. I am sending this marvel of American technology to you directly because I'm so damn mad I can barely see straight.

As you will observe, the grill doesn't work. The cooking element somehow malfunctioned, the control mechanism and cord overheated, and the resulting electrical surge nearly burned the house down. While trying to unplug the grill, I managed to burn my left hand, though not seriously.

Since we live in a cold climate and it's not often possible to get out in the backyard and grill a steak, I thought this new "GrilleMaster" of yours was just the answer we'd been looking for. I guess not. This was just another $79.95 plus tax tossed away on a badly made product— and a potentially dangerous product, at that.

I took the grill to Penobscott Hardware here in Portland, but they said the manufacturer is responsible for the item, not them. They were sympathetic but couldn't seem to help. I'm sending this grill to you so that you will know what poorly designed products you're turning out, and so that you will take a look at the design of this thing before someone else gets hurt.

Wake up, Farberware! America won't settle for third-rate merchandise any longer. As I look for another smokeless grill, I'll be sure to see if I can find one with a Japanese label.

Sincerely,

Angus MacGregor

◈

Case 5–3 VOLVO OF NORTH AMERICA, INC.

BACKGROUND NOTE

Managers occupying junior-to-middle level positions in large organizations are often called upon to resolve disputes. Some of these are disagreements between lower-level supervisors and employees; some are disputes with supervisors or distributors; others, like the dispute in this case, are between the organization and a customer.

Every customer has a value to an organization, and every customer has a price to that organization. Customers are, of course, the lifeblood and source of revenue to a business, but not all customers are worth saving. Some, in fact, may be more trouble and expense to maintain than they are worth.

Dealing with customers—or with anyone else who is in disagreement with your organization—requires patience, tact, and a certain measure of skill. A variety of response modes is open to the manager who faces an angry customer, along with a range of options in dealing with the case.

This case requires two documents in response: a one-page communication strategy memo and an action document. The strategy memo is directed to the Vice President, Consumer Affairs, Volvo of North America, Inc., and describes in some detail how you plan to handle this case and why. The action document implements the strategy. That might be a letter to the servicing dealer, or perhaps a letter addressed directly to the customer. Your strategy may well involve more than just one letter, but your response to this case requires just one memo and one letter.

Assume that you are an assistant manager in the Consumer Affairs Department, responsible for New York, New England, and the northeastern United States. Your memorandum and action document must be in finished form, dated, signed, and ready to transmit.

June 9, 2000
311 Haddonfield Drive
DeWitt, NY 19310

Volvo of North America
Rockleigh Industrial Park
Rockleigh, NJ 07647-0913
ATTN: Consumer Affairs Department

Dear Volvo of North America:

I am the owner of a 1998 Volvo 800-DL. It's my second Volvo automobile and I've been very pleased with the car until just recently.

My car has a manual, 5-speed transmission and about ten days ago, while driving home from work, I discovered that I couldn't shift the car into second gear. The clutch worked fine, and the shift lever would move into any gear except second. The next day I took the car back to the dealer, Gary Ortman Imports, 2117 West Genesee Street, in Syracuse. After examining the transmission, their chief mechanic said the receiving fork in the shift linkage was bent and would have to be replaced.

With parts and labor, the repairs came to $787.65. I wouldn't be so upset about this, but the warranty on the car expired June 1, 1998. I took delivery of the car June 1, 1998, and the sales agreement has a 24-month, 24,000-mile limited warranty. The odometer now reads 18,471 miles.

Mr. Barry Quinlevan, the service manager at Ortman Imports tells me that it is most unusual for a shift fork to fail anytime during the first ten years of operation in this model automobile. I am a careful driver and certainly haven't abused the car in any way. He was sympathetic, but said he wouldn't be allowed to submit the part for a warranty claim.

I am angry and more than a little frustrated about this. It just doesn't seem right that I should get stuck with a bill for $312 in parts, $154 in labor, and $21.65 tax, all because that part failed less than a week after my warranty expired. Is there something you can do for me, or should I have bought a Lexus?

Sincerely,

PAUL A. KEENAN

6

LISTENING AND FEEDBACK

W e have all grown to understand how valuable communication is to the success of any business. And few of us would argue with the value of being skilled as a communicator on a personal level. We make friends, establish relationships, pass ideas, and accomplish the work that earns our living each day. Yet, strangely, the communication skill most central to our success—personally and professionally—is the one we're least likely to study in a formal way.

According to Professors Nichols and Stevens of the University of Minnesota, the average person spends about 70 percent of each day engaged in some type of communication. More specifically, researchers report that of all the time we spend communicating each day, 45 percent is spent listening, 30 percent speaking, 16 percent reading, and only 9 percent writing.[1]

More recent studies have shown that adults now spend more than half their daily communication listening to someone else speak. Even though it's clearly a crucial skill, very few people, according to Professor James Floyd, know how to do so efficiently and effectively.[2] Nichols warns, however, that "listening is hard work. It is characterized by faster heart action, quicker circulation of the blood, a small rise in bodily temperature." The implication is simple: If you are not motivated to work at listening, you are not likely to improve.[3]

Studies of listening skill have repeatedly shown that the average North American adult listens at an efficiency rate of just 25 percent. Your mother was right: For most of us, literally three-quarters of what we hear goes in one ear and out the other. We retain and understand just a fraction of what's going on around us.[4]

There is a substantial difference, though, between hearing and listening. On the one hand, hearing is merely an involuntary physical response to the environment. Listening, on the other hand, is a process that includes hearing, attending to, understanding, evaluating, and responding to spoken messages. It's a sophisticated communication skill which can be mastered only with considerable practice. It is fair to emphasize, however, that while improving one's listening skills is difficult, demanding, and challenging, it can be immensely rewarding.[5]

Why have most of us become so resistant to careful listening? "It's because of our fast-paced world," says Kathy Thompson of Alverno College. "We're always in a hurry. Mentally we're saying, 'Get to the point.' We don't have time to hear the whole story. We're running from house to job to store to church. Good listening takes time."[6]

That's part of it, according to Wick Chambers, a partner in Speechworks, an Atlanta communications-training firm. "But also, people think listening is boring; it's more fun to talk." Still others blame TV and radio, which allow people to combine listening with so many other activities that simply listening—to music, for example—seems like a waste of time.[7]

"When you watch television," says Sheila Bentley, a Memphis, Tennessee, communications consultant, "you're listening in a way that doesn't require you to retain anything and doesn't object if you leave the room. And because it's interrupted by commercials, you don't have to develop sustained attending skills. With people spending six hours a day doing that kind of listening, it's no wonder there's concern that we're becoming a nation of poor listeners."[8]

WHY LISTEN?

Poor listening can cause disasters, as it did in the 1977 runway collision at Tenerife Airport in the Canary Islands, when misunderstood instructions caused 583 deaths. But more often, poor listening results in millions of little time-wasting mistakes a day—the wrong coffee order, credit card charge, or telephone number. Ms. Bentley spends hours with medical managers because of the massive liability awards doctors and hospitals can pay in response to poor listening. "People are realizing," she says, "that a lot of mistakes we attributed to other things are actually listening problems."[9]

At Starbucks Coffee Company stores, where a customer can order a "double-shot decaf grande iced half-skim vanilla dry cappucino," employees are taught a procedure for hearing and calling orders developed by the company five years ago. It systematizes the sequence of words describing the drink—size, flavoring, milk, decaf—with automatic defaults. Then the person making the drink echoes the order aloud. "We expect our employees to listen," says Alan Gulick, a Starbucks spokesman. "It's an important component of customer service."[10]

Listening is the central skill in the establishment and maintenance of interpersonal relationships. No matter what type of relationship—professional, personal, neighborly, romantic—listening is the skill that forms the bond and keeps the relationship moving forward. Harvard psychologist Daniel Goleman says, "Listening is a skill that keeps couples together. Even in the heat of an argument, when both are seized by emotional hijacking, one or the other, and sometimes both, can manage to listen past the anger, and hear and respond to a partner's reparative gesture."[11]

THE BENEFITS OF BETTER LISTENING

James J. Floyd, who has taught and written on this subject for many years, offers four specific benefits you'll obtain from becoming a better listener: increased knowledge, job success, improved interpersonal relations, and self-protection.[12]

Scholars of human behavior have shown a steady tendency during the last half of the twentieth century in the United States toward more passive learning technique and more passive leisure activities. As a society, we spend more time watching television, movies, and videos, and less time reading. Coincidentally, we also spend more time these days listening to CDs, tapes, and radio.

A study conducted by Sperry Corporation (now UNISYS) reported that students spend 60 to 70 percent of their time in a classroom listening.[13] Professors Nichols and Stevens found in their studies at the University of Minnesota that every group of students receiving instruction in listening improved by at least 25 percent, while some groups improved by as much as 40 percent.[14] Without some instruction in listening improvement, however, it appears that the listening abilities of most people actually decline from elementary school on.[15]

A number of other good reasons exist for you to improve your listening:

Listening Demonstrates Acceptance   The very act of listening to another person demonstrates that you value him or her and care about what he or she is saying. If you show that you *don't care* about others, they'll quit talking to you. Good, perhaps, in the short run, but disastrous in the long-term.

Listening Promotes Problem-Solving Abilities   Good managers are often asked to do what bartenders, cab drivers, and counselors have done for years: allow someone the time and attention to talk through a problem. Rather than providing advice and solutions right away, most successful managers encourage employees to arrive at solutions on their own. By listening carefully and reflectively, a supervisor can guide a subordinate to a solution that has a greater chance for success and substantially greater levels of employee buy-in.

Listening Increases the Speaker's Receptiveness to the Thoughts and Ideas of Others   The best ideas don't always come from yourself or your immediate staff and colleagues. Often, you'll find great ideas where you least expect them. They may come from your customers, your employees, your suppliers and business partners, and (interestingly) from people who refuse to do business with you. You might be genuinely surprised at what your competitor's customers are saying about you, if only you'd take the time to listen to them.

Listening Increases the Self-Esteem of the Other Person   You are not personally responsible for the self-esteem of everyone in your organization, but think about it for a moment. Isn't it easier to come to work, concentrate on the tasks at hand, and compete successfully if you feel good about yourself? Sales managers have known intuitively for years that self-esteem is crucial to a sales representative's ability to succeed. They hear "no" so often that they come to accept failure as an inevitable part of the job. Having a manager who'll listen to them willingly and uncritically can be enormously helpful.

Listening Helps You Overcome Self-Consciousness and Self-Centeredness   A little instruction and some practice in active listening can help talkers to shut up and the self-consciously shy to open up. Working more toward the center of the "listening-talking" continuum can be especially helpful to junior managers who are inclined to offer opinions when the demand for them is not especially brisk.

Listening Can Help to Prevent Head-On Emotional Collisions   If you concentrate on your own needs to the exclusion of other people's needs and interests, you will find that others will return the favor: they will focus on their own interests and not yours. The key to preventing the sort of emotional train-wrecks that are destructive to any organization is to put other people's needs ahead of your own. Find out what their concerns and interests are first—by listening carefully to them—and you will likely get what you want sooner and with substantially less angst.

By taking responsibility for successful communication through active and reflective listening, you can become more successful at those activities that depend on communication, including your personal and professional life. You can learn more, improve your relationships with others around you, and increase your chances for success. Careful listening is no guarantee, of course, but it's a wonderful place to start.

THE ROLE OF INEFFECTIVE LISTENING HABITS

Ralph Nichols, followed by a number of other researchers, was early to discover that many of us employ listening habits which are ineffective and may interfere with learning. The problem is not that we *can't* listen or *don't* listen. It's far more likely that we've learned to listen *haphazardly* and in ways that are simply counterproductive.

The first step in becoming a more effective listener, both in the workplace and in our personal lives, is to identify the poor listening habits we've developed over a lifetime and replace them with effective, productive habits.

AN INVENTORY OF POOR LISTENING HABITS

Here, then, are a few habits that hinder rather than help as we try to listen to what others are telling us:

Being Preoccupied with Talking, Not Listening   Among the most successful CEOs, board chairmen, military generals, university presidents—that handful of enormously talented high achievers who run large and complex organizations, each one—without exception—is far more interested in listening to what others have to say than they are in talking. When they talk, they invariably ask questions—to gather information, to solicit opinion, to "take the pulse" of the organization. When they speak, the sentences tend to be brief, cogent, and terse. They succeed by gathering up what others know and sharing what they know selectively.

Calling the Subject Uninteresting   We've all done it. You can probably recall doing it in algebra class or, perhaps, during a lecture on a subject you had little interest in knowing anything about. Many have paid dearly for this error by declaring that everything from cost accounting to microeconomics just "isn't especially interesting." If you declare a subject to be dull, you virtually guarantee that you'll learn nothing about it. Some subjects may be a bit duller than others, but in order to learn anything at all, you'll have to be somewhat selfish about this and tell yourself, "This may not be fascinating, but there's something in here that's important for me to know." Taking an interest in the subject is the first step.

Letting Bias or Prejudice Distort the Messages You Hear   We all have biases. They are an important, almost inescapable part of who we are, and the kind of lives we've led. By filtering incoming messages through these biases, stereotypes, or prejudices, however, we put another speaker's intentions at risk. We hear what our biases tell us to hear, and not what's being said. The best advice is not to rid yourself of your preferences, but simply to know what they are. Don't let your views on a particular subject or about a particular speaker interfere with what you're hearing.

Oversimplifying Answers or Explanations   This is really a form of uncritical listening. It comes from an all-too-understandable desire to reduce the complex to something simpler, to eliminate detail, to tighten-up arguments that depend on important detail. Listen carefully to what's being said and later examine those parts of the explanation or answer that may be eliminated, keeping what's most valuable or useful.

Yielding to External Distractions   It's certainly easy to be distracted. If you work in a cubicle rather than a private office, you may be exposed to half-a-dozen or more conversations at once. Carol Hymowitz of The *Wall Street Journal* says, "In this open-space era, aimed at flattening hierarchies and promoting teamwork, managers . . . have to adapt to less privacy and more contact, to being constantly seen and heard as they make decisions and deals." Learning to focus on the task at hand, whether it's a phone conversation or a face-to-face meeting with an employee, is crucial to success as a listener.[16]

Yielding to Internal Distractions   These can come from anywhere, even (or especially) when you're isolated and trying to concentrate. Put aside your personal concerns—everything from car payments to your next appointment—and devote just a few minutes to the listening task at hand, and you will find far fewer problems in your life. A few minutes spent concentrating on the words you are hearing will pay big dividends all week.

Avoiding Difficult or Demanding Material   This problem is akin to the first one we talked about—it's just as bad to say that a subject is difficult as it is to say it's dull or uninteresting. By staying with subjects and material you know and are already comfortable with, you limit your ability to grow intellectually. Any debate or forensics coach will tell you that listening is a skill, just like putting in golf or a free throw in basketball. If you are unwilling to work at it, you are unlikely to get any better.

Rationalizing Poor Listening   There are certainly enough people or circumstances to blame your poor listening habits on: "No one taught me how to do this." "This office is filled with noise and distractions." "I've never paid much attention to listening as a skill." Don't give up. And don't accept that 25 percent efficiency rate as something you can't do anything about. Effective, active listening is important and you can improve.

Criticizing the Speaker's Delivery   Rather than focus on the speaker's accent, pacing, or phrasing, concentrate instead on the message they carry. Look for both cognitive and emotional content, but give the speaker a break. Most people haven't had much formal training in public speaking and, in the course of casual conversation, directional changes and fluency breaks are common. Concentrate on *what's* being said, rather than *how* it's said.

Jumping to Conclusions   Formulating a response prematurely may disrupt the speaker's thoughts, may take the conversation in an unintended direction, or may reveal that you do not understand what the speaker has been trying to say. Rather than predicting the direction or outcome of a conversation, give your partner an opportunity to get to the point. Relax and let him or her talk for a little while.

Getting Over-Stimulated   If you're more concerned about your response than about what's being said to you, chances are good that you will miss much of what you are hearing. "There's the old joke," says communications consultant Wicke Chambers. "The opposite of talking isn't listening. It's waiting to talk. That's what a lot of people do," she says. "They just wait to talk." The advice? Take it all in, think about it, then formulate a response. Go one step at a time.

Assigning the Wrong Meaning to Words   This sounds remarkably simple, but we do it everyday, at home, at work, and at school. Some words have specific meaning and you can, in fact, look them up. (*Enormity* meaning "excessive wickedness" or "beyond all moral bounds," rather than "largeness" or "big.") Others require interpretation. ("The customer says he needs this right away." Does that mean twenty minutes from now? By the close of business? Or, will sometime this week be okay? You'd better ask.)

Listening Only for the Facts   On the face of it, this doesn't sound like such a bad idea. ("I wish he'd get to the point.") The problem, however, is that if we listen *only* for the facts, that's all we'll have—facts. We won't have any real understanding of why the issue is important, how it's linked to other issues, or what the implications or outcomes may be. Along the way, you have to listen for context, connections, and those rhetorical ligatures that link facts to human experience.

Trying to Make an Outline of Everything We Hear   This is not a good idea because so little of what we'll hear from one day to the next is really organized in any systematic way. Not many extemporaneous speeches and very few impromptu conversations are based on any sort of organized outline. Don't force what you hear into artificial patterns. Just take it in, sort it out as you go along, and try as best you can to make sense of what the speaker is saying.

Faking Attention to the Speaker   This is a skill learned in high school and college classrooms all over the country, later developed as a high art form in business meetings everywhere. You don't want to seem impolite, so you smile and nod. The speaker thinks you not only understand, but agree! The fact is, you haven't heard a word that's been said. But you've given the impression that you have. As a direct result, the speaker is unlikely to repeat herself, offer additional examples or illustrations, or seek questions from those who might appear confused or curious.

Letting Emotion-Laden Words Throw Us off the Track   Most intelligent speakers know well enough to avoid racist, sexist, or profane language precisely because it is offensive to so many people. But what about words or phrases that have some emotional attachment for you that a speaker would have no clue about? Sometimes the attachment is personal (a date or a song title, for example); more often, it's a topic or subject reference that can set you off (taxes, for instance). It's easier said than done, but stay in control of your emotions and pay attention, at least until the conversation or speech is finished.

Resisting the Temptation to Interrupt   One of the by-products of the imbalance between talkers and listeners is interruption, with three or four people talking and no one listening. "We have become a nation of interrupters," says Professor Kathy Thompson. It's as true at home as it is in business, where several people may be vying for the boss's attention, and none much cares what his or her competitors are saying. According to Sam Nelson, director of debate at the University of Rochester, "People want to take credit for things. If you're the first person to get it out, it's your's. So you go into the meeting thinking, 'I'm going to get this out if it kills me.' " That also helps explain the disappearance of the pause from many people's speech. Many experts see the value of pausing, however, saying that it signals a sense of confidence. If you are confident in your ideas, confident in your position, it will probably pay for you to wait your turn and avoid interrupting others.

Wasting the Differential Between the Rate at Which We Speak and the Rate at Which We Think If all this weren't bad enough, biology also works against attentive listening. Most people speak at a rate of 120 to 150 words a minute, but the human brain can easily process more than 500 words a minute, leaving plenty of time for what Cynthia Crossen calls *mental fidgeting*. "If the speaker also happens to be slow, monotonal and wordy," she adds, "it requires a heroic effort to stay tuned instead of simply faking it."[17]

DEVELOPING GOOD LISTENING HABITS

Researchers at Sperry Corporation (now UNISYS) have identified ways in which you can review your ineffective habits, identify those you should replace, and substitute more effective strategies for listening, learning, and remembering. In fact, they have identified more than a dozen habits you may wish to consider for your own inventory of communication skills.

Stop Talking This doesn't occur to many people, but it is effective.

One Conversation at a Time You can't talk on the phone and have a conversation with someone in the room at the same time. Choose the conversation you most want to have and tell the other person you'll be available in a few minutes.

Empathize with the Person Speaking Put yourself in his or her shoes; try as best you can to see it from their point of view. It's not easy to listen empathetically, but it's important to try.

Ask Questions If you are confused, lost, or need information, ask for clarification. Simple questions that seek data, positions, or intentions can be especially helpful.

Don't Interrupt Asking questions may be useful, but initially at least it may be more helpful simply to let your conversation partner talk for a bit. If the conversation has any substance at all, it won't be long before you have an opportunity to react.

Show Interest Demonstrate complete interest in what's being said to you. Look the talker in the eyes, show interest with your facial expression, and maintain an open and nonthreatening posture. Show that you care.

Give Your Undivided Attention If you can, close the door, hold your calls, and give all of your attention to whoever is speaking. If privacy isn't possible, at least put aside what you're working on, reading, or doing. If you really need some conversational privacy and your office isn't set up for that sort of thing, you might consider going for a walk. Low tones and a steady pace will usually provide you with an opportunity to speak in confidence.

Evaluate Facts and Evidence   Listen critically. Ask yourself (and, perhaps, your conversation partner) how you know this is true. What's the source of your confidence in the data? Ask whether the evidence is recent, reliable, accurate, and relevant to the subject.

React to Ideas, Not to the Speaker   It's tough to separate the message from the messenger, but give it a try. We often choose to believe what we hear, based on who we hear it from. Wherever possible, look beyond your assessment of the speaker to the ideas contained in the speech.

Wishing Doesn't Make It So   Just because you want to hear it doesn't mean that is what the speaker is saying. Shakespeare's phrase "The wish is father to the thought" means simply that we don't listen very carefully because we're often engaged in a great deal of wishful thinking.

Listen for What Is *Not* Said   If you expect to hear something and don't, perhaps it's time to ask why you haven't. Match your expectations of the speaker's content against what you actually hear, and think carefully about what hasn't been said.

Listen to *How* Something Is Said   We told you earlier not to criticize the speaker's delivery and that's still a useful rule. You should consider listening, however, for the emotional content, for hints of sarcasm, cynicism, or irony in what you hear. Often a speaker will downplay criticism or make light of a key point simply with a shift in his or her tone of voice. Tune in to the speaker's mood and intention, as well as the content of the speech.

Share the Responsibility for Communication   It's not entirely the speaker's responsibility to make sure you understand what's being said. You have an obligation to seek out information that's useful or important to you. Focus, concentrate, ask questions, pay attention to what's going on.[18]

THE FIVE ESSENTIAL SKILLS OF ACTIVE LISTENING

To become an effective, empathetic, and skilled listener, you must participate in the dialogue. This is a much more active process than the one you use when listening to speeches, lectures, or in meetings. This is a process that involves you and one or two other people engaged in direct conversation. To increase your probability of success, here are four skills you should practice and master.

Paraphrase Others as They Speak   From time-to-time in a conversation, it will be useful for you to summarize what others are saying. It's helpful to use your own words to do this, but you must do it to their satisfaction in order to convince them you are really listening. Such summaries often begin with a phrase similar to this: "If I understand you correctly, what you're saying is . . ," or "In other words, you're telling me that . . ."

Reflect Feelings   Some managers will look intently for the meaning in a spoken sentence without paying much attention to the emotional load attached to it. Try, as best you can, to grasp the affective intent of the speaker. Summaries that reflect feeling might sound like this: "You're not very confident about this, are you?" or "You seem determined to see this through."

Reflect Meaning   This is the cognitive or logical content of a discussion. It's always helpful for a manager to focus on the facts at hand, how they're organized, and how they bear on the topic being discussed. Consider this reflection of a conversation's meaning: "When you say you will need help with this project, am I correct in assuming you mean you will require additional support staff, particularly in the start-up phase?"

Reflect Conclusions   Discussions can ramble far and wide and can include a great deal of information that may not be directly relevant. It's often useful to review what you have agreed to or concluded, particularly as a conversation is drawing to a conclusion. A summary reflecting the conclusion of a conversation might sound like this: "So, considering the cost of the upgrade and our other immediate needs, am I right in assuming you are not in favor of the purchase?"

Follow Through   Important as listening is, follow-through is even more so. Professor Calvin Morrill, professor of sociology at the University of Arizona, cautions that once you have asked for feedback, "unless you take steps that show your employees that you've listened to them and intend to take action, they will never speak again. In cases like those," he says, "the manager would have been better off never having asked at all."[19]

A SYSTEM FOR IMPROVING YOUR LISTENING HABITS

The time you spend preparing for your quarterly or semiannual performance review might be a good time to review your communication habits in general and your listening habits in particular. In you're serious about becoming a better listener, consider this four-step process.

Review Your Listening Inventory   Make a few notes about those habits and behaviors that dominate your communication from day to day. Think, in particular, about those which you most often use and which seem to work best or work least for you.

Recognize Your Undesirable Listening Habits   If you display, even occasionally, any of those habits we have listed above as undesirable, make a note of them: which ones, how often, and under what circumstances (that is, one-on-one conversations with employees, during meetings with colleagues and coworkers, and so on).

Refuse to Tolerate Undesirable Habits   Even if the undesirable habits you list are infrequent and don't seem particularly serious, refuse to tolerate them as a part of your communication skill inventory. Tag them for removal and get to work on them.

Replace Undesirable Habits with Effective Ones   For every unproductive, undesirable, or negative listening habit you have, identify a positive habit or skill to replace it. Don't simply tell yourself you won't daydream during a lecture; work out a system to use the spare time effectively.[20]

Becoming a good listener carries some risks. Talkers can attach themselves to you like barnacles to a boat, and detaching them isn't easy. Good listeners can also find themselves on the receiving end of other people's problems, even when they may have little to offer in the way of support or counsel. But the rewards can be enormous for developing this skill, both for you as an individual and for the organization that employs you. Remember: Putting other people's needs ahead of your own may seem counterintuitive, but doing so will help both you and others achieve your goals sooner, more efficiently, and less stressfully. It's in your best interest to care about how well you listen.

GIVING AND RECEIVING FEEDBACK

When he was mayor of New York City, Ed Koch frequently walked the streets of his hometown asking his constituents, "How am I doing?" The question wasn't simply rhetorical; nor was it a ritualistic greeting for his faithful supporters. He asked the question of friend and foe alike. He cared about the responses he received because his ability to perform as that city's mayor depended on *feedback*—direct, honest, current, unfiltered feedback. If he wasn't doing well, New Yorkers let him know about it. When he performed to their satisfaction, they told him. For a public official, honest feedback is almost as important as campaign contributions. It is no less important to a manager in the private sector.

Good feedback doesn't just happen. It's the product of careful, deliberate communication strategies, coupled with good interpersonal communication skills. You can significantly increase the probability of communication success if you understand the role of feedback in both personal and professional communication.[21]

GUIDELINES FOR CONSTRUCTIVE FEEDBACK

Now that you have improved your listening skills, it may be time to focus on how and when to provide feedback to others. Here are a few suggestions.

Acknowledge the Need for Feedback   The first thing we each must recognize as communicators is the value of giving and receiving feedback, both positive and negative. Feedback is vital to any organization committed to improving itself, because it is the only way for managers and executives to know what needs to be improved. Giving and receiving feedback should be more than just a part of an employee's behavior; it should be a part of the whole organization's culture.

You will need high-level feedback skills to improve your organizational meetings, and, more generally, interactions between employees. These skills will also help you communicate more effectively with customers and suppliers. In fact, you will find many opportunities to apply these skills across your working environment.

Give Both Positive and Negative Feedback   Many people take good work for granted and give feedback only when they encounter problems. This is a bad policy; people will more likely pay attention to your complaints if they have also received your compliments. It is important to remember to tell people when they have done something well.

Understand the Context   The most important characteristic of feedback is that it always has a context: where it happened, why it happened, what led up to an event. You should never simply walk up to a person, deliver a feedback statement, and then leave.

Before you give feedback, review the actions and decisions that led up to the moment. Every communication event exists in a context and if you don't understand the context to the events you're thinking of criticizing, your comments are unlikely to have a positive effect on others.

Provide Definitions   Don't assume that the person you are counseling or offering feedback to will understand the words, phrases, or terms you're using. Make certain that the language you use is both acceptable to the person you're speaking with and appropriate for the circumstances. More to the point, make sure you're using words whose meaning you both clearly understand and agree on.

A simple example may help: *The American Heritage Dictionary of the English Language* lists 93 separate and distinct meanings for the word *get*. When you use that word in conversation, what do *you* mean? Some scholars now say the 500 most commonly used words in our language have more than 14,000 dictionary definitions. The fact is, the more meanings assigned to a word, the less it means. Make sure people understand you by providing definitions, examples, and illustrations. You may even need to provide exceptions and limits. Make sure people understand the language you're using as you provide feedback to them.[22]

Use a Common Language   Don't speak in a language that your conversation partner is likely to misunderstand, misconstrue, or misinterpret. Use words, phrases, terms, and ideas that are in line with what you know about that person. If you are sure she understands an acronym or company jargon, it's probably okay to use it, but if you're dealing with someone who doesn't share the same frame of reference you do, avoid language that will cause confusion.

Don't Assume   Making assumptions invariably gets you into trouble. During interpersonal communications, it is dangerous to make the assumption that the other person either thinks or feels as you do at that moment. Communication consultant Tony Alessandra says, "The other person may have a frame of reference that is totally different from your own. She reacts and perceives according to what she knows and believes to be true, and that may be different from your own reactions, perceptions and beliefs." To avoid the problems inherent in assumptions, ask for direct feedback, check on facts, examine underlying assumptions, and use a healthy dose of skepticism before you say, "I know exactly what you mean."

Focus on Behavior Rather than People   When people receive feedback, especially feedback from a supervisor or superior, they are often defensive, fearful, and likely to take anything you say as a personal assault. Defuse the hostility, minimize the fear, and depersonalize the conversation by focusing your comments on the behavior involved and not the people. If you say, "These trip reports need additional information," that's substantially less threatening than saying, "Why can't you fill out a trip report correctly?"

Know When to Give Feedback   Before deciding to offer feedback, determine whether the moment is right. You must consider more than your own need to give feedback. Constructive feedback can happen only within a context of listening to and caring about the other person. If the time isn't right, if the moment isn't appropriate, you can always delay briefly before offering your thoughts. Don't wait too long or you'll find that feedback won't be helpful, but choose your moments wisely.

Deborah Lake is a manager at SC Johnson Wax who moved from a traditional office to a cubicle last year at the company's Commercial Markets headquarters. She quickly figured out that she had to unlearn advice on speaking forcefully in business conversations. Everyone, in fact, had to lower their voices in the open space to preserve their privacy and avoid disturbing the person in the adjacent cubicle. She doesn't hesitate to speak loudly, however, when giving positive feedback. "I want others to hear if I tell someone they've done a wonderful job, because I want that person to be recognized," she says. But if it's negative feedback, she speaks quietly.[23]

Know How to Give Feedback   Providing constructive, useful feedback involves more than simply responding to people as they speak to you. Effective feedback involves an understanding of the language, people's intentions as they speak (or choose not to speak), the context in which the communication takes place, and your objectives as a manager.

KNOWING WHEN *NOT* TO GIVE FEEDBACK

You shouldn't attempt to give feedback to another person when:

- You don't know much about the circumstances of the behavior.
- You don't care about the person or will not be around long enough to follow up on the aftermath of your feedback. Hit-and-run feedback is not fair.
- The feedback, positive or negative, is about something the person has no power to change.
- The other person seems low in self-esteem.
- You are low in self-esteem.
- Your purpose is not really improvement, but to put someone on the spot ("gotcha!") or demonstrate how smart or how much more responsible you are.
- The time, place, or circumstances are inappropriate (for example, in the presence of a customer or other employees).

KNOWING HOW TO GIVE EFFECTIVE FEEDBACK

These suggestions should make it easier for you to provide feedback that works to another person:

Be Descriptive   Relate, as objectively as possible, what you saw the other person do or what you heard the other person say. Give specific examples, the more recent, the better. Examples from the distant past are more likely to lead to disagreement over the facts.

Be Objective   This may not be possible, but it's worth trying anyway. Do what you can to remove subjectivity from your discussions with others when you're providing feedback, at least at the beginning of the discussion. When it's time to offer personal opinions or subjective observations, identify them as such and explain that "it's only my view." Wherever possible, stick to the facts and focus on what you know for sure.

Don't Use Labels   Be clear, specific, and unambiguous. Words such as *immature, unprofessional, irresponsible,* and *prejudiced* are labels we attach to a set of behaviors. Describe the behavior and drop the labels. For example, say "You missed the deadline we had all agreed to meet," rather than "You're being irresponsible and I want to know what you're going to do about it."

Don't Exaggerate   Be exact. To say "You're always returning late from your lunch break" is probably untrue and, therefore, unfair. It invites the feedback receiver to argue with the exaggeration rather than respond to the real issue.

Don't Be Judgmental   Or at least don't use the rhetoric of judgment. Words such as *good, better, bad, worst,* and *should* place you in the role of a controlling parent. This invites the person receiving your comments to respond as a child. When that happens, and it will most of the time, the possibility of constructive feedback is lost.

Speak for Yourself   Don't refer to absent, anonymous people; don't attempt to speak for your supervisor or for people much higher up the line. Avoid such references as "A lot of people here don't like it when you . . ." Don't allow yourself to be a conduit for other people's complaints. Instead, encourage others to speak for themselves. You must take responsibility for your own job, but don't attempt to speak on others' behalf.

Talk First About Yourself, Not About the Other Person   Use a statement with either the word *I* or the word *we* as the subject, not the word *you.* This guideline is one of the most important and one of the most surprising. Consider the following examples regarding lateness:

1. "You are frequently late for meetings."
2. "You are very prompt for meetings."
3. "I feel annoyed when you are late for meetings."
4. "We appreciate your coming to meetings on time."

The first two statements begin with second-person pronouns. People can become defensive when criticism begins with *you* and may be less likely to hear what you say when feedback is phrased as direct criticism. The last two statements begin with first-person pronouns and can help to create an adult/peer relationship. People are more likely to remain open to your message when the criticism does not appear to be aimed directly at them. Even if your rank is higher than the feedback recipient's, strive for an adult/peer relationship. Try using first-person statements (*I* or *we*) so the effectiveness of your comments is not lost in the accusation.

Phrase the Issue as a Statement, Not as a Question   Contrast "When are you going to stop being late for meetings?" with "We can't begin the meeting on time when you are late." The question is controlling and manipulative because it implies "You, the responder, are expected to adjust your behavior to accommodate me, the questioner." Most people become defensive and angry when spoken to in this way. On the other hand, *I* or *we* statements imply, "I think we have an issue we must resolve together." The *I* statement allows the receiver to see what effect the behavior had on you.

Encourage People to Change   Feedback must focus on things the recipient has the power to change. Most people can't change such basic personality preferences as shyness or a preference for openness over closure. But they can change the behavioral outcomes that affect the workplace. Leaving a set of sensitive documents scattered across a desktop is an outcome that a manager can focus on, regardless of personality preferences. Focus on those issues that are both important to improvement and well within the power of the other person to change.

Restrict Your Feedback to Things You Know for Certain   Don't present your opinions as facts. Speak only of what you saw and heard and what you feel or think. If you're not sure or can't say so with certainty, hold your comments. Feedback based on speculation or second-hand information may be far more destructive than you imagine. Make sure of what you know and then act on it.

Build Trust   While people occasionally learn valuable lessons from those they don't get along with, feedback is always more readily accepted if it comes from a trusted source. The psychological research on trust has shown that persuasive messages from a trusted source always produce greater impact and longer-lasting results. Skillful managers will use each opportunity for feedback to establish useful working relationships and build long-term trust.

Help People Hear and Accept Your Compliments When Giving Positive Feedback   Many people feel awkward when told good things about themselves and will fend off the compliment ("Oh, it wasn't that big a deal. I just helped another manager put together a proposal.") Sometimes they will change the subject. It may be important to reinforce the positive feedback and help the person hear it, acknowledge it, and accept it.[24]

KNOWING HOW TO RECEIVE FEEDBACK

There may be a time when you receive feedback from someone who does not know feedback guidelines. In these cases, *help your critic refashion the criticism* so that it conforms to the rules for constructive feedback ("Tell me what we can do to improve the conditions in your department."). When reacting to feedback:

Breathe   This is simple but effective advice. Our bodies are conditioned to react to stressful situations as though they were physical assaults. Our muscles tense. We start breathing rapidly and shallowly. Taking full, deep breaths forces your body to relax and allows your brain to maintain greater alertness.

Listen Carefully   Don't interrupt. Don't discourage the feedback-giver. You can't benefit from feedback you don't hear.

Ask Questions for Clarity   You have a right to receive clear feedback. Ask for specific examples. ("Can you describe what I do or say that makes me appear hostile to you?") If you don't understand terminology or references, request an explanation.

Acknowledge the Feedback   Paraphrase the message in your own words to let the person know you have heard and understood what was said. Don't simply sit there silently. Provide the other person with both verbal and nonverbal indicators that you've heard and understand what's been said. Remember, this isn't any easier for the other person than it is for you.

Acknowledge Valid Points.   Agree with what is true. Agree with what is possible. Acknowledge the other person's point of view ("I understand how you might get that impression") and try to understand their reaction. Agreeing with what's true or possible does not mean you agree to change your behavior. You can agree, for instance, that you sometimes jump too quickly to a conclusion without implying that you will slow down your conclusion-making process. Agreeing with what's true or possible also does not mean agreeing with any value judgment about you. You can agree that your work has been slow lately without agreeing that you are irresponsible.

Don't Be Defensive   Most of us don't take direct criticism well. We often spend part of the conversation planning our response (or defense), rather than listening carefully to what's being said. Don't listen *passively;* ask questions, inquire about issues that you don't understand or that aren't clear to you. But avoid the temptation to draw your sword and do battle then and there. Most feedback provided to you by a superior is carefully thought out in advance and is designed with your best interests and improvement in mind. Take it for what it's worth: an opportunity to improve your performance and chances for success.

Try to Understand the Other Person's Objectives   Whether you're listening to your subordinates or to your own boss, you'll never fully understand what they're saying unless you set aside your own goals and objectives and focus on theirs. Try to see the world from their viewpoint and appreciate what motivates their comments.

Take Time Out to Sort Out What You Heard   You may need time for sorting out or checking with others before responding to the feedback. It is reasonable to ask the feedback-giver for time to think about what was said and how you feel about it. Make a specific appointment for getting back to him or her. Don't use this time as an excuse to avoid the issue.[25]

Communication is clearly a two-way process. People who serve in management positions must accept the responsibility for both providing and seeking out information which will be useful in correcting and improving the processes involved. The place to begin is with the recognition that feedback is both a useful and productive part of communication. And with some careful application of productive listening skills as you interact with others in the workplace, your chances for success are greater.

Endnotes

1. Nichols, R. G. and L. Stevens. *Are You Listening?* New York: McGraw-Hill, 1957.

2. Floyd, J. J. *Listening: A Practical Approach.* Glenview, IL: Scott, Foresman and Company, 1985, pp. 2–3.

3. Nichols, R. G. "Listening Is a 10-Part Skill," in Huseman R. C., et al., (eds), *Readings in Interpersonal and Organizational Communication,* Boston: Holbrook Press, 1969, pp. 472–479.

4. Crossen, C. "The Crucial Question for These Noisy Times May Just Be: 'Huh?' " *Wall Street Journal,* July 10, 1997, p. A1.

5. Wolvin, A. D. and C. G. Coakley. *Listening.* Dubuque, IA: Wm. C. Brown, 1982.

6. Crossen, "The Crucial Question," p. A1.

7. Ibid.

8. Ibid.

9. Ibid.

10. Ibid.

11. Goleman, D. *Emotional Intelligence.* New York: Bantam Books, 1995, p. 145.

12. Floyd, *Listening,* pp. 2–8.

13. Sperry Corporation. *Your Personal Listening Profile,* 1981.

14. Nichols and Stevens, *Are You Listening?* p. 15.

15. Landry, D. L. "The Neglect of Listening." *Elementary English* 46 (1969), 599–605.

16. Hymowitz, Carol. "If the Walls Had Ears, You Wouldn't Have Any Less Privacy." *Wall Street Journal,* May 19, 1998, p. B-1.

17. This collection of ineffective listening habits was assembled from ideas presented in Nichols and Stevens, *Are You Listening?* "Listening is a 10-Part Skill," pp. 472–479; and Floyd, *Listening,* pp. 2–3. See also Alessandra and Hunsaker, *Communicating at Work.* New York: Simon & Schuster, 1993, pp. 54–68.

18. This collection of effective listening habits was assembled from ideas presented in Sperry Corporation, *Your Personal Listening Profile.* See also Floyd, *Listening;* and Alessandra and Hunsaker, *Communicating at Work,* pp. 54–68.

19. Carvell, T. "By the Way . . . Your Staff Hates You." *Fortune,* September 28, 1998, pp. 200–212.

20. Floyd, J. J., *Listening,* pp. 34–43.

21. For a discussion of the role feedback plays in theoretical communication models, consult Rogers, Everett M. *A History of Communication Study.* New York, NY: The Free Press, 1997, pp. 396–399.

22. Claiborne, Robert. *Our Marvelous Native Tongue: The Life and Times of the English Language.* New York, NY: Times Books, 1983, pp. 3–24.

23. Hymowitz, Carol, "If the Walls Had Ears," p. B-1.

24. For an extended discussion of feedback technique and applications, see Wolvin and Coakley, *Listening,* pp. 97–99, 214–219, and 223–238.

25. For a discussion of feedback applications in the workplace, see Alessandra and Hunsaker, *Communicating at Work,* pp. 79–90.

For Further Reading

Burley-Allen, M. *Listening: The Forgotten Skill (A Self-Teaching Guide),* 2nd ed. New York, NY: John Wiley & Sons, 1995.

Robertson, K. "Mind Your Listening Manners." *The Toastmaster,* Vol. 64, No. 7 (July 1998), 15.

◇♫

Case 6–1A   EARL'S FAMILY RESTAURANTS: THE ROLE OF THE REGIONAL SALES MANAGER

Among the more difficult to master, yet less obvious of human communication skills is that of listening. For many managers, listening often seems more of a luxury than a necessity. Time is short, pressures to accomplish work goals are substantial, and communication takes on a one-way character: It's my job to speak; it's your job to listen.

As managers rise from junior to more senior positions in an organization, they gradually discover that more and more of their time is spent in interpersonal communication, face-to-face with subordinates, peers, and superiors. They are less task oriented, more process oriented. Gathering information is far less difficult than figuring out what it means.

The key to many management problems often lies in another's perspective. Finding out what others think of an issue, how they view the matter at hand, is frequently useful to a manager. The danger lies in wasted time or misspent effort in such conversations. Somehow learning to make listening a more structured, productive activity becomes increasingly important to managers who have the talent and the will to succeed.

Listening and hearing are not the same thing. Surprisingly, most North American adults listen at an efficiency rate of no more than 25 percent. Yet much of what we need to make decisions, to understand our circumstances, and to solve the problems we face comes to us in an aural form.

Becoming an active listener, a reflective, skilled communicator is not easy, but it's certainly within reach for the average manager. Acknowledging bad listening habits is a good way to begin the process, systematically replacing such habits with productive, useful listening skills. Knowing that it's possible to become more skilled in this process makes listening one of the central talents that managers must concentrate on early in their careers.

THE ROLE OF THE REGIONAL SALES MANAGER

The case of Earl's Family Restaurants involves two roles, each played from a different perspective. One is the regional sales manager for a food service manufacturing firm in the midwestern United States; the other is the chief buyer for a mid-size chain of restaurants, also in the Midwest.

The facts of this case are the same for both participants. As is usual, though, both people see the facts through slightly different eyes. Each has a perspective unique to the position he or she occupies, and each has a set of objectives and goals that accompany the job. As you read the relevant facts in this case and assume your role, keep in mind that you are evaluated by your supervisor on the extent to which you can achieve those job-related goals. Keep in mind, as well, that communication may be one of the tools you can use to reach your objectives.

YOUR TASK

Please read and familiarize yourself with the information in this case. You have been selected to participate in a role-playing exercise designed to demonstrate the importance of communication skills in practical everyday human interaction. Your portion of this exercise involves *only* the role of the regional sales manager for Exceptional Food Products, Inc.

Make whatever assumptions you need to in order to play your role, but be convincing as you create your character. The other person involved in this exercise knows many of the same facts about the incident, but may have a different perspective on those facts. Do your best to communicate effectively.

THE FACTS OF THE CASE

You are the regional sales manager for Exceptional Food Products, Inc. of Chicago. You have seven territorial sales representatives who work directly for you, covering a five-state area in the midwestern United States. Your region includes Illinois, Wisconsin, Iowa, Michigan, and Indiana. Your seven-person team handles more than 200 accounts; you have reserved several, special accounts for yourself and you handle those customers personally.

Among your more important accounts, both in dollar volume and in years of service, is Earl's Family Restaurants. Your grandfather, who established Exceptional Food Products, Inc., was a personal friend of Mr. Earl Tolliver of Indianapolis, the founder of Earl's Family Restaurants. Your two families have been doing business together for many years.

About six weeks ago, because of the growing volume of work in your office, you felt it safe to assign the account to your most successful territorial sales representative. This individual is relatively new to restaurant food sales, but seems bright, energetic, and eager to succeed. He took the account gladly and, for the moment at least, appears to be doing well with it.

Exceptional Food Products, Inc. provides a full range of packaged goods to restaurants, clubs, schools, institutions, and military installations throughout the country. Your region is one of the more important to the firm and, occasionally, your team leads the nation in sales volume. Your team regularly leads in market penetration. In recent months, however, problems have begun to arise. Customers have complained to delivery people, to your territorial sales representatives and, lately, to you.

Institutional complaints have not been as frequent or as great as restaurant complaints, but they're growing. Among the more routine complaints is one that alleges customers aren't getting what they ordered. On occasion, delivery people will leave a substitute product or two

without notifying the restaurant or seeking permission to do so. Deliveries have been late in recent days to a number of customers; your boss tells you a Teamster's job action (a work-to-rule slowdown) in the transportation division and some maintenance problems have slowed things down. That should improve soon, though, he says.

You have lost some customers in recent months to several new market entrants. They seem strongly customer-oriented and are working hard to take away your business. One of the top people in finance at Exceptional Food Products, Inc. tells you that your top new competitor is now a subsidiary of a very large firm, Cub Foods, Inc., that is engaging in a deliberate policy of undercutting you on price. They're willing to lose money for an unspecified period of time in order to push you out of several lucrative markets. Frankly, this is a worrisome development.

The chief buyer for Earl's Family Restaurants has called and asked to meet with you. He is concerned about a number of things that have happened recently and he concludes the phone conversation with this: "Look, if you guys can't do any better than you've done over the past six weeks, we may just have to look somewhere else for a supplier."

Your objective in meeting with the buyer from Earl's is to save that account for Exceptional Food Products and, if possible, convince him that you will be able to beat the competition on both price and service before long. You simply cannot afford to lose this account—it means nearly 15 percent of total sales for the region.

From your perspective, the problems in this case are primarily—though not entirely—about cost. You are under pressure to cut costs yet deliver the most competitively priced products possible to restaurants that face narrow margins and tough competition.

This case was prepared from public sources by James S. O'Rourke, concurrent associate professor of management, as the basis for class discussion rather than to illustrate either effective or ineffective handling of an administrative situation. Personal and corporate identities have been disguised.

☙

Case 6–1B EARL'S FAMILY RESTAURANTS: THE ROLE OF THE CHIEF BUYER

Among the more difficult to master, yet less obvious of human communication skills is that of listening. For many managers, listening often seems more of a luxury than a necessity. Time is short, pressures to accomplish work goals are substantial, and communication takes on a one-way character: It's my job to speak, it's your job to listen.

As managers rise from junior to more senior positions in an organization, they gradually discover that more and more of their time is spent in interpersonal communication, face-to-face with subordinates, peers, and superiors. They are less task-oriented, more process-oriented. Gathering information is far less difficult than figuring out what it means.

The key to many management problems often lies in another's perspective. Finding out what others think of an issue, how they view the matter at hand, is frequently useful to a manager. The danger lies in wasted time or misspent effort in such conversations. Somehow learning to make listening a more structured, productive activity becomes increasingly important to managers who have the talent and the will to succeed.

Listening and hearing are not the same thing. Surprisingly, most North American adults listen at an efficiency rate of no more than 25 percent. Yet much of what we need to make decisions, to understand our circumstances, and to solve the problems we face comes to us in an aural form.

Becoming an active listener, a reflective, skilled communicator is not easy, but it's certainly within reach for the average manager. Acknowledging bad listening habits is a good way to begin the process, systematically replacing such habits with productive, useful listening skills. Knowing that it's possible to become more skilled in this process makes listening one of the central talents that managers must concentrate on early in their careers.

THE ROLE OF THE CHIEF BUYER

The case of Earl's Family Restaurants involves two roles, each played from a different perspective. One is the regional sales manager for a food service manufacturing firm in the midwestern United States; the other is the chief buyer for a mid-size chain of restaurants, also in the Midwest.

The facts of this case are the same for both participants. As is usual, though, both people see the facts through slightly different eyes. Each has a perspective unique to the position he or she occupies, and each has a set of objectives and goals that accompany the job. As you read the relevant facts in this case and assume your role, keep in mind that you are evaluated by your supervisor on the extent to which you can achieve those job-related goals. Keep in mind, as well, that communication may be one of the tools you can use to reach your objectives.

YOUR TASK

Please read and familiarize yourself with the information in this case. You have been selected to participate in a role-playing exercise designed to demonstrate the importance of communication skills in practical everyday human interaction. Your portion of this exercise involves *only* the role of the chief buyer for Earl's Family Restaurants.

Make whatever assumptions you need to in order to play your role, but be convincing as you create your character. The other person involved in this exercise knows many of the same facts about the incident, but may have a different perspective on those facts. Do your best to communicate effectively.

THE FACTS OF THE CASE

You are the chief buyer for Earl's Family Restaurants of Indianapolis. Your 54-restaurant chain extends throughout the Midwestern United States, with most of your establishments concentrated in Illinois, Indiana, Michigan, and Wisconsin. You have a few restaurants in Kentucky and Ohio. Your firm is publicly held, but the majority shareholder is Earl Tolliver, III, grandson of the restaurant chain's founder. You have been closely associated with the family for many years and have been employed with the firm since you left business school.

Exceptional Food Products, Inc. of Chicago is one of your principal suppliers of packaged goods. You buy most of your condiments, table supplies, canned and packaged restaurant supplies from them. They have done well for you and your firm for many years. Lately, though, you've had some trouble with Exceptional Food Products.

For one thing, your account was assigned about six weeks ago by the regional sales manager at Exceptional Food Products to a territorial sales representative. This person is loud, obnoxious, rarely available, and doesn't seem to know your business particularly well. This sales rep is new to the area and has been in the food business for just three years.

You could put up with this new salesperson if it were just the personality that seemed to get in the way of a good working relationship. After all, there is no interaction with your customers; the only contact is with you and your central buying office. Lately though, other, more serious problems have arisen. Shipments have been late. Often, Exceptional Food Products will show up late on Fridays at your restaurants in northern Indiana and southwest lower Michigan, just in the nick of time to restock for the weekends. Friday nights, Saturdays, and Sunday breakfasts are typically your busiest times, both in volume and cash flow.

On several occasions, Friday deliveries in South Bend, Benton Harbor, Grand Rapids, and Fort Wayne have simply been postponed until Monday. Last weekend, your Benton Harbor restaurant ran out of several crucial condiments and had to telephone the South Bend restaurant and ask for an emergency transfer by automobile.

Lately, Exceptional Food Products has pulled another clever stunt on you by leaving substitute brands that you didn't order. When your restaurant managers confront the delivery person, he simply says: "Look, here's what's on the invoice. I got no control over what the invoice says or what they load on my truck. I'm just here to deliver what they tell me to deliver."

Your restaurant managers have been stuck with generic labels and off-brands when they clearly specified the national brand of several products. Worse, you have been billed for the national brand. You regard that as a kind of double-whammy: inferior products at name-brand prices. Your contacts with the new territorial sales representative have been entirely unsatisfactory. You would really like to do business with the regional sales manager once again, but have had trouble getting together. You have called Exceptional Food Products, Inc. and asked for a meeting with the regional sales manager from Chicago.

Your objective is to let these people know, in no uncertain terms, that their behavior has been unacceptable. You have spent far too much time and money straightening out the account with them and you want them to know that Exceptional Foods is causing more grief than your restaurant managers need.

From your perspective, the problems are entirely about the relationship between the supplier and your company, and are focused on deficiencies in service. Exceptional Foods' task, in your view, is to make life easier for your managers, not harder. If things don't turn around soon, you're considering taking your business to another supplier. The fact that you have been doing business with Exceptional Foods for longer than anyone can remember makes no difference to you or to the Tolliver family. Business is business.

One last item: *Don't* let the sales manager go until you get an apology from their firm for their behavior. You want their service (and their prices) to improve, but you really want them to recognize what they have done to your business, and an apology is in order.

❧

Case 6–1C EARL'S FAMILY RESTAURANTS: THE ROLE OF THE OBSERVER

Among the more difficult to master, yet less obvious of human communication skills is that of listening. For many managers, listening often seems more of a luxury than a necessity. Time is short, pressures to accomplish work goals are substantial, and communication takes on a one-way character: It's my job to speak; it's your job to listen.

As managers rise from junior to more senior positions in an organization, they gradually discover that more and more of their time is spent in interpersonal communication, face-to-face with subordinates, peers, and superiors. They are less task-oriented, more process-oriented. Gathering information is far less difficult than figuring out what it means.

The key to many management problems often lies in another's perspective. Finding out what others think of an issue, how they view the matter at hand, is frequently useful to a manager. The danger lies in wasted time or misspent effort in such conversations. Somehow learning to make listening a more structured, productive activity becomes increasingly important to managers who have the talent and the will to succeed.

Listening and hearing are not the same thing. Surprisingly, most North American adults listen at an efficiency rate of no more than 25 percent. Yet much of what we need to make decisions, to understand our circumstances, and to solve the problems we face comes to us in an aural form.

Becoming an active listener, a reflective, skilled communicator is not easy, but it's certainly within reach for the average manager. Acknowledging bad listening habits is a good way to begin the process, systematically replacing such habits with productive, useful listening skills. Knowing that it's possible to become more skilled in this process makes listening one of the central talents that managers must concentrate on early in their careers.

THE ROLE OF THE OBSERVER

The case of Earl's Family Restaurants involves two roles, each played from a different perspec-
tive. One is the regional sales manager for a food service manufacturing firm in the midwestern United States; the other is the chief buyer for a mid-size chain of restaurants, also in the Midwest.

The facts of this case are the same for both participants. As is usual, though, both people see the facts through slightly different eyes. Each has a perspective unique to the position he or she occupies, and each has a set of objectives and goals that accompany the job. As you read the relevant facts in this case and assume your role, keep in mind that you are evaluated by your supervisor on the extent to which you can achieve those job-related goals. Keep in mind, as well, that communication may be one of the tools you can use to reach your objectives.

YOUR TASK

Please read and familiarize yourself with the information in this case. You have been selected to observe a role-playing exercise that is designed to demonstrate the importance of communication skills in practical everyday human interaction. Your task is to observe what happens during the conversation between two people playing the roles of the chief buyer for Earl's Family Restaurants and the regional sales manager for Exceptional Food Products, Inc.

Observe and take note of as much as you can during the conversation. Pay particular attention to both verbal and nonverbal communication issues. Note the direction and pace of the conversation. Who takes the lead in speaking? Who responds? What's the general tone of the exchange? Is this a conversation among friends? Are these people colleagues or business partners in a successful enterprise?

What's the nature of the relationship between these two people? Does either participant emerge from the conversation having achieved the goals they had set for themselves in advance? Does this exchange between two people involve winners and losers, or are they able to accommodate each other's needs to reach a satisfactory compromise?

THE PERSPECTIVE OF THE REGIONAL SALES MANAGER

The regional sales manager for Exceptional Food Products manages the work of seven territorial sales representatives over a five-state area in the midwestern United States. That seven-person team handles more than 200 accounts. Among the more important of those accounts, both in dollar volume and in years of service, is Earl's Family Restaurants.

About six weeks ago, because of growing volume, the regional sales manager assigned the Earl's Family Restaurant account to a successful territorial sales representative. This individual is new to restaurant food sales, but seems bright, energetic, and eager to succeed. From the sales manager's perspective, the new rep seems to be doing well with the account.

Exceptional Food Products, Inc. provides a full range of packaged goods to restaurants, clubs, schools, institutions, and military installations throughout the country. The midwestern region is one of the more important to the firm and, occasionally, leads the nation in sales volume. This sales team, in fact, regularly leads in market penetration. In recent months, however, problems have begun to arise. Customers have complained to delivery people, to sales reps, and lately, to the sales manager.

Institutional complaints have not been as frequent or as great as restaurant complaints, but they are growing. Among the more routine complaints is one that alleges customers aren't getting what they ordered. On occasion, delivery people will leave a substitute product or two without notifying the restaurant or seeking permission to do so. Delivery truck drivers seem to feel that an occasional substitution is preferable to not delivering a much-needed product.

Deliveries have been late in recent days to a number of customers; the regional sales manager has been told by the national sales manager that a Teamster's job action (a work-to-rule slow-down) in the transportation division, along with some maintenance problems, have slowed things down. According to company officials, that should improve soon.

The company has lost some customers in recent months to new market entrants. They seem strongly customer-oriented and are working hard to take away business. A top new competitor is a subsidiary of a very large firm, Cub Foods, Inc., and they are engaging in a deliberate policy of undercutting Exceptional Food Products, Inc., on price. They're willing to lose money for an unspecified period of time in order to push Exceptional Foods out of several lucrative markets. This is a worrisome development.

The chief buyer for Earl's Family Restaurants has called and asked to meet directly with the regional sales manager for Exceptional Food Products. He is concerned about a number of things that have happened recently and he concludes the conversation with this: "Look, if you guys can't do any better than you've done over the past six weeks, we may just have to look somewhere else for a supplier."

From the regional sales manager's perspective, the problems are entirely about cost. The sales manager is under pressure to cut costs yet deliver the lowest-priced products possible to restaurants that face narrow margins and tough competition.

THE PERSPECTIVE OF THE CHIEF BUYER

The chief buyer for Earl's Family Restaurants resides in Indianapolis and supervises purchasing for a 54-restaurant chain located throughout the midwestern United States. The firm is publicly held, but the majority shareholder is Earl Tolliver, III, grandson of the company's founder. The chief buyer, incidentally, is married to a member of the Tolliver family and has been with the company since graduating from college.

Exceptional Food Products, Inc., of Chicago is one of the company's principal suppliers of packaged goods. The company buys most of its condiments, table supplies, canned and packaged restaurant supplies from them. They have done well for Earl's Family Restaurants for many years. Lately, though, the company has experienced trouble with Exceptional Foods.

One bone of contention is the assignment of a new sales representative at Exceptional Foods to the account. For many years, the regional sales manager had personally overseen the Earl's account. And, from the perspective of Earl's chief buyer, the new sales rep is loud, obnoxious, never available when needed, and doesn't seem to know the restaurant business particularly well. The new sales rep, in fact, has been in this business for just three years.

Lately, more serious problems have arisen. Shipments have been late. Often, Exceptional Food Products will show up late on Fridays at Earl's restaurants, just in the nick of time to restock for the weekends. Friday nights, Saturdays, and Sunday breakfasts are typically the company's busiest times, both in volume and cash flow. On several occasions, deliveries have been postponed until Monday.

One other contentious issue is the delivery of generic labels and off-brands when the customer clearly specified the national brand of several products. Worse, Earl's has been billed for the national brand. The chief buyer has heard and seen enough and has asked for a personal meeting with the regional sales manager for Exceptional Foods. From the chief buyer's perspective, the problems are entirely about the relationship between the supplier and the restaurant chain, and are focused on deficiencies in service.

This case was prepared from public sources by James S. O'Rourke, concurrent associate professor of management, as the basis for class discussion rather than to illustrate either effective or ineffective handling of an administrative situation. Personal and corporate identities have been disguised.

☙

Case 6–2A THE KROGER COMPANY: THE ROLE OF THE STORE MANAGER

Among the more difficult to master, yet less obvious of human communication skills is that of providing feedback to others in the workplace. For many managers, feedback must often wait for specified, formal counseling occasions, such as a performance review. Time is short, pressures to accomplish work goals are substantial, and communication often takes on a one-way character: feedback is used, not to improve communication, but to correct job-related performance issues.

As managers rise from junior to more senior positions in an organization, they gradually discover that more and more of their time is spent in interpersonal communication, face-to-face with subordinates, peers, and superiors. They are less task-oriented, more process-oriented. Gathering information is far less difficult than figuring out what it means.

The key to many management problems often lies in another's perspective. Finding out what others think of an issue, how they view the matter at hand, is frequently useful to a manager. The danger lies in wasted time or misspent effort in such conversations. Somehow learning to make feedback a more structured, productive activity becomes increasingly important to managers who have the talent and the will to succeed.

Feedback is more than simply sending messages or issuing orders. Often, the process involves soliciting information from others so that you can first understand their perspective or point of view. Then, under planned and carefully controlled conditions, information regarding both performance and communication can assist both managers and subordinates in achieving organizational goals.

Knowing that it's possible to become more skilled in this process is the first step. Recognizing that, managers must concentrate early and often at improving their ability to both solicit from and provide feedback to others.

THE ROLE OF THE STORE MANAGER

This case involves two roles, each played from a different perspective. One is the manager of a mid-size Kroger store in the Louisville Kroger Marketing Area. The other is the sales manager for a local Pepsi-Cola bottler.

The facts in this case are the same for both participants. As is usual, though, both people see the facts through slightly different eyes. Each has a perspective unique to the position he or she occupies, and each has a set of objectives and goals that accompany the job. As you read the relevant facts in this case and assume your role, keep in mind that you are evaluated by your supervisor on the extent to which you can achieve those job-related goals. Keep in mind, as well, that communication may be one of the tools you can use to reach your objectives.

YOUR TASK

Please read and familiarize yourself with the information contained in this case. You have been selected to participate in a role-playing exercise designed to demonstrate the importance of communication skills in practical everyday human interaction. Make whatever assumptions you need to in order to play your role, but be convincing as you create your character. The other person involved in this exercise knows many of the same facts about the incident, but may have a different perspective on those facts. Do your best to communicate effectively.

THE FACTS OF THE CASE

You are the manager of the Rosewater, Kentucky, Kroger store, a mid-size store that's been in operation for seven years. The store is profitable and has shown strong sales growth over the past three years, despite competition from two other regional chains, one of which opened a year ago, and another which has been in place for five years.

You have been in the retail food business for 11 years, serving as manager of the Rosewater store for the past three months. This is your first store manager's job and you are determined to show the Louisville marketing director that you have management potential.

Soft drink vendors have long been difficult to deal with for several reasons: First, they supply you with high-turn items that are nationally advertised and very popular with your customers; second, they are in constant competition with their rivals for display and shelf space; and, finally, soft drink vendors are often under great pressure from their distributors to push the product.

The local Pepsi-Cola sales manager is a fellow named Roger Willis. He works for a company called Southland Beverages, Inc., and is well-known within the company for moving high volumes of product, but for his temper, as well. His drivers rarely speak back to him and are under considerable pressure to comply with his tight schedules, large delivery loads, and nearly impossible quotas. You have spoken with Mr. Willis several times on the telephone but have not yet met him in person.

You can deal with the drivers; after all, they have to earn a living, too, and most of them do a fine job of keeping your store stocked with fresh products at regular intervals. The local Pepsi vendor, however, is another story. Over the past six months his drivers have routinely dropped products you don't want on your loading dock, they're often late with deliveries, they have left quantities you can't sell, and they have been entirely uncooperative with your receiving staff on the dock. Often, they're just rude.

As you ask one of your department heads what happened last Friday, he tells a story that other Kroger employees regard as familiar. "We had a new route man for Pepsi last week and this guy just wouldn't listen to us."

"How so?" you ask. "What'd he do?"

"Well," your employee replies, "in the first place, he dropped nine flats, instead of the three that we asked for. Most of the order was 12-packs, and we're running low on 6-packs. And he arrived right at a shift change, so nobody was really able to spend much time with him."

"What did you say?"

"When I saw nine flats, I asked him 'Why so many?' He just said, 'I'm stocking you up for the weekend.' Man, I'm tellin' you, we couldn't sell nine flats in a week, much less by Monday."

You pause for a moment, then ask, "Did you ask him to re-load six of those flats on the truck?"

Your department head replies, "I sure did, but he said 'Look, here's what's on the invoice. I got no control over what the invoice says or what they load in my truck. I'm just here to deliver what they tell me to deliver. Besides, it'd take me half the night to re-slot all this stuff back in the warehouse.'"

"Well," you say, "I think we can fix this."

"That's not all," your employee adds. "He installed that new Pepsi endcap display a week early. The Coke guy saw it this morning and had a fit. He's upset and wants to talk with you about it."

"A couple more phone calls to make," you think to yourself. "I think it's time I met Roger Willis."

YOUR MEETING WITH MR. WILLIS

Your objective is to let Mr. Willis know, in no uncertain terms, that their behavior has been unacceptable. You have spent too much time already dealing with the antics of his drivers. You really want three things from him: First, you want his unconditional assurance that his employees will quit delivering more product than you order and will begin complying with your request for an appropriate product mix.

Second, you want him to arrange for a Southland Beverages, Inc., employee to disassemble the endcap display *today*. Their special promotion isn't scheduled for another week and the display space belongs to another vendor just now. Finally, you want an apology from them for the way they have behaved. Being an assertive business person is one thing; being rude and arrogant is another. You want his service to improve, but you also want him to recognize what he is doing to your store, and an apology is in order.

This case was prepared from public sources by James S. O'Rourke, concurrent associate professor of management, as the basis for class discussion rather than to illustrate either effective or ineffective handling of an administrative situation. Personal and corporate identities have been disguised.

Case 6–2B THE KROGER COMPANY: THE ROLE OF THE PEPSI-COLA SALES MANAGER

Among the more difficult to master, yet less obvious of human communication skills is that of providing feedback to others in the workplace. For many managers, feedback must often wait for specified, formal counseling occasions, such as a performance review. Time is short, pressures to accomplish work goals are substantial, and communication often takes on a one-way character: feedback is used, not to improve communication, but to correct job-related performance issues.

As managers rise from junior to more senior positions in an organization, they gradually discover that more and more of their time is spent in interpersonal communication, face-to-face with subordinates, peers, and superiors. They are less task-oriented, more process-oriented. Gathering information is far less difficult than figuring out what it means.

The key to many management problems often lies in another's perspective. Finding out what others think of an issue, how they view the matter at hand, is frequently useful to a manager. The danger lies in wasted time or misspent effort in such conversations. Somehow learning to make feedback a more structured, productive activity becomes increasingly important to managers who have the talent and the will to succeed.

Feedback is more than simply sending messages or issuing orders. Often, the process involves soliciting information from others so that you can first understand their perspective or point of view. Then, under planned and carefully controlled conditions, information regarding both performance and communication can assist both managers and subordinates in achieving organizational goals.

Knowing that it's possible to become more skilled in this process is the first step. In recognizing that, managers must concentrate early and often at improving their ability to both solicit from and provide feedback to others.

THE ROLE OF THE PEPSI-COLA SALES MANAGER

You are the territorial sales manager for Southland Beverages, Inc., a nonunion regional Pepsi-Cola bottler. While your firm handles other products—including Mountain Dew and Dr. Pepper—Pepsi-Cola, Diet Pepsi, and Pepsi One are clearly your most important products and account for nearly two-thirds of your company's revenues.

The soft drink business isn't easy. After all, you're in constant competition with the local Coca-Cola bottler, the RC Cola vendor, and another beer and soft drink distributor who sells Seven-Up products. Your margins are narrow, largely because of your cost structure. Most of your expenses come from delivery operations: ownership, maintenance and operation of your delivery fleet and your wage structure. To cut your fixed costs just a bit, you have convinced

your general manager to let you implement a program of driver incentives. Their hourly wages are lower by one-third, but they get a percentage of every product *flat* (a term used to describe a shipping container) they deliver.

Your general manager likes the idea of driver incentives and is pushing you to lower your costs even further with less frequent deliveries. Fewer stops at each retail outlet, combined with longer stock leads will mean lower costs and more profit for Southland. In general, the drivers are happy with the scheme, but they have encountered some resistance from store managers with limited storeroom and loading dock space.

"Keep it up, Roger," says your boss. "You're doin' a great job. I'm really pleased with the way we've been able to get control of our delivery costs."

"Thanks," you say. "I was pretty sure this system would work. Not everybody's happy, but—hey—that's life. Right?" Just as your general manager departs and closes the door to your office, the intercom beeps. It's your assistant, Darleen.

"Mr. Willis? It's Pat Hanson from Kroger on line two."

"Thanks," you say. "Hello. This is Roger Willis."

"Mr. Willis," says the voice on the other end, "this is Pat Hanson in the Rosewater Kroger Store. If you have a few minutes today, I'd really like to meet with you about some problems we've been having. I'd also like to show you something in your Pepsi display area. Can we get together today?"

"I suppose," you say. "How does four o'clock sound? I can be there by four, but I don't have much time."

"This won't take long," Hanson replies. "I'll see you at four."

❧

Case 6–2C THE KROGER COMPANY: THE ROLE OF THE INSTRUCTIONAL FACILITATOR

This case involves two roles, each played from a different perspective. One is the manager of a mid-size Kroger store in the Louisville Kroger marketing area. The other is the sales manager for a local Pepsi-Cola bottler.

Please read and familiarize yourself with the issues addressed in the background note, as well as the facts contained in both roles. The facts in this case are the same for both participants. As is usual, though, both people see the facts through slightly different eyes. Each has a perspective unique to the position he or she occupies, and each has a set of objectives and goals that accompany the job. As you read the relevant facts in this case and assume your role, keep in mind that you are evaluated by your supervisor on the extent to which you can achieve those job-related goals. Keep in mind, as well, that communication may be one of the tools you can use to reach your objectives.

YOUR TASK

Your task is to facilitate a role-playing exercise designed to demonstrate the importance of communication skills in practical everyday human interaction. Make whatever assumptions you need to in order to assist the role players, but be flexible as they create their characters and play out the details of the case. Each person involved in this exercise knows basically the same facts about the incident, but each has a slightly different perspective on those facts.

Before the Role-play Begins. Select two members of the class who would be willing to participate in a role-playing exercise. You can either ask the class as a whole for volunteers, or you can select two people based on your knowledge of their personality, cooperativeness, and communication skill.

Give one copy of the store manager's role to one person and one copy of the Pepsi-Cola

sales manager's role to the other. Have each person read their roles separately. If possible, give out the roles the day before you plan to conduct this exercise.

Please ask the two students who have agreed to participate in this exercise *not to read the other role player's role.* Ask that they confine their reading only to the role they've been assigned, and to play the role with sincerity and conviction. Please ask them, as well, not to collaborate or to share information with each other. The success of this exercise depends, in part, on each person seeing the communication situation from his or her own perspective.

As the Role-play Begins. Tell all members of the class that two of their classmates have volunteered (or were selected) to participate in a communication exercise. Ask them all to observe carefully and, if they care to, take notes on what they see and hear. Then, tell the two role players to simulate the first meeting between the Kroger store manager and the Pepsi-Cola sales manager, beginning with introductions.

As the two role players begin, step back and observe the interaction carefully. They shouldn't be reading from their case instructions, but should assume the manners and actions of their character directly. Let the interaction go on for as long as you think it is productive. Most volunteers will play the character roles with enthusiasm and conviction and will carry the meeting through to some logical conclusion. If your players become frustrated, angry, or confused, *step in and stop the roleplay.*

When the Role-play Concludes. Take control of the classroom once again and, before you do anything else, thank the players for their time, effort, and talent. A small round of applause usually makes each of them feel better about the experience. Then, ask the class as a whole about several issues.

1. *Cognitive Listening.* What *facts* arose during the discussion? Did either of the players come to the meeting with differing *assumptions?* Where did the discussions begin? Did either player ask the other to back up and review any details?

2. *Affective Listening.* What *emotions* arose during the discussion? Were either of the players angry, frustrated, or upset? Did each maintain a professional manner? Were they courteous to one another? Did either player change his or her emotional tone as a result of the meeting?

3. *Nonverbal Listening.* What was the *body posture* and *gesturing* like during the interaction? Did both players exhibit open posture with arms unfolded, palms open or uplifted? Was the nonverbal communication essentially negative: arms folded, body posture at an angle, head down? What happened with *eye contact* during the meeting? Did both players look directly at each other, or did one search the ceiling or floor during the conversation? How close were they to one another? Did one of them back away

from the other at some point? Did one interrupt the other at any point?

4. *Listening for Meaning.* Did each player understand the other? Did they work from the same set of intentions? Did both players reach some sort of mutually satisfactory agreement by the end of the meeting? What could each of them have done to make the meeting more successful? Give each member of the class an opportunity to comment and then observe that, while no two conversations are ever the same (different people, different subjects, different moments), a number of basic considerations can make each of us more effective listeners and, ultimately, communicators.

5. *Quality of Feedback.* Look for the quality of feedback provided by each participant in the exercise. Is the information being exchange of any real value to the other participant in the conversation? Does emotion contribute to success in the exercise or hinder success? Is each participant saying and doing those things which will most likely lead to a successful resolution of the dispute?

Case 6–3   THREE FEEDBACK EXERCISES

Organize the class into groups of three people each. Two people in each group will play roles defined for them in the exercises. The third person in each group will serve as the observer/ recorder. The instructor should take 3 to 4 minutes to explain the role-playing exercise and assign roles to each of the participants.

Participants should take 10 to 12 minutes to read the exercise requirements and play their respective roles. Each group observer/recorder should then take 2 to 3 minutes to brief their observations to the entire class.

FEEDBACK EXERCISE #1: THE DISGRUNTLED ANALYST

RELATIONSHIP: A supervisor and an employee who reports directly to him or her.

CONTEXT: You are an employee who joined the company eighteen months ago as an entry-level analyst. You have a bachelor's degree in finance and some prior work experience in sales. You had other job offers but accepted this one because you though it would offer the greatest challenge and most opportunity for growth and advancement. You are now no longer the most junior employee in the organization; others with similar education but less experience are assigned to your division.

THE ANALYST: You feel that you are stuck doing all of the most basic grunt work in the division: gathering and organizing data sets that everyone uses, dealing with ground-level maintenance problems, and producing report documents that newer employees can claim credit for but contribute less to.

THE SUPERVISOR: You think the analyst is doing acceptable work, but it's far from top-level performance. During the past 30 days, you have had to counsel this individual twice about late "after market" reports and misrouted reports. You think this person might eventually make a good trader, but first must "grow up" and begin accepting responsibility on the job.

FEEDBACK EXERCISE #2: THE WITHHOLDING COWORKER

RELATIONSHIP: Two coworkers who both report to the same supervisor.

CONTEXT: You and a coworker are members of the same marketing department in a *Fortune 500* firm. You have worked closely with this other person for the past eight months and have developed a casual relationship outside of working hours. You both enjoy your work, seem to like the company and the industry, and are dedicated to seeing your organization succeed. One of the reasons you like the work is that others who have preceded you in these positions have quickly moved on to "bigger and better things" within the company.

ISSUE: You feel that your coworker does not share information with you that is essential for you to be an effective department member. You suspect, in fact, that your coworker may occasionally withhold information (changes in team meeting times and locations, scheduling details, feedback from field visits) so that you don't look as good in the eyes of your supervisor. You have asked to meet with your coworker to talk about this.

FEEDBACK EXERCISE #3: THE IMPERILED LINE EXTENSION

RELATIONSHIP: Two coworkers who report to different superiors.

CONTEXT: You and another employee who is about your age work in different divisions of a large packaged goods firm. You have been assigned to work on a product line extension together. Your target launch date is eight months from now. Needless to say, a considerable amount of time, effort, and money are being devoted to the success of this project.

ISSUE: You feel that your coworker (from another division) has simply not cooperated with you in gathering the information you'll need to make your launch window. Unless you can secure the cooperation of this person, key issues, including packaging, transportation, advertising and promotion, and retailer incentives, may be in jeopardy. You have asked to meet with your coworker to talk it over.

This case was prepared from public sources by James S. O'Rourke, concurrent associate professor of management, as the basis for class discussion rather than to illustrate either effective or ineffective handling of an administrative situation. Personal and corporate identities have been disguised.

7

COMMUNICATING
NONVERBALLY

⤫

Getting dressed for work used to be a snap for executive Ron Demczak. Then his company went casual—every day. With 30 suits and little else in his closet, Demczak spent several thousand dollars buying a new, sporty wardrobe. He learned to call ahead to clients to make sure he didn't wear corduroys when they were wearing suits. And he dreaded the mornings.

"I hated it because every morning I had to have my wife match new outfits to wear," said Demczak. He is the liaison for U.S. customers of drugmaker Warner-Lambert. "Now," he adds, "I'm getting a little better at it."[1]

He's not alone. Robert Park is a manager at Ernst & Young, LLP in northern California. For his firm the switch to full-time casual dress was spurred by a desire to blend in. In that region, the accounting firm's clients were mostly from Silicon Valley, where software engineers and other young techies practically invented casual office wear. "We used to stick out like sore thumbs, being the only ones in suits and ties," he said. "Everybody knew we had to be the accountants or the bankers."

Still, Park keeps a traditional wardrobe for use when meeting outsiders who expect suits and ties. Some managers even stow suits in their cars so they won't be uncomfortably surprised. "That's when it gets complicated," said Wendy Liebmann, president of WSL Strategic Retail consultants. "Do I go by my code or theirs?"[2]

Why would executives feel uncomfortable in casual clothes? What's so complicated or difficult about being dressed differently from others you're doing business with? The answers to these and thousands of other questions about how humans interact with one another is related directly to how we communicate. And for Ms. Liebmann, Mr. Park, and everyone else in the workplace, the questions they are asking have very little to do with language and a great deal to do with *nonverbal communication.*

If I look you directly in the eyes while we're speaking is that a sign of respect or defiance? If you stare at a new employee while she's eating lunch, is that a sign of affection or harassment? When you speak with a friend, how far apart should you stand? How close should you be when the boss asks you a question? If the boss reaches out to pat you on the shoulder, would it be acceptable for you to reciprocate?

Some workplaces, like the commodities exchange, encourage people to speak up and raise their voices. Others demand quiet. Some offices provide private space with doors that close, while others simply push desks together in huge, open rooms. In many instances, understanding what coworkers mean when they speak depends on your ability to understand whether they're being serious, sarcastic, or humorous.

How can so much information be conveyed without using language? And, perhaps more importantly, how can one person possibly understand all the rules? What means one thing here may very well mean something else there, and what's seen as harmless in one company may be strictly forbidden in another. Clearly, understanding nonverbal communication is not simply useful for a manager. It's essential.

A FEW BASIC CONSIDERATIONS

Communication experts have established the fact that less than a third of the meaning transferred from one person to another in a personal conversation comes from the words that are spoken. The majority of meaning comes from nonverbal sources, including body movement; eye contact; gestures; posture; vocal tone, pitch, pacing, and phrasing. Other messages come from our clothing, our use of time, and literally dozens of other nonverbal categories. Learning how to read and understand such wordless messages isn't easy, but may be essential to understanding everyone from your customers to your supervisor to your spouse.

Nonverbal communication is widely regarded as the transfer of meaning without using verbal symbols. That is, *nonverbal* refers in a literal sense to those actions, objects, and contexts that either communicate directly or facilitate communication without using words.[3] As communication professionals and casual observers alike will testify, though, separating the effects of verbal and nonverbal behavior is never easy, largely because they tend to reinforce each other, contradict each other, or are in some way *about* each other.

It's also important to note that, with the exception of emotional displays and certain facial expressions, virtually all nonverbal communication is culturally based. That is, we learn to behave and communicate in certain ways, and to interpret the meanings of those behaviors, as we grow up in our culture. Being *enculturated,* as we will see in the next chapter, means acquiring values, beliefs, possessions, behaviors, and ways of thinking that are acceptable to others and, in fact, expected of us as members of our society. So, what may be strictly forbidden in one culture—exposing an adult woman's face to strangers in public—may be perfectly normal in another. As members of a global community, we must not only learn and abide by the rules of the society we grew up in, but also come to understand and appreciate the rules of other societies, as well.

NONVERBAL CATEGORIES

In a series of early studies of nonverbal communication,[4] communication researchers outlined three basic categories of nonverbal language.

Sign Language   This can be as simple as the extended thumb of the hitchhiker or as complex as the complete system of sign language for the deaf.

Action Language   This includes all movements that are not used exclusively for communicating. Walking, for example, serves the functional purpose of moving us from one place to another, but it can also communicate, as when we decide to get up and walk out of a meeting.

Object Language   This includes all objects, materials, artifacts, and things—ranging from jewelry, clothing, and make-up to automobiles, furniture, and artwork—that we use in our daily lives. Such things, including our own bodies, can communicate, whether we intend them to or not.

THE NONVERBAL PROCESS

Nonverbal communication is really a three-step process involving a cue, our own expectations, and an inference.

Cue   We look first for a wordless cue—a motion, perhaps, or an object. On arriving at work, you notice a coworker who is glum, sullen, and withdrawn. You say "Good morning," but he doesn't reply.

Expectation   We then match the cue against our expectations, asking what seems reasonable or what seems obvious, based on our prior experiences. Since your coworker is normally cheerful, talkative, and outgoing, your expectations are at odds with the cue you've just perceived.

Inference   Having picked up the cue and measured its importance and meaning against our expectations, we *infer* meaning. Since we can't see an attitude or intention directly, we must draw an inference based on the nonverbal cue and our own expectations. Given the cue and our expectations of this particular coworker, we conclude that he's unhappy, upset, or depressed for some reason. Note that this conclusion is based on observation alone and not an exchange of verbal information between two people. If we are careful and observant, we can learn a great deal without the use of language. We should be careful, though, because our confidence often exceeds our ability when it comes to accurately interpreting nonverbal cues.

READING AND MISREADING NONVERBAL CUES

"The great majority of us are easily misled," says Dr. Paul Ekman, a psychologist at the University of California at San Francisco. "It's very difficult, and most people just don't know what cues to rely on." To be sure, research shows that people can usually read someone else's feelings from the facial expression. "Most of us are fairly accurate in the rough judgments we make based on nonverbal cues," says Dr. Miles Patterson, editor of the *Journal of Nonverbal Behavior* and a psychologist at the University of Missouri at St. Louis.[5]

The new research is pointing to areas where people's confidence in reading nonverbal cues outstrips their accuracy. In 1991, Dr. Robert Gifford reported finding specific nonverbal clues to such traits as aloofness, gregariousness, and submissiveness. His report, which appeared in the *Journal of Personality and Social Psychology,* also found that though there are such reliable clues about character, "people read much into nonverbal cues that just isn't there, while missing much that is," says Dr. Gifford.[6]

While people are right about their reading of character some of the time, especially for more obvious traits like gregariousness, the problem, according to Dr. Gifford, is that they are overly confident and assume that they are equally adept at reading more subtle aspects of character when they are actually misjudging. For example, in a recent study of people applying for a job, Dr. Gifford had videotapes of the applicants evaluated by 18 seasoned interviewers, most of them personnel officers.

Before going for their interviews, each applicant had taken tests that gauged their degree of social skills and how highly motivated for work they were. The test for motivation, for instance, asked such questions as how willing they would be to work unusual hours if it were necessary. The interviewers were far more accurate about the applicant's self-evident social skills than about their motivation, a more subtle trait important in employment decisions.

The nonverbal cues that made the interviewers decide whether an applicant had high motivation included smiling, gesturing, and talking more than other applicants. In fact, though, none of those nonverbal patterns was a true indicator of motivation. The practical result of such mistakes is that many people are hired on a misreading of their personality traits, only to disappoint their employers. "Social skills are far more visible than motivation, but coming across well in your job interview is no guarantee of other traits that might matter in your day-to-day job performance," Dr. Gilford said. "People are being hired for some of the wrong reasons." While a clever applicant might make a point a smiling, gesturing, and talking a lot during a job interview, a savvy interviewer would be cautious about reading too much into that show of outgoingness.[7]

FUNCTIONS OF NONVERBAL COMMUNICATION

Nonverbal communication can serve any number of important functions in our lives, but researchers have identified these six as major functions.

Accenting Nonverbal communication often highlights or emphasizes some part of a verbal message. A raised eyebrow might accompany an expression of surprise; a waving finger might underscore an expression of disapproval.

Complementing Nonverbal communication also reinforces the general tone or attitude of our verbal communication. A downcast expression and slumping posture might accompany words of discouragement or depression; upright posture, a smile, and animated movement might reinforce a verbal story about winning a recent promotion.

Contradicting Nonverbal communication, on the other hand, can contradict the verbal messages we send, sometimes deliberately, sometimes unintentionally. Tears in our eyes and a quiver in our voices might involuntarily contradict a verbal message telling friends and family that we're doing all right. A wink and a nod might deliberately send the nonverbal message that what we're saying just isn't so. The fact is, when verbal and nonverbal messages contradict, we tend—for a number of reasons—to believe the nonverbal. In the last analysis, it's simply much easier to lie than it is to control a range of nonverbal reactions: our facial expression, pupil dilation in our eyes, tension in our vocal cords, pulse rate, sweating, muscle tone, and many others. Control of such things is, for most of us, well beyond our voluntary reach.

Regulating Certain nonverbal movements and gestures are used to regulate the flow, the pace, and the back-and-forth nature of verbal communication. When I want you to speak to me, I'll face you, open my eyes, open my arms with hands extended and palms facing upward, and look expectantly into your eyes. When I want you to stop speaking so I can either talk or think of what I'm about to say, I will turn slightly away from you, fold my arms, put one hand out with palm facing forward, and either close my eyes or turn them away from yours.

Repeating   Nonverbal messages can also repeat what verbal messages convey. With car keys in hand, coat and hat on, I can announce: "I'm leaving now," as I walk toward the door. You might hold up three fingers as you ask: "Is that the best you can do? I've gotta buy three of them."

Substituting   Nonverbal communication can also substitute for, or take the place of, verbal messages, particularly if they're simple or monosyllabic. As a youngster looks toward a parent on the sidelines during an athletic contest, a quick "thumbs up" can substitute for words of praise or encouragement that might not be heard from a distance or in a noisy crowd.[8]

PRINCIPLES OF NONVERBAL COMMUNICATION

Fifty years of research and five thousand years of human experience with nonverbal communication have identified six principles thought to be universally true.

Nonverbal Communication Occurs in a Context   Just as context is important to the meaning of verbal messages, so is context important to our understanding of nonverbal messages. Folded arms and laid-back posture may mean disinterest or boredom on one occasion, but may signify introspective thought on another. Professor Joseph DeVito of Hunter College says, in fact, that "Divorced from the context, it is impossible to tell what any given bit of nonverbal behavior may mean. . . . In attempting to understand and analyze nonverbal communication . . . it is essential that full recognition be taken of the context."[9]

Nonverbal Behaviors Are Usually Packaged   Nonverbal behavior, according to most researchers, occurs in *packages* or *clusters* in which the various verbal and nonverbal messages occur more or less simultaneously. Body posture, eye contact, arm and leg movement, facial expression, vocal tone, pacing and phrasing of vocal expressions, muscle tone, and numerous other elements of nonverbal communication happen at once. It's difficult to isolate one element of the cluster from another without taking all of them into account.

Nonverbal Behavior Always Communicates   All behavior communicates and, since it is literally impossible not to behave in some way, we are always communicating, even when we aren't speaking with or listening to others. Even the least significant of your behaviors, such as your posture, the position of your mouth, or the way you've tucked (or failed to tuck) in your shirt say something about your professionalism to others around you. Other people may not interpret those behaviors in the same way, or in the way you might want them to, but like it or not, you're always communicating, even if you're just sitting there "doing nothing." Doing nothing, in fact, may communicate volumes about your attitude.

Nonverbal Behavior Is Governed by Rules   The field of linguistics is devoted to studying and explaining the rules of language. And, just as spoken and written language follow very specific rules, so does nonverbal communication. A few forms of nonverbal behavior, such as facial expressions conveying sadness, joy, contentment, astonishment, or grief, are universal. That is, the expressions are basically the same for all mankind, regardless of where you were born, raised, educated, or enculturated. Most of our nonverbal behavior, however, is learned and is a product of the cultures in which we are raised. A motion or hand gesture that means one thing in my culture may well mean another in yours. The thumb and forefinger in touching to form a circle is often raised in North America to signify everything's "A-okay." In Latin America, that same gesture is used to illustrate the anal sphincter muscle and is employed as a powerful insult.

Nonverbal Behavior Is Highly Believable   Researchers have discovered what we have known individually for quite some time: we are quick to believe nonverbal behaviors, even when they contradict verbal messages. When an employee's eyes dart away quickly, or search the floor as he thinks of an answer to the supervisor's question, most of us would suspect the employee is not telling the truth. Try as we might, there are many nonverbal behaviors we cannot fake. We might convincingly write or speak words that are untrue, but it's much more difficult to behave nonverbally in ways that are false or deceptive.

Nonverbal Behavior Is Metacommunicational   The word *meta* is borrowed from Greek and means "along with, about, or among." Thus metacommunication is really communication *about* communication. The behaviors we exhibit while communicating are really about communication itself, and nonverbal communication occurs in reference to the process of communicating. Your facial expression reveals how you feel about the meal you've just been served; your handshake, vocal tone, and eye contact tell us what you think about the person you've just been introduced to.[10]

DIMENSIONS OF THE NONVERBAL CODE

When we talk about nonverbal communication, we're really talking about the codes we use to encode our messages and the signals that contain them. The code we use in verbal communication is language, and through thousands of years of human interaction, we've established rules to guide us and a structure for employing and interpreting the messages that language permits us to send and receive. With nonverbal communication, however, the code is neither as clear nor is it as precise, primarily because the meaning of our messages must be inferred without the benefit of feedback.

The code itself is divided into more than a dozen dimensions, each with the power to encode and carry messages from one person to another. Each has different characteristics: some appeal to just one sense, others appeal to several; some have a limited range of possible meanings, others have a huge span of subtleties for encoding human intentions; some belong to the environment—both its physical and psychological aspects—of the communication event, while others belong to the participants in those events.

The Communication Environment   This refers to that collection of nonhuman factors that can, and often does, influence human transactions. People often change environments in order to accomplish their communication goals: the choice of a restaurant for a business meeting, or a resort hotel to conduct a conference. Often, people will simply say, "Let's go somewhere quiet where we can talk."

This category concerns those factors that can influence a human relationship, but are not, in Professor Mark Knapp's words, "directly a part of it." This would include such factors as the furniture, architectural style, interior decorating, lighting conditions, colors, temperature, background noise, or music. It may be something as small as an ashtray or dish left on a table you plan to use, or something as grand as the city in which you are meeting.[11]

Body Movement   The study of human motion in communication, often referred to as *kinesics* or *kinesiology,* is concerned primarily with movement and posture. The way we walk, sit, stand, move our arms, hands, head, feet, and legs tells other people something about us. This dimension also includes such areas of interest as facial expression, eye contact, and posture. The five basic categories of human movement include:

> *Emblems.* These are nonverbal acts which have a direct verbal translation or dictionary definition, sometimes a word or two or a brief phrase. The thumbs-up sign, the extended middle finger, and the hitchhiker's thumb are three well-known examples.
>
> *Illustrators.* These are gestures that often complement our verbal signals, helping to illustrate what's being said verbally. We can count off the number of items we want on our fingers, or measure distance with the space between our hands.
>
> *Affect displays.* These are behaviors that indicate the type and intensity of the various emotions we feel. Facial expressions, hand and arm movements are commonly used to communicate emotional or affective states of mind.
>
> *Regulators.* These are body movements that help to control the flow of communication. Hand movement, arm positioning, and eye contact can easily maintain or regulate the back-and-forth nature of personal conversation, for example.
>
> *Adaptors.* These are movements or behaviors that involve personal habits and self-expressions. They are methods of adapting or accommodating ourselves to the demands of the world in which we live. We usually engage in these behaviors in private, but sometimes under pressure we will resort to twisting our hair, scratching, adjusting our glasses, or, perhaps, picking our noses if we think no one's looking.

From a workplace perspective, a trend toward incivility is fostering a backlash, especially in response to unwelcome or rude nonverbal behavior. During tense talks in Chicago courts, Southwest Airlines Chief Executive Herb Kelleher crouched and slowly flipped his middle finger toward a pilots' union lawyer. "It was a joke," he explained. But other companies are cracking down on crude nonverbal behavior. Cleveland-based American Greetings Corporation has banned obscene talk and gestures. And an official of Roadway Services, an Akron, Ohio, freight hauler, says truckers are told to practice restraint.[12]

Eye Contact   This human behavior is really a part of kinesics, but often deserves separate attention because of the importance it plays in human interaction. Direction, duration, and intensity of gaze are often seen as indicators of interest, attention, or involvement between two people. Keep in mind, however, that nonverbal mannerisms are culturally based, and eye contact is just one example of a human behavior that can vary from one society to another.

In Japan, for instance, looking a supervisor directly in the eyes is a sign of defiance, even insubordination. In the United States and Canada, supervisors expect direct and frequent eye contact as a sign of respect. A senior leader in a large organization once remarked, "I won't hire a man who won't look me in the eye." Why would he feel that way? Largely because in this culture we draw inferences about honesty and integrity from eye contact; if people look down or look away when we're speaking to them, we assume they are ashamed or being untruthful. Honesty and eye contact are, of course, unrelated behaviors, but people in our society make judgments about them, nonetheless.

A Communicator's Physical Appearance   This area is not concerned with movement, as kinesics is, but with aspects of our bodies and appearance which remain relatively unchanged during the period of interaction. Such things as body type (ectomorph, mesomorph, or endomorph), height, weight, hair, and skin color or tone are included. Some researchers have also focused on physical attractiveness and people's reaction to personal appearance. A number of studies, in fact, have shown that people readily attribute greater intelligence, wit, charm, and sociability to those people whom they judge to be very attractive.

Another new study has found that good looks can yield substantial rewards. Economists Daniel Hamermesh of the University of Texas and Jeff Biddle of Michigan State University have found that education, experience, and other characteristics being equal, people who are perceived as good looking earn, on average about 10 percent more than those viewed as homely. And, surprisingly, men are more likely than women to pay the penalties of below-average appearance. Men who are below average in attractiveness, the study found, tend to make about 9 percent less, while below-average women make only 5 percent less.[13]

Naomi Wolf, author of *The Beauty Myth,* agrees with Hamermesh and Biddle's conclusions, but argues that women often face greater discrimination when it comes to appearance. One recent study looked at earnings of MBA graduates over their first 10 postdegree years. Ratings of beauty based on school photographs correlated positively with starting and subsequent salaries for men. There seemed to be no relationship between the starting salaries of women and their beauty, but attractive women experienced faster salary growth. Dr. Hamermesch suggests that better-looking people may have high self-esteem—from years of compliments—that translates into better performance on the job.[14]

Independent of such studies, conventional wisdom tells businesspeople that others make judgments about them based on their appearance, including everything from hairstyle to body weight, clothing style to skin tone. How you perform on the job may well be the most important aspect of your behavior in the workplace, but if you don't make a favorable first impression, you may not be given the chance to show what you can do. On the other side of that coin: judging a coworker or prospective employee by appearance may seem intuitive and useful, but may also prove inaccurate. While it is true that you can make some judgments about a book by its cover, you may wish to withhold judgment until you have an opportunity to gather more information.

Artifacts   These are objects that are human-made or modified. The number and kind of things we might call *artifacts* is enormous, ranging from clothing, jewelry, and eyeglasses to the objects we own and decorate our offices with. Certainly the way we dress denotes how we feel about an occasion or those whom we're with. Every family, for instance, has at least one cousin who will show up at a wedding wearing a corduroy sport coat; it's not that he can't afford dinner clothes or a tuxedo, it's just that he's thumbing his nose at the rest of the family.

People in the business world make judgments about those they deal with as a result of the artifacts they see in their offices and in the communication environment. A friend once asked if I would trust a stockbroker who drove a '82 Toyota to work each day. The implication was that a "successful" broker would have enough money to buy and drive an expensive automobile. And, while there is no connection at all between investment success and taste in motor cars, the majority of adults in the marketplace make such judgment-links with great regularity.

Touch   This is among the more widely discussed and, perhaps, least understood aspects of human behavior. Numerous studies have shown that physical contact is essential to human existence. Adults need it for social and psychological balance; children need it for stimulation, security, and reassurance. Many infants, in fact, will fail to thrive if they're not regularly offered the reassuring warmth of human touch. Needless to say, touch is conducted on many levels and for many reasons by each of us, with functional, professional, social, and sexual implications for each kind of touch. Perhaps more than any other dimension of the nonverbal code, touching is a culturally determined, learned behavior. The relationship between the two people touching and the norms of the society in which they live—or were enculturated—will determine the length, location, intensity, frequency, acceptability, and publicness of their haptic behavior.

The *rules* regarding touch in the North American workplace have changed in recent years from liberal to conservative—from frequent touch to little or no touch. Back-slapping, arm-grabbing, and other forms of behavior that ranged from affectionate friendship to adolescent horseplay, are now widely banned in most businesses, largely from a fear of lawsuits. A colleague who returned to work following a maternity leave was cheerfully welcomed by friends and coworkers in her office, but no one would touch her until she spoke up, "It's alright to give me a hug. I would appreciate that."

The best advice regarding touch is to assume that if people extend their hand, it's probably alright to shake it. Touching any other parts of their bodies would be considered inappropriate unless you're specifically given permission to do so.

These are probably unfortunate developments—largely the result of abusive behavior in the workplace, mostly aimed at women—in view of numerous recent studies presented to the Society for Neuroscience, finding that touch—direct human contact—can have a positive influence on the production of a hormone affecting the body's reaction to stress. Abnormal levels of the hormone, in fact, have been linked to changes in a part of the brain involved with learning and memory.[15] The value of human touch is undisputed. The issue for managers is one of exhibiting good sense and good manners when touching others.

Paralanguage   This term refers, very simply, to *how* something is said and not to *what* is said. It deals with the whole range of nonverbal vocal cues involved in speech behavior, including voice qualities, vocal characterizers, vocal qualifiers, and speech segregates. These are sometimes referred to as *vocalics.*[16]

Often, the only real clues we have to a person's actual intent as we listen to him or her speak are found in paralanguage. If your supervisor approaches you just before lunch one day and says, "Lisa, we need to talk about the LaSalle account," your reaction to those words may depend on a number of factors, including the communication environment and context, as well as your expectations. But your sense of urgency—how quickly you offer to set up a meeting, whether you postpone a lunch date to talk about the account—may well depend on *how* those words were spoken. Your cue is often contained in your interpretation not of the words themselves, but the pacing, phrasing, tone, pitch, and intensity of your supervisor's delivery.

Vocal qualifiers are contained in the speech of every human and are an integral part of every spoken word. They are, in fact, our principal cue to identifying and interpreting sarcasm and cynicism. When you ask a coworker in a meeting if he thinks a new cost-control measure will work, and the response is "Oh yeah—You bet—No problem with that plan," you're faced with a brief dilemma. Was your coworker being sarcastic just then, or does he genuinely believe that plan will succeed? Your reaction to his words will depend entirely on how you interpret the tone of his voice.

Paralanguage not only serves to help listeners identify emotional states in the speaker, but also plays an important role in conversational turn-taking. People often signal others in a conversation that it's their turn to talk, or that they would like a turn to speak, or that they aren't yet done speaking. Much of the signaling is done nonverbally through vocalics: rate, pacing, pitch, tone, and other vocal, subverbal cues.[17]

Space   Often referred to in the research literature as proxemics, this refers to the study of how humans use space, including the areas in which we work, live, socialize, and conduct our lives. We know intuitively that space communicates in many ways in the business world, especially when we examine the subject of office space. Professor Joseph DeVito says, "We know, for example, that in a large organization, status is the basis for determining how large an office one receives, whether that office has a window or not, what floor of the building the office is on, and how close one's office is to the head of the company."[18]

Workers in large organizations have faced two interesting, sometimes discouraging, trends in the allocation of office space: shrinking cubicles and disappearing personal space. With office space becoming more expensive per square foot, facility managers have looked for increasingly creative ways of dealing with the demand for workspace and privacy. The trend over the past 25 years away from huge office spaces with many desks and no privacy brought portable wall dividers known as *cubicles* into the workspace. The arrangement provided for a minimum of privacy, or in some cases, an illusion of privacy.[19]

A second trend has developed in recent years, known as *hoteling,* to provide office space on demand for workers who have an infrequent need for private or semiprivate space. Greg Bednar is an Audit Partner in the accounting firm of Ernst & Young, LLP in Chicago. "We began 'hoteling' several years ago," Bednar said, "but expanded the program dramatically in October of 1997." The entire Chicago office of Ernst & Young, according to Bednar, including more than 3,000 people and 500,000 square feet of office space between the 11th and 17th floors of the Sears Tower were affected.[20]

"It seemed like a great idea at first," he said, "because we were able to save so much money. We got an instant economic benefit from giving up 100,000 square feet of workspace. We also wanted a more technology-literate workforce. People had to be plugged into the system and into our clients. Additionally, we were hoping to develop a more flexible workforce." What Ernst & Young got was a huge, temporary saving on office space rental, but a workforce that felt disenfranchised from the company.[21]

Each morning, Ernst & Young employees report to work by checking in at the concierge desk in the outer lobby. Once properly identified, they receive access to a cubicle, known as a "four pod," so called, because four workers occupy one workspace about 20 feet square. They each have a desk and chair, a telephone, and a network connection for their laptop computers. The cubicle offers no overnight storage space, no opportunity to put up pictures, bookshelves, or personal items, and virtually zero privacy.[22]

"It's become a morale issue," said Bednar. "What we've gained in revenue by renting less floorspace, we've lost in teaming, mentoring, and social interaction. We have no 'water cooler chats,' and very little informal interaction with each other. Frankly, no one knows where anyone else is on any given day." Wayne Ebersberger, also a partner in Ernst & Young's Chicago office, says, "The loss of this personal space is an important matter. It isn't just a workspace or productivity issue any longer. We're losing some of the fabric of our culture."[23]

Categories of Personal Space Cultural anthropologist Edward T. Hall has observed and classified four categories of distance, each of which helps to define the relationship between the communicators.

- *Intimate.* This ranges from actual touching to a distance of about 18 inches. At this distance, the presence of other individuals is unmistakable: each individual experiences the sound, smell, even the other's breath. To be given permission to position yourself so closely to another implies a personal relationship involving considerable trust. Often, though, we're forced to stand or sit next to someone, perhaps actually touching them, without really wanting to do so—in an elevator, a subway car, or an airline seat. Most North Americans feel some level of discomfort at such closeness when they don't really know the other person. People try to avoid eye contact at this distance, focusing instead on distant or nearby objects.[24] While most people feel uncomfortable at this distance from strangers or casual acquaintances, most are willing to briefly tolerate such closeness in order to get what they need—a trip to the top floor in an elevator, transportation to the next subway stop, or lunch in a crowded cafe.
- *Personal.* Each of us, according to Dr. Hall, carries a protective bubble defining our personal distance which allows us to stay protected and untouched by others. In the close phase of personal distance, about 18 to 30 inches, we can still hold or grasp each other, but only by extending our arms. In the far phase (about 30 inches to 4 feet), two people can touch each other only if they both extend their arms. This far phase, according to Professor DeVito, is "the extent to which we can physically get our hands on things; hence, it defines, in one sense, the limits of our physical control over others."[25] The common business phrase "arm's-length relationship" comes from the definition of this distance, meaning that a proper relationship with

customers, suppliers, or business partners might be one in which we are not so close as to be controlled or unduly influenced by them.

- *Social.* At a distance of about 4 to 12 feet, we lose the visual detail we could see in the personal distance, yet we clearly are aware of another's presence and can easily make eye contact. You would have to step forward, however, in order to shake hands. Note that during most business introductions, people do just that: step forward, make eye contact, shake hands, then step back. The near phase of social distance (4 to 7 feet) is the range at which most business conversations and interactions are conducted. In the far phase (7 to 12 feet), business transactions have a more formal tone and voices are raised just slightly. Many office furniture arrangements assure this distance for senior managers and executives, while providing the opportunity for closer contact, if participants decide it's necessary.[26]
- *Public.* In the close phase of public distance, about 12 to 15 feet, we feel more protected by space. We can still see people, observing their actions and movements, but we lose much of the detail visible at closer distances. We can move quickly enough to avoid someone and are not forced to make eye contact with people we do not know. In the far phase, more than 25 feet, we see people not as separate individuals, but as part of the landscape or scene in the room. Communication at this distance is difficult, if not impossible, without shouting or exaggerated body movement.[27]

Our use of space varies greatly, depending on where we live and how we were raised, but it varies even more from one culture to another and is a frequent source of difficulty for people who move to another culture as adults. The next chapter, which deals with international and intercultural communication, will explain more about how U.S. business managers adapt to changes in such important nonverbal behaviors as proxemics.

Time   Our use of time and how we view its role in our personal and professional lives, speaks volumes about who we are and how we regard others. This, too, is culturally determined to a large extent, since the use of time involves extensive interaction with other people in our societies.

In North America, we place considerable importance on punctuality and promptness, announcing to anyone who'll listen that "time is money." U.S. and Canadian, and to a lesser extent European, society see time as a commodity that can be saved, wasted, spent, or invested wisely. Mediterranean, Latin, and Polynesian cultures, on the other hand, see time in a much more seamless fashion, moving past them in an inexorable stream. Lateness in South American nations is not only acceptable, but often fashionable—a view that regularly frustrates North American businesspeople who experience it for the first time.[28]

Anthropologists have demonstrated how people from various parts of the world view time in very different ways. Edward T. Hall has written at length about people who see the world in monochronic ways, that is, with one kind of time for everyone, while others see the world in polychronic ways, with many kinds and uses of time. U.S. and Canadian citizens, as well as those who live in Germany, Switzerland, and the industrialized nations of the G-8, tend to work in precise, accountable ways with an emphasis on "saving time," and being "on time" for appointments and meetings.

People who live and work along the Mediterranean, in Latin America and the Middle East, and in more traditional, developing economies often view time from a multifaced or polychronic perspective. While being on time for a business meeting may be important in Latin America, it may not be *more important* than a conversation with a friend who has been ill or whom you haven't seen in some time. Additionally, the pace of life as well as business in such societies can vary considerably, but is invariably slower than the pace of activity in Western Europe or North America.[29]

Color Color, shading, and hue as subtle and powerful message-senders have a long and, well . . . colorful history. We signal our intentions ("This project has the green light"), reveal our reactions ("That move prompted red flags throughout the organization"), underscore our moods ("I'm feeling a little blue today"), and call our emotions to the surface ("She was green with envy"). We coordinate and carefully select (for the most part) the colors we use in our offices, our homes, our automobiles, our clothing, and even our hair. We even use color to stereotype and categorize others ("She's that blonde from marketing," and "He's one of the original graybeards in this company").

New marketing research has shown what we have suspected for some time—that color plays an important role in our perceptions of food packaging and food purchase decisions. According to Cooper Marketing Group in Chicago, health-conscious consumers are likely to think that any food, from cookies to cheese, is probably good for them as long as it comes in green packaging. A trip down the fat-free food aisle in your local supermarket will confirm those findings: the top brands, from Snackwell's cookies to Healthy Choice meals, use green packaging. Hershey Foods spokeswoman Natalie Bailey says, "Green is becoming recognized as a low-fat color." Elliot Young of Perception Research Services adds, "It's a risk not to use green. It makes it easier for the shopper to distinguish low-fat items."[30]

"Color serves as a cue," according to Dr. Russell Ferstandig, a psychiatrist whose company, Competitive Advantage Consulting, advises marketers about the hearts and minds of consumers. "It's a condensed message that has all sorts of meanings." Some are no more than fads, such as clear drinks like Crystal Pepsi or Coors' Zima, while others are more enduring, including everything from Raspberry Jell-O to traditional school colors.[31]

Food companies are usually aware of the meanings they send and tend to rely on certain colors until circumstances require a change. According to color researchers, there are no inherently good or bad colors; the context affects the meaning. White, for instance, is seen as a good color, but no longer in bread, where brown is becoming preferred because of its more healthful and natural connotations. In packaging, the most popular colors have been red and yellow, according to John Lister, a partner in the New York design firm of Lister Butler. "People tend to be attracted to the warmth of these colors, he added. "They are cheery and friendly."[32]

Smell A primitive perceptive capability, smell is a powerful communicator reaching far and wide throughout human emotion and experience. Though it is less understood and more subtle than most other dimensions of the nonverbal code, our sense of smell plays an important part in our ability to communicate.

We wear perfume, cologne, and after-shave lotions to signal others that we are freshly scrubbed and desirable. We use deodorants and antiperspirants to mask natural body odors. We use breath mints to cover the smell of bacteria growing in our mouths, and we use room fresheners to disguise the odors of everyday living trapped in our homes, cars, and offices. Smells can be highly evocative and very emotional, in part because they're associated with one of our most primitive and least-developed sense organs. Everything from the aroma of mom's pot roast or apple pie cooking in the kitchen to the scent of leather seats in a new Mercedes can have an emotional effect on each of us.[33]

From a marketing perspective, human response to aromas is very personal and highly emotional. According to Dr. Trygg Engen, a professor at Brown University, "Aromas are learned in association with a moment and remain inextricably linked to the mood of that moment."[34] Researchers have found that a whiff of baking bread is enough to transport many people back to an idealized childhood. Others are perked up by the smell of lemon or lulled by jasmine. Still others report allergic reactions to smells.

Aromatic mood manipulation is an area of increasing interest among productivity consultants, moving well beyond mom's spice jar and the romantically scented candle. Junichi Yagi, a senior vice president of Shimizu Technology, says "If you have a high-stress office environment, you want to soothe and stimulate alertness. In a hotel, you might want to create a relaxed mood." To perk people up, Mr. Yagi has experimented with central air circulation systems to alter or enhance the moods of everyone from office workers to shopping mall customers. Peppermint, lemon, rosemary, eucalyptus, and pine have been shown to increase alertness, while lavender, clove, floral, and woodlands scents create a relaxing effect. Experiment participants describe feeling refreshed in the presence of a light citrus mixture.[35]

From a workspace perspective, most personal scents are deemed acceptable if they are insufficiently powerful to extend beyond intimate distance. Employees, customers, and others have complained—and in some cases succeeded in court—about being exposed to various odors including food, perfumes, tobacco smoke, and unvented product odors. To protect themselves against unwanted and expensive litigation, many business organizations have published policies asking employees to be respectful of others with whom they must share the workspace, keeping colognes, perfumes, and other personal scents to a minimum.

Taste   Closely related to our sense of smell is our ability to taste. It's limited to a small grouping of sensations that include salty, sweet, bitter, and other tastes located in a collection of small, flask-shaped sensors in the epithelium of the tongue. It's a complex response system that involves our abilities to see and smell, as well, and one—much like color and touch—that is highly subjective in nature. What is "bitter" to some is "rich and full bodied" to others. For still others, such things as espresso coffee, broiled asparagus, and scotch whiskey are "acquired tastes." Our appreciation for the taste of various food and drink is a function of both age and enculturation and, like our use of space, can pose problems when we move from one culture to another.

As the demographic make-up of our society changes, it's important to note that our taste in food is changing along with it. Picante sauce now outsells catsup, and commercially prepared food, ranging from fine dining to take-out is available in cuisines ranging from Mexican to Italian, Greek to French, and Thai to Szechuan.[36]

Sound   The study of acoustics and its effects on communication is now an important part of nonverbal research. Public speakers are particularly conscious of whether they can be heard by everyone in the room, and those who use amplification and public address systems are involved in a constant struggle with audio system feedback, acoustical bounce, and other peculiarities of microphones, amplifiers, and speakers.

Sound comes in other forms, too, including the melodic ranges of the human voice, the sounds produced by nature as well as mankind and our machines (jets, cars, jack-hammers, boom boxes), and of course, there's music. Culture and, more often, subculture can determine our reaction to musical compositions and performances. The melodies of a big band or an orchestra may be attractive to some, but sappy and dull to their grandchildren, whose tastes in music may run to salsa, reggae, or rock 'n' roll.

Silence   The absence of speech or sound may be used to communicate as powerfully and directly as any verbal code. Some researchers liken silence to acoustics in the same way that facial expressions are related to kinesics. Silence can be used both positively and negatively: to affect, to reveal, to judge, or to activate. Asian cultures, in particular, make extensive use of silence during business meetings and contract negotiations.

Research in interpersonal communication has revealed that silence may serve a number of important functions.

To provide thinking time. Silence can offer an opportunity for you to gather your thoughts together, to assess what's just been said by others, or to weigh the impact of what you might say next. United States Ambassador Mike Mansfield once observed that he carried his pipe and tobacco with him for so many years because they gave him something to do while the room grew quiet. "I was never at a loss for words," he said. "I was just reluctant to say the first few that came to mind."[37] Somehow guests or colleagues were more willing to tolerate the tobacco smoke than the silence.

To hurt. Some people use silence as a weapon to hurt others. Giving someone the silent treatment can be particularly powerful, especially if they expect to hear from you and speak with you. In many business organizations, a dropoff in communication can be an early indication of trouble; often, the recipient of the silent treatment is being eased out of the decision-making processes and, perhaps, the company itself.

To isolate oneself. Sometimes silence is used as a response to personal anxiety, shyness, or threats. If you feel anxious or uncertain about yourself or your role in an organization, particularly if you are new to the company or are junior in rank to others in the group, silence is a common response. Eventually, even the most junior or introverted of managers will be asked to speak up on important issues. The key is knowing when to speak and how much to say.

To prevent communication. Silence may be used to prevent the verbal communication of certain messages. An executive may impose a "gag order" on employees to prevent them from discussing sensitive information with others inside or outside an organization. In other circumstances, silence may allow members of a negotiating team or collective bargaining group time to "cool off." If words have the power to inspire, soothe, pro-voke, or enrage, then silence can prevent those effects from occurring.

To communicate feelings. Like the eyes, face, or hands, silence can also be used to communicate emotional responses. According to Professor DeVito, silence can sometimes communicate a determination to be uncooperative or defiant. "By refusing to engage in verbal communication," he says, "we defy the authority or legitimacy of the other person's position." In more pleasant situations, silence might be used to express affection or agreement.[38]

To communicate nothing. While it remains true that you "cannot not communicate," it is equally true that what you wish to communicate on occasion is that you have nothing to say. Keep in mind that receivers in the communication process will interpret silence, just as they interpret words, motion, and other forms of communication, in their own way. They, not you, will assign meaning to what you are not saying, to whom you are not saying it, and the occasion on which you are not saying anything. From a manager's perspective, it may be a good idea to call someone and say, "I don't have an answer for you yet, but I'll find one and get back in touch with you before the end of the week." That might be preferable to no contact at all. A customer might think you don't care about him; a supplier might think you have lost interest in doing business; an investment analyst might believe you have something to hide if you're not talking.

The Effects of Nonverbal Communication Here are six general outcomes that are important for every manager to know.

Nonverbal cues are often difficult to read. During the 1970s, a number of popular books introduced the general public to nonverbal communication. One popular volume, written by a journalist, described the nonverbal studies of several researchers.[39] That best-seller was followed by others that simplified and popularized research in this area; many of them, however, oversimplified the behavioral science behind the findings in the interest of making a sale, detecting a liar, attracting members of the opposite sex, and so on.

According to Professor Mark Knapp, "Although such books aroused the public's interest in nonverbal communication . . . readers too often were left with the idea that reading nonverbal cues as *the* key to success in any human encounter; some of these books implied that single cues represent single meanings. Not only is it important to look at nonverbal *clusters* of behavior, but also to recognize that nonverbal meaning, like verbal, rarely is limited to a single denotative meaning."[40]

Nonverbal cues are often difficult to interpret. What may mean one thing in one context, culture, or circumstance may mean something entirely different in another. Professor Knapp goes on to say, "Some of these popularized accounts do not sufficiently remind us that the meaning of a particular behavior is often understood by looking at the context in which the behavior occurs; for example, looking into someone's eyes may reflect affection in one situation and aggression in another."[41] The importance of reading context, just as we would with verbal expression, is especially important. The meaning of all communication, after all, is context-driven.

Nonverbal behaviors are often contradictory. Our posture and vocal tone may say one thing, but our eyes may say another. We try to stand up straight and portray a dominant, confident posture, but our hands fidgeting with a pen may say something entirely different. Nonverbal behaviors do come "packaged" together, and we must often examine several behaviors before we begin to discern a coherent picture of the person before us. The problem with such packages or clusters of behaviors is that they're not always consistent and not always complementary. Which one should we believe?

Some nonverbal cues are more important than others. As we examine several behaviors clustered together—vocal pace, tone, and pitch; body posture; pupil dilation; arm and hand movement—it often becomes clear to careful observers that some cues are more important than others. For the most part, the relative importance of a given cue is dependent on habits and usual behaviors of the speaker. In other words, are the behaviors I'm observing usual or unusual for this person? If they're unusual, do they contradict verbal portions of the message? And, finally, it's important to note that some portions of our anatomy are simply easier to control than others: even a nervous person can sit still if she makes a determined effort to do so, but few among us can control the dilation of our pupils. Many can control facial expression, but few can determine when tears will flow, or when our voices will choke with emotion.

We often read into some cues much that isn't there, and fail to read some cues that are clearly present. We often look for cues that seem most important to us personally: whether a person will look us directly in the eyes as we speak, or which direction they've crossed their legs. Such cues may be meaningless. We can also misread cues if we have insufficient information on which to base a judgment. Business leaders seen nodding off in a conference may be judged as indifferent by their hosts; in reality, it may be jetlag that's caught up with them.

We're not as skilled at this as we think we are; our confidence often exceeds our ability. Caution is the byword in dealing with nonverbal communication. Even though a substantial portion of what we learn from a human transaction—between two-thirds and three-quarters of all meaning—comes from nonverbal cues, we simply aren't as skilled at this as we'd like to be. It's easy to misinterpret, misread, or misunderstand someone. It's equally easy to jump to conclusions from just a few bits of evidence. The best advice for any manager would be to withhold judgment as long as possible, gather as much information—verbal as well as nonverbal—as possible, and then reconfirm what you think you know as frequently as possible. The stakes are high in business transactions, almost as high as the chances for error in decoding nonverbal cues.

Endnotes

1. Jackson, M. "Some Workers Uncomfortable with Trend Toward Casual Clothes." *South Bend Tribune,* January 8, 1998, p. C7. See also Lee, L. "Some Employees Just Aren't Suited for Dressing Down." *Wall Street Journal,* February 3, 1995, pp. A1, A6.

2. Jackson, "Some Workers Uncomfortable," p. C7. See also Berger, Joseph. "Black Jeans Invade Big Blue: First Day of a Relaxed IBM," *Wall Street Journal,* February 7, 1995, pp. A1, B4. See also Bounds, W. and J. Lublin. "Will the Client Wear a Tie or a T-Shirt?" *Wall Street Journal,* July 24, 1998, pp. B1, B8.

3. Knapp, M. and J. Hall. *Nonverbal Communication in Human Interaction,* 3rd ed. Fort Worth, TX: Holt Rinehart and Winston, Inc., 1992, pp. 5–6.

4. Ruesch, J. and W. Kees. *Nonverbal Communication: Notes on the Visual Perception of Human Relations.* Los Angeles, CA: University of California Press, 1956.

5. Goleman, D. "Non-Verbal Cues Are Easy to Misinterpret." *New York Times,* September 17, 1991, B5.

6. Ibid.

7. Ibid., pp. B5-6.

8. Eckman, P. "Communication Through Nonverbal Behavior: A Source of Information About an Interpersonal Relationship," in Tomkins, S. S. and C. E. Izard (eds.), *Affect, Cognition and Personality.* New York, NY: Springer and Co., Publishers, 1965.

9. DeVito, J. *The Interpersonal Communication Book,* 5th ed. New York, NY: HarperCollins, 1989, p. 215.

10. Ibid., pp. 214–226.

11. Knapp and Hall, *Nonverbal Communication,* pp. 13–16.

12. "Be Civil. There Is a Clampdown on Obscene Gestures in the Office and on the Field." *Wall Street Journal,* July 5, 1994, p. A1.

13. Harper, L. "Good Looks Can Mean a Pretty Penny on the Job, and 'Ugly' Men Are Affected More Than Women." *Wall Street Journal,* November 23, 1993, p. B1.

See also Brody, J. "Ideals of Beauty Are Seen as Innate. The Ideal Face Transcends Culture, Study Says." *New York Times,* March 21, 1994, p. A6.

14. Ibid., p. B1. See also Newin, T. "Workplace Bias Ties to Obesity Is Ruled Illegal. Federal Judges Back a 320-Pound Woman." *New York Times,* November 24, 1993, p. A10.

15. Rubin, R. "The Biochemistry of Touch." *U.S. News & World Report,* November 10, 1997, p. 62.

16. Knapp and Hall, *Nonverbal Communication,* p. 16.

17. DeVito, *Interpersonal Communication,* p. 265.

18. Ibid., p. 247.

19. Hymowitz, C. "If the Walls Had Ears, You Wouldn't Have Any Less Privacy." *Wall Street Journal,* May 19, 1998, p. B1.

20. Bednar, G. Partner, Ernst & Young, LLP, Chicago, in a telephone interview with the author, August 17, 1998.

21. Ibid.

22. Ibid.

23. Ebersberger, W. Partner, Ernst & Young, LLP, Chicago, in a telephone interview with the author, August 17, 1998.

24. For an excellent extended discussion of the role of space in social interaction, see Hall, E. T. *The Hidden Dimension.* New York, NY: Doubleday, 1982.

25. DeVito, *Interpersonal Communication,* p. 248.

26. Ibid., p. 249.

27. Ibid., pp. 249–250.

28. Ferraro, G. *The Cultural Dimension of International Business,* 3rd ed. Upper Saddle River, NJ: Prentice-Hall, 1998, pp. 93–95.

29. For an excellent discussion of the role of time in human affairs, see Hall, E. T. *The Dance of Life.* New York, NY: Doubleday, 1989.

30. Reiss, T. "Hey, It's Green—It Must Be Healthy." *Business Week,* July 13, 1998, p. 6.

31. Hall, T. "Marketers Seek the Color of Delicious." *New York Times,* November 4, 1992, p. A13.

32. Ibid., p. A19.
33. Hall, E. T. *The Hidden Dimension,* pp. 45–50.
34. Engen, T. *Odor Sensation and Memory.* New York, NY: Praeger (no date).
35. O'Neill, M. "Taming the Frontier of the Senses: Using Aroma to Manipulate Moods." *New York Times,* April 4, 1993, pp. B2, B6.
36. Willoughby, J. "The Tip of Your Tongue Knows the Bitter Truth: Flavor Can Be Painful," *New York Times,* April 27, 1994, pp. B1, B5.
37. Mansfield, M. United States Ambassador to Japan, in a personal interview with the author in the U.S. Embassy in Tokyo, May 1983.
38. DeVito, *Interpersonal Communication,* pp. 258–261.
39. Fast, J. *Body Language.* New York, NY: M. Evans, 1970.
40. Knapp and Hall, *Nonverbal Communication,* p. 27.
41. Ibid.

For Further Reading

Archer, D. and R. Akert. "Words and Everything Else: Verbal and Nonverbal Cues in Social Interaction." *Journal of Personality and Social Psychology,* Vol. 35 (1978), 443–449.

Argyle, M. *Bodily Communication,* 2nd ed. London, UK: Methuen. 1998

Buck, R. "A Test of Nonverbal Receiving Ability: Preliminary Studies." *Human Communication Research,* Vol. 2 (1976), 162–171.

Christensen, D., A. Farina, and L. Boudreau. "Sensitivity to Nonverbal Cues as a Function of Social Competence." *Journal of Nonverbal Behavior,* Vol. 4 (1980), 146–156.

Leathers, D. G. *Successful Nonverbal Communication: Principals & Applications.* Boston, MA:Allyn & Bacon, 1996.

Morris, Desmond. *Bodytalk: The Meaning of Human Gestures.* New York, NY: Random House, Inc., 1994.

Rogers, Everett M. (ed.). *A History of Communication Study: A Biographical Approach.* New York, NY: The Free Press, 1994.

Case 7–1 OLIVE GARDEN RESTAURANTS DIVISION, GENERAL MILLS CORPORATION

Managers occupying junior-to-middle level positions in large organizations are often called upon to resolve disputes. Some of these are disagreements between lower-level supervisors and employees; some are disputes with suppliers or distributors; others, like the dispute in this case, are between the organization and a customer.

Every customer has a value to an organization, and every customer has a price to that organization. Customers are, of course, the lifeblood and source of revenue to a business, but not all customers are worth saving. Some, in fact, may be more trouble and expense to maintain than they are worth.

Dealing with customers—or with anyone else who is in disagreement with your organization— requires patience, tact, and a certain measure of skill. A variety of response modes is open to the manager who faces an angry customer, along with a range of options in dealing with the case.

This case requires two documents in response: a one-page communication strategy memo and a letter to the customer. The strategy memo should be directed to the president of the Olive Garden Restaurants Division and should describe in some detail how you plan to handle this case and why. The letter to the customer explains what you have chosen to do.

Assume that you are the director of customer service and report through the vice president for sales and marketing to the president. Your memorandum and customer letter should be in finished form, ready to transmit.

[Dated Three Days Ago]
51588 River Forest Dr.
South Bend, IN 46617

Mr. Ronald N. Magruder
President
Olive Garden Restaurants Division
General Mills Corporation
5900 Lake Ellenor Drive
Orlando, FL 33809

Dear Mr. Magruder,

Last week, my family and I had a genuinely unpleasant experience in an Olive Garden Restaurant. My first instinct was to dismiss it as an other example of bad customer service and forget about it. The truth is, I can't forget about it. The experience was bad enough that I thought you should hear about it.

On Tuesday evening of last week, I selected the Olive Garden Restaurant at 6410 Grape Road in Mishawaka, Indiana for a mid-evening meal with my father and two daughters. We've had good experiences and great food in Olive Garden Restaurants before and, in fact, think your facilities are generally well run.

We arrived at the restaurant about 8:15 p.m. and were surprised to discover that very few customers were seated for dinner. No one was waiting in the entryway to greet us—something we have come to expect at Olive Garden. After waiting more than ten minutes for a hostess, I went into the bar and asked if someone could seat us. A hostess, clearly annoyed at the prospect of additional customers, offered us a table in an area my father couldn't walk to. He is an amputee and walks, with great difficulty, on crutches.

After an extended discussion about why we couldn't take a table in the upper seating area, the hostess showed us a table—not cleaned off—and left the menus. We discovered that I had a luncheon menu and there were no children's menus available.

Our next challenge was finding a waiter. After an extended wait (10 to 12 minutes), a young man appeared and wanted to know if we had been helped. He indicated that this table wasn't "in his station," but offered to take our orders, anyway. We ordered our meals and I asked for a glass of wine. Twenty minutes later (nearly 45 minutes after our arrival), our meals arrived (cold) and I was told that the bar was out of wine. Two additional requests produced silverware and napkins.

Mr. Ronald N. Magruder
[Dated Three Days Ago]
Page Two

When we sampled our meals and discovered they were cold, I asked to see the manager—a large, officious man who was equally annoyed with the prospect of customers at that hour. The meals were prepared exactly as we had ordered and were fine, except that our waiter had forgotten about them. My cannelloni was cold—there is no other way to describe it. My father's meal was the same but he asked me not to complain. The girls simply ate their meals (equally cold) and didn't want to become involved in a verbal exchange with the manager. Please keep in mind that I haven't sent back a meal twice in the past thirty years. I'm not a complainer.

I was given a second plate of cannelloni and the waiter departed—apparently for the evening. We never saw him again. We finished our meals and waited—it was nearly ten o'clock in the evening on a Tuesday with just one other couple seated in the dining room. Coffee and dessert were out of the question. I just wanted a check and, if possible, a brief discussion with the manager about what had happened.

Again, I had to go into the bar to find an employee and wait—5 to 7 minutes—for my check. The manager was absolutely confrontational when I told him what I have just related to you. "What do you want me to do about it?" he said. "Tell your employees that I'm a customer and not a nuisance in their evening," I answered. Then, unbelievably, he asked "Are you lookin' for a free meal or somethin'?" I was stunned.

I signed the American Express charge slip and turned to leave. Your manager mumbled, just loud enough for me to hear, "No tip, huh?" I turned and said to him, "I've got a tip for you, friend. Get out of the food business."

It's been nearly a week since the event and I'm still upset, partly because of his behavior and the experience my father and children went through, and partly because I genuinely like Olive Garden Restaurants. I must tell you, in all honesty, I cannot now imagine returning to that one.

Thanks for listening to my story. I know it's not easy to listen to a customer with a "bad service" story, but I feel better having shared it with you.

Sincerely,

Martin A. Wallace, M.D.

❧

Case 7–2   WAUKEGAN MATERIALS, INC.

Managers are often called on to recognize the achievements and accomplishments of their employees and others within their organizations. Public acknowledgment of exceptional work, career milestones, and special events in people's lives is important, not only to those being recognized, but to others who carefully observe how the organization treats its people.

Those who have worked in and for large, complex organizations will often acknowledge that it's difficult to monitor and properly appreciate individual achievements. Many financial, sales, production, and profit goals are predicated on group activities; individuals often are made to bask in the reflected glory of group membership.

Among the more useful observations regarding letters of appreciation are these: if it isn't worth writing as a personal, individual document, it isn't worth receiving. Generic, one-size-fits-all letters are frequently the subject of employee scorn. Letters of appreciation, in general, should be brief, warm, and specific. They should probably not extend beyond two or three paragraphs, they should reflect a controlled enthusiasm for the message recipient, and they should comment specifically on the achievements or accomplishment for which the receiver is being recognized.

Waukegan Materials, Inc., is a regional distributor in the building and construction industry. They conduct both wholesale and retail operations and are a nonunion firm. You may assume that you are general manager of the Lakefront Division. This case requires two documents: a one-page transmittal memorandum and a letter of appreciation to an employee. The memo should be directed to the company president and should respond to the president's questions posed in the case. Both documents should be in final form and ready to dispatch.

This case was prepared from public sources by James S. O'Rourke, concurrent associate professor of management, as the basis for class discussion rather than to illustrate either effective or ineffective handling of an administrative situation. Personal and corporate identities have been disguised.

WAUKEGAN MATERIALS, INC.
3400 Sheridan Road
Waukegan, Illinois 60620

DATE: [Today's Date]

TO: General Manager, Lakefront Division

FROM: Paul Magers

                    President, Waukegan Materials, Inc.

SUBJECT: Employee-of-the-Quarter Awards

Your suggestion that Waukegan Materials, Inc., begin a program of employee recognition was a good one. As you know, we have had more than two dozen nominations for the first of our quarterly employee recognition awards, and it's been difficult to select just one who is more deserving than the others for this honor. After several long and very trying sessions, the awards committee has selected our first recipient.

The Waukegan Materials Employee-of-the-Quarter is Mr. Delbert R. Finch of our roofing supplies branch. Finch is an all-around good fellow with a very impressive work record. In fact, he hasn't missed a day's work in the nine years he has been with Waukegan. He tracks the ordering of materials in our roofing supply branch, arranges for shipment to retailers and construction contractors, supervises stock assortment and reshelving operations, and generally keeps an eye on things in the Lakefront Warehouse.

Please help me and the committee by providing us with a letter to recognize Mr. Finch's good work. I would like to present him with the letter and some sort of appropriate gift or memento at our quarterly supervisors' luncheon next month. I don't want to spend a fortune on this program, but I do want the gift to be both appropriate and suitable. The letter should be a good one, too; I'm thinking about having it framed for him and giving a copy to the local newspapers.

Tell me what you plan for us to give him, what this will cost, and how much you think we should spend annually on the program. Please draft a letter today acknowledging his achievements. I'd like to see something by the close of business. Thanks for your help.

8

COMMUNICATING IN INTERCULTURAL AND INTERNATIONAL CONTEXTS

The world you inhabit in the twenty-first century will be a vastly different place from the one you came to know as a child of the twentieth century. The industrialized nations of the world will experience change of an unprecedented sort, and the United States will gradually but inevitably become very different from the nation your parents and grandparents lived and worked in.

What will be different? Almost everything, from the food you eat to the technology you use to the work you do. The organizations that will employ you are changing, restructuring, and transforming themselves. The products and services they provide are changing, as are the skills needed to produce them. The community in which you live will change, as will the people who live there.

The people who inhabit this nation, in fact, will change more profoundly and more quickly than at any previous time in our history, bringing with them fundamental cultural shifts that will redefine what it means to be an American, what *work* is, what *business* means, and what we mean by a *family*. In sum, life in the twenty-first century will not be "business as usual."

Let's look first at some areas we know will change dramatically in the years just ahead and then examine what we mean by culture and diversity. If you understand the circumstances you are likely to face as you tackle the task of managing a business in a highly competitive, global business environment, your chances for success are greater. And, more than anything else—more than technology, science, law, the environment, or systems of government—the social norms and new rules of our society will affect how your business will operate and the challenges you will face as a manager.

INTERCULTURAL CHALLENGES AT HOME

Ethnicity   According the U.S. Bureau of the Census, profound shifts in the next few decades will leave this country older and far more ethnically diverse than ever before. By the middle of the twenty-first century, the United States will no longer have a "majority" race, but instead will be a nation of multiple ethnic groups. Non-Hispanic whites will account for just half of our population. Hispanics will comprise about one-quarter of this country's people, while African-Americans will grow slowly to just over 13 percent. Asian Americans are projected to become about 8 percent of the nation's citizens.[1]

Population Growth   The current U.S. population of 268 million is projected to reach 300 million around the year 2010 and nearly 400 million by midcentury. That increase may sound huge, but it will actually reflect an all-time *low growth rate* after the year 2025. Put simply, the large group of aging baby boomers—those 76 million Americans born between 1946 and 1964—will begin dying faster than new Americans are born, reducing net population increases.[2]

Age   In the next decade alone, the number of people in the United States over the age of 50 will increase by half. In July 1983, the number of Americans over the age of 65 surpassed the number of teenagers. And, with continuing improvements in lifestyle and medical technology, the over-65 population in this country is likely to be more than 50 million by the year 2010—a figure that represents between one-fourth and one-fifth of our population. Today, in fact, more than 50,000 Americans are over the age of 100. And, by the middle of the twenty-first century, that number may approach a million.[3]

   At the same time that the average age of the population and the workforce are rising, the pool of young workers entering the labor market is shrinking. The average worker's age in the United States in 1987 was 36. By 2010, that average will be nearly 41. And workers in the 16- to 24-year-old age group will shrink by several million, or nearly 8 percent of the population.

Families   The shape, size, and even the definition of American families has changed over the past 30 years. Since 1970, they have become smaller; more of them are led by just one parent, and more have mothers who work outside the home. According to Ken Bryson of the U.S. Bureau of the Census, "In the 1970s and 1980s, we had a big shift from married couples with children to one-parent families and people living alone."[4] A recent study which he supervised found that the number of married couples with children under 18 shrank from 40 percent of all households to 25 percent. Divorce rates have soared, and the number of single-person households has climbed from 17 percent to 25 percent.[5]

Women in the Workforce   More women are entering the workforce than at any time since the end of World War II. Since 1998, two-thirds of all new workers in the U.S. have been female. And by 2010, nearly two-thirds of all working age women will be employed. Today, the United States has a workforce that is about 46 percent female, compared with smaller figures in Japan and Mexico, but larger percentages in Sweden and Denmark. A U.S. Labor Department study shows that 43 percent of all executive, administrative, and managerial jobs in the United States are held by women. By comparison, women hold just 17 percent of all managerial positions in Sweden and less than 10 percent in Japan.[6]

   Noteworthy as well is that while working women in the United States are doing better in terms of opportunity and advancement than the vast majority of their counterparts in other nations, they are still paid about 75 percent of what men in comparable positions receive. In addition, working women still bear a disproportionate share of the burden of child care and household duties. Some 42 percent of working moms, in fact, have children under seven years of age.[7]

CULTURAL CHALLENGES ABROAD

A New World Order   Among the more important events of the twentieth century was the fall of the Berlin Wall in 1988. In the decades that followed the collapse of communism and the disintegration of the Soviet Union, we have witnessed a flowering of freedom in Eastern Europe, the establishment of a single European currency, and a lowering of restrictions on the movement of capital, labor, and finished goods. The world has seen its exchanges and bourses integrate into a seamless, global marketplace for money. Jobs flow to areas with lower-priced, competent labor. Capital flows to investment opportunities which best balance risk with return. And the definition of "made in America" now depends on which part of the product or process you examine. At the dawn of the twenty-first century, the market never sleeps. And the manager who plans to participate only in a domestic economy will have few places left to work.

International business is a fact of life today as never before. And in order to succeed, whether as a manager in a transnational corporation, or as an entrepreneur in a small business hoping to sell your goods and services to people in other nations, you will need thorough understanding of the people in your company, your industry, and the global marketplace. The key to understanding them is an understanding of their culture.

Customs and Culture Abroad   In Hungary, men customarily walk on the left side of women or anyone of greater status, like a boss. It's considered intrusive to ask a man from the Middle East about his wife or female members of his family. It's also considered impolite for a woman to pour wine in Italy. Why? Well, as you will discover, different cultures promote different ways of thinking and behaving. What's considered customary for you at home may well be unacceptable overseas. And, of course, what's perfectly natural for people—even professional businesspeople—in other countries may be considered peculiar or offensive here.

   Some mistakes can be worse than embarrassing. Anthropologist Margaret Nydell tells of an American woman in Saudi Arabia who slid into the front passenger seat of a car and planted a friendly kiss on the cheek of the man at the wheel. Public displays of affection don't play well there. The gesture was spotted by a captain of the Saudi National Guard who demanded to know if the couple was married. They were, but not to each other. As a result, the woman was expelled from the country and the man, who argued with the lawman, spent some time in jail.[8]

   In 1995, Bill Richardson, then a U.S. Congressman from New Mexico, traveled to Baghdad, Iraq, to meet with Saddam Hussein to try to secure the release of two Americans who had been imprisoned after accidentally straying into Iraqi territory. Richardson greeted Hussein with a handshake, then sat down and crossed his legs. Hussein stood up abruptly and left the room, ending the meeting before it began. Richardson's offense? He'd displayed the sole of his shoe, a serious insult in many Arabic and Eastern countries because the bottom of the foot is considered to be the dirtiest part of the body. The Americans were eventually released, but Richardson's opening gambit didn't help the process.[9]

   Nonverbal communication can be as much a source of misunderstanding as verbal, according to American business consultant, Elizabeth Ulrich. "The classic example is the 'A-OK' gesture which is positive in the United States," she says, "but obscene in much of the rest of the world." That same gesture in France means "worthless." It is impolite to point to people in Japan or to give the split-fingered "victory" sign knuckles out in England. It is offensive to use the "thumbs-up" sign in Nigeria, or to eat with your left hand in most Arab countries.[10]

Mary Murray Bosrock, author of a series of international etiquette books, says showing up on time for a dinner party in South America could be a disaster—no one expects anyone to be less than half-an-hour to an hour late. She says you are liable to find your host or hostess still getting dressed if you actually arrive at the hour printed on the invitation.[11]

In many Asian cultures, particularly Japan, saying "no" is considered very impolite. In fact, it's unusual to the point of being rare, particularly in business negotiations. According to Philip R. Harris, an international business consultant, and Robert T. Moran, a professor of international management, indirect and vague approaches are more acceptable than direct and specific references. "Sentences are frequently left unfinished so that the other person may conclude them in his or her own mind. Conversation often transpires within an ill-defined and shadowy context, never quite definite so as not to preclude personal interpretation."[12]

Japanese businesspeople are reluctant in the extreme to say "no" to a direct question, even when the answer is, in fact, "no." Instead, you may hear, "These things often take much time," "Issues of this sort, as you understand, are sometimes difficult," or "We are sorry that things have developed in such a fashion." Often, a Japanese businessperson will simply change the subject or direct an unrelated question back to you. In the most extreme conditions, if you ask for a "yes" or "no" response, you will receive only silence, usually accompanied by head nods, tightened lips, and a break in eye contact with you. A senior, experienced Japanese trade negotiator puts it this way: "It is true that we Japanese try diligently to prevent any situation from becoming what we call *tairitsu,* a confrontation, whether in our personal lives or in business and politics."[13]

Being culturally sensitive is essential to your success. In Japan, for example, the presentation of a business card is done with reverence, almost like an intricate dance. Cards, which represent the person's importance to the company and personal identity within the community, are gently presented with two hands and accomplished with a bow. Businesspeople exchanging cards always face each other, holding their cards on the upper two corners. The recipient is expected to take the card and, with studied seriousness, examine it thoroughly before carefully and respectfully putting it in a cardholder. During business meetings, cards are often kept out in the open and used respectfully as a reference point during conversations.[14]

In the United States, according to Roger E. Axtell, former marketing vice president for Parker Pen Co., "We just stuff them in our pockets or even write on them." During a business trip to Japan, Axtell saw an American businessman picking his teeth with a business card. "I thought, 'Hey, that's my personal identity there!' "[15]

One further caution regarding business cards: bring enough for everyone. You'll find that not only do the principals in a meeting want your card—everyone in the room expects one. Americans traveling in Asia should expect to hand out 200 cards a week. You'll get bonus points if your card is translated into the local language on the reverse side. To make absolutely certain the translation is precise and correct, ask your U.S.

Chamber of Commerce contact for advice on having your cards printed on the backside before you arrive.

You've undoubtedly heard or read about the elaborate rituals of gift-giving in Japan, where just about every business occasion demands an exchange of gifts. You know some numbers are unlucky in China, or that some colors are inappropriate for gifts or flowers in the Middle East. But the rules are many and varied, so if you are traveling to a new part of the world to try to make money—or even as a tourist—you are well advised to learn something of the culture and the local customs.

BUSINESS AND CULTURE

Whether you are dealing with issues of marketing, management, finance, or even the details of accounting for a firm's assets and business activities, the success or failure of your company abroad will depend on how effectively your employees can exercise their skills in a new location. That ability will depend on both their job-related expertise and each individual's sensitivity and responsiveness to a new cultural environment. Among the most common factors contributing to failure in international business assignments, according to Professor Gary P. Ferraro of the University of North Carolina, "is the erroneous assumption that if a person is successful in the home environment, he or she will be equally successful in applying technical expertise in a different culture."[16]

Research has shown (Tung, 1988; Black, Gregersen and Mendenhall, 1992) that failures in an overseas business setting most frequently result from an inability to understand and adapt to foreign ways of thinking and acting, rather than from technical or professional incompetence. At home, U.S. businesspeople equip themselves with vast amounts of knowledge about their employees, customers, and business partners. Market research provides detailed information on values, attitudes, and buying preferences of U.S. consumers. Middle- and upper-level managers are well versed in the intricacies of their organization's culture, and labor negotiators must be highly sensitive to what motivates those on the other side of the table. Yet, when North Americans begin doing business abroad, they frequently are willing to work with customers, employees, suppliers, and others about whom they know and understand very little.[17]

DEFINITIONS OF CULTURE

So, what exactly *is* culture and how does it affect the way we do business? *Culture is everything that people have, think, and do as members of their society.* Culture affects and is a central part of our society, our economy, and the organizations which employ us. Culture is, thus, composed of the following.

Material Objects Everything you own, lease, borrow, or use is defined as a part of your culture, from the automobile you drive to the clothing you wear. We make judgments each day, often without even being aware we are doing so, about the people we meet and do business with. Many, if not most, of those judgments depend on what we think about the way people are dressed, whether their shoes are polished, how their offices are furnished, the sort of wristwatch they wear or briefcase they carry, and so on. People, in turn, judge us by the material objects we use and surround ourselves with.

Ideas, Values, and Attitudes.   We also tend to categorize people according to the ways they think, the ideas they believe, or the basic values they hold to be true. Sometimes the categories are easily described, such as *liberal* or *conservative.* Other ideas, including religious beliefs, or fundamental ideas about family, society, and self are not so easy to categorize.

Expected Patterns of Behavior   Every society has certain *cultural norms* regarding behavior. In the United States, women expect equal treatment under the law, but in many Middle Eastern nations, such as Saudi Arabia, women do not have voting privileges and are not permitted to drive an automobile. Cultural norms in that part of the world are very closely tied to Islamic religious doctrine and prescribe a wide range of expected behaviors ranging from what clothing is permissible to when and with whom a woman might be away from her home.

In many ways, culture defines how we look at life in general, and it guides how we respond to characteristics such as race, ethnicity, physical attributes, age, social class, education, and many other factors. It also shapes our responses to these qualities, both within ourselves and in other people.[18] At the broad social level, culture tells us who we are (what groups we belong to), how we should behave, and ". . . gives us attitudes about 'them,' the people who are different from us. It tells us what should be important as well as how to act in various situations."[19]

Culture surrounds us so completely, and from such an early point in life, that we often do not realize that there are other ways of dealing with the world, that others may have a different outlook on life, a different logic, or a different way of responding to people and situations.[20]

SOME PRINCIPLES OF CULTURE

Here, then, are a few ideas about culture that have been shown to be true across time and across both national and cultural boundaries.

Culture Is Learned   In 1861, Giuseppe Garibaldi played a pivotal role in the uniting of feudal kingdoms and principalities into the modern nation-state of Italy. As the populace of Southern Italy acclaimed Garibaldi as their ruler, he told the cheering throngs, "Now that we have founded the nation of Italy, we must all learn to be Italian."[21] Few of us would give a moment's thought to *learning* how to be American, Italian, Mexican or any other culture. If you were born into a culture, you learned from the moment you began to see, hear, and breathe. Our first culture is so closely defined with each of us that we're barely aware we *have* one. Learning a second culture, though, is clearly more difficult. The older we become, the closer to impossible the task becomes.

Culture Is Universal to Human Society   Everyone has a culture, regardless of where they were born, raised, educated, and civilized. For some among us, the idea of a *specific* culture is not as easy as it may look. My college roommate was born and raised in Syracuse, New York. His wife, Mary, was born and raised in northern

California. Following their marriage in the early 1970s, they moved overseas and have lived in the Philippines; in Kenya, East Africa; in Greece; in Italy; and in England. No matter where they move, however, and no matter how many different cultures they're exposed to, they'll always be thoroughly American. Their vocabulary and preferences in food have changed a bit, but not their basic culture. For their two boys, Jim and John, culture is a different matter. Even though they grew up with U.S. passports and American parents, they lived in societies very different from those their parents grew up in. They were educated in British schools and, for all intents and purposes, they've really become British by culture and "citizens of the world" by experience.

All societies exhibit an interest in passing along cultural values and norms to their children. It's really the similarity of those values and norms that collectively creates and defines a culture. Thus, no matter where you travel, you'll find people with cultures of their own—interesting, diverse, rich cultures—different from the one in which you grew up.

Culture Is Constantly Undergoing Change   Among the basic truths about culture is that none is ever static. The clothing people wear, the transportation they use, the books they read, the topics they talk about, the food they eat, the music they listen and dance to, all will change over time. Compare the lives your grandparents led to the life you are leading, and you'll get some sense of how your own grandchildren will look at you. Change *is* the constant in every culture. There are those who insist that whatever is new in a culture (what sort of music *is* your little brother listening to?) is inferior to whatever came before. True or not (and, usually, it's a matter of opinion about whether change is an improvement), the elements that make us who we are will constantly remain in flux.

Cultures change because of *internal* forces, such as discovery, invention, and innovation. They also change because of *external forces,* including the diffusion of innovation across space and time, and borrowing the traits, habits, or customs of another culture.

Some Cultures Change More Quickly than Others   Some societies are isolated by geography—vast oceans or tall mountain ranges. Others are isolated by preference. The more keenly tuned-in a society is to the interests and preferences of other cultures, the more quickly change will come. If fashions change quickly in Paris each spring, can New York and Los Angeles be far behind in producing copies? Life in parts of the American Midwest and South change more slowly, in part because of geography, and in part because of preference. Some people prefer things as they are and try to preserve life as they know it; others prefer change and will move to cities or other nations in search of that change.

Los Angeles, California, is nearly 3,000 miles from New York City, but culturally the two cities are not vastly different. Residents will point to a faster pace in New York and a more laid back style in LA, but they are both metropolitan centers of business, politics, media, publishing, fashion, food, and much more. Victorville, California, is no more than 75 miles from Los Angeles, but culturally it's light years away. The pace of life, the food available in local restaurants, the clothing worn there, and everything else from entertainment to commerce are vastly different. The people of Victorville proudly point to the fact that little has changed in their little town over the past 50 years, and they like it that way. Life in Los Angeles can, and probably will, change in significant ways before you have lunch tomorrow.

Five factors influence the *rate* of change as well as the *kind* of change a culture may experience. These factors include:

- *Relative advantage.* Is it superior to what already exists? If the change isn't superior in some way to existing habits, the innovation is unlikely to catch on.
- *Compatibility.* Is it consistent with existing cultural patterns? Some changes are superior to current practices but they may be at odds with existing culture patterns. If what's new is not compatible with the ways in which the majority of people think and behave, change may be slow to occur.
- *Complexity.* Is it easily understood? Desktop computers represent a clearly superior means of communicating and processing both text and data, but their general complexity held back widespread adoption for the better part of a decade in our society.
- *Trialability.* Is it testable? Can we try it out experimentally? The difference between hair dye and a tattoo is that one is temporary, while the other is permanent. Cultural change comes more quickly when people can experiment a bit without making irrevocable decisions.
- *Observability.* Are the benefits clearly visible to those affected by change? If you can't see its value, you may be unwilling to try it.[22]

Culture Is *Not* Value-Neutral   The diversity movement in this country, for all the good and positive change it has brought to American business and higher education, has passed along one subtle *untruth* that is frequently repeated: "We must respect all other cultures, because our culture is really no better than theirs. Ours is simply different."

Our culture certainly *is* different from others, but that's not the same as saying that all cultures are equally moral, equally fair, or equally humane. Amnesty International annually publishes a list of cultures in which people are denied basic human rights. And the Conference Board develops a list of nations each year which are rank-ordered according to level of corruption. The United States, by the way, is among the least corrupt nations on earth, but is still some distance from the top of the list. In 2000, Norway was listed as *the* least corrupt among nations.

With human rights and corrupt behavior as basic considerations, we must also understand that many factors from ancient tradition to religious belief can produce human behavior that you and I may well regard as offensive or outrageous. At the dawn of the twenty-first century, women are still not allowed to vote or own property in many nations, and in other nations they are often ritualistically mutilated or sold into slavery. The very fact that such practices are accepted in those societies and simultaneously shock us is a sign that our values and theirs aren't the same. Our cultures may well be quite different from one another, but they are not equal or interchangeable in all respects. Culture, in fact, is *not* value-neutral.

Not All Cultures Are Equally Complex   Because of size, geography, distance from great population centers, and other factors, some cultures are more simple in their patterns of organization, behavior, and belief than others. Vast sections of Sub-Saharan Africa, the Polynesian islands of the South Pacific, the dense interior of South America's jungles and rain forests, and the frozen tundra of the Arctic have developed cultures that are both ancient and rich in their heritage, but not terribly complex. Many still depend on barter to survive and small councils of elders for adjudicating legal problems. The modern G-8 nations have legal systems and tax codes so complex that no lawyer or accountant could claim expertise in all of them.

Virtually All Cultures Permit the Development of Subcultures   Within each culture, small groups of people inevitably develop separate and specialized interests: hikers, bikers, baseball fans, gourmet cooks, bible readers, bird-watchers, and volunteer firemen. The list is potentially endless, as people gather together in the same room, on the telephone, or the Internet to pursue their common interests. The tolerance of some societies is not endless, however. Highly repressive cultures permit very little in the way of deviation from doctrine. Cuba, for example, banned the celebration of Christmas from 1959 until 1998. Even the United States officially bans certain activities by hate groups, even though the U.S. Constitution protects their right to exist. The more complex the culture, the greater the likelihood and the greater the number of subcultures that will exist and flourish.

Culture Can Influence Biology and Biology Can Influence Culture   This may not seem self-evident at first, but culture can—and does—have an enormous influence on human biology. The most striking example can be seen in the dramatic increase in average height and body weight of the Japanese people during the last 50 years of the twentieth century. Men in their third decade of life now weigh substantially more than their grandfathers did and are, on average, several inches taller. The gains in women's physiognomy are equally impressive.

   Other illustrations abound, from facial scars and body adornment in West Africa to breast implants and plastic facial surgery in the United States. Even such issues as fat content in our diets can affect how big we grow and how fit we are. The United States, to counterbalance a culture which had grown soft and averse to exercise in the 1950s and 1960s, has actively portrayed exercise and fitness as desirable and worthwhile. Not only have people worked themselves into generally better physical condition, several new industries have grown up around them, offering sportswear, exercise machines, high-tech shoes, and high-energy diets.

FUNCTIONS OF CULTURE

Cultures universally respond to human problems and challenges by developing systems to deal with them. Most successful cultures develop economic systems, marriage and family systems, educational systems, and supernatural belief systems. These systems are more complex and intricate in some cultures than in others, but for the most part, people collectively establish rules for economic value and trade, systems for assigning responsibility, for establishing and raising families, for educating children, and for a belief in God or an afterlife. Individual beliefs may vary somewhat, but it is the culture itself that establishes how most people in a society think, believe, and behave.[23]

ETHNOCENTRISM

All cultures—to one degree or another—display *ethnocentrism,* or the tendency to evaluate a foreigner's behavior by the standards of one's own culture and to believe that one's own culture is superior to all others. We take our culture for granted. We're born into it, live with its rules and assumptions day in and day out. We quickly come to believe that the way we live is simply "the way things should be."

As a result, we see our behavior as correct and others' as wrong. Keep in mind what we've said about culture *not* being value-neutral. We have very good reasons for believing and behaving as we do, but that doesn't necessarily mean that others are "wrong."

All cultures are ethnocentric, some more so than others. Ethnocentrism, in fact, can enhance group solidarity within a society and is often used by corrupt national or ethnic leaders as a means of building or consolidating power and excluding outsiders. Clearly, ethnocentrism can foster prejudice, contempt, stereotypes, and conflict.[24]

CROSS-CULTURAL COMMUNICATION SKILLS

One set of skills essential to success in a global economy, then, is the ability to communicate across cultures. According to a number of authors on this subject, the skill set you need involves several personal capacities:

- The capacity to accept the relativity of your own knowledge and perceptions. We each tend to judge people, events, and ideas against our own education, background, and beliefs. Simply recognizing that some of these are bound to be different from those of other cultures is a useful starting point.
- The capacity to be nonjudgmental. Make personal judgments, if you wish. Just keep them to yourself.
- A tolerance for ambiguity. The less you understand about something, the more problematic your views will be for other people.
- The capacity to communicate respect for other people's ways, their country, and their values without adopting or internalizing them.

This also involves the capacity to display empathy, to be flexible (particularly under conditions of high ambiguity or uncertainty), to take turns (or wait your turn, if you're uncertain of the protocol), and the humility to acknowledge what you do not know or understand.

Clearly, understanding what motivates the people you hope to do business with will be crucial to your success. Technical competence in your line of work is important, but so is an understanding of the culture, customs, norms, and beliefs of others, whether domestically or internationally. Curiously, as we find the world's economy becoming more global and interdependent, we also find our own nation undergoing similar changes. The only constant in the years ahead, it seems, will be change itself.

Endnotes

1. Friedman, D. and K. Pollack. "Ahead: A Very Different Nation." *U.S. News & World Report,* March 25, 1996, p. 8.
2. Seelye, K. Q. "Future U.S.: Grayer and More Hispanic." *New York Times,* March 27, 1997, p. A-18.
3. Rimer, S. "As Centenarians Thrive, 'Old' Is Redefined," *New York Times,* June 22, 1998, pp. A-1, A-14.
4. Kilborn, P. T. "Shifts in Families Reach a Plateau, Study Says," *New York Times,* November 27, 1996, p. B-1.
5. Ibid.
6. Thomas, P., V. Reitman, D. Solis, and D. Milbank. "Women in Business: A Global Report Card." *Wall Street Journal,* July 26, 1995, p. B-1.
7. Ibid.
8. Maxa, R. "How to Avoid Cultural Blunders: For Business Travelers, a Few Rules Can Go a Long Way." MSNBC. *http://www. msnbc.com/ news/224480/asp.* 12/23/1998, 5:00 p.m.
9. Ibid.
10. Adams, D. "Don't Get Upset if Foreign Executive Holds Your Hand." *South Bend Tribune,* December 20, 1998, p. B5.
11. Bosrock, M. M. *Put Your Best Foot Forward.* Minneapolis, MN: International Educational Systems, 1995.
12. Harris, P. R. and Moran, R. T. "Doing Business with Asians—Japan, China, Pacific Basin, and India," in *Managing Cultural Differences: High Performance Strategies for a New World of Business.* Houston, TX:

Gulf Publishing Company, 1991, pp. 393–406.
13. Barnlund, D. *Communicative Styles of Japanese and Americans: Images and Realities.* Belmont, CA: Wadsworth Publishing Company, 1989, pp. 156–157.
14. Adams, "Don't Get Upset," p. B5.
15. Ibid.
16. Ferraro, G. P. *The Cultural Dimension of International Business,* 3rd ed. Upper Saddle River, NJ: Prentice-Hall, Inc., 1998, p. 7.
17. Ibid.
18. Harvey, C. and Allard, M. J. *Understanding Diversity: Readings, Cases, and Exercises.* New York, NY: HarperCollins College Publishers, 1995, p. 7.
19. Simons, G. *Working Together: How to Become More Effective in a Multicultural Organization.* Los Altos, CA: Crisp Publications, 1989, p. 5.
20. Harvey and Allard, *Understanding Diversity,* p. 7.
21. See Harris, W. H. and J. S. Levey. *The New Columbia Encyclopedia.* New York, NY: Columbia University Press, 1975, p. 1046. See also Trevelyan, G. M. *Garibaldi and the Making of Modern Italy,* 1911, reprinted 1948.
22. Ferraro, *The Cultural Dimension,* pp. 25–30.
23. Ibid. pp. 22–25.
24. Lustig, M. and J. Koester. *Intercultural Competence: Interpersonal Communication Across Cultures.* New York, NY: Addison Wesley Longman, Inc., 1999, pp. 146–149.

For Further Reading

Axtell, R. *Dos and Taboos Around the World.* New York, NY: John Wiley & Sons, 1985.

Black, J. S., H. B. Gregersen, and M. Mendenhall. *Global Assignments: Successful Expatriating and Repatriating International Managers.* San Francisco, CA: Jossey-Bass Publishers, 1992.

Guy, V. and J. Mattock. *The International Business Book.* Lincolnwood, IL: NTC Business Books, 1995.

Hall, E. T. and M. R. Hall. *Understanding Cultural Differences: German, French, and Americans.* Yarmouth, ME: Intercultural Press, 1990.

O'Hara-Devereaux, M. and R. Johansen. *Globalwork: Bridging Distance, Culture and Time.* San Francisco, CA: Jossey-Bass, 1994.

Ricks, D. *Blunders in International Business.* Cambridge, MA: Blackwell, 1994.

Tung, R. L. *The New Expatriates: Managing Human Resources Abroad.* Cambridge, MA: Ballinger Publishing, 1988.

Urich, E. *Speaking Globally: Effective Presentations Across International and Cultural Boundaries.* Exeter, NH: Kogan Page, 1998.

❧

Case 8–1 OAK BROOK MEDICAL SYSTEMS, INC.

Jacqueline Harris has been an employee of Oak Brook Medical Systems for about 12 years. For the past 18 months, she has been director of strategic planning for the Hospital Supply Division, a segment of Oak Brook Medical Systems which has grown at the phenomenal rate of nearly 35 percent per year over the past 3 years.

The division is relatively new, having been formed just seven years ago as a result of changes in the healthcare marketplace. The division's growth has been the direct result of good products, solid customer service, and the quality focused people the company has managed to attract. The people working for the Hospital Supply Division are, for the most part, self-starters—entrepreneurial, competitive types who are dedicated and hard-working. The people in Jackie's division and the corporate leadership pride themselves on making things happen for their customers.

Jackie is considered a very valuable asset to her division and is widely credited with developing the strategy that resulted in a $40 million business for the company. She is also considered a no-nonsense, results-oriented manager with a history of being able to get things done. Jackie is also known for her directness and, on several occasions, has had problems interacting with her colleagues. According to friends and coworkers, she is known to be curt with colleagues as well as subordinates.

JACKIE'S COLLEAGUES AND COWORKERS

Others in the division see her as being defensive and, at times, overwhelming. They say she overwhelms people with data when presenting an idea or making a point. Another person has been quoted as saying that "I feel like I am being talked down to when I have a conversation with her." As a result of these perceptions, some feel that she is unapproachable and tough to work with. In the last couple of years, her difficulty in communicating with colleagues has been a greater concern during discussions of her future in the division. To date, however, no one has brought this to her attention directly.

Jackie has experienced the difficulty of communicating with her colleagues, but she considers this simply to be a part of getting the job done. In fact, she thinks she is behaving in a manner comparable to the successful people who have preceded her. Jackie has grown increasingly frustrated, though, because of a lack of attention from senior management.

Despite her highly successful performance with the strategic plan, no one seems to be talking with her about a promotion, and she cannot understand why she is being overlooked. Increasingly, she thinks it is a result of her manager (a division vice-president) and the president of the division not wanting to promote her because she is African-American. She won't say it aloud, but she is beginning to suspect that subtle forms of racism are holding her back.

This frustration has grown more acute, at least to her thinking, because she has always known success. She graduated in the top 10 percent of her engineering class at a large, well-known midwestern university. She was in the top 5 percent of her MBA class in the Sloan School of Management at MIT. Jackie has always taken pride in her work and has always worked toward excellence in whatever tasks she took on. She selected this division of Oak Brook Medical Systems, in fact, because it was fast-paced, results-oriented, and the market was growing dramatically for its products and services. This was an industry and a company, Jackie thought, that could provide job opportunities for people who could do good work and produce results.

This division, however, has had very little representation of women and people of color in its management ranks. At first, Jackie thought this would work to her advantage, creating opportunities for her to move up quickly. Now she was beginning to suspect that there were few women and no people of color in division upper management because those in power don't want them.

Both Jackie and other senior management officials recognized the shifting demographics in their customer base and the positive implications of having someone in the division who could identify with such customers and bring a different perspective to the business. With this in mind, she decided to remain with the division. Before long, though, it became plain to those around her that she was not happy.

THE NEED FOR ACTION

As her manager, how would you approach Jackie with your concerns about her problems in communicating with others? How would you help her with her professional development and career growth within the division? In assisting her, you may wish to consider these questions:

- What are the assumptions being made about Jackie by her colleagues and managers?
- What growth opportunities do you see for Jackie which could address the issue of communication with other employees?
- What do you see as obstacles that could get in the way of Jackie's growth and development in the Hospital Supply Division? How do you think the environment in the division may have contributed to the difficulties she is experiencing?
- What should you as her manager do to provide support and communicate that support to her? How would you go about challenging your assumptions about her? What would you do to confront her assumptions about others in the division?
- If you would find it helpful, describe some examples of the sort of feedback you might provide for Jackie regarding her work and her interactions with others in the division.

At a *minimum,* in your response to this case, please identify:

- Business and management issues
- Legal issues
- Cultural issues

In your response to this case, you *must* also answer two additional questions:

- What must I do *right now* to solve the problem? What actions do I take immediately?
- What advice would I offer to senior management about this matter? Have any company policies (or lack of policies) contributed to the events described above?

This case was prepared by Ms. Kay Wigton with the assistance of James S. O'Rourke, concurrent associate professor of management, as the basis for class discussion rather than to illustrate either effective or ineffective handling of an administrative situation. Personal and corporate identities have been disguised.

❧

Case 8–2   BIG DOG SOFTWARE, INC.

Todd Batey returned from lunch with high hopes for a productive afternoon. Two large, long-term projects had just been completed and this would be his opportunity to dig through that stack of unopened mail, deferred memos, file folders, journals, and magazines he simply hadn't found time to read.

Among the larger, more important projects Batey had worked on during the past several months was a new product launch in the company's enterprise software division. At the same time, he had been working with Big Dog Software's senior team on a highly confidential and potentially profitable strategic alliance: Big Dog executives were targeting several Japanese firms for a joint venture that would permit the company to distribute its famous "S-4" supply chain management software in Japan and, perhaps, throughout much of Asia.

COMPANY BACKGROUND

Big Dog Software, Inc., is a small but rapidly growing firm located outside of Silicon Valley in LaJolla, California. This quirky back-bedroom start-up had grown from $8 million in capital with no revenues just five years ago to a $150 million, publicly held firm that specializes in enterprise software, customized applications, and innovative thinking in systems integration and supply-chain management. Chad Lucas and his college roommate, Joshua Flynn, had converted an interest in management information systems into a successful business long before most of their classmates had paid off their college loans.

Virtually all of their efforts had been internal, however. Lucas and Flynn hired half-a-dozen of the smartest young programmers and systems engineers in Southern California and began developing a product line. Perhaps their brightest move was to hire Todd Batey, a recent Santa Clara grad who specialized in marketing. Piece-by-piece, the team of Lucas and Flynn had put together a very strong business, but now things were beginning to move much more quickly. If they were to take advantage of the window of opportunity now open in the Far East, they would need more than bright programmers and a young marketing director. They would need a business partner who knows the territory.

OPPORTUNITY KNOCKS

As Batey tossed his soft drink cup in the recycling bin, one of the interns stuck her head in Todd's cubicle. "Chad and Josh need to see you."

"What's up," he asked?

"No clue," she replied. "I just know something's happening and you're next on the agenda."

Batey grabbed his Palm Pilot and headed down the hallway. With just 75 employees, Big Dog Software didn't take up much space: two floors of a modern office building where Torrey Pines Road meets the I-5. On a nice day (and they were almost all nice) you could see Pacific Beach from the windows in Batey's cubicle. Not much privacy, but a great view.

Batey walked into Chad Lucas's office without knocking. Formality was about as common around Big Dog Software as neckties. "You need to see me?" he asked.

"Hey, Todd," came the reply, "have a seat."

"We just got a fax from Masahiro," said Lucas. "Our endless series of trips to Tokyo has finally paid off." The fax in question was from Masahiro Fudaba, a senior vice president with Ichi Ban Heavy Industries of Japan.

"Really?" asked Batey.

"Finally." said Flynn. "We're going into partnership with Ichi Ban to form a joint venture. Their shareholders, business partners, bankers, and Keiretsu executives have finally bought off on the deal." He paused for a just a moment. "Looks like the Big Dog is going to Japan."

"First, though, we're going to have some Japanese visitors," said Lucas. "The word from Masahiro is that Kazushi Yakura and a team of eight Japanese managers will be here next week to begin the process of organizing our new, jointly owned company. Apparently Mr. Yakura will be here for just a few days. The transition team, however, is planning to stay until we have all the details worked out."

"How can I help?" asked Batey.

"Well," said Flynn, "we're engineers. You're the marketing guy, so we figured you would be the logical person to help make these folks feel welcome."

"More to the point," said Lucas, "we need to help the people on Ichi Ban's transition team understand a bit more about us. They know our business, our market, and our industry, but I'm not sure how much these guys know about the United States, about California, or about doing business with Americans. According to Masahiro," he added, "only Mr. Yakura has been to the United States. Most of the others have never been out of Japan."

"Interesting," said Batey. "What else do we know about them?"

"Here's a list of people they've identified for the visit," said Lucas. "We have ages, job titles, and a little bit of background, including education and prior work experience, but not much else."

"What do you want them to know?" asked Batey.

"It's clear to me that we have to reduce their anxieties, eliminate their fears, and raise the level of mutual trust," said Flynn. "I know that you understand something about intercultural communication, so we'll leave the details up to you." He paused for a moment, then said. "Let's make it more than a Padres' game and a day at the Zoo."

"No problem," said Batey. "I'll have a preliminary plan worked up for you by the close of business tomorrow."

Lucas and Flynn thanked the young marketing manager and expressed complete confidence in his ability to make the Japanese managers' visit productive and successful. Todd left Lucas's office and, heading down the hallway, thought to himself. "No problem? Maybe there is a problem here. What are we gonna do with these guys?"

DISCUSSION QUESTIONS

1. Assume that your cubicle is near Todd Batey's and he has asked you for some advice on this subject. What would you say to him?

2. What objectives or measurable outcomes should Batey specify for his immersion into American culture for these visitors?

3. What American concepts can you safely assume these managers know and understand? What concepts do you think they *absolutely must* understand in order for the joint venture to succeed?

4. How would you go about showing them what the United States is all about? Where would you take them? What would you show them?

5. How can you be sure what your visitors will understand when they're ready to go home?

6. What sort of budget would you need for this program?

7. How much do you suppose other Big Dog employees understand about Japan and Japanese culture? Should any of them be involved in your effort to introduce North America to your new Asian business partners?

This case was prepared by James S. O'Rourke, concurrent associate professor of management, as the basis for class discussion rather than to illustrate either effective or ineffective handling of an administrative situation. All names are fictional and identities have been disguised for purposes of case discussion.

9
MANAGING CONFLICT
❧

The workplace of the twenty-first century—much like the workplace of the last century—is filled with tension and strife. Conflicts arise under pressure-cooker deadlines, increased workloads, fear of layoffs, and the unrelenting demand for higher productivity. Under such stress, workplace violence has been increasing. (See Glossary: "going postal.") And even in calm settings, routine business negotiations often turn ugly.[1]

Some organizations don't seem interested in peace. General Motors Corporation lost more than $2.2 billion trying to win a labor struggle with the United Auto Workers union in the late-1990s. According to one industry analyst, "GM and the UAW are like oil and water. They just cannot get along." Threats, intimidation, walkouts, lockouts, and inflexible positions have characterized their relationship over the years. "GM ought to have learned from this strike that it can't win labor showdowns," says auto analyst Maryann Keller. "They've had 24 strikes since 1990, and it hasn't solved anything."[2]

Conflict can arise from a variety of sources, but many experts see it as a function of such workplace variables as personality, personal and professional relationships, cultural differences, working environments, demands of the marketplace, and of course, competition. "Workers today compete for schedules and projects, for money and training," says Marilyn Moats Kennedy, a career coach in Wilmette, Illinois.[3] And, as organizations move increasingly to teams and teamwork to accomplish specific objectives, differences among team members can lead to conflict.

"Conflict in any endeavor that requires the input of two or more people is a real possibility," says Jeanne Gulbranson, president of Key Performance International in Las Vegas, Nevada. "As the scope of a project increases, the likelihood of differences in opinion and approach increases as a function of the number of tasks involved and the amount of time spent by the staff in the resolution of the project." These conflicts, according Gulbranson, may arise because of people's natural resistance to change, scheduling pressures, perceived difficulties in reporting procedures, or simply because things aren't working well.[4]

Not *all* conflict within an organization is unhealthy, but conflict between and among people within an organization can quickly become counterproductive, divisive, and destructive if not properly managed. In some quarters, most notably high-tech companies, conflict is actually encouraged as a catalyst for creativity. An idea is turned loose on the company's intranet and other employees begin to examine it for flaws. In the best of circumstances, a good idea can be turned into a great idea with creative input and reflective critical thinking from those who must take ownership of the project. At its worst, such conflict can encourage predators in the electronic jungle to "flame" the idea's creator with derisive e-mail messages and the struggle for idea supremacy begins.[5]

A DEFINITION OF CONFLICT

Not surprisingly, we have even seen conflict over how to define conflict.[6] Most experts agree, however, that while *opposition, incompatibility,* and *interaction* are important ingredients in conflict, *a perception of conflict* is essential. In other words, if no one thinks a conflict exists, there probably isn't one.[7]

We can define conflict, then, as a process that begins when someone perceives that someone else has negatively affected, or is about to negatively affect, something that the first person cares about. In practical terms, says Erik Van Slyke of HR Alliance, a Greensboro, North Carolina, consulting firm, "conflict is any time we disagree to the point where we can't go forward." Unchecked, he thinks, small matters can quickly mutate from a business conflict to a personality issue.[8] And from there, everything from productivity to working relationships to share price can suffer.

CONFLICT IN ORGANIZATIONS

The Traditional View   This perspective assumed that all conflict was bad. Conflict in an organizational setting was viewed negatively and was often used synonymously with words such as violence, destruction, and irrationality to reinforce the negative image. Conflict was assumed to be the result of poor communication, a lack of openness and trust between workers and management, and a failure on the part of managers to be responsive to the needs and aspirations of their employees.[9] Naturally, good managers would do all in their power to avoid conflict. A workplace without conflict was assumed to be a happy, productive workplace.

The Human Relations View   Popular from the 1940s to the 1970s, this viewpoint assumed that conflict was a natural occurrence in all groups and organizations. And, since conflict was inevitable, industrial and labor psychologists argued in favor of simply accepting conflict. They rationalized its existence: it can't be eliminated; it may even be beneficial. Embrace it, they said. It's a natural part of every organization.

The Interactionist View   This perspective, which emerged in the social science literature during the 1980s and 1990s, was a bit more radical than its predecessors. The interactionist approach actually *encourages* conflict on the grounds that a harmonious, peaceful, tranquil, and cooperative group may become static, apathetic, and unresponsive to a need for change and innovation. Without a minimum level of conflict, they reason, no organization can change, adapt, and survive the rigors of the marketplace.[10]

In theory, the idea of ongoing minor conflict as a stimulus to creativity sounds good. But does it work in practice? Is it really a good idea to have people at each other's throats just for the sake of a few new market initiatives? "Never underestimate the power of a good idea," says business journalist Michael Warshaw. "Most people in most companies want to do the right thing. Give them an opportunity to make a positive contribution and chances are that they will." Warshaw, who writes for *Fast Company* magazine, also thinks people will work hard in order to leave their mark on a project or an organization. But, "most new-idea champions aren't in a position to order people to participate in their projects," he says.[11] Often, resources are scarce, values compete, and colleagues are looking for visibility in the company. The result is conflict. Properly managed, however, conflict *can* have a beneficial effect on a business. The important questions concern *why* conflict arises and *how* the process should be managed.

SOURCES OF CONFLICT IN ORGANIZATIONS

Conflict may develop over any number of issues or factors, but these five seem to appear regularly in the social psychology literature.

Limited Resources   People in organizations large and small often confront one another over resources which are either scarce or dwindling. These might include issues such as managerial responsibility, supervision of other employees, office or storage space, budget, tools and equipment, training, and access to superiors. If one person perceives another to have some advantage (fair or not), conflict may arise over that perception. It may be something as simple as whose copier budget is bigger or as complex as who will lead the organization in a new, high-visibility product launch.

Values, Goals, and Priorities   Confrontation often occurs because of differences in speciality, training, or beliefs. Karen A. Jehn of Pennsylvania's Wharton School demonstrated in a series of experimental field studies that if people share the same basic values, they're less likely to experience conflict, regardless of task or working conditions.[12] Harvard Business School professor Linda Hill notes that "It is easier to develop relationships with those who share your background, values, interests, or working styles than those who do not. Many studies," she says, "have shown that most of you are more comfortable and prefer to spend time with those similar to you. For instance, it is no surprise that conflicts in organizations often occur between different functional departments. People from different functional areas are likely to have different educational and career histories and, perhaps, values and working styles. Finding common ground and a mutually comfortable way of working can be challenging."[13]

Poorly Defined Responsibilities   Conflict may result from differences between formal position descriptions and informal expectations on the job. "The book" says one thing, but "the job" demands another. In many instances, job design problems arise from ill-defined, vague, or imprecise descriptions that are linked to everything from scheduling to compensation to performance review systems.

Change   Among the few constants in organizational life is change itself. Everything, including annual budgets, organizational priorities, lines of authority, limits of responsibility, restructuring, mergers, divestitures, and layoffs can induce anxiety, uncertainty, and conflict in a business.

Human Drives for Success   Conflict may also be a byproduct of the natural sense of goal orientation that every human experiences. Virtually all organizations, even those in the not-for-profit sector, produce competition among its members by employing many competitors striving for very few rewards. The greater the imbalance between competitors and rewards, the greater the potential for conflict. In a retail establishment, access to walk-in customers may produce significant conflict if compensation schemes are linked directly to sales. In a military organization, where salaries are determined by rank and seniority, competition develops for fewer and fewer available promotions as competitors move up the chain of command.

SENSING CONFLICT

It doesn't take a social psychologist to find conflict in a business. It takes many forms and manifests itself in a number of ways—most of them easily visible, others not. Each manager in a business must assume responsibility for identifying conflict, both potential and actual, within the work environment and using appropriate means for managing or resolving differences which are unhealthy to the life of the organization.

As we saw a few moments ago, conflict can be potentially healthy or destructive to a business. Social psychologists draw a distinction between *functional* and *dysfunctional* conflict. A healthy disagreement about when to act, how much to spend, who to hire, or which path to take is essential to the survival of a business. Conflict becomes dysfunctional, however, when it impedes or prevents managers and their employees from achieving the organization's business objectives. Here are some ways to sense day-to-day conflict in the workplace.

Visualize   Try to visualize or imagine how your actions or those of others might cause, or are causing, conflict. Ask yourself the sort of questions a journalist might ask in reporting a news story: *Who? What? When? How? Why?* Sometimes those self-enquiries begin with *if:* "If I were to change the production schedule to assist the folks in shipping, how would *my* crew react?" You can't always know the answers, but knowing what questions to ask can help prevent serious conflict before it begins.

Give Feedback   The amount, accuracy, and timeliness of information that you can provide to an employee will help you to understand his or her point of view. Sharing your thoughts and feelings first, in a nonthreatening way, often encourages others to tell you what's on their minds. Your employees may not like a particular set of circumstances, but they are likely to be more accepting if they think they know the whole story.

Get Feedback   Take the time to find out what your associates are thinking and feeling. Don't wait until the last moment to discover that you have trouble. Probe for more information by asking questions such as: *How so? In what way? Why? Can you tell me more?* The quality of the feedback you receive, particularly from subordinates and those who are not in your reporting chain, will be a direct function of the level of mutual trust you are able to establish. Harvard professor Linda Hill concludes that balancing advocacy with inquiry is essential. "Managers are trained to be advocates," she says. "They are rewarded for being problem solvers—for figuring out what should be done, putting forth plans for action, and influencing others to adopt them. By contrast, inquiry skills—the ability to ask questions—have gone relatively undeveloped and unrecognized. But as managers rise in their organizations, and the issues they confront become more complex and divergent from their personal experiences, inquiry skills become essential. Managers need to access and embrace the diverse expertise and perspectives of other people. They need to learn how to balance advocacy and inquiry to promote mutual learning."[14]

Define Expectations   Meet regularly with your associates to determine priorities for the day ahead or the coming week. Any major discrepancies or misunderstanding between your expectations and theirs will alert you to potential conflict. Managers often discover that, as they define their expectations for employees in clear easily understood terms, they will receive information in return about what team members and associates expect. Such conversations may be among the few opportunities for supervisors and subordinates to exchange both objective and subjective views of the workplace and the tasks at hand.

Review Performance Regularly   When supervisors and employees communicate openly about how they are (or are not) working together, they reduce the opportunity for serious conflict and help to build stronger working relationships. Most businesses require annual performance reviews for managerial employees and more frequent reviews—semiannual or quarterly—for hourly employees. Experts say that when such reviews are seen by all participants as fair, objective, and professional, morale and workplace satisfaction are likely to be high.

THE BENEFITS OF DEALING WITH CONFLICT

Both you and the organization you work for will benefit if you deal directly with conflict. For you, personally, the benefits are important.

Stronger Relationships   You will be able to build stronger interpersonal relationships as a result of being comfortable expressing your true thoughts and feelings.

Increased Self-Respect   You will be able to feel good about yourself and learn not to take every small bit of criticism personally. A key element in the definition of a professional is that she is able to accept feedback and handle criticism in a professional, rather than personal, manner. It's not *about* you. It's about the organization, the task at hand, and serving those who depend on you.

Personal Growth and Development   When you break down some of your own invisible barriers and become more assertive in resolving or preventing conflict, you will invariably learn more and gain support from others. And if others in the organization come to know that they can depend on you when it really counts, team bonds are strengthened and success is that much easier to realize.

Dealing professionally with conflict in the workplace benefits not only you, but the organization that employs you. Those benefits might include:

Improved Efficiency and Effectiveness   Employees will be able to do their jobs more effectively, and probably with greater levels of efficiency and productivity, by focusing their efforts where they will produce the greatest results. Rather than waste time and energy on workplace conflict, they can do what they were hired to do in the first place.

Creative Thinking   By encouraging people to share and learn from their mistakes, the organization will reap the benefits of creative thinking and a dramatically improved learning curve. By confronting potential conflict before it has an opportunity to paralyze the organization, managers can lower the level of apprehension and fear in the workplace, as well. An important consideration for any employee who is thinking about looking for work elsewhere is whether her work is valued over the long term by management. Advertising the fact that your organization is not a "one-mistake outfit" can help people become less fearful of making mistakes and more confident in trying new ideas and new ways of thinking.

Synergy and Teamwork Managers and associates will be able to focus on serving customers and clients by helping each other. We often hear in the United States that "the customer is number one." In many Asian societies, however, executives have come to realize that "the employee is number one." By taking care of your employees, developing a sense of teamwork and organizational loyalty, you can be assured that they, in turn, will take care of your customers. And those customers, whose loyalty and business you've worked so hard to earn, will take care of your shareholders.

STYLES OF CONFLICT MANAGEMENT

Not everyone approaches conflict in quite the same way. Some welcome the opportunity for a good dust-up. Others duck into the shadows and do their best to avoid confrontation. The style you adopt should reflect a deliberate, thoughtful view of the reasons why people may be in conflict, the culture of your organization, and the personalities of those involved. Figure 9-1 represents author Kenneth Thomas' view of conflict management arrayed along two separate dimensions: *cooperativeness* and *assertiveness*. Thomas defines cooperativeness as the degree to which one person tries to satisfy another person's concerns, while assertiveness is seen as the degree to which one person tries to satisfy her own concerns.

With cooperativeness arrayed from low to high along the horizontal axis, and assertiveness arrayed from low to high along the vertical axis, these two dimensions form a 2 3 2 matrix which can be used to plot a manager's conflict response style. The "conflict-handling intentions" as he calls them are *competing, collaborating, avoiding, accommodating,* and *compromising.*[15]

FIGURE 9-1   Five Styles of Conflict Management

Source: K. Thomas, "Conflict and Negotiation Processes in Organizations," in M.D. Dunnette and L.M. Hough (eds.), *Handbook of Industrial and Organizational Psychology,* 2nd ed., Vol. 3. Palo Alto, CA: Consulting Psychologists Press, 1994.

Competing   This style of conflict management involves people who are both assertive and uncooperative. People who try to satisfy their own interests at the expense of others involved are regarded as competitive. It's a strategy that works when dealing with other participants in the marketplace, but it's often seen as counterproductive inside an organization. Internal competition often produces impressive results but it certainly does not promote teamwork or the cooperative behaviors required of teammates. This approach clearly produces winners and losers.

Collaborating   This style involves people who are assertive but cooperative. If those involved in a situation with the potential for conflict express a desire to fully satisfy the concerns of all others, we're likely to see cooperation and a search for mutually beneficial outcomes. In collaborating, the intention is to solve the problem by clarifying differences rather than by accommodating various points of view. This approach seeks win-win solutions that incorporate the viewpoints of all those involved.

Avoiding   This conflict management style involves people who are both unassertive and uncooperative. When a manager chooses to withdraw from a discussion or a situation in which conflict is likely, his choice is based on a desire to avoid a fight as well as those with whom he may disagree.

Accommodating   This style involves people who are unassertive but cooperative. A manager seeking to appease an opponent or an employee may be willing to place that other person's interests above her own, usually for the sake of maintaining a good working relationship. In spite of personal misgivings or doubts, accommodators are willing to "give in" and "get along," either to promote the goals of the other person or for the sake of group harmony. Consistent accommodation to the needs and interests of others is sometimes seen as another form of conflict avoidance.

Compromising   This approach involves people who are at the midpoint on both assertiveness and cooperativeness. Compromise occurs when each party to a conflict demonstrates a willingness to give up something in order to promote a solution. When sharing of this sort occurs, there are no clear winners or losers. Rather, there is "a willingness to ration the object of the conflict and accept a solution that provides incomplete satisfaction of both parties' concerns."[16]

SO, WHAT SHOULD YOU DO?

In approaching the challenge posed by conflict in your organization (or any organization, for that matter), it seems clear that a single approach simply won't work. To succeed—that is, to achieve many different goals and balance the tug among opposing values—you may have to demonstrate skill at each of the five styles of conflict management we've just discussed. In some situations, you may need to accommodate to keep a valued employee. In other circumstances, you wish to compromise on an issue that's not especially important to you in order to get what you want. On other occasions, you may be faced with situations in which there are many competitors and few rewards; to stay in the game, your approach may be thoroughly competitive. On still other occasions, you may decide to pack up your armor and avoid a fight altogether.

As you gather information and assess the situation, however, negotiation and conflict experts have identified a number of additional important considerations and suggestions.

Listen, Listen, and Then Listen Some More   That helped Los Angeles attorney Alan Liker navigate the sensitive negotiations for the purchase of Budget Rent-a-Car from Ford Motor Company by a group of licensees he represented. In such deals, he says, you have to find out what people are sensitive about, and you can do that only by listening carefully. Then, you can adjust negotiation terms "so that it's perceived as a win-win situation."

It takes a great deal of discipline to be a good listener, according to William P. Dunk, a management consultant in Chapel Hill, North Carolina. "You're tempted to start speaking and intervening," he says, unwisely taking ownership of the problem. "By talking too much, even if you're not posing a solution, you're not pushing the employee into self-awareness."[17]

Separate the People from the Problem   Having clarified the mutual benefits to be gained by successfully concluding a negotiation, it may be useful to focus attention on the real issue at hand—solving the problem. Negotiations are more likely to conclude satisfactorily if the parties involved depersonalize the discussions. You're much more likely to get what you want if "one upmanship" or revenge aren't part of your agenda. How can you do that? Begin to see the other party as an advocate for a point of view, rather than an adversary or a rival. It's far better to say, "I can't support that solution," than it is to say, "I can't support you."[18]

Focus on Interests, not Positions   Positions are demands that a negotiator makes. Interests are the real reasons behind the demands. Experience shows that it is easier to establish agreement on interests, given that they tend to be broader and multifaceted. You should also recognize that a negotiating position may be driven more by emotion than logic. It may be useful to inquire about that: "Can you tell me why you feel that way?" Or, perhaps a simple, declarative statement will prompt the response you're looking for: "Help me understand why you are advocating that position."[19]

Recognize and Accept the Feelings of the Individuals Involved   Irrational feelings are often generated in the midst of controversy, even though the participants don't always want to recognize this fact. Each wants to believe that she is examining the problem objectively. Recognizing and accepting feelings such as fear, jealousy, anger, or anxiety may make it possible for the participants to accept their own true feelings. Effective managers don't adopt a critical attitude, saying "You have no right to feel angry." Rather, they accept those feelings for what they are and work to communicate empathy for those people involved.[20]

Keep Your Own Emotions in Neutral   When John Day headed the transition team that closed down pharmaceutical manufacturer Sterling Winthrop in New York, after its parts were sold to four different companies, he was faced with the anger of employees who were losing their jobs. "You've got to keep your cool and keep busy and focus on the positive side," he says. "After they got their point across, I'd say, 'I'm in the same situation. Here's what I'm trying to do.' " All the parties involved in a conflict have to focus on what they're going to do next to begin solving the dilemma, says Mr. Day, who is now an executive with Ingersoll Rand. "That defuses the situation."[21]

Track the Conflict to Its Source   Conflicts may arise from a manager's personality or style. Outside influences may also contribute. "Maybe an employee's got a sick parent in Georgia or a horrible two-hour commute," says William Dunk. "An effective executive at any level must realize both the drain on productivity and the incremental amount of conflict coming from forces outside the workplace." Then, he says, you can get the employee some help in dealing with them.[22]

Communicate Continually and Frankly   In the Sterling Winthrop negotiations, the transition team communicated as much as possible. "We had constant meetings and newsletters, even if there wasn't much to tell them," says John Day. That made employees feel involved and helped lessen the tension of the company's difficult, final days. Day's team was also brutally honest, telling employees it was unlikely they would be hired by the acquirers. That sort of honesty brought them credibility when other conflicts arose. "On reflection," Mr. Day says, "that was a big thing."[23]

Get People Together on the Small Stuff First   When disagreements crop up, get the parties together and decide on three or four small measures that everyone can agree on and work on those. If people can agree on at least a few things, experts say, the big issues won't be quite as difficult. Moreover, if you establish a harmonious negotiating environment, a little goodwill can help to carry difficult conversations on other, larger issues.[24]

Devise Options for Mutual Gain   This will involve some creativity on your part as a manager. By focusing your collective attention on brainstorming alternative mutually agreeable solutions, the conversational dynamic shifts from competitive to collaborative. This can demonstrate to others than you are a person of goodwill whose perspective does not necessarily require winners and losers. Additionally, the more options, alternatives, and combinations you have to explore, the greater the probability of reaching a solution that will please everyone involved.[25]

Define Success in Terms of Gains Rather than Losses   If a manager seeking a 10 percent raise receives only 6 percent, that outcome can be seen as either a 6 percent improvement (over current income) or a 40 percent shortfall (over desired outcome). The first interpretation focuses on gains, while the second focuses on losses (in this case, unrealized expectations). The outcome is the same, but the manager's satisfaction with it varies substantially. It is important to recognize that our satisfaction with an outcome is affected by the standards we use to judge it. A sensible manager might ask, "Is this a meaningful improvement over current conditions?"[26]

Follow Up to Ensure Success   Review all of the issues, definitions, discussions, data, and details with everyone involved. Make sure that you're in agreement on the solution you plan to implement and the ways in which you plan to go about it. Establish some means of determining whether your solution is working. If possible, quantify outcomes. Agree to revisit the problem at a specific point in the future if the solution you have chosen doesn't seem to work.

Know When to Cut Your Losses   Sometimes, the conflict has simply gone too far and you have to decide where and when to start cutting. "All conflicts don't get resolved," says management consultant William Dunk, "and all people aren't worth saving."[27]

Having said all of this, keep two important things in mind: first, many—if not most—conflicts resolve themselves before they become generalized workplace dilemmas. Most people of goodwill are willing to work with one another for the benefit of the organization, as long as they can see their own best interests linked in some way with those of the organization. And second, managers get paid to listen to their employees, gather useful information, resolve disputes, make tough decisions. The more of it you do, the better you'll get.

If all else fails, consider the advice of Canadian Zen master Albert Low. "Zen teaches that fundamental conflicts exist in every being and that striving to reconcile them is the cause of all suffering, and all life," Low explains. "Conflict abounds in business, too—in the turf wars between departments and in the competing demands of shareholders, employees, customers, and community. The conventional approach to settling the strife with trades-offs actually kills the only sources of growth." The director of the Montreal Zen Centre and author of *Zen and Creative Management* says, "Managers are always choosing between two or more equally desirable resolutions, but all of them are in conflict. The real management charter," he says, "is to harness the energy of opposing forces. And that requires a really creative act. Responding is about trying to catch up. Acting takes you to the future."[28]

Endnotes

1. Lancaster, H. "Solving Conflicts in the Workplace Without Making Losers." *Wall Street Journal,* May 27, 1997, p. B1.

2. Bernstein, A., P. Galuszka, and R. Barker. "What Price Peace? GM Lost a Lot to the UAW, and Labor Relations Are Still Bad." *Business Week,* August 10, 1998, pp. 24–25.

3. Warshaw, M. "The Good Guy's (and Gal's Guide to Office Politics)." *Fast Company,* April 1998, p. 156.

4. Gulbranson, J. E. "The Ground Rules of Conflict Resolution." *Industrial Management,* Vol. 30, No. 3, (May–June 1998), 4.

5. Lancaster, H. "Solving Conflicts."

6. See, for instance, Fink, C. F. "Some Conceptual Difficulties in the Theory of Social Conflict." *Journal of Conflict Resolution,* December 1968, pp. 412–460.

7. Robbins, S. P. *Organizational Behavior: Concepts, Controversies, and Applications,* 8th ed. Upper Saddle River, NJ: Prentice-Hall. 1998, p. 445.

8. Thomas, K. W. "Conflict and Negotiation Processes in Organizations," in Dunnette, M. D. and L. M. Hough (eds.), *Handbook of Industrial and Organizational Psychology,* 2nd ed., Vol. 3. Palo Alto, CA: Consulting Psychologists Press, 1994.

9. Robbins, S. P., *Organizational Behavior,* p. 445.

10. Ibid., pp. 446–447.

11. Warshaw, M., "The Good Guy's," p. 156.

12. Jehn, Karen A. "Enhancing Effectiveness: An Investigation of Advantages and Disadvantages of Value-Based Intragroup Conflict." *International Journal of Conflict Management,* Vol. 5, No. 3 (July 1994), 223–238.

13. Hill, L. A. *Building Effective One-on-One Work Relationships.* Harvard Business School reprint, 9-497-028, October 13, 1996, p. 3.

14. Ibid., p. 4.

15. Thomas, K. W., *Handbook.*

16. Robbins, S. P., *Organizational Behavior,*" *pp. 451–453.*

17. Lancaster, H., "Solving Conflicts," p. B1.

18. Whetten, D. A. and K. S. Cameron. *Developing Management Skills: Managing Conflict.* New York, NY: HarperCollins College Publishers, 1993, p. 35.

19. Ibid.

20. Schmidt, W. H. and R. Tannenbaum, "Management of Differences," in *Harvard Business Review on Negotiation and Conflict Resolution.* Boston, MA: Harvard Business School Press, 2000, pp. 18–19.

21. Lancaster, "Solving Conflicts," p. B1.
22. Ibid.
23. Ibid.
24. Ibid.
25. Whetten, and Cameron, *Developing Management Skills,* p. 35.

26. Ibid., p. 36.
27. Lancaster, "Solving Conflicts," p. B1.
28. Green, W. "Zen and the Art of Managerial Maintenance." *Fast Company,* June 1996, p. 50.

For Further Reading

Bornstein, G. and I. Erev. "The Enhancing Effect of Intergroup Competition on Group Performance." *The International Journal of Conflict Management,* Vol. 5, No. 3 (July 1994), 271–283.

De Dreu, C. K. W. "Productive Conflict: The Importance of Conflict Management and Conflict Issue," in De Dreu, C. K. W. and E. Van de Vliert, *Using Conflict in Organizations.* London, England, UK: Sage Publications, Ltd., 1997.

Drory, A. and I. Ritov. "Effects of Work Experience and Opponent's Power on Conflict Management Styles." *The International Journal of Conflict Management,* Vol. 8, No. 2 (April 1997), 148–161.

Evans, Sybil. "Conflict Can Be Positive." *HR Magazine,* May 1992, pp. 49–51.

Janssen, O. and Van de Vliert. "Concern for the Other's Goals: Key to (De-)escalation of Conflict." *The International Journal of Conflict Management,* Vol. 7, No. 2 (April 1996), 99–120.

Rahim, M. A. and R. T. Golembiewski (eds.). *Styles of Managing Organizational Conflict: A Critical Review and Synthesis of Theory and Research.* Greenwich, CT: JaiPress, Inc., 1997.

Ritov, I. and A. Drory. "Ambiguity and Conflict Management Strategy," *The International Journal of Conflict Management,* Vol. 7, No. 2 (April 1996), 139–155.

Thomas, K. W. "Conflict and Conflict Management," in Dunnett, M. D. (ed.), *Handbook of Industrial and Organizational Psychology.* Chicago, IL: Rand-McNally, 1976, pp. 889–966.

Thomas, K. W. "A Survey of Managerial Interests with Respect to Conflict." *Academy of Management Journal,* June 1976, pp. 315–318.

Van de Vliert, E. and C. K. W. De Dreu, "Optimizing Performance by Conflict Stimulation," *The International Journal of Conflict Management,* Vol. 5, No. 3 (July 1994), 211–222.

⚜

Case 9–1   HAYWARD HEALTHCARE SYSTEMS, INC.

Bob Jackson is the news operations manager of the distribution center for Hayward Healthcare Systems, Inc., a mid-size, nonunion company located in California. The distribution center is an $80-million-a-year operation that has 50 employees, including 15 minorities and 18 females in the workforce.

Jackson was transferred from another operations position in the company to fill this position because of some serious performance problems in the distribution center that had resisted all attempts at improvement. The center had experienced a very high level of defects (4,000 per month) and an unacceptable rate of errors in the orders taken from client hospitals. Jackson accepted the assignment knowing that top management would expect him to improve the performance of the distribution center in a relatively short period of time.

Jackson's first few weeks on the job were revealing, to say the least. He discovered that the five supervisors that his predecessor had selected to lead the center's workforce had little credibility with the employees. They had each been selected on the basis of their job seniority or their friendship with the previous manager.

The workforce was organized into three categories. *Pickers* identify supplies by code numbers in the storage area, remove packaged items from the shelves, and sort them into baskets. *Drivers* operate forklifts and electric trucks, moving baskets and boxes of supplies to different locations within the distribution center. *Loaders* transfer supplies onto and off of the forklifts and delivery trucks.

THE SITUATION MR. JACKSON ENCOUNTERED

Jackson found that his employees were either demoralized or had tough, belligerent attitudes toward management and other employees. Part of the problem, he soon learned, was a lax approach to background checks and prior job references. Seven employees were convicted felons who had been imprisoned for violent assaults on their victims. The previous manager had made all of the hiring decisions by himself without bothering to check on the applicants' references or backgrounds.

Jackson soon discovered that it was not unusual for employees to settle their differences with their fists or to use verbally abusive language to berate people who had offended them. His predecessor had unintentionally encouraged these disruptive activities by staying in his office and not being available to the other workers. He had relied largely on his discredited supervisors to handle their own disciplinary problems. Before long, the employees at the center felt they could handle their own affairs in any way they wanted, without any interference from management.

THE LOADING DOCK INCIDENT

While sitting in his office, planning to make several policy changes to improve the efficiency of the distribution center, one of Jackson's supervisors entered and reported that two of the loaders had just gotten into a heated dispute, and the situation on the loading dock was tense.

The dispute was between Ed Williams, a black, male employee, and Buddy Jones, a white, male employee, and focused on which radio station to play on the loading dock sound system. Williams is the only black employee who works on the loading dock. The company's policy permits employees to listen to music while they work and, in recent years, workers have considered listening to music to be a benefit that improves their working conditions.

Williams insisted that he couldn't stand to listen to the country music that Jones preferred to play. For his part, Jones claimed that Williams' choice of rap and hip-hop music was offensive to him and made working conditions difficult. An emotional and angry argument developed between the two men over their choices in music, and each yelled racial slurs at the other. Neither the company nor the division have a policy governing the choice of music permitted in the workplace. Apparently, whoever gets to work first chooses the music for the day.

Both Jones and Williams were known as tough employees who had previous disciplinary problems at Hayward Hospital Supply. Jones had been incarcerated for 18 months prior to being hired by the company. Jackson knew that he should take immediate action to resolve this problem and to avoid a potentially volatile escalation of the conflict. His supervisors told Jackson that, in the past, the previous manager would simply have hollered at the two antagonists in the conflict and then departed with no further action.

Jackson's objectives in resolving the conflict included the establishment of his own control in the workplace. He knew that he would have to change "business as usual" in the distribution center so that employees would respect his authority and would refrain from any further unprofessional conduct.

RESOLVING THE PROBLEM

In determining the most appropriate solution to the dispute between Jackson's employees, you should consider the following questions:

1. What seems to be the cause of the conflict?
2. What style of conflict management are the distribution center's employees using in this case?
3. What style of conflict management have Hayward Healthcare System managers used in the past?
4. What should Mr. Jackson do to settle the conflict? Should either or both of the employees be punished for their behavior?
5. What can Mr. Jackson do over the long term to ensure that incidents such as the one described in this case are less likely to occur?
6. What can Mr. Jackson do to develop a group of supervisors who can provide the support he requires and who can properly direct the work of the employees in the distribution center?
7. How important is communication in this case? What should Mr. Jackson do to improve the quality of communication in the distribution center?

This case was prepared by Ms. Kay Wigton with the assistance of James S. O'Rourke, concurrent associate professor of management, as the basis for class discussion rather than to illustrate either effective or ineffective handling of an administrative situation. Personal and corporate identities have been disguised.

❧

Case 9–2   DIXIE INDUSTRIES, INC.

Middle managers are frequently called upon to draft documents, including letters, memoranda, position papers, background reports, and briefing documents for senior people in their organizations. Sometimes, senior managers will ask subordinates not only to prepare a document for signature, but to gather the relevant supporting information, as well.

Often, the preparation of such documents requires no more than a quick referral to a balance sheet, database, or filing system to gather the information needed. Sometimes, though, a management response requires that the company—often in the person of the chief executive or president—take a position on an issue. It is in such circumstances that middle managers can reveal who among them is most perceptive, thoughtful, and insightful.

Some management problems are easily resolved. The issues are clear, the resources are available, and implementation is not difficult. Other problems are more difficult. Resources may be limited, intentions and agenda may not be clear, and more than one audience may be paying attention to the response.

The issue at hand deals with corporate policy, corporate actions in regard to that policy, and with the public perceptions of both. This case requires two documents: a brief (two- or three-page) communication strategy memorandum and a letter to an employee. The strategy memo should be directed to the president of Dixie Industries, Inc., and should describe in detail how you plan to handle the case and why. The letter will help to implement the strategy.

Assume that you are the vice president for human resources and report directly to the president of the firm. Dixie Industries, Inc., is a midsize, nonunion textile company located in the American South. The author of the study referred to by your president is a loom operator with ten years' experience and six years of job tenure with the firm. Your memorandum to the president and letter to Ms. Feldman should be in finished form and ready to transmit.

This case was prepared from field interviews by James S. O'Rourke, concurrent associate professor of management, as the basis for class discussion rather than to illustrate either effective or ineffective handling of an administrative situation. Personal and corporate identities have been disguised.

DIXIE INDUSTRIES, INC.

3128 Northeast Industrial Park Road
Meridian, Mississippi 39201

DATE: [Today's Date]

TO: Vice President, Human Resources

FROM: Keith Harkins
            President, Dixie Industries, Inc.

SUBJECT: Dixie Industries Women's Group Study of Company Promotion Practices

BACKGROUND

As you know, Dixie Industries, Inc., recently has been accused by an ad-hoc committee of employees of "a continuing and pervasive bias in promotions in favor of men." You may recall that Ms. Linda Feldman, founder and chairperson of the Dixie Industries Women's Group, has produced a so-called study of this problem and has demanded that we respond. The DI Executive Committee has read her study (such as it is) and asked for my response. I have attached a copy of her letter.

As far as I can determine, we now have four women in positions *above* that of assistant department head. None of the senior executive positions, other than your own, has ever been filled by a female, but we're certainly open to hiring some as positions come open.

Now you know, of course, that more than 40 percent of our 1,800 employees are female—all of them industrious and hard-working. Many of them are quite loyal to the company, but many others (Ms. Feldman included) come and go with some frequency. We have experienced 23 maternity leave requests in the past 12 months. Others have poor attendance records (sick children, school problems, etc.).

OUR OFFICIAL POSITION

My position, and the position of Dixie Industries, Inc., is this: we will promote the most deserving individual who is available to fill a particular vacancy. We will certainly consider any qualified woman (or any qualified man, for that matter) when a job in the executive ranks comes open. Our long-standing policy of promoting from within remains firm. We go outside the company only when no fully qualified applicants are available in-house.

Ms. Feldman's complaint ignores a number of important points, including the fact that few, if any, of our loom operators and plant floor personnel have the education and background to become managers. Also, a number of the figures she cites in the study are simply wrong. She does have a point, however, in that we have *very few* women in management or executive positions.

The other issue she ignores is the fact that we haven't had much turnover in management or executive positions in the past five years. In 25 positions, we've had one retirement and one resignation. The retirement resulted in an internal promotion (to VP, finance from comptroller), and the resignation resulted in an external hire. We have such low turnover, in my view, because of employee loyalty. And, as you know, we are well ahead of the industry in this regard.

Dixie Industries Women's Group Study of Promotion Practices
Page 2 of 3
[Today's Date]

ISSUES TO BE RESOLVED

I am concerned about several issues here.

- **Unionization.** If Ms. Feldman manages to get enough of our hourly wage employees excited about this issue, we could be looking at a petition for establishment of a collective bargaining unit—probably with the ILGWU. That's a distraction that would be costly and counterproductive.
- **Publicity.** This is just the sort of thing that could hurt our image in the local community and, ultimately, drive our stock price down even further. We just cannot afford to have employees airing their grievances in the newspapers. We could use a little positive publicity for a change.
- **Job Action.** We have had a difficult time over the past 18 months in recruiting and retaining dependable loom operators. I'm concerned that Ms. Feldman and her group may instigate a slow down, a walkout, or some other job action that will impair this company's ability to respond to customer orders and remain competitive. As you know, margins in this industry are shrinking every year because of foreign competition.
- **Productivity.** We are consistently below industry standards in productivity and have been for more than a year. We simply cannot afford to spend more time worrying about issues like this. Instead, we must work on absenteeism, turnover, and unit productivity.
- **The Right Thing to Do.** I am also concerned about more than simple appearance here. I want this company to do the right thing, whatever that may be. The problem, of course, is that I'm not at all certain what the right thing might be. We can't promote high-school educated loom operators to management positions simply because we don't have many women in management.

Give me your best thoughts on this. What should we do? Shall we confront Ms. Feldman and her group? Or, should we try to work with her to resolve the issues we face?

I'm ready to move on this issue. Please prepare a plan for me that will respond to Ms. Feldman, address her concerns, and do what you can to help us calm this situation. Please let me know whether or not you think we should meet with this women's group. Involve whichever members of the staff you think are appropriate and copy them on your memo. Make it confidential but don't leave our key players in the dark.

Additionally, I would like you to prepare a letter for my signature to Ms. Feldman. I don't want any publicity about this matter, and I certainly don't want any lawsuits. Let me see your draft within 48 hours.

###

10
BUSINESS MEETINGS THAT WORK

❧

Say the word in a small group of your colleagues. Go ahead, say it. "Meeting." Suggest that your group schedule a meeting; tell them that you think they can resolve the issue they're discussing by setting up a meeting. Now watch the nonverbal reactions: eyes roll, noses scrunch up, people begin hyperventilating. Eyes that don't roll begin to glaze over.

You know the reason: no one likes meetings. "Too many of them are a waste of time," says Marge Boberschmidt. "Too many people walk out of too many meetings feeling that they didn't accomplish anything." Boberschmidt is a former public relations executive at AT&T who now runs her own consulting firm—planning meetings. "My greatest fear is that people will leave a meeting I've planned—having spent time, money, energy, and all sorts of lost opportunity—and come to the conclusion that it just wasn't worthwhile."[1]

Boberschmidt's reactions are common among managers who know that people and productivity are at the top of their list of current concerns. "People are my most important asset," says Bill Mountford, owner of a chain of Midwestern restaurants called *Studebagels*. "And I know that, even though I have information to share with them and they have information to share with me, I'm almost certain that having a meeting is among the least productive things I can do."[2]

Meetings are the most universal—and universally despised—part of business life. But bad meetings do more than ruin an otherwise pleasant day. William R. Daniels, senior consultant at American Consulting & Training in Mill Valley, California, is adamant about the real stakes: bad meetings make bad companies. "Meetings matter because that's where an organization's culture perpetuates itself," he says. "Meetings are how an organization says, 'You are a member.' So if every day we go to boring meetings full of boring people, then we can't help but think that this is a boring company. Bad meetings are a source of negative messages about our company and ourselves."[3]

It's not supposed to be this way. In a business world that is faster, tougher, leaner, and more downsized than ever, you might expect the sheer demands of competition (not to mention the impact of e-mail and groupware) to curb our appetite for meetings. In reality, according to author Eric Matson, the *opposite* may be true. As more work becomes teamwork, and fewer people remain to do the work that exists, the number of meetings is likely to increase rather than decrease.[4]

WHAT'S THE MOTIVATION FOR MEETING?

So why do people have meetings? Most management experts tell us that there are really three reasons: first, because they're scheduled and attendance is not optional; second, because participants have ulterior or non-meeting-related motives for attending (those meetings are usually in nice hotels located far from the company headquarters); and third, because they have no other options for achieving their goals.

In some industries where product development and marketing programs rely heavily on teamwork across departments, meetings are simply unavoidable. Survey results published by the Annenberg School of Communications at the University of Southern California and the University of Minnesota's Training & Development Research Center show that executives, on average, spend 40 percent to 50 percent of their working hours in meetings. Further evidence of the pervasiveness of meetings comes from facility consultant Jon Ryburg, who says he advises corporate clients to provide twice as much meeting space as they did 20 years ago.[5]

According to a recent survey by MCI, managers now attend an average of 60 meetings a month, more than a third of which they say are difficult or unproductive.[6] In some professions, that percentage is much higher. "I must spend three-quarters of my working day in meetings," says Nancy Hobor. "I meet with our CFO regularly. I meet with my staff, with investment analysts, with mutual fund managers, with dozens of different people during the day." Hobor is vice president for corporate communications and investor relations at W.W. Grainger and Company in Lake Forest, Illinois. "Time to myself is a luxury, so I have to use it wisely. I also have to use my meeting time wisely, as well as the time I take from other people."[7]

SO, WHY MEET?

An unspoken but widely accepted rule of business meetings is this: you should never, ever call a meeting—especially one that involves the time, energy, and budget of a considerable number of people—unless you have no other choice. A formal meeting is a communication alternative available when you cannot accomplish your goals or objectives in any other way. It is, in other words, the communication tool of last resort, after you have considered and discarded other forms of information exchange.

Professional meeting consultants see five legitimate reasons for taking people's time, spending their company's money, and devoting both energy and effort into a meeting.

- *To motivate.* A sales force, for instance, may get the jump-start it needs to begin a highly competitive new season by meeting with people who can provide both motivation and methods for successful selling.
- *To educate.* An investor relations manager may meet with analysts or fund managers to brief them on new earnings growth projections, an update to the company's strategic plans, or a proposed product line.
- *To recreate.* Team building exercises often take place off-site in a hotel or conference center setting, or—increasingly—in a wooded, outdoors setting designed to build confidence and unity.

- *To initiate.* Gathering employees together prior to a new product launch or brand line-extension might help to explain product features and the market position management is hoping to sell to customers.
- *To network.* Members of professional societies and trade associations often gather to meet and speak with each other as much as they do to hear scheduled speakers or participate in carefully planned panel discussions or breakout sessions.
- *To reward.* Management can show employees that they genuinely care about them by offering a trip—often with family members accompanying them—to a company meeting in a desirable location (think warm in the winter, cool in the summer). A resort hotel or theme park can combine the professional and social goals of meeting very nicely, as long as costs are kept within reason and recreational goals are specified as an important part of the meeting agenda.[8]

WHAT IS A BUSINESS MEETING?

A business meeting is a gathering in which a purposeful exchange or transaction occurs among two or more people with a common interest, purpose, or problem. Many meetings, of course, turn out to be neither purposeful nor productive, but the best of them can help to solve problems, build consensus, gather opinion, and move an organization forward. Many, in fact, are not only productive, but actually fun.

WHEN SHOULD I CALL A MEETING?

As we've already noted, people meet for a variety of reasons. Generally, they gather together to move group actions forward. That's often referred to as a *task focus*. To do this, participants usually do two things in meetings: they present information to others and they collaborate. That is, they review, evaluate, discuss, solve problems, decide what to do next. When any of these actions is essential to your business, consider a meeting.

And, as we've also noted, people want to meet for social reasons. Numerous studies have shown that people gather in meetings because they feel a need to belong, a need to achieve or make a difference of some sort, or because of a desire to communicate, to build and share a common reality.[9]

Why else should you consider meeting? Here are 10 more reasons why a meeting may be your best communication option:

- Talk about goals.
- Listen to reports.
- Train people.
- Explain plans and programs.
- Tell people what they're supposed to do and how they're to do it.
- Build morale.
- Reach a consensus.
- Discover or solve problems.
- Gather opinions.
- Keep things moving.

WHEN SHOULD I *NOT* CALL A MEETING?

You should consider some other communication alternative when a phone call, a memo, or an e-mail message would do just as well. Frequently, managers think they must meet with people—usually their employees and coworkers—in order to simply pass along information. If the flow of information is entirely one-way, you certainly should consider alternative routes for it. Unless the information is very sensitive or personal—the death of a colleague or the sale of the company—a face-to-face meeting is usually not necessary.

You should also not plan a meeting when:

- A key person is not available. Often, a substitute can fill in for a colleague, but in some instances, it simply makes no sense to meet without a particular person in the room.
- Participants don't have time to prepare. If the group needs certain data or information to guide its discussion, make sure you have time to gather and distribute it. If preliminary reading or small-group discussions must take place first, don't short-circuit your intentions by scheduling a meeting before all of that can happen.
- Personality conflicts or the plans of higher management might make the meeting a waste of time. If the issue you plan to discuss has become highly polarized in your organization, gathering people on opposite sides of the issue may provoke conflict rather than discussion. Preliminary, one-on-one meetings may be necessary to smooth the way for larger discussions to follow. And, of course, if you know (or think you know) that organizational executives have other plans, a meeting to discuss the issue *may* be unproductive. Planning a rebuttal or response might be a good reason for meeting, but if the issue has already been resolved higher up in the organization, save your time and energy. Cancel the meeting.

WHAT SHOULD I CONSIDER AS I PLAN FOR A MEETING?

Three issues—the objective, the agenda, and the participants—are essential to the success of any meeting, regardless of size, length, or purpose.

The Objective   Your foremost consideration should be your purpose in getting together. What is the meeting's objective? Why is this important? If participants aren't clear on your purpose for meeting, they'll make up one of their own. When that happens, it's easy to lose control and watch your participants wander off in a dozen different directions.

How can you build clarity into your purpose for meeting? Christopher Avery, a communications consultant who owns Partnerwerks in Austin, Texas, thinks the following steps may help.

First, consider why you want people to meet. Ask yourself what you will accomplish face-to-face (or via conference call) that you wouldn't accomplish otherwise. Are you meeting to share information, build relationships, make decisions, design something, or solve a problem? After you know the objective of the meeting, think about the outcomes you're hoping for and write down at least two of them: What is the *perfect* outcome for this meeting? What is your *minimum acceptable* outcome?

Next, validate the objective and outcomes to the best of your ability. Can you reasonably expect this group to produce your outcome in the time allotted? What can they achieve? What sort of preparation will they need? Include others whom you trust in this process if it will help you achieve clarity. Finally, start the meeting by clearly stating the objective and outcomes. Make sure all of the participants understand the objective and are willing to work toward it.[10]

The Agenda   Create a solid agenda. It's nothing more than an outline of things to be discussed at the meeting, along with a time budget for each item. To create an effective agenda, ask yourself three questions: To achieve our objectives, what do we need to do in this meeting? What conversations will be important to the people who attend? What information will we need to begin?

Two important considerations: first, prioritize your agenda items. Make sure you don't spend most of your time on more immediate but less important issues. Leaving the most crucial or urgent items until last runs the very real risk of running out of time and not considering them at all. Second, assign realistic amounts of time to each agenda item. When you have exhausted the time allocated for discussion of a particular item, the meeting chair must gently nudge the group: "Any other thoughts on this? It's time to move on."

What's the most effective use of your agenda? Conventional wisdom says that agendas should be created and distributed in advance. For formal meetings and meetings requiring preparation, that approach makes considerable sense. For informal meetings or for those called in the midst of change, however, you can easily build an agenda as you begin. Simply poll the participants on topics they think should be covered, establish a set of priorities, and budget the meeting time.[11]

The most important thing you can do with your agenda, once it's written, is to stick to it. In too many meetings, too many participants wander off topic, spending too much time discussing issues irrelevant to the reason they are in the room. Michael Schrage, a consultant on collaborative technologies, acknowledges that most meetings in most companies are decidedly agenda-free. "In the real world," he says, "agendas are about as rare as the white rhino. If they do exist, they're about as useful. Who hasn't been in meetings where someone tries to prove that the agenda isn't appropriate?"[12]

Agendas are worth taking seriously. Intel Corporation, the Silicon Valley semiconductor manufacturer, is fanatical about them. They've developed an agenda template that everyone in the company uses. A typical Intel agenda, which circulates several days before a meeting to let participants react to and modify it, lists the meeting's key topics, who will lead which parts of the discussion, how long each segment will take, and what the expected outcomes will be.

Of course, even the best of agendas can't ensure the success of a meeting. The challenge, according to Kimberly Thomas, director of communications for small business services at Ameritech in Chicago, is to keep meetings focused without stifling creativity or insulting participants who stray. "When comments come up that aren't related to the issue at hand," she says, "we record them on a flip chart labeled 'The Parking Lot.' We always track the issue and the person responsible for it," she adds. "We use this technique throughout the company."[13]

The Participants   The people on your participant list should be only those people who are directly related to the goals for the meeting. Failing to invite key decision makers or influencers invites frustration and failure. Including people either because they're interesting or simply to fill up chairs in the room is a waste of your time and theirs. So who should you include? Think carefully about inviting people who:

- will have to carry out or implement what's been decided
- have valuable information or good ideas
- can approve the results
- can act as an advocate on behalf of the group's ideas at a higher level
- represent divergent views or traditionally excluded viewpoints
- are indispensable to the success of the decision

Once you know whose input is needed, as well as those whose buy-in will be necessary to move forward, you're ready to secure the facilities and issue invitations.

HOW DO I PREPARE FOR A SUCCESSFUL MEETING?

We mentioned three essential considerations as you plan for a meeting—the objectives, the agenda, and the participants—but there's more. Here are some additional steps you should think about carefully.

Arrange for a Meeting Time, Date, and Place   Think carefully about what times and dates would be most convenient for everyone concerned. In the absence of convenience, when can people be there? While it may not be possible to accommodate literally *everyone's* schedule as you plan for a meeting, be as flexible as possible in trying to arrange a time that the largest number of participants will find workable. Mealtimes are often used as an opportunity to get an otherwise difficult-to-assemble group together. Most people have at least something to eat at breakfast and lunch each day and, if you offer to buy, they may be willing to join you.

Keep in mind that it's generally a bad idea to convene a meeting outside of normal business hours. There are times when you must, but the editors of the *Harvard Management Communication Letter* say such occasions should be reserved for real emergencies. "People who schedule meetings for evenings and weekends are merely advertising the embarrassing fact that they have no life—and they're expecting others to give up theirs. That kind of person should not be allowed to run anything, much less part of a modern corporation, because they lack the basic humanity to do a good job."[14]

Selecting a location for your meeting can be just as important as drafting your objectives and drawing up a participant list. "If people are meeting for recreational reasons, or are being rewarded in some way by the company, think very carefully about where you want to meet," says meeting consultant Marge Boberschmidt. "A world-class hotel or even a nice corporate conference center can often compensate for an otherwise uninspired panel of speakers or weak agenda."[15]

Coordinate Details at the Meeting Site   "The small stuff will always come back to bite you," says Boberschmidt. "Pay attention to the size of the room, the quality and comfort levels of the seating, the conference table, projection equipment, lighting, temperature controls, refreshments, and anything else that will influence a participant's frame of mind."[16] Everything from parking to pencils and pads will affect how people feel about the experience of being in a meeting room, she says, and all of it is worth considering.

Consider, as well, all of those issues related to travel requirements, location, and cost. Make absolutely certain that every participant knows how to find the meeting location. Anticipate commonly asked questions, then provide a telephone number for last-minute questions or unanticipated problems. Having a real human being to talk with can be comforting as a busy manager tries to pull his act together at the last minute before an important business meeting.

And, if you're responsible for planning the meeting, talk to or meet with those responsible for supporting or carrying out your plans, including audiovisual technicians, caterers, front-desk managers, and banquet and meeting managers. Make certain they know how to find you—no matter what the hour—and be explicit about what you want. Be pleasant to them, though. Keep in mind that they are probably overworked and underpaid, and the success of your meeting is in their hands. A generous tip at the right moment wouldn't hurt, either.

Announce the Agenda   Unless secrecy is essential, your meeting is more likely to succeed with a published agenda that everyone has had an opportunity to examine and think about in advance. State your objectives and explain the outcomes you're hoping for. Be sure to include all relevant detail in the announcement, including, themes, topics, speakers, times, dates, places, directions, and the specific responsibilities of the participants. If you e-mail the agenda, ask for a return receipt to make sure everyone received and displayed the document. If you are at all nervous about getting everyone on the same page, follow up with paper copies and, perhaps, a phone call to assure them that this is a high-priority event.

Assign Roles   An important part of the planning process involves the assignment of roles. Any well-run meeting will involve at least four important roles.

- Facilitator
- Recorder
- Leader
- Participant

Some meeting planners like to add a fifth role, the timekeeper, so that each agenda item gets its fair share of attention and the discussion stays on track. Different people can play each of these roles, or one person can play them all. But they all have to be accounted for if the meeting is to flow well and produce results. Determining role assignments at the beginning engages everybody in the process and—if done properly—validates each participant's expectations and contributions.[17]

WHAT FORM OR MEETING STYLE WILL WORK BEST?

Each organization has its own style which is based, in part, on the personalities of both the leadership and participants, as well as the organizational culture. The style you select has to fit the preferences of those who will participate as well as the business needs of the organization. Here are three styles or meeting forms that are well suited to smaller business-oriented meetings.

The Staff Conference   This military-style meeting often works well if you clearly outrank everyone else in the room. In this format, each team member reports to you on how his or her project is going, answers your questions, and makes recommendations. The two of you then discuss strategy, usually with very little input from other team members. (The meeting that kicked off each episode of the 1980s TV drama *L.A. Law* was a good example of the staff conference style).

This style keeps everyone informed of what each team member is doing, forces all team members to be ready with reports and to be accountable in front of their peers, and lets you control the flow of the meeting. Disadvantages include a limited exchange of ideas, an autocratic management style, and the potential for conflict if participants' responsibilities overlap.

The "Congressional" System   If you're chairing an association meeting, where officers are elected and all members are of equal standing, your role in the chair will be that of a presiding officer rather than an executive. In this case, a parliamentary format is almost always the right choice. In this style of meeting, people don't just talk when they please: it's hands up, like in school, and when everyone's had their say, they vote.

This system is useful if you have particularly argumentative members or if the issues to be discussed are especially contentious. As chair of a parliamentary meeting, you must be careful not to take sides publically. If you want something specific to happen, you'll have to ensure that other members bring the matter up and get it passed with very little help from you. You can't let participants think that you're forcing your own agenda through.

This meeting style allows input from whoever wants to give it; it encourages people to think before speaking; and agreed-upon rules of order make it easier to maintain decorum. To prevent interruptions or side-tracking, the chair simply says, "Hold that thought, Jeff. Carolyn has the floor." An obvious disadvantage is that the chair has severely limited power, and it does encourage a certain amount of intrigue and power-brokering in advance of the meeting.

The "House of Commons" System   In the British House of Commons, the Prime Minister is the head of government, but he sits on the floor of the House like any other member; he does not preside. If you're clearly the ranking person present, but want to make the meeting as democratic as possible, appoint (or have elected) another member to chair the meeting. Remind the presiding officer beforehand that she is to shut you up if you're out of order, just as she would any other member.

One obvious advantage to this approach is that you will spend less time planning the meeting. It also provides leadership experience to other members and encourages subordinates to speak frankly. If the newly elected (or appointed) meeting leader isn't careful, however, this approach can create the impression that no one is in charge.[18]

HOW DO I KEEP A MEETING ON TRACK?

Meetings don't actually go off-topic, people do. It usually takes at least two people adrift to take the meeting off course. Sometimes, a participant with ulterior motives can try to hijack a meeting and use it for his own purposes, but that's a less common threat than these three.

Topic Drift   Almost any meeting can attract comments or observations from participants that will take the discussion in an unintended direction. Sometimes a brief discussion of nonagenda items can lighten the mood in the room and may, in fact, be helpful in getting certain people to speak, but you can tolerate such diversions for just so long. When this happens, the meeting chair has a couple of choices: call the group back on topic, "OK, let's see if we can focus on the problem we need to solve. . . ." Or, the chair can ask if the group would like to consider the new topic separately: "This discussion seems to be outside the scope of the agenda. Can we table this for now or do we need to add this as a separate discussion item?"

Breaking Time Agreements   This can happen if the meeting doesn't start or end at the times advertised in the agenda. It can also happen if the time budgeted for a given agenda item isn't honored. Either one can be a serious problem that prevents the group from reaching its goals. Dealing with the agenda time budget is generally easier, since the chair can either continue the discussion and reschedule other agenda items, or limit the discussion and move on to the next item.

What happens if people don't show up on time, leave early, or—worse—just don't show up at all? Improving the "crispness" of a meeting means getting participants to take them seriously. How often have you heard someone declare at the end of a gathering, "Well, meeting's over. Let's get back to work." The mind-set at Intel Corporation is that "meetings *are* work." They're an important part of the job and each participant has to take them seriously. Other companies punish latecomers with a penalty fee or reprimand them in the minutes of the meeting for being late or absent.

Subgroup Focus   Sometimes agenda items will spawn dialogue among members of a small group who have important views and ideas to share with each other. When other participants have no interest in that conversation, however, they become bystanders at their own meeting. How should the meeting chair handle such conversations? She has two choices: first, ask subgroup participants to rejoin the main discussion or, if that approach is unsuccessful, ask those involved in the spontaneous breakout session if the topic they're exploring is something that would interest the entire group. Either way, the leader must reassert control or risk losing the direction and commitment of the larger group.[19]

WHAT SHOULD I LISTEN FOR?

Some people have such a deep-seated need to be right that they simply can't stand evidence to the contrary. They are the ones who work overtime to prove others are wrong and disparage anyone who offers a different point of view. These folks make meetings difficult because, for them, meetings become a win-lose occasion, an opportunity to show other people just how wrong they really are. If they can't argue the evidence, they'll debate the procedure. If that doesn't work, they'll attack or threaten others in the room. They'll bluff, bluster, pull rank, and—if all else fails—they'll get up and leave.

How do you get people to listen? Well, that's not an easy question to answer. The key is showing them how cooperating with others is in their own best interest. At a minimum, you can lead by example, trying to improve your own listening behavior in meetings.

- Consider all of your knowledge, ideas, and opinions as functions of your unique perspective. Consider each other person's knowledge, ideas, and opinions as functions of their perspective. Each person is entitled to his or her own point of view, though they are not entitled to their own set of facts.
- Pay attention to your own point of view, especially as it relates to others. Doing this will help you discern your own beliefs and values and be more comfortable with them.
- Remember that considering an issue from many different viewpoints is what makes a team smart. Value the opportunity to meet with people who see things differently than you do.
- Practice what collaboration consultant Christopher Avery calls "playback listening." Pay careful attention to what others say so that you can play-back their words to them exactly. This powerful practice will help you develop the capacity to acknowledge others' points of view and help them to be heard.
- Hear others with the intention of integrating your point of view with as many others as you can. To do this, though, you must be willing to hear and validate all other points of view. And, not just when you agree with them, but consistently over time.
- Try not to think in terms of *right* and *wrong,* but rather in terms of what works and doesn't work. Think about outcomes for the group and achieving the groups' goals, not merely your own goals of contributing to the process.[20]

WHAT SHOULD I LOOK FOR?

Have you ever been to a meeting where, even though the leader said she wanted high participation, she stood at the end of the table and "talked at" the participants, each of whom was seated silently down both sides? It's not all that uncommon. Leaders who don't plan for participation in a meeting won't get it, no matter what they say they want. Standing at the end of a long table sends a strong nonverbal message: Don't talk, just listen. It's a great setup for discouraging participation.

As you saw in Chapter 7, actions not only speak louder than words but often speak in ways that words simply cannot. Think about what that means as you look around your meeting room and where people will sit. In his book *Silent Messages,* Albert Mehrabian tells us the words we say account for just 7 percent of total message communication. Our tone of voice accounts for another 38 percent. But body language, including such issues as eye contact, posture, gestures, hand movement, and position in the room, account for 55 percent—more than half—of all received communication in an interpersonal setting.[21]

Deliberately conveying nonverbal messages is not all that difficult. When you are the leader and you need to maintain control of a meeting, run the meeting yourself to signal that you have both authority and control. Stand while others are sitting to signal that you have the floor. And, of course, sit at the head of the table to show that you are in charge.

On the other hand, if you want a more participative or collaborative meeting, ask a team member or facilitator to run the meeting. That would signal shared control. Sit while others are sitting to signal that your views are equally important. And consider taking a seat along the side of the conference table to demonstrate that you're one of them, rather than in charge of them.[22]

You can even defuse confrontation by changing the furniture in the room. A living room atmosphere with sofas, upholstered chairs, and low-rise coffee tables is likely to encourage people to speak up in a more participate way. Conference tables clearly denote authority and who outranks whom.

To minimize participation and interruptions:

- Set up a long, narrow table for a smaller meeting, placing the leader at the end.
- Choose a seating arrangement that minimizes eye contact between participants (classroom-style seating), where one presenter faces the audience.
- Create an expectation that speech only comes from the front of the room.

To maximize participation and collaboration:

- Choose a round or square table, with the leader seated as a member of the group.
- For longer meetings, set up chairs in a U-shape, instead of using classroom-style row seating, so that participants face each other.
- For large groups, arrange banquet-style seating to accommodate five to eight people, using as many round tables as necessary.[23]

WHAT SHOULD I WRITE DOWN?

In every meeting, someone should be designated to take notes. At the very least, the names and titles of those present, the agenda items discussed, the participant comments, and the ideas generated should find their way onto paper. If the group leader is to follow up on decisions, new ideas, or opportunities discussed during the meeting, a simplified, streamlined method of recording and sharing the minutes of each meeting must be a priority.

Increasingly, technology has begun to play a role in note-taking during meetings. 3M Corporation has developed a digital whiteboard that's as simple to write on and erase as a traditional whiteboard. The difference? The board captures a complete record of the evolution of ideas during a meeting. Every board full of information can be saved as a page on your personal computer, ready to edit, print, e-mail, and cut and paste into other applications.

In too many organizations, discussions are held and ideas are written onto flip charts, chalk boards, and white boards, but somehow, nothing happens. Decisions don't get turned into actions. According to Michael Schrage, a consultant on collaborative technologies, the best way to avoid that is to convert from *meeting* to *doing*—where the doing focuses on the creation of shared documents that lead to action. At most computer-enabled meetings, the most powerful role for technology is also the simplest: recording comments, outlining ideas, generating written proposals, projecting them for the entire group to see, and printing them so people leave with real-time minutes.

"You're not just having a meeting," says Schrage, "you're creating a document. I can't emphasize enough the importance of that distinction. It is the fundamental difference between ordinary meetings and computer-augmented collaborations. Comments, questions, criticisms, insights should enhance the quality of the document. That should be the group's mission.[24]

HOW CAN I MAKE MY MEETINGS MORE PRODUCTIVE?

Technology may be one answer. Gordon Mangione, a product-unit manager at Microsoft Exchange Group, uses video technology to improve the experience for his team in Redmond, Washington. "Daily meetings are a valuable tool for keeping projects on track," he says. "But as the number of participants grows—our team includes about 60 key managers—we face a dilemma: How do we ensure real-time interaction, keep everyone informed, and maintain cohesiveness—without tying up the whole team?"

Team meetings are critical at Microsoft. "Teams come together, review daily builds, and identify any developments from the past 24 hours. We haven't found an 'enabling technology' that works better than face-to-face conversation," he observes. "But when meetings turn into standing-room only affairs, the disadvantages are overwhelming."

Mangione's answer is a hybrid meeting, part physical and part virtual. "We still hold the daily meeting in our conference room, but now just 20 people sit in the room. The other 40 'attend' from their offices." Three technicians make the meetings work. Video cameras and microphones in the conference room and on everyone's computer screen allow 'virtual' and 'physical' participants to see and hear one another. A large-screen TV captures presentations which are broadcast to the desktops, and people pass notes to one another via instant messaging technology.[25]

Microsoft isn't alone in embracing new technology to improve meetings. WebEx of San Jose, California, now offers software that plugs into your browser, permitting people in different physical locations to look at the same document and discuss changes as they are being made. They can talk on the phone, even though the calls are being sent via the Web.[26] Technology, of course, can do more than just bring people in different locations together. It can also increase productivity—that is, help generate more ideas and decisions per minute. One of the main benefits of "meetingware" is that it allows participants to violate the first rule of good behavior in most other circumstances: *wait your turn to speak.* With Ventana Corporation's *GroupSystems V,* the most powerful meeting software available today, participants enter their comments and ideas into workstations which, in turn, organize the comments and project them onto a monitor for the whole group to see. Nearly everyone who has studied or participated in computer-enabled meetings agrees that this capacity for simultaneity produces dramatic gains in the number of ideas and the speed with which they are generated.[27]

Other companies have tried different methods for making meetings more productive and more interesting. Kaufman and Broad Home Corporation, one of the top home builders in the United States, recognized that the grind of workday pressures made group meetings especially difficult. Their solution? The "After Five" meeting. Jeff Charney, senior vice president of marketing and communications, began gathering his team for freewheeling brainstorming sessions after 5:00 o'clock P.M., when the workday normally concludes. "Without all the day-to-day pressures," says Charney, "it's much easier to engage our imaginations and let them run wild."

During one of their "After Five" sessions last year, the team devised a major promotional campaign that used a full-scale replica of the home of Marge and Homer Simpson—a marketing gambit that got worldwide media attention. "Nine-to-five," says Charney, "we're in a taking-care-of-business mode. By holding the meeting at the day's end, we can switch gears and leave behind phones and pagers. Those things just kill creativity."[28]

Still others have tried an updated version of an old military stand-by: the "7:30 A.M. Stand-Up." Researchers at the University of Missouri wanted to test the notion that one way to make better, certainly shorter, meetings was to take away the chairs. And sure enough, after comparing outcomes for 111 meetings, they found that those conducted while the participants were seated lasted an average of 34 percent longer than meetings in which the participants remained standing. More importantly, they discovered the quality of decision making was the same for both formats. Dr. Mary Waller, a professor who specializes in organizational behavior at the University of Illinois, and who was not involved with the study, added: "I think it's a pretty important finding. If I were consulting with an organization, I would probably suggest that they combine sit-down and standing-up meetings."[29]

The Ritz-Carlton hotel chain—the only hotel company ever to receive a Malcolm Baldrige National Quality Award—uses the same idea with considerable success. Every day at precisely 9:00 A.M., about 80 of the company's top executives gather for a 10-minute stand-up meeting in the hallway outside the office of President and COO Horst Schulze. Just as important, within 24 hours, every hotel from Boston to Bali, and the rest of the company's 16,000 employees, get the same concentrated dose of the Ritz credo at their daily shift meetings. "We prepare a monthly calendar of lineup topics," says Leonardo Inghilleri, senior vice president for human resources, "ranging from the opening of a new hotel in Dubai to meeting-planner programs—and e-mail them weekly to each hotel. For one critical moment each day," he says, "the entire organization is aligned behind the same issue."[30]

CAN BUSINESS MEETINGS EVER IMPROVE?

There's certainly hope, according to Bernard DeKoven, founder of the Institute for Better Meetings in Palo Alto, California. "People don't have good meetings because they don't know what good meetings are like. Good meetings aren't just about work. They're about fun—keeping people charged up. It's more than collaboration. It's 'col-iberation'—people freeing each other up to think more creatively."[31]

Endnotes

1. Boberschmidt, Marge. Personal communication, January 6, 2000.
2. Mountford, William. Personal communication, September 19, 1999.
3. Matson, Eric. "The Seven Sins of Deadly Meetings." *Fast Company,* April 1996, pp. 122–128.
4. Ibid.
5. "Making Meetings Work." *The 3M Meeting Guides,* available online from 3M Corporation at *http://www.3M.com/meetings/.*
6. "Men and Women Fall Back into Kids' Roles at Corporate Meetings." *Wall Street Journal,* December 15, 1998, p. B-1.

7. Hobor, Nancy. Personal communication, January 7, 2000.
8. Boberschmidt, Marge. Personal communication.
9. "Anatomy of Great Meetings." *The 3M Meeting Guides,* available online from 3M Corporation at *http://www.3M.com/meetings/.*
10. Avery, Christopher M. "Clear Objectives Make Powerful Meetings." *The 3M Meeting Guides,* available online from 3M Corporation at *http://www.3M.com/meetings/.*
11. "Building Great Agendas." *The 3M Meeting Guides,* available online from 3M Corporation at *http://www.3M.com/meetings/.*
12. Matson, Eric. "The Seven Sins," pp. 122–128.
13. Ibid.
14. *Harvard Management Communication Letter,* Vol. 2, No. 11, November 1999, pp. 1–3.
15. Boberschmidt, Marge. Personal communication.
16. Ibid.
17. "Anatomy of Great Meetings."
18. "Chairing a Meeting: To Keep Order, Be True To Form," (no author listed) *New York Times,* September 22, 1999, p. C-25.
19. "Keeping a Meeting on Track." *The 3M Meeting Guides,* available online from 3M Corporation at *http://www.3M.com/meetings/.*
20. Avery, Christopher M. "Listening to Others in Meetings." *The 3M Meeting Guides,* available online from 3M Corporation at *http://www.3M.com/meetings/.*
21. Mehrabian, Albert. *Silent Messages: Implicit Communication of Emotions and Attitudes.* Belmont, CA: Wadsworth Publishing Co., 1981.
22. "Nonverbal Messages in Meetings." *The 3M Meeting Guides,* available online from 3M Corporation at *http://www.3M.com/meetings/.*
23. Ibid.
24. Matson, Eric. "The Seven Sins," pp. 122–128.
25. Olofson, Cathy. "So Many Meetings, So Little Time." *Fast Company,* January–February 2000, p. 48.
26. Mardesich, Jodi. "Putting the Drag in WebEx's Ad Campaign." *Fortune,* January 10, 2000, p. 174.
27. Matson, Eric. "The Seven Sins," pp. 122–128.
28. Olofson, Cathy. "Open Minds After Closing Time: Meetings I Never Miss." *Fast Company,* June 1999, p. 72.
29. Berger, Alisha. "The All-Rise Method for Faster Meetings." *New York Times,* June 22, 1999, p. D-7.
30. Olofson, Cathy. "The Ritz Puts On Stand-Up Meetings." *Fast Company,* September 1998, p. 62.
31. Matson, Eric. "The Seven Sins," pp. 122–128.

For Further Reading

Creighton, James L. and James W. R. Adams. *Cyber Meeting: How to Link People and Technology in Your Organization.* New York, NY: Amacom, 1998.

Doyle, Michael and David Straus. *How to Make Meetings Work.* New York, NY: The Berkley Publishing Group, 1993.

Frank, Milo O. *How to Run a Successful Meeting in Half the Time.* Washout Publishing Company, 1995.

Fricks, Holly. "The Five W's: Tips for Planning Your Company Meeting." *Indiana Business Magazine,* July 1998, pp. 34–37.

Goldberg, Matt. "The Meeting I Never Miss." *Fast Company,* February 1997, pp. 28–30.

Kopytoff, Verne G. "The Necessary Art of the Impromptu Meeting." *New York Times,* August 24, 1997, p. A-11.

Mosvick, Roger K. and Robert B. Nelson, *We've Got to Start Meeting Like This: A Guide to Successful Meeting Management.* Indianapolis, IN: Jist Works, 1996.

Schrage, Michael. *No More Teams! Mastering the Dynamics of Creative Collaboration.* New York, NY: Doubleday, 1995.

☙

Case 10–1 SEQUOIA MEDICAL SUPPLY, INC.

BACKGROUND NOTE

Among the more difficult and distasteful aspects of management is the task of collecting money from people. Most organizations centralize this function and delegate collections to specialized units within a comptroller's division.

The management of assets, however, including accounts receivable, is the responsibility of the organization's officers. While certain staff employees may be enlisted to assist in tracking accounts, communicating with clients and customers, and accounting for funds within the business, very few people are available to tell a manager just how to deal with a delinquent customer and when to act.

A range of options, from computer-produced reminders to telephone calls to the delinquent customer, is available to managers who must intervene in a collection case. Who says what to whom, though, and in what tone of voice and with what effect is entirely a matter of judgment.

Some cases can be resolved with a simple note or phone call. Others may require more stern measures, including, perhaps, a threat of legal action. Some recalcitrant clients might need the nudge that a collection agent can provide. But even that comes at a cost.

Sequoia Medical Supply, Inc., is a mid-sized, regional vendor of equipment and goods ranging from prepackaged disposable supplies to high-tech, noninvasive diagnostic equipment. Their customer base includes hospitals, clinics, and physicians.

The case at hand involves a delinquent, out-of-state corporation. The memorandum from the vice president for finance to you includes two attachments: a statement of account and a recent credit report. This case requires two documents:

a brief (no more than two to three pages) communication strategy memorandum and a letter.

Please assume that you have recently joined the company as accounts receivable manager. Your memo should be addressed to the vice president for finance and should detail what you plan to do with this account and why; the letter may be addressed to the customer or to another party who will assist in collecting the overdue funds.

ADDITIONAL INFORMATION

Corporate Cash Flow. Sequoia Medical Supply is a mid-sized firm with US$18.5 million in annual sales. Disposable medical supplies, including glass and polystyerene containers, syringes, tubing, catheters, tape, and specialty packaged items account for about two-thirds of sales. Noninvasive diagnostic equipment, monitors, analyzers, OR equipment, and examining room equipment comprise the remaining one-third of sales.

Receivables. The amount past due from Findlay Laboratories represents 80 percent of all past due receivables. Currently, about 95 percent of the firm's receivables are current.

Ratios & Formulas. To give you some perspective on the amount of persuasion that may be needed in this case, you may wish to look at several totals and their attendant ratios, including accounts receivable, receivables past due, and receivables turnover.

Accounts Receivable Past Due:
 100% / 80% × Findlay Lab Account Past Due
Total Annual A/R:
  100% / 05% × A/R Amount Past Due
Total (unaveraged) A/R Turnover:
  Total Annual Sales / Total Annual A/R

SEQUOIA MEDICAL SUPPLY, INCORPORATED

• One Sequoia Parkway • Kalamazoo, Michigan 49003 •

DATE: [Today's Date]

TO: Manager
              Accounts Receivable

FROM: Thomas J. McDermott
              Vice President, Finance (Ext. 1-8397)

SUBJECT: Delinquent Account, Findlay Laboratories, Inc.

A recently completed internal audit of our accounts receivable has revealed a serious pattern of delinquency in the Findlay Laboratories account. Please take the appropriate steps to resolve this matter at once.

I have attached several documents that may be helpful to you. I know you are relatively new here, but I assume that, by now, you are familiar with the details of this case, so it shouldn't be difficult to do what's necessary. At the same time, it may be useful for us to examine the way in which this case has been handled.

In particular, I have these questions:

- How did this account get so far delinquent without sounding alarm bells?
- How did we manage to grant so much credit to these people with such inadequate financial information on the customer?
- Are our own credit and debt-recovery policies adequate?

Please provide me with a detailed review of this account and the actions you have taken, or would recommend, to resolve this. Two issues are of concern here: first, solving the problems associated with this account and, second, making sure this sort of thing does not happen again.

These people have been good customers for some time, but the account is seriously overdue and, without question, the sums involved are much larger than they should be. Do whatever is necessary and get the documents to my desk by COB Friday.

###

This case was prepared from public sources by James S. O'Rourke, concurrent associate professor of management, as the basis for class discussion rather than to illustrate either effective or ineffective handling of an administrative situation. Personal identities have been disguised.

STATEMENT OF ACCOUNT
Findlay Laboratories
896 Morley Drive
Suite #4
Findllay, Ohio 45839

Source	Debit	Credit	Balance
Unresolved discrepancies, 1998–99	23,654.13		
December 1, 1999 #2316	73,600.00		97,254.13
January 5, 2000 #2379	25,279.27		122,533.40
February 2, 2000 Check #1193		46,250.00	76,283.40
March 1, 2000 #3873	963.78		77,247.18
March 7, 2000 Credit Memo #A4279		42.63	77,204.55
April 5, 2000 #4156	8,026.56		86,231.11
May 3, 2000 #4183	1,000.09		87,231.20
June 7, 2000 #5300	7,624.00		$94,855.20

Current balance: $ 94,855.20

Amount past due: $ 94,855.20

Last payment: February 2, 2000

HEALTHCARE INDUSTRY CREDIT ASSOCIATION
Toledo, Ohio
Credit Report

SUBJECT: Findlay Laboratories, Inc.   DATE: [One week ago]
896 Morley Drive, Suite #4
Findlay, OH 45839   RATING: Unrated

Subject is a closely held entity (C-corp.) incorporated in March 1995 under the laws of Ohio. The officers:

T.R. Baskin, M.D., Fostoria, OH, president.

Gertrude Bergen, M.D., Findlay, OH, vice president.

Lloyd Bergen, Findlay, OH, secretary and registered agent.

Dr. Baskin, an obstetrician in Fostoria, OH, is active in the operation of subject laboratory only in a policy-making capacity.

Dr. Bergen is a pathologist at Findlay Community Hospital. She is active in the operation of the laboratory, though day-to-day operation is now supervised by a hired office manager.

Lloyd Bergen is a Findlay, OH, attorney and is the husband of Gertrude Bergen.

Subject was organized to supply computer-assisted analysis and other laboratory services to physicians throughout the county. Subject is reported to have entered into a contract to supply services to Findlay Community Hospital as well.

Business is conducted in a clean and well-maintained brick building, owned by and rented from Gertrude and Lloyd Bergen. Seven medical technicians, a business manager, and an office clerk are employed.

Baskin and Bergen maintain generally good credit ratings in their separate medical practices. Findlay Laboratories, however, is unrated because of their separate incorporation from the practices of Baskin and Bergen and because they have been in operation for less than two years. One supplier reports a balance in the high four figures, with very slow payment. Another reports an initial order of $25,000, with payments running 60 to 90 days slow. A third supplier has suspended shipments subject to pending resolution of a $19,000 account.

Dr. Baskin declined to furnish financial information on the subject except to say it was adequately capitalized. There are reports that the business was largely financed by a loan from the Farmers and Merchants Bank of Findlay, secured by chattel mortgage. Two reliable sources also indicate that several local physicians hold financial interest in the subject.

❧

Case 10–2 SPARTAN INDUSTRIES, INC.

BACKGROUND NOTE

Managers are often called on to recognize the achievements and accomplishments of their employees and others within their organizations. Public acknowledgment of exceptional work, career milestones, and special events in people's lives is important, not only to those being recognized, but to others who carefully observe how the organization treats its people.

Those who have worked in and for large, complex organizations will often acknowledge that it's difficult to monitor and properly appreciate individual achievements. Many financial, sales, production, and profit goals are predicated on group activities; individuals often are made to bask in the reflected glory of group membership.

Promotions are one means of rewarding employees who have performed especially well, but promotions are given for just two reasons: a vacancy exists in a position that must be filled, and the company has identified an individual with demonstrated potential to serve in that position. Promotion announcements are generally carefully guarded secrets within a business until the moment they are made public. This is usually the case because a promotion for one employee often means that others were considered but not selected.

Promotion letters must convey several pieces of information: the fact of the promotion, the new position or title, and the effective date. Additionally, such letters often convey congratulations to the recipient of the promotion, along with appropriate expressions of appreciation for past accomplishments.

Spartan Industries, Inc., is a mid-sized manufacturer of specialty metal products, most of which are used in the automotive industry. They produce lathed and stamped metal products to contract specifications for both domestic and overseas manufacturers of automobiles and automotive equipment. Spartan Industries, Inc., is a nonunion firm.

You may assume that you are an assistant manager in the metal specialties stamping division of the Jackson, Michigan, plant. The company retains a firm in Detroit, Michigan, specializing in manufacturing and labor law to handle all legal matters.

Spartan Industries, Inc., conducts no internal public relations work other than a monthly desktop newsletter produced by the human resources division. You may entertain any reasonable structural or procedural assumptions in this case.

This case requires three documents:

- a communication strategy memo (one-and-a-half to two pages in length). The memo should be directed to the company's general manager, with appropriate copies to other officers/agencies, and should respond to the questions posed in the case.

- a letter to the employee selected for promotion.

- a sample letter addressable to those employees who were considered but *not* selected for promotion.

All three documents should be in final form and ready to dispatch.

SPARTAN INDUSTRIES, INC.
2200 Spring Arbor Road
Jackson, Michigan 48138 USA

DATE: [Today's Date]
TO: Assistant Manager
            Metal Specialties Stamping Division
FROM: William A. Bissell
            General Manager, Jackson Plant
SUBJECT: Employee Promotion Announcements

I am pleased to inform you that we're going to promote several people in the Jackson plant, and one of the employees to be promoted is a member of your division.

Robert S. Johnson currently serves as lead operator in the punch press section of the stamping division and, effective the first of next month, will assume the responsibilities of punch press foreman.

Bob has been with us seven years and has performed superbly in his duties. You may recall that he served on our safety committee following a series of accidents last year. He's been indispensable to the company, and I want to make sure we not only retain our best people, but put our very best people in positions of responsibility. It seems to me, based on your recommendations and his work record, that Johnson is the right employee for the foreman's job.

Now, as you know, we interviewed and considered several other current employees for that position. I want them to know how much we appreciate their work, but there is only one opening at the moment, and the job goes to Johnson. I'd like your help with a couple of matters related to this promotion:

- First, draft a letter to Johnson telling him of the promotion. Congratulate him on my behalf and explain how valuable he is to us. Say whatever else you think may be necessary or important.

- Second, give me your thoughts regarding notification of the employees. What should we say to those whom we considered but did not select? And, how should we go about it? Prepare a sample letter for them; I want to know what you think we should say.

- Third, when should we let Johnson know about this—before or after we tell the others? Give me some sense of timing and your best judgment on how we should handle a general announcement to the entire plant.

- Finally, I am interested in garnering some positive publicity for the Jackson plant. I would think a promotion of this type would be of some interest to the local news media. Please give me your specific suggestions regarding this. How should we go about placing this story in the local press?

I think we should move quickly on this. There is no real point in delaying the notifications. I would like to see your thoughts no later than tomorrow morning. As always, your help is indispensable to me. Please accept my thanks for your good work.

—WAB—

11

DEALING WITH
THE NEWS MEDIA

S ome people are simply better than others at saying what they mean and sounding sincere in the process. When a federal grand jury accused Chrysler Corporation of odometer tampering some years ago, it was clear to Chairman Lee Iacocca that there was only one way to stem public concern: confront it head on and nip it in the bud. So he called a news conference, apologized for "breaking the law of common sense," and pledged to fix the mistakes.

Iacocca told reporters that Chrysler had done nothing illegal. But in his familiar, blunt style, he also pointed a finger at his own company for "dumb" and "stupid" practices. "Did we screw up? You bet we did," he admitted. He outlined how Chrysler would make it right with their customers, and he promised it wouldn't happen again.

Apparently it worked. Four days after the charges were announced, 55 percent of adult Americans polled in a public opinion survey thought Chrysler faced a serious problem. In a follow-up survey four days after the press conference, 67 percent of those contacted felt Chrysler had adequately dealt with the issue. Chrysler officials added that there had been no ill effect on vehicle sales or stock prices.[1]

INTRODUCTION

Maintaining a positive, honest, accessible relationship with the news media who report on your industry and your company will never be easy, but it will be essential. Few managers and virtually no executives will make it through a career successfully without responding to the media—in good times and in bad.

More than 30 years ago, management consultant and former CBS News President Chester Burger said:

> A corporate president is not chosen for his outstanding ability to articulate corporate problems. He is selected by his board of directors because of his management know-how, or his financial expertise, or his legal proficiency, or whatever particular combination of these talents may be required by the immediate problems facing the company. In utilizing his own skills, he is usually very good indeed.
>
> But the skills of management are not the same as those required to deal with the news media. Reporters, whether they are employed by television (where most people get their news these days), newspapers, magazines, or

radio, are trained in their ability to talk with someone and unearth a newsworthy story, one that will stimulate their viewers or readers. That is why they were selected; that is their surpassing talent; and that is precisely what unnerves corporate managers who choose to face their questions.[2]

Most media relations and corporate communication experts will acknowledge that reporters are not only well-trained in their profession, but most are quite good at the process of asking good questions in pursuit of a newsworthy story. What few outsiders understand, however, is that managers and executives have faced others—many of them better informed and better prepared to ask tough questions—whom they respect but do not fear.

"There's little in this world tougher than a bond road show," says Jordan Industries President and COO Tom Quinn. "The people in that audience have money to invest and plenty of tough questions about what you're planning to do with it." In many respects, investors in the debt market are sharper than equities investors. "People who manage mutual funds, retirement plans, or insurance companies know dozens of tough questions to ask and they take their measure of you as you sit there on a stool or stand in front of them with nothing but your wits and charm to defend yourself."[3]

The fact is, managers get paid to answer difficult questions every day, from people who know the facts, understand the business, and are familiar with the products and services involved. Everyone from worried or irate shareholders to curious government regulators have posed questions that managers must answer—many of them on the spot, without reference to files, databases, or conversations with others in the organization.

The relationship between the media and business is essentially adversarial. That's simply part of doing business in a democratic society. NBC reporter and later ABC news commentator David Brinkley once said, "When a reporter asks questions, he is not working for the person being questioned, whether businessman, politician, or bureaucrat, but he is working for the readers and listeners."[4] He also once said, "News is what you don't want to tell me. Everything else is public relations."

Can you do it? Are you equal to the challenge of facing a reporter and straightforwardly answering questions about your business? Sure you are. It won't be easy, but you certainly have the talent and the motivation to do the job. What you need is the preparation.

OVERVIEW

This chapter will look at why it will be in your best interest to cooperate with reporters and editors who wish to interview you, and will suggest specific ways for you to prepare yourself. Specifically, we'll examine six issues that face any manager who faces the prospect of a press interview, whether for good news or bad.

- Why interviews are important
- Should I or shouldn't I?
- A look at the media
- Getting ready
- Making it happen
- Follow-up

WHY INTERVIEWS ARE IMPORTANT

They Are a Chance to Reach a Large Audience   An interview with a reporter is an unparalleled opportunity to reach a very large audience. You simply cannot attend enough Kiwanis Club breakfasts or Rotary Club luncheons to tell your story directly. Those events, by the way, are wonderful opportunities, and you should take advantage of every invitation you receive to speak before such groups. They represent a chance to network, to meet community leaders, and to put your message forward in a direct and unfiltered fashion. The disadvantage is that they offer a limited audience for your message.

If you must reach thousands or millions of people with your message in a short period of time, you have very few choices. One choice is to take out newspaper and magazine advertisements (television advertisements are usually too expensive and inappropriate for most corporate information campaigns). People usually look at such ad campaigns as one-sided and biased and pay little attention to the content of the message.

If you need to speak to a metropolitan, statewide, or national audience, the mass media are—or should be—your first choice. Arranging for dinner or luncheon speeches will be helpful, as will the information you plan to post on your company's Web site. But there is simply no substitute for speaking directly to a newspaper or television reporter. Their reach is global, their speed is near-instantaneous, and their reputation for objectivity is your guarantee that "informed attenders" in the public (those who read newspapers and watch national television newscasts) will see, hear, or read your message. It may not be pleasant, but you have few other choices.

They Represent an Opportunity to Tell Your Story   For better or worse, most people in your target audience really don't know much about you. If your company is typical, many people will recognize the company's name, some will know of your products and services, a few will understand issues related to ownership, organization, or the industry in which you complete, and no one will seem to understand much about the very issues that worry you the most. Like it or not, most people are basically ignorant about your people, your mission, and your goals as an organization.

Is this all bad? Not necessarily. Anonymity can have its rewards. The owner of a small bookshop near a college campus once remarked, "Whenever some stink about book publishing, censorship, or objectionable publications hits the news, reporters in this town always go over to interview the manager at Barnes & Noble. Good," she said. "I don't want to answer those kinds of questions." Being anonymous, however, often means you must fight to be noticed when it's important for the public to know who you are.

They Are an Opportunity to Inform   Talking to a reporter is a chance for you, as a manager, to establish yourself as an expert on certain subjects, or at least as a specialist who knows something about the market, the product category, or the industry. Being friendly with those who are in search of information to support a newsworthy story can buy some goodwill for you when times are more difficult and the story is about you, rather than someone else.

If you make it a regular practice to offer information to the news media about your company and your industry, chances are much greater that the readers and viewers of those news outlets will associate your name, your company's name, and your product or service line with such important attributes as quality, currency, value, and desirability. You can't afford to be shy when the media come looking for a comment on a story related to your business, even if it doesn't involve you directly.

They Offer an Opportunity to Address Public Concerns   The public at large are worried about a number of things, including the environment, the economy, job opportunity, working conditions, and product safety. Where does your company fit into those concerns? Do you know what concerns are most important to people across the nation or in your own community? If not, you should, because those are most likely to become the motivating factors that frame a reporter's questions.

You should be ready with little or no notice to address questions that concern how your company treats the environment. Do you produce hazardous waste or non-biodegradable by-products? How do you dispose of those? How does your company treat its workers? What are the wages, conditions of employment, or benefits for those who make your products or deliver your services? If a company across town or somewhere else in the country makes an unsafe product, and you happen to compete in the same industry, are you ready to answer detailed, direct questions in an honest and believable manner?

A number of surveys have shown that when people watch television news interviews—particularly in a crisis or during a breaking news story—they tend to ask one question of themselves as they observe a businessperson responding to a reporter: "Is anyone smart in charge here?" If so, they go on about their own business and don't think much about yours. They're confident in the knowledge that some smart young man or woman is taking care of that messy business they saw on television. If the answer is "no," then the viewer tends to think less of the company involved, and may decide that company shouldn't be permitted to do business in their community any longer.

Keep in mind that just because you may have a license to do business—to assemble things, to transform raw materials into finished goods, or to store or process various materials, doesn't mean you'll be in business forever. Your real license to continue what you're doing depends directly on the goodwill and permission of the people who live in your community, who work in your facilities, and who buy your products and services. If they lose confidence in you, you're done. It's up to you to convince them that someone smart is in charge.

They Give You an Opportunity to Set the Record Straight   While it's true that many people know little (and some want to know even less) about your company and its business practices, much of what some people know just isn't so. American humorist Will Rogers once said, "It ain't what he don't know that bothers me. It's what he knows for sure that just ain't so that I'm worried about."

You'd be surprised, indeed, if you were to speak directly with many people about your business or your industry. Misconceptions, stereotypes, distortions, and often some disinformation will form the bulk of what they "know for sure." A news media interview is an opportunity to set the facts straight, to offer your own perspective, and to refute allegations or stories that are simply untrue.

When Jim Tolley was vice president for public affairs at Chrysler Corporation, he often focused on providing the company's perspective, particularly for a bad-news story or for a set of details that could easily be misinterpreted.

Say you have an off quarter. If you get up and drone through the figures and sit down, you're apt to see someone else's negative interpretation of the results in your morning paper. But show them how you invested some of those bucks that never got to the bottom line, and the story takes an up-beat turn. For example, Chrysler spent $600 million (US) on plants and products in the first quarter of this year. That's a lot of money—so much that it loses its meaning without a frame of reference. So [we] put it in these terms: "We just spent more money in 90 days on plant and product than Chrysler made net between 1925 and 1982."[5]

They Are an Opportunity to Reinforce Credibility   When the public stops believing in you, you're finished. An important part of your task as a manager is to reinforce public belief in what you do, what you make or provide, and in who you are as an organization. How do you do that? One easy way for a manager to find credibility for his or her statements to the press is to cite the speeches, public pronouncements, or public statements of the company's executive team.

Where will you find such statements? In your company's advertising brochures, on your corporate Web site, in the annual report, or in the company's 10K and 10Q filings with the Securities and Exchange Commission. You needn't spend a great deal of time inventing clever things to say about your organization; people have already done that for you, including public relations and advertising firms, the corporate communication staff, and the company's senior team. Read those documents, look for ideas, phrases, and concepts that you can easily include in a conversation with a reporter. Remember, the more often you say it, the more likely it is a reporter will eventually use it in a story.

SHOULD YOU OR SHOULDN'T YOU?

In deciding whether or not to respond to a reporter's request for an interview, or whether to call a press conference to attract attention to your message, here are a few basic considerations.

There Are Few Blanket Rules   One of the most important rules is this: "Never talk to strangers." If your mother passed along that bit of wisdom to you as a child, consider yourself well-raised. Your mother was wise, indeed. Dealing with strangers is a high-risk proposition, especially in the news media.

If you are approached by a reporter and asked to respond to a series of questions about your company, your products or services, or the industry, do what you can to gather some basic information first: who is the reporter? Which organization does he or she work for? What sort of deadline is the reporter working against? Then ask for some time to gather information, consult with others, and formulate a decision about participating.

Public relations expert Vic Gold once said, "There are no blanket rules in this business, except one: If Mike Wallace calls, hang up."[6] Did the venerable CBS journalist do something to anger or upset Mr. Gold? Probably not, but the advice is useful, anyway. His point is simple: *60 Minutes,* the program for which Mr. Wallace is a reporter is *not* a news program. It's owned and operated by the News Division of the CBS Television Network. The program employs journalists and former reporters—Leslie Stahl,

Morely Safer, Ed Bradley, and others—to report the stories you see on air. Executive producer Don Hewitt and his staff are long-experienced in the business of television news. So why isn't *60 Minutes* a news program? What makes it different?

60 Minutes is merely the longest-running and most successful of a television genre that includes such programs as *NBC Dateline,* ABC's *20/20, PrimeTime Live,* and a host of equally profitable but less reputable programs such as *Hard Copy, Inside Edition, American Journal,* and many others. These are clearly not news programs. They are entertainment programs. Often, they are dressed up to look like news: well-known news reporters are hired to speak into the camera; news editing techniques are employed to create movement and tension in their stories; and studio sets as well as field reporting techniques create the impression for the audience that these are news programs. Nothing could be further from the truth.

The objective standards and search for the truth that characterize legitimate news operations are strangers to these programs and those who produce them. Stories on such programs are usually chosen more for their emotional value or their salacious audience appeal than their news value. Producers often agree to accept an assignment or begin reporting on a story because of preconceived views or an ideologically driven perspective.

The truth about such programs as *60 Minutes* and others is that they are wonderfully entertaining. But as you smile or nod when Ed Bradley disassembles some poor soul on camera, think to yourself: "That could be me." Few people have the skills or abilities to present themselves and their argument in a fashion that a producer could not edit to suit his or her own taste. Even experienced politicians, long skilled in the arts of dealing with the press, have been eaten alive by the interviewers and producers of these "magazine format" shows.

Some businesspeople have agreed to *60 Minutes* interviews and have lived to tell of it. Others have emerged successfully: they've told their stories to a large audience; they were treated fairly; the facts were presented in an even-handed and professional manner. Joseph and William Coors of Coors Brewing Company made the deliberate decision to be interviewed by CBS *60 Minutes* in the midst of an on-going labor dispute and emerged looking like conscientious, caring, responsible businessmen. Keep in mind, they are an exception to the rule.

The same general considerations we've discussed here also apply to print publications that pass themselves off as newspapers. They include *The National Enquirer, The Globe, Midnight, Weekly World News,* and other supermarket tabloids. Even their most loyal readers admit that they don't buy those publications for serious news; they see them for what they are: entertainment. Some focus on celebrities, others on the bizarre, and still others on the near-believable. It would be difficult, indeed, to see how you and your company could benefit from being quoted or featured in an edition of one of these papers.

Ask Your Public Affairs or Corporate Communication Office for Help
Unless you work in a very small company, chances are good that the firm employs people who do this for a living. Your organization, no doubt, will have people who are experienced professionals, able to advise you in making your decision to participate in an interview.

"Why doesn't the public affairs person do the interview?" you ask. The reason is simple enough: no self-respecting reporter wants to talk to a public affairs specialist.

They know full well that the Public Affairs office or corporate communication media specialists have an agenda to discuss. Reporters understand that experienced public affairs and public relations people will say only what they want a reporter to hear and report.

Should that make you cautious? It should, primarily because a reporter will feel more comfortable with you, hoping for more candid and revealing statements. In a reporter's eyes, you will have more credibility because you're closer to the action in the organization; you are on the front lines where business decisions are made and the essence of the business happens each day.

Your Public Affairs or Corporate Communication office can still be of great help to you, though, as you search for information, bring yourself up-to-date on the story, and gather details that will be useful in determining whether to participate in the interview. Ask them for assistance—they won't say "no."

Get Some Background Before Committing   Among the many things you'll want to know before agreeing to a press interview is whether this story is primarily about you and your business, or whether it's simply an industry trend story that you're being asked to comment on.

It will be especially useful for you to know the background of the story before saying "yes" to an interview. Simply ask the reporter, "What's the backdrop here? How did this story develop?" You should also consider asking who else is participating in this interview. What sources has the reporter consulted? If you know a competitor is talking to him or her, that may influence your decision to participate. If you know that a well-recognized industry critic or media gadfly is being quoted, that may influence your decision as well.

Gut Feelings Are Important   If the story is sufficiently negative, or if you think the news organization you are dealing with won't give you an opportunity to tell your story accurately, fairly, and completely, you may well decide not to participate. If a reporter has deceived you about his or her identity, affiliation, or intentions, you might not want to cooperate. If your experience with the news organization that this reporter works for has an unsavory reputation, that may influence your feelings.

You have to trust your instincts. They have taken you a long way in life and have served you well. They have helped you get through college, find a job, and get into business school. They usually won't fail you if you simply let them work on your behalf. Don't agree to participate if

- You don't trust the reporter;
- You aren't clear on the direction or intent of the story;
- A reporter tries to high-pressure or blackmail you into cooperation;
- The nature of the story is so strongly negative that you do not want your name or your company's name associated with the report.

Remember, if you don't participate, you won't have an opportunity to tell your side of the story, from your perspective, or to set the record straight on issues that are most important to your firm. On the other hand, if you honestly think you won't get a fair shake from the reporter or the news organization, you're perfectly within your rights as a citizen and an employee to back off and think about it. The advantage is that your remarks won't be misquoted or taken from context, and you won't be a part of a story you consider unseemly. The disadvantage may be that others set the tone and direction of the story, and you may be running to catch up.

A LOOK AT THE NEWS MEDIA

In order to know what you're getting into, we should examine a few basics about the news media.

It's a Business First and foremost, news is a business; it is not a philanthropic enterprise. Newspapers, magazines, television stations and networks, and radio broadcasters make money not by selling news, but by selling airtime and space to commercial advertisers. It's a straight-forward exchange of audience for money. The greater the audience for commercial advertisements, the more the publisher or broadcaster can charge for the time or space.

One interesting aspect of this arrangement is that many businesspeople sign contracts with broadcasters without knowing exactly how much the ads they run will cost them. They know what the rate per thousand households will be, but they won't know until the rating estimates have come in just how much they will pay for the privilege of airing their commercial announcement. Again, the greater the audience, the larger the invoice.

If broadcasters want greater revenues for the airtime they sell, the easiest way to obtain it is to increase the size of the audience that watches their programming. In the case of news broadcasts, that may mean anything from a new hairdo for the news anchor to new graphics or a dramatic new set design. It may also mean more controversial news stories—stories designed to pique the interest of the audience and draw in more viewers. Newspapers do it with dramatic headlines ("Mom Locks Tot in Trunk at JFK"), more stories about celebrities ("Brolin and Babs Wed in Malibu Ceremony"), sports figures (O.J. Simpson, Frank Gifford, Marv Albert), and other people who really don't matter.

Journalist and newspaper editor Pete Hamill recently wrote:

> True accomplishment is marginal to the recognition factor. There is seldom any attention paid to scientists, poets, educators, or archaeologists. Citizens who work, love their spouses and children, pay taxes, give to charities, and break no laws are never in a newspaper unless they die in some grisly murder. Even solid politicians, those who do the work of the people without ambitions for immense power, and do so without scandal, are ignored. The focus of most media attention, almost to the exclusion of all other subjects, are those big names.[7]

Does this mean you can't get into the news unless you're famous? No, although it certainly helps to be famous if you want attention. Chrysler Corporation's Jim Tolley has said: "[Lee] Iacocca's prominence and personality put us in an unusual and enviable situation. Other professionals spend their careers trying to get publicity for their company or client; at Chrysler, we get paid to cope with it."[8]

News organizations are also eager to boost ratings by searching for bad guys, wrong-doers, and companies whose products bring people to grief. Of course, that's good. You would expect that the media would perform a public watchdog function, looking out for our best interests. But what if they have got the story wrong? What if someone has fed a reporter some details about your company or your products which are simply not true? To keep from becoming a ratings booster for a news program or a local paper out to do good for the community and its readers, you should consider taking the initiative with a story, demonstrating both good citizenship and good sense by helping a reporter see your company's perspective.

Markets and Sophistication Most market areas are served by broadcasters and newspaper publishers who are loathe to mistreat businesspeople, and for good reason. Those very same businesspeople are the lifeblood of their advertising program. If word gets around that the local paper has misquoted, misrepresented, or mishandled a business or its management, the publisher will hear about it. And, in turn, so will the editors and reporters.

News gathering and advertising are supposed to be separate, but rarely ever are. That doesn't mean that reporters will spike a legitimate investigation or important news story just because an advertiser is involved. Nor does it mean that a businessperson can buy his or her way off the front page with a healthy advertising account. But it does mean that in a small- to medium-sized market of 50,000 to 750,000 people, you can generally expect courteous, fair, and professional treatment most of the time.

In large markets of one million or more people, life is a bit different. For one thing, it's tougher to get your story into the news when you want exposure for your company or your products. Announcing good news is difficult in a large market because it's usually a much bigger deal to those who generate it than it is to those who report it. And in a large market there's simply a lot more news, good and bad.

Reporters in large markets are also much less sensitive to the relationship between advertising and profits. When they smell a good story, they'll go after it with little regard for the names involved. Big cities also produce a certain amount of "hit and run" journalism in which reporters will do anything to get the details or the pictures of a story, including climb the fence to your property, pay a gate guard to get past him, or hassle your employees until they've found one who's disgruntled enough to talk. Once the story is done, they don't need you any more and you have little leverage with them. If you're located in a metropolitan area and become involved in an important breaking news event, you should seek professional help from your corporate communication office or a professional public relations firm at once. Even a few hours' delay can be disastrous.

Another aspect of market size and sophistication is that media outlets in smaller markets can rarely afford to develop reporters who are genuine specialists. In New York, financial and economics reporters often know more about the market and the issues than the people they are interviewing. In Detroit, dozens of reporters focus exclusively on the automotive industry and have a professional lifetime's experience in writing about autos and carmaking. In San Francisco, literally hundreds of journalists specialize in the computing hardware and software industry; many of them have advanced degrees and are highly sophisticated in their approach to the issues they write about.

You get the picture. If you live and work in a big city, you can and should expect the journalists you deal with to know a great deal about your business. Be careful: They know the issues in your industry, they understand the vocabulary, and they know the questions to ask. The real danger here is not that you will be misquoted. The danger is that you'll say something dumb and they will get it right. Worse yet, a broadcast journalist will save the videotape.

In a smaller market—say Syracuse, New York; Montgomery, Alabama; or South Bend, Indiana—the danger is just as great for a manager, but it's danger of a different type. The risk in small-to-medium markets is that a general assignment reporter will know little or nothing of your business or industry. That means if she gets it wrong in the story that appears on tonight's six o'clock news, or in tomorrow's newspaper, it's probably your fault.

In such cases, you're dealing with a bright, curious, capable journalist, but one who is probably overworked, underpaid, and has a car wreck and a cat show to cover later in the same day. Your story is just one stop along the way. It's up to you to explain the story in simple, everyday terms that the audience will understand. It's your job to make complex issues simple, to make difficult terms clear, and to turn a confusing story into one that's easy to understand. You can do so by offering your company's perspective early and often in the interview and by flagging the interview with easy-to-follow cues: "The key issue here, Maureen, is . . ." or "If there's one thing I think is more important for your viewers to understand than any other, Mark, it's this . . ."

They Do Make Mistakes   Daily newspapers contain literally millions of facts and dozens of opinions. Occasionally, a reporter will simply get it wrong. She will copy down the wrong fact, transpose numbers, or worse, she'll speak with someone who doesn't know anything.

This sort of thing happens from time to time, even in large markets with sophisticated and highly regarded news operations. The reporters who make such mistakes rarely ever do so because of malice or bad feelings about the source. Mistakes most often occur because of naivete or pressure to get a story done before deadline. Occasionally, reporters feel a kind of internal pressure to sensationalize a story when hype or hyperbole aren't called for.[9]

If it happens to you, if you are misquoted or your words are taken from context, if the facts in the story about your company are distorted or just plain wrong, you should respond, but should do so carefully.

Deal first with the reporter. On the telephone, or in person, ask if she misunderstood you, or if you weren't clear in your response to her questions. Try to begin such conversations with this phrase: "I know you don't want your readers to be misinformed, so. . . ." Complete the thought with words such as these: "I thought you should know that some of what appears in your story on page three this morning is inaccurate."

Demanding a Retraction   You should never, ever, under any circumstances, demand a retraction or threaten a reporter. For one thing, it won't work. For another, it puts you in a position of obligation to a reporter who's just misquoted you. In exchange for retracting the incorrect story, you now "owe him one." Additionally, reporters are threatened all the time; they have grown accustomed to hearing threats from news sources. Your best bet is to appeal to a reporter's sense of integrity and credibility. Without credibility, a reporter has nothing. Stories about journalists making up details of a story or inventing sources for feature reports invariably end with the notation that the reporter has been fired by the paper or the television station. Once you have a reporter's full attention, give him or her the details or the perspective you hope to reach the public with, and conclude the conversation with the phrase, "Thanks. I know you'll do the right thing."

If dealing directly with the reporter who wrote or broadcast your story doesn't work, your next step is the news director (in broadcasting) or the managing editor (in newspapers). The approach should be exactly the same: "I know you don't want your viewers to be misinformed, so . . ." Editors and news directors are seasoned professionals who know their business and who want very much to see that the sources and subjects of their news stories are treated fairly.

Your last resort is the publisher or station manager, but it's unlikely they will be of much help. Such executives are reluctant to back a version of the truth other than the one presented to them by their news managers. Only in rare circumstances of willful misconduct will publishers or general managers back down, apologize, or retract a story. If all else fails, you can threaten to sue, but that's a very lengthy, expensive process that often ends in disappointment. Only in the most egregious cases do publishers or broadcasters end up losing in court.

Facts vs. Opinions   If the mistake is an error in fact, editors and news directors will be quick to correct it, and will usually do so with a sincere and direct apology to the person or organization who was misrepresented. If the mistake, however, is a matter of opinion, perspective, or viewpoint, it will be much more difficult—if not downright impossible—to get a correction or response from the paper or broadcaster. Editors and news directors feel very deeply that they are entitled to report opinion, even if it's a minority viewpoint, and, as long as it's labeled as such, they owe an irate reader or viewer very little in the way of an apology. Bill Moyers of CBS News once said, "Our business is truth as much as news."[10] And, while facts can be easy to produce and easy to correct, truth can be highly subjective. One man's "ecological calamity" can be another man's "routine clean-up."

Few Reporters Are Decision Makers   While it's important that you deal directly with and try to make friends of the reporters who cover your business and your industry, it's important to note that very few reporters are influential enough to make key decisions about the stories they cover. Tom Brokaw can decide if a story is big enough for him to be there personally, but Ann Thompson cannot. Reporters, even big-name anchormen, are responsive to the decisions made by their managing editors and news directors. Some stories become big enough, fast enough for general assignment reporters to be bumped aside in favor of a bigger name on the byline. On other occasions, reporters know they are in the doghouse with their bosses because of the insignificance or remoteness of the stories they have been assigned to cover.

It's useful for business executives to cultivate the friendship and favor of certain reporters. In fact, unless they involve breaking news or a crisis of some sort, most news stories rarely get any attention when they're first suggested to a media outlet. Corporate communication professionals will tell you it may take six months to a year to convince someone at *Fortune, Barrons,* or *Business Week* to cover a *soft feature.* But you should know that reporters rarely make the decisions that lead to extensive reporting, the investment of photography or research talent, or the assignment of air-time or print space to a story. Those decisions are made by news management professionals, and regardless of what you do for a living, you should make it your job to get to know them.

Get to Know Local Management If you work in a metropolitan market, the professionals in your corporate communication department will help you and others in the organization tell your story through the media. Follow their lead. If you work in a smaller market, you may need to take the initiative to meet and speak with news professionals on your own.

You should systematically set about, with the assistance of your corporate communication people, meeting radio and television news directors, newspaper managing editors, and—if your community has a business news weekly—the editors of that publication. Meeting with them may take no more than 20 minutes, and you may do little more than offer them your business card, a brief overview of your business and its products and services, and an offer to help if a story should ever develop on a subject related to your business. Conclude the conversation by asking for an opportunity to comment on any story, whether it deals directly with your company or not. "Call me," you should say. "Give me a chance to help you tell the story accurately, fairly, and completely."

If you maintain a regular, steady dialogue and keep open lines of communication with local editors and news directors, you're unlikely to be surprised by bad news. And you're unlikely to have serious disagreements with them about how a story should be covered. Do your part and respond each time you are asked for a comment. Be there ahead of their deadline and respect their rules; you won't get to edit your own comments, nor will you get to look over a story before it goes to press. That simply won't happen. But you certainly can get a news organization into the habit of calling you back to check a quote or ask for additional details if you treat them as intelligent professionals and respect the work they do.

GETTING READY

Preparing to meet with a reporter or to be interviewed by a journalist will involve some homework on your part, beginning with your strategy. If you don't have a strategy, it means that you don't know what your objectives are; if you have no specific objectives, you shouldn't agree to the interview.

Develop a Strategy Both your supervisor and your Public Affairs office should know of your interest in meeting with and working with local news managers, and you should go about cultivating a good working relationship with a strategy in mind. That strategy should specify, in very clear terms:

- The goals you hope to achieve by working with local news professionals
- The general content of your message
- The intended audience for your message
- The visuals or photo opportunities you intend to offer
- The timing and sequence of events involved in your story
- What makes this story different from others
- What makes your story newsworthy
- The media you plan to work with to tell your story

Your strategy should be committed to paper as soon as you have a story to tell. Keep in mind that a strategy on paper is not a commitment to one course of action; it should be a living, changing document as you discover new ways to tell the story, new ideas for promoting your message, and new opportunities to use the news media to your advantage. Review it and revise it as often as you need to.

Research the Reporter   Make a point of getting to know the reporter you've agreed to interview with. Find out as much as you can: writing and reporting style, story types, experience, general reputation in the community. The best place to start is with the media relations staff of your Corporate Communications office. They'll know something about nearly every reporter who takes an interest in your company and can help prepare you.

If you have the time, look at some of this reporter's previous stories. Read some clips from the company archives and get a sense of the reporter's style. Does she frequently use direct quotes? Is the style friendly, professional, or aggressive? Should you prepare background information on your company and its products or services to take with you to an interview? Would this reporter welcome a tour of your facilities?

The same is true of television reporters. If time permits, consider gathering a few videotapes of your reporter's work. If you've been invited to a regularly scheduled local program for an interview, make certain you watch at least one episode of the program in advance to get some idea of the style the interviewer uses with his or her guests.

Refine and Practice Your Message   Even the most experienced of professionals can benefit from practice occasionally. CEOs, board chairmen, and senior managers will often draft a message they want to convey during a press interview, edit it carefully, review it, and rehearse it. Most important, they will work on *sound bites,* those ten- to twelve-second memorable phrases that they hope will appear again and again on television and in the newspaper.

Do you know the *central theme* to your message—the one nugget of truth that you really want a reporter to record or write down? Begin with your central theme and work from there to develop *examples, illustrations,* and *anecdotes* to support that message. Make sure all of the evidence you plan to use is *accurate, current,* and *easy to understand.*

Speak in terms of the public's interest, not the company's. Don't talk about what the company wants or needs, but speak instead of how this will benefit the community, the consumer, your customers, and others, including your employees. Speak in personal terms, showing how you and your coworkers are involved in making better products, providing better services, building a better community.

Rehearse the words you actually plan to use during a press interview. Don't assume that you'll be able to ad lib the content of your interview when the pressure is on. You won't. You'll rely on what you know, what you have rehearsed, and what you feel most comfortable with. Practice your message until you know it so thoroughly you would feel comfortable conducting the interview in the middle of the night.

And, when all else fails: go to the mission statement. Make sure you know your company's mission statement, because when you really can't think of another thing to say, you can always offer the mission statement and then show how the subject at hand is related to the company's basic goals. It'll give you time to think and an opportunity to link the basic vision, values, and beliefs of your firm to the subject of the interview.

Confirm the Details and Ground Rules   Double-check the time, day, date, and location of the interview. If it's a studio interview and you've never been to that location before, you might consider driving by that location *before* you actually need to be there. Can you find the studio or offices you've agreed to meet in? Do you know where you can park? Do you know how long it will take you to get there? Will traffic patterns be different at the time of day you've agreed to meet?

If you've arranged for a telephone interview, make sure you tell the reporter upfront how much time you can devote to the conversation. Make certain you know whether or not the interview is being recorded. In a face-to-face interview, it's not a bad idea for you to bring along a microcassette recorder so that you'll have your own copy of what you were asked and what you said in response. The very presence of the recorder will keep a reporter honest. If she knows you have a copy of the conversation, there will be little temptation to get inventive with a direct quote, a fact or figure, or some important element of the story. If you're using a telephone and plan to record the interview, both parties must know of and agree to the recording. Otherwise, you may be in violation of one or more wiretap laws.

As you double-check the rules, ask if you can stop or correct quotes as you speak. Almost all reporters will allow this. And inquire about what the reporter's interests are one more time. Is there anything in particular that she'd like to talk about?

Review the News of the Day   Even if your interview is scheduled early in the day, make sure you check the morning paper, watch the headlines on CNN, and briefly tune in to the local news. If you have the time and network access, you may want to check the Internet to see if any stories regarding your company or your industry are on the net. You never want to be surprised.

If a reporter offers a story or a headline to you that you haven't seen or heard before, you aren't obligated to respond. You can never be certain that the report is accurate, or that you've been told the whole story. Journalists sometimes ask you to respond to a quote from someone else. If you haven't seen or heard that quote before, say so. "I'm sorry, Heather, I haven't seen that story yet. I'd rather read the full story before I respond." Don't be goaded into responding to a quote or a story you haven't read and haven't had an opportunity to think about.

Remember, *You* Are the Expert   Often lost in all of the anxiety and rush to prepare for an interview is the idea that you know more about the subject than the reporter does. Granted, some financial and business press journalists know a great deal about the subject, but it's rare that they would know your company, your projects, your products, your services, your strategy, and your plans for the future as well as you. Rely on the confidence and detailed preparation that got you this far to take you one step further.

MAKING IT HAPPEN

When the moment of the interview arrives, here's a final checklist to consider.

A Prepared Pocket Card May Help   Many executives carry a small 3" × 5" (or slightly larger) index card to record and review important details. A manufacturing facility manager in Michigan carries a card in his jacket pocket which contains the number of acres inside the perimeter fence, the square footage on the plant floor, the number of employees per shift, the hourly output in each division, production goals for the week, and other important, quantifiable information.

What's most important about your work? Can you jot down a few things that are unlikely to change in the next few days and keep them on hand? What about those issues related directly to the reason your being interviewed? Write down one or two main points you hope to impress the reporter with. Include supporting detail, numbers, and examples, if you can. Think about jotting down several key points you could talk about if the interview runs long. What *good news subjects* would you like to talk about if time permits?

Arrive Early, Check Out the Setting   Again, if you're being interviewed at a studio, the offices of a newspaper or magazine, or at some neutral location, plan to arrive early. Even if your schedule is busy that day, squeeze out a few extra minutes so that when the interviewer arrives, or it's your turn to go on, you're calm, relaxed, and familiar with the surroundings.

Appearance and Make-Up Are Important   Television is a visual medium and it's one that favors close-up shots. If a production assistant offers you an opportunity to apply make-up, take it. Men: Swallow your pride and let the make-up artist improve your looks. A little light powder will help to reduce glare produced by perspiration under the studio lights and, most importantly, it will help to prevent dark shadows from forming under and around your eyes. Women: If you routinely wear make-up, don't do anything differently for a television appearance. If you don't routinely wear make-up, follow the same rules offered for men.

One reminder: Make sure you stop in the rest room on your way out and remove the make-up. If you show up at work wearing make-up, the staff may not understand.

Get Your Points in Early   Most interviews, especially in broadcasting, will move *very* quickly. Lead with your main point. Rephrase it in the next sentence. Then, mention your key issues or principal concerns again before a minute has elapsed. Don't assume that a reporter will get around to asking you what you want to say. He may *never* get around to asking you about those subjects you would most like to talk about. Raise your principal concerns early and often.

Take the Mother-in-Law Test   This is a simple test that asks whether or not your mother-in-law would understand the explanation you've just given. Does your response to a question or does your prepared statement for the press contain acronyms, technical terms, and industry lingo? Is it filled with insider jargon?

Remember that those people watching your interview, or reading the report of your conversation with a journalist, are generally pretty smart, but they probably don't know much about your business. Use everyday terminology, simple explanations, direct declarative sentences. Draw pictures for them, tell stories, use anecdotes. Do what you can to make the subject both real and interesting for them. And, if you don't have a mother-in-law, borrow mine. She's a lovely woman named Edna who'd be more than happy to tell you if she understands what you have just said.

Be Yourself   Unless you're the Boston Strangler or someone with a personality no one would want to meet, you're much better off simply being yourself. Don't pretend, don't posture, and don't try to be someone you're not. A great reservoir of goodwill exists in this country for ordinary people who look and act like they're honest. The audience will give you the benefit of the doubt, as long as you act like yourself and play it straight.

STAYING IN CONTROL OF AN INTERVIEW

Among the worst things that could happen is for you to lose control of an interview. It's no different than managing a project or a business event. If you lose control, you cannot determine the outcome; other people will do that for you.

The Importance of Staying in Control   This means simply that you must focus on your goals for the interview and offer responses that are directed toward those goals. Keep your objective in mind, get your key points in early, and repeat them as often as you can. Don't let a reporter take the interview in a direction that is negative, counterproductive, or off-topic.

Say what you want to say. If they don't use it, you're only out the time and effort you spent preparing. If you say something in response to a question that you hadn't planned on or didn't intend to say, you're asking for trouble. If a reporter asks you a question you don't want to answer, answer a question you wish he had asked. If a journalist asks you a question you can't answer, say why it is you can't offer an answer ("That information is confidential," "We don't yet know what caused the accident," or "Those details are protected by the Privacy Act.").

Avoid responding with simple "yes" or "no" responses, even if the questions are posed in that way. Use the opportunity to seize control of the interview and get your key points across. It's free airtime or print space that's at stake here. Use it to your best advantage.

You Don't Have to Accept a Reporter's Premise   If a reporter begins a question with the phrase, "Isn't it true . . .," watch out. What usually follows is often not true and is usually designed to put you on the spot. Don't accept what a reporter says as gospel truth, even if the reporter seems especially well informed. Stick to what you know and repeat your most important contentions. If a reporter uses words you wouldn't use, or phrases you wouldn't say, don't repeat them, even to deny the accusation.

Tell the Truth   Being completely truthful is a novel idea for some managers, but it's one that usually works. If you've done what you are accused of doing—unless your attorney advises otherwise—admit it, but explain in the very next breath what you'll doing to correct the problem or improve the issue. Don't invent, embellish, stretch, or puff up the facts. Reporters are exceedingly good at finding the truth in most stories; they're trained professionals in research and investigation. If they smell a liar, they'll come after you like a pack of dogs. You needn't reveal everything, of course, but what you do say should be honest, accurate, and truthful.

Avoid Arguments   Don't pick a fight. Journalists are trained in the techniques of combative interviews, and you are unlikely to win. If you get angry and lash out at a reporter, he or she will likely remain quiet and let you look foolish. Stay calm, under control, and professional. You'll win the respect of the reporter and the audience in the process.

You Are *Always* on the Record   People who watch television shows about reporters often think they can go *off the record* to tell an interviewer something confidential, hoping that it won't make it into the story. People who tell reporters something off the record usually have an ulterior motive: "You can use this information any way you want, just don't attach my name to it." Reporters are *very* suspicious of sources who pass along information that is off the record.

Bob Franken, who was assistant managing editor of *The Arizona Republic* for many years, once said, "If you don't want it to appear in the paper, don't ever say it to a reporter." He meant very simply that saying something to a reporter will somehow, someday eventually work its way to the surface and appear in print, on the air, or in public. If you're concerned about keeping something secret, don't say it. You can't fault a reporter for using something you've said, even though you tried to preface (or backpedal) the words, "off the record." In every successful manager's career, there is no room for off the record comments to a reporter.

Use Examples, Illustrations, Brief Anecdotes   People respond to stories, especially those with circumstances they can easily envision or identify with. Illustrate your response or press statement with tales that will capture the hearts and imagination of those listening or reading. Rather than talk about how many metric tons of snow were removed from your company's property during last week's blizzard, relate a story that involves one of your employees; talk about how long he worked and what the experience was like. Examples and stories will work much better than dry facts, figures, and statistics.

If You Can't Speak to the Questions, Speak to the Issue   Individual questions may be phrased in a way that makes them tough to answer. More important, your response to this particular question may be of little help in assisting the audience to understand the larger issue. You may need to deflect the question slightly: "That would be interesting to know, Jay, but the more important issue at the moment is . . ." Or, you may simply need to refocus the question: "The number of units involved in this recall is much less important than the overall issue of product safety. . . ."

Above All Else, Stay Likeable   If the audience doesn't like you, you're dead meat. As you read a few minutes ago, there is a great reservoir of goodwill and understanding out there for people who work hard, play by the rules, and respond honestly to a question. If the audience decides that they like the reporter better than they like you, it will be all but impossible to win any friends for your company or your cause. Use humor, be self-effacing, stay humble. You've got a lot to lose if you don't.

FOLLOW-UP

After it's over, you shouldn't simply put the experience behind you. Each press interview should be an opportunity to learn, grow, and improve your abilities. Another event, another product roll-out, another small crisis may be just around the corner.

Review the Article or Tape   Read what's been written about you, watch the videotape, and look carefully at the way the story came together. Did the reporter get it right? Are the key facts there? If most of it's right and if your company is cast in a generally favorable light, be glad. That's the most you can ask. Very few reporters will get every detail exactly right; even fewer will say things the way you'd have said them if you wrote the story yourself.

Inform the Chain of Command   No surprises. Keep your boss informed about every interview you do. Tell the people in Corporate Communication how it went; they may wish to pass along information to others in the company who may be contacted for an interview. No one expects perfection from each encounter with the media, but no one in higher management wants to be blindsided by employee quotes or statements in the press.

Provide Feedback   It's not a bad idea to pick up the phone and call the reporter who interviewed you. He or she will likely enjoy hearing from you, especially if the experience was a good one. If it didn't work out the way you had planned or hoped, talk with the reporter and see what went wrong. If it did work, consider a follow-on opportunity. Perhaps there's another story in your organization that would be of interest to that reporter or another opportunity to show what your company can do.

Leave a Record for Your Successor   Don't walk away from an encounter with the Fourth Estate and simply press on with business as usual. Take a few minutes to draft a memo for the record, explaining how the request for an interview developed, what the key issues were, who was involved, where the interview took place, and what your impressions were. Include a copy of the newspaper or magazine clipping, or—if possible—include a copy of the videotape. The more information your successor has to work with, the greater the chances for success if the same reporter or news outlet should call again.

Endnotes

1. Tolley, James L. "Iacocca Still Charms the Media." *ABC Communication World,* September 1987, p. 22.
2. Burger, Chester. "How to Meet the Press." *Harvard Business Review,* July–August 1975, p. 63.
3. Quinn, Thomas. President and Chief Operating Officer, Jordan Industries, Inc., Chicago, Illinois, in a personal interview, Thursday, November 20, 1997, Notre Dame, Indiana.
4. Burger, "How to Meet the Press," p. 62.
5. Tolley, "Iacocca," p. 22.
6. Gold, Vic. "If Mike Wallace Calls, Hang Up: Ten Rules for Dealing with Today's Journalists." *The Washingtonian,* September 1984, pp. 87–89.
7. Hamill, Pete. *News Is a Verb: Journalism at the End of the Twentieth Century.* New York, NY: The Ballantine Publishing Group, 1998, p. 80.
8. Tolley, "Iacocca," p. 21.
9. Hamill, *News Is a Verb,* pp. 79–94.
10. Lichter, S. Robert, Stanley Rothman, and Linder S. Lichter. *The Media Elite: America's New Powerbrokers.* Bethesda, MD: Adler & Adler, 1986, p. 132.

For Further Reading

Cutlip, Scott M., Allen H. Center, and Glen M. Broom. *Effective Public Relations,* 6th ed. Englewood Cliffs, NJ: Prentice-Hall, 1985.

Evans, Fred J. *Managing the Media: Proactive Strategies for Better Business—Press Relations.* Quorum Books, 1997.

Hilton, Jack. *How to Meet the Press: A Survival Guide.* Dodd, Meade, 1987.

Hoover, Judith D. *Corporate Advocacy: Rhetoric in the Information Age.* Greenwood Publishing Group, 1997.

Marlow, Eugene. *Electronic Public Relations.* Wadsworth Publishing Company, 1996.

Matthews, Wilma. *How to Create a Media Relations Program.* International Association of Business Communicators, 1997.

Mayhew, Leon H. *The New Public: Professional Communication and the Means of Social Influence.* Cambridge University Press, 1997.

Moore, Simon. *An Invitation to Public Relations.* Cassell, 1996.

Robinson, James W. *Winning Them Over.* Prima Publishing, 1986.

Wade, John and Tony Hicks. *Dealing Effectively with the Media.* Crisp Publications, 1992.

Ward, Sue. *Getting the Message Across: Public Relations, Publicity, and Working with the Media.* Pluto Press, 1993.

Yale, David R. *Publicity and Media Relations Checklists.* NTC Business Books, 1995.

ॐ

Case 11–1 BUON GIORNO ITALIAN FOODS, INC.

Please read and familiarize yourself with the information contained in this case. You have been designated to serve as an official representative of your firm and can expect to be interviewed by broadcast or print reporters on the incident described here. You may keep this fact sheet at hand during an interview and, if necessary, refer to it. Be aware that your credibility depends, to a degree, on your familiarity with the facts. Be aware, also, that a reporter may ask related questions not addressed by the information provided by this sheet. Do your best.

BACKGROUND

You are a senior production manager with Buon Giorno Italian Foods, Inc., of Mishawaka, Indiana. Your supervisor, Mr. Anthony Delgado, is vice president for production for the firm. Your company has just one plant but grosses nearly $3,000,000 per year, producing specialty Italian food items for wholesale distribution through food brokers to restaurants. Your company has recently launched a highly successful line of similar food items under the Buon Giorno label that are designed for retail sale through supermarkets and specialty food shops.

Your new line of specialty Italian soups has proven particularly successful throughout the midwestern United States. The Mishawaka plant now produces more than 2,000 cases a month of the soups, including pasta e'fagiole, minestrone, and rigatoni aribiata. Your retail sales of these soups have tripled in the past six months and now account for 15 percent of sales. The national and North American markets appear virtually unlimited.

Your firm purchases ingredients for your specialty food line from a number of different importers, most of them in New York and New Jersey. Your largest supplier of pasta is Dellafina Imports of Secaucus, New Jersey. Many of the fresh food stocks, including beans, onions, and other vegetables come from local and regional green grocers. Specialty items, such as anchovies, pimentos, dill, and other ingredients come from literally dozens of small food brokers in the Midwest and along the East Coast. Such items are price sensitive and you shop for the best bargains wherever they may be found.

THE FACTS OF THE CASE

Your supervisor called you this morning and told you that the company president, Mr. Carmine Matuso, was notified by the Michigan public health commissioner that your company's food products have been implicated in a series of mysterious deaths in the Midwest. The Michigan Public Health Service and several Michigan county coroners have quickly begun gathering data and reviewing autopsies dating back several months.

The link, according to Michigan Public Health Commissioner, Dr. Viola Nelson, was established tentatively over the weekend in Detroit when three people became seriously ill after eating what they claim were cans of your company's soup. Dr. Nelson has notified the FDA and regional public health officials, and contacted your CEO, Mr. Matuso, three days ago. Since that time, one additional death has been recorded under similarly suspicious circumstances in the Birmingham, Michigan, area. Your boss has delayed telling you about this until today.

Health officials now suspect the culprit may be a deadly botulism bacterium in one or more batches of your Minestrone Milano. A quick series of telephone calls to production supervisors in the Mishawaka plant reveals that your people had heard rumors over the weekend and, in fact, several phone calls from Detroit area hospitals had been received.

THE EXECUTIVE COMMITTEE DECISION

Following an executive committee meeting this morning at Buon Giorno Foods, the company has decided to begin an immediate recall of all Minestrone Milano. Some 6,000 cans of the soup are thought to be on supermarket shelves and in consumer cupboards throughout a seven state area. The Minestrone Milano in question bears the lot number G-7114-AB9. That number is stamped on the bottom of the cans.

The committee has decided not to recall any other soup lines or any of the company's other products. Supermarkets are being asked to pull their shelf stocks and return them to the broker who supplied them. Consumers are asked to return the soups to the stores where they bought them. Above all, the committee feels, no one should panic over this matter. After all, no definitive link has yet been established between your products and the illnesses and deaths in Michigan.

The company has retained the service of Blank, Hobbes, Harter and Freeman, a Chicago law firm specializing in product liability. Your firm has also contracted the services of an epidemiologist and a pathologist from St. Joseph Hospital, South Bend, Indiana. They're planning to examine your production and processing equipment and packaging facilities, perhaps as early as tomorrow. Your task is to explain this to the press and the public.

This case was prepared from public sources by James S. O'Rourke, concurrent associate professor of management, as the basis for class discussion rather than to illustrate either effective or ineffective handling of an administrative situation. Personal identities have been disguised.

Case 11–2   O'BRIEN PAINT COMPANY

Please read and familiarize yourself with the information contained in this case. You have been designated to serve as an official representative of your firm and can expect to be interviewed by broadcast or print reporters on the incident described here. You may keep this fact sheet at hand during an interview and, if necessary, refer to it. Be aware that your credibility depends, to a degree, on your familiarity with the facts. Be aware, also, that a reporter may ask related questions not addressed by the information provided by this sheet. Do your best.

THE FACTS OF THE CASE

A fire broke out early this morning in the Western Avenue plant of the O'Brien Paint Company. A night security officer smelled smoke in one of the bulk storage facilities and called local fire officials on the 911 emergency line. When the officer returned from the telephone to the scene of the fire, he saw flames and immediately recognized the danger to various paints and chemicals stored in the area. He removed a handheld fire extinguisher from the wall unit in the storage facility and attempted to extinguish the flames himself; he was largely unsuccessful.

A pumper unit, a hook-and-ladder unit, one rescue unit, and a command vehicle responded to the fire call from the Fire Department's #7 Station, located at 1616 Portage Avenue. Those units were under the command of Fire Captain Cazimir Pelazinski and arrived on the scene 4 minutes and 30 seconds after the emergency call was received, at approximately 3:25 A.M.

By the time the fire units arrived, flames had spread from the bulk storage area to a production unit, a packaging room, and a box and dry-storage facility. Because of the spreading flames, Capt. Pelazinski upgraded the fire designation from one alarm to three and called for two back-up pumper units from Fire Station #6 at 4302 West Western Avenue; those units were on scene by 3:41 A.M.

Fire officials briefly considered evacuating the surrounding neighborhood, mostly low-income, single-family dwellings and a few low-rise apartment buildings, because of the toxic nature of smoke and fumes from the fire. A significant danger of explosion from paint, chemicals, varnish, turpentine, and other products also existed at the time.

For a variety of reasons, fire officials elected not to evacuate the neighborhood. The fire was eventually brought under control by approximately 7:20 A.M. but has not yet been declared fully extinguished.

The security officer, Rupert J. Watson, 37, of 819 Christiana Street, was unhurt in the incident. He has been employed by O'Brien Paints, Inc., since October 14, 1992, as a security specialist. Mr. Watson is a native of the local area and a veteran of the U.S. Army; he served as a combat infantryman in Persian Gulf during Operation Desert Storm in 1990–91.

Your supervisor, Mr. Fredrick J. McQuethy, who is assistant vice president for production, spoke with you by telephone this morning for several minutes. At this point, apparently, no cause for the fire can be specified, though both you and Mr. McQuethy are aware that several small fires have broken out in the Western Avenue Plant in recent months, none of them causing extensive damage.

Mr. McQuethy is personally convinced that militant trade unionists in the plant set the fire.

The collective bargaining agreement with members of International Brotherhood of Oil, Atomic and Chemical Workers, local 326, is set to expire in less than 30 days. The union is adamant about renegotiating elements of the contract dealing with compensation, job security, and working conditions in the Western Avenue plant.

The building was last inspected 11 months ago by a local fire marshal and was due for inspection in about 30 days. Several minor fire safety discrepancies were noted in the previous inspection but were corrected in a matter of weeks. The production area was equipped with a fire suppression system that functioned satisfactorily. The storage units, however, were equipped a bit differently. They were protected by a sprinkler system that apparently failed, permitting a substantial amount of damage to occur. All areas were in compliance with state and local fire ordinances.

One last item: The police have been called in by the fire department within the past hour to investigate the charred remains of an individual found in the fire rubble. As far as you know, that individual is not an employee of the firm. The security officer, Mr. Watson, claims no knowledge of anyone on the plant grounds last evening and has told investigators he has no idea how someone could have gotten in the building without his knowledge or permission. Police, thus far, are silent on this matter.

Damage to portions of the plant is extensive, but production could probably resume within a week to ten days, depending on the findings of the fire investigators. Most short-term orders could be filled by the O'Brien Paint plants in Alameda, California and Linden, New Jersey, until that time.

Your task is to explain all of this to the press and the public. Keep in mind that the news media may have interests which are different from those of the immediate neighborhood, the community at large, O'Brien Paint employees, and O'Brien shareholders.

This case was prepared from public sources by James S. O'Rourke, concurrent associate professor of management, as the basis for class discussion rather than to illustrate either effective or ineffective handling of an administrative situation. Personal identities have been disguised.

☙

Case 11–3 AMERICAN RUBBER PRODUCTS COMPANY, INC.

THURSDAY, MARCH 4, 1993

As the clock in his study struck 10:00 P.M., Jeff Bernel stood up, stretched, and walked over to the window. The lake-effect snow blowing in from Lake Michigan had picked up intensity and was beginning to accumulate on the lawn. Wet, slippery snow on the streets and roadways wouldn't be far behind. "It's nice to be home tonight," he thought, "even if I still have another ninety minutes of finance ahead of me."

Jeff Bernel, chairman, president, and chief executive officer at American Rubber Products Company, headquartered in northwest Indiana, was also an executive MBA student at the University of Notre Dame, 40 miles to the east. Late nights, team study meetings, telephone conferences, and group projects were a fact of life for a second-semester MBA.

As he settled back into his finance text, the phone rang. It was Mark Dilley, his executive vice president and chief operating officer. "Jeff," he said, "there appears to have been an accident at work. Some kind of explosion. We have to get there." A brief pause followed and Bernel responded, "See you there."

Bernel bounded down the steps, grabbed a coat, and left a note for his wife, Liz. As he backed out of the driveway, he knew in an instant the usual two-mile drive would take more than a few minutes.

THE COMPANY JEFF BERNEL LEADS

American Rubber Products Company is a mid-size manufacturing firm with annual revenues in excess of $35 million. The firm employs 600 people at four locations in Indiana, Michigan, Kentucky, and New York. The company was founded in 1933 and is a supplier of seals and gaskets to the North American Original Equipment Manufacturers and first tier automotive markets.

THE SCENE AT THE LAPORTE PLANT

When he arrived at the LaPorte, Indiana, headquarters of American Rubber Products, he was certainly unprepared for what he saw: fire trucks, ambulances, rescue vehicles, police cars, chaos, and considerable confusion. The main gate was blocked with a pumper unit, so he pulled around to the side entrance on Tipton Street. As he did, a familiar face greeted him.

Sheriff's deputy Greg Bell, a friend from church, knocked on the car window. "You've had a boiler explosion, Mr. Bernel. You have two fatalities." The news was stunning. In 20 years of business experience and 6 years of submarine duty in the Navy, Jeff had never experienced anything like this.

He pulled his car into the parking lot, grabbed a flashlight from the glove box, and went through the center door to Press Room C. There, he ran into Ida Allen, press room supervisor. "Give me an update," he said. Mrs. Allen, a loyal employee of more than dozen years, gave Bernel an accounting of all those at work. "We were just at the end of the second shift, Jeff. We had about 40 people in the building."

"It could have been a lot worse," he thought to himself. "If this had been the first shift, we'd have had 60 or 70 people in here, plus another 40 in an adjoining area."

Mrs. Allen, obviously shaken and upset, continued with her update for Bernel. She detailed where each employee had been, where the injured were, and how she had rung 9-1-1 and then cared for the most seriously injured until help arrived. Though visibly shocked, she used full names for the five injured and described in detail what had happened. Among those hurt, two were critical, two were in serious condition, the other was listed by paramedics as "fair."

The two deceased employees had been in the press room adjacent to the boiler room when the accident occurred. "They were press operators," Bernel later recalled, "who took raw pre-formed rubber stock and placed it in a mold attached to a steam press. The press would close hydraulically for whatever length of time it would take to shape and cure the rubber into auto gaskets."

The presses at American Rubber Products were timed to open after each cure cycle. Press operators would remove cured gaskets and put them on a conveyor to a posttreatment trim area. Operators would then clean the mold with a brush and an air gun. That process would be repeated three-to-five times each hour. One person is charged with responsibility for six-to-ten presses, producing from 100-to-300 gaskets per hour, depending on the size and weight of the product.

"These are semiskilled laborers," Bernel said later. "They receive on-the-job training from senior mold/press operators responsible for new employees. We also supply problem-solving training and statistical process control training for each." On the evening of Thursday, March 4, 1993, Press Room C was staffed by about a half-dozen employees. It was 10:30 P.M. and now two of them were dead: a 32-year-old mother of two and an 18-year-old woman hired earlier in the week as a temporary employee.

THE BOILER ROOM EQUIPMENT

The boiler room adjacent to Press Room C is essentially a barrel on its side, measuring 10-to-12 feet in diameter and 30 feet long. According to industry experts, it's known as a *marine boiler,* which uses natural gas fed through tubing at one end. An electrically controlled gas burner fires the combustion gasses down a 20-inch pipe called a *Morrison Tube.*

As they move horizontally through the boiler, the combustion gasses are blown down the Morrison Tube, then diverted 180 degrees through hundreds of small tubes, each one-and-a-half inches in diameter, directing the gasses back toward the burner. These tubes are surrounded by cool, fresh water. Gasses in the stainless steel tubes heat more than 20,000 pounds of that water to create steam. Gasses are then diverted 180 degrees again at the burner end and passed through another set of tubes before being vented out an exhaust stack more than 100-feet high.

The boiler, manufactured by The York Shipley Company of St. Louis, Missouri, features two large compartments: one containing low pressure, the other containing high pressure. In the low-pressure compartment, atmospheric pressure aided by blower fans totals approximately 10 pounds per square inch (ppsi). The high-pressure compartment is where water is heated to 125 ppsi. The higher the water pressure, the hotter the steam.

THE BOILER'S HISTORY

A marine boiler, properly maintained is considered to have a useful lifetime of approximately 30 years in continuous service. Because of the risk posed to human life in their operation, marine boilers are licensed by Occupational Safety and Health Administration authorities in all 50 states. And, because of the number of moving parts, high steam pressure, and extremely high temperatures involved in a boiler's operation, state-licensed inspections are mandated at regular intervals. The frequency of those inspections varies according to state regulation, boiler type, and variety of operational uses.

The boiler at American Rubber Products Company was slightly more than 15 years old on the day of the accident. Five years prior to the accident, Power Plant Services of Fort Wayne, Indiana, had installed a new, more efficient gas burner. Annual and semiannual safety inspections were performed each summer by Hartford Steam Boiler Insurance Company under a license issued by the State of Indiana. During those inspections, the boiler was completely disassembled, both ends were opened, and all internal parts were examined. A state-specified series of inspection parameters was then tested for by Power Plant Services, who also performed any repairs deemed necessary.

As far as Jeff Bernel knew, the boiler was in good condition, conformed to the operational specifications of the State of Indiana, and—until a few minutes ago—posed no threat or hazard to his employees. Although he was an engineer who understood the inner workings of the boiler, Bernel left the inspection and certification of the equipment in his plant to the state-certified experts from Power Plant Services and Hartford Steam Boiler Insurance.

EVERY EXECUTIVE'S NIGHTMARE

"As I exited the building by the South entrance," Bernel recalled, "people were everywhere." LaPorte Hospital, by sheer coincidence, has just completed a disaster preparedness exercise and the trauma team was already on site. "An emergency technician confirmed that ambulance response was just nine minutes to the scene. Within 20 minutes, all injured were in the hospital, receiving treatment." After his brief tour of the darkened, powerless building, he gathered one, final situation report from employees, fire and police officials. Competent professionals were there doing their jobs, but could Bernel do his?

As he walked back to his car, Bernel noticed that reporters and cameras crews from South Bend and Chicago were already on-scene. The parking lot was filling up with gawkers and media-types and he had to do something, fast. As he slipped into the driver's seat and slammed the door, one thought came to him: "I've got to get help."

At that point, he got out his cell phone and called David Haist, lead attorney with Barnes & Thornburg. As the phone rang at Haist's home, it was 11:30 P.M.

Haist was quick with a reply: "I can't help you, Jeff, but Doug Dieterly can. He's our best product liability lawyer and you should talk with him tonight." After an exchange of telephone numbers, Bernel dialed Dieterly and explained as much as he could. By this point, the car was growing cold.

"Do you think it's your fault?" Dieterly asked?

"No," Bernel replied, "I really don't. We've done everything we were supposed to do. We've followed the state safety guidelines scrupulously. That boiler is torn down and inspected semiannually and certified as safe by State of Indiana boiler inspectors."

"If you're not at fault," Dieterly counseled, "appoint someone to speak, open the doors, and tell them everything you know." After a pause, he added: "If you are at fault, or think you may be, lock the doors, gather all management employees and direct them not to speak to anyone." Dieterly's final words were clear: "Don't practice conjecture."

Dieterly had instructed Bernel that, under Indiana law, worker's compensation insurance provides that a company cannot be held liable unless gross negligence is proven. If it is, litigants can pierce the corporate veil and claim the assets of the shareholders and officers.

Bernel rubbed his glove against the car window to clear the condensation, and realized that meeting the media was just the first of many problems he would face. The tools in his LaPorte plant were the property of his customers—the Big Three domestic automakers and a handful of important overseas customers. If he couldn't produce steam to cure rubber in ten days, his customers would simply reclaim the molds, and American Rubber Products would be out of business.

More than talking to the press, Bernel was faced with two basic issues, one dealing with people and the other dealing with his business. The people issue was more pressing, more urgent. "How do I keep this group together?" he thought. "How do I care for the wounded and deceased, and their families? And how in the world do convince them it's safe to return to work?"

The other issue was his business. If he couldn't restore manufacturing capacity soon, he wouldn't have a business. It was too late to draft a crisis response plan now. As he glanced at his watch, he could see that it was 12:05 A.M. Tomorrow had already come.

This case was prepared from personal interviews and public sources by James S. O'Rourke, concurrent associate professor of management, as the basis for class discussion rather than to illustrate either effective or ineffective handling of an administrative situation.

ANALYZING A CASE STUDY

Among the many tools available to business educators, the case study has become increasingly popular. Professors use it to teach the complexities of many different, modern business problems. That's not a surprising development. Beyond the fundamentals, memorization and description will take you just so far. The real test of whether you are ready to manage a business will come when you are asked to assume the role of a manager, step into an authentic business situation, make sense of the circumstances you see, draft a plan, and take action.

WHY STUDY CASES?

Schools of law have studied cases for many years as a means of exploring legal concepts and understanding the practices of the courts. Harvard Business School began inviting executives and managers into their classrooms after the First World War, hoping to provide students with some insight into the thinking of successful businessmen. Not long afterward, professors of business began writing down the narratives of these business managers in an effort to capture the ambiguities and complexities involved in the day-to-day practice of commerce and administration.

The idea spread to other schools of business and migrated from graduate to undergraduate programs. Today, many business educators use case studies because their narratives are so valuable in developing analytic and critical thinking abilities, as well as organizational and communication skills. You can memorize lists, procedures, and attributes. You can occasionally guess successfully at the answer to a multiple-choice question. But you cannot memorize the answer to a problem you have never encountered, nor can you guess at the options available to a manager who must resolve a complex, difficult, often ambiguous situation.

TYPES OF CASES

Although each case is different, you are likely to encounter three basic types of case studies, depending on the subject you are studying: field cases, library cases (sometimes referred to as *public record cases*), and armchair cases.

Field Cases   Field cases are written by professors and students of business with the cooperation of managers and executives who experienced the events and problems described in the case. They involve extensive interviews with people who are often identified by name as the narrative unfolds. Information contained in these cases is known best—and sometimes only—to insiders in a business. Newspaper accounts and descriptions of events contained in the business press may play a role in establishing key facts, but the sequence of events, what was said to whom, what each manager knew at the time, and which managerial options were open to the principals of the case are often a mystery to the public-at-large.

Extensive interviews with employees, managers, and executives will often reveal more. Careful examination of business records and databases can provide background and context for the events. And, frequently, the active cooperation of a company is the only way a case author will ever know exactly what happened with any measure of certainty.

Field cases are often more extensive and thorough than other case types, but present a dilemma for the case writer: what does the company have to gain by granting access to its premises, its records, and its employees? Is this merely an attempt to make executives look good after the fact? Are such cases an attempt at public relations when things go wrong in a business? Often, to gain access to a business, a case writer must have some special relationship with those who own or manage it, and must have a reputation for reporting on events in an accurate and fair manner. One disadvantage of such cases is that, once they are published, they are difficult to modify and may quickly become dated.

Library Cases   Unlike a field case, library or public record cases do not involve special access to the businesses being studied. They do not involve interview material or direct quotes which are unavailable elsewhere. And they most often do not include figures, data, or information which are not somehow a part of the public record, available to anyone with a library card and basic research skills.

Companies that have failed somehow—blown a great opportunity, overlooked the obvious, chosen the wrong path, or failed to act when they should—are understandably reluctant to permit case writers to speak with their employees or look at the evidence. If they've done something terribly wrong—committed a crime or imperiled the public welfare—a company may do all it can to withhold, obscure, or cover up what has happened. That is precisely the challenge facing most business reporters as they gather information for publication each day. Journalist David Brinkley once said, "News is what you don't want to tell me. Everything else is public relations."

Writers who produce library cases, however, have a wealth of information available to them. In addition to stories produced for broadcast, print, and online news organizations, business case writers can look to numerous government documents and other sources, particularly for publicly held firms. Annual filings with the Securities and Exchange Commission, such as forms 10-Q and 10-K, can be very helpful. When one company declares its intention to acquire another, or is sued in federal court, numerous documents relevant to the issues at hand may become a part of the public record. When a company prepares to launch an IPO or float a bond offering, numerous public disclosures are required. Case writers have a high degree of confidence in the accuracy of such records, since the penalty for falsifying them may involve heavy fines or jail time.

Armchair Cases   These are fictional documents about companies that don't really exist and events that have never really occurred. While they bear some resemblance to authentic cases, they are often lacking in the richness of detail and complexity that accompany real events. They may be useful, however, in introducing basic concepts to students or in provoking a discussion about key issues confronting businesses.

Business educators produce armchair cases when they are denied access to the people and data of real businesses, or when they wish to reduce very complex events to a series of simple decision opportunities. Armchair cases are often useful to begin a discussion about change management, the introduction of technology, or a rapidly unfolding set of events in other cultures. A principal advantage of these cases is that they can be modified and updated at will without securing the permission of the fictional companies and managers they describe.

PRODUCING A CASE SOLUTION

To produce a case solution that demonstrates you are ready for management-level responsibility will involve the following steps.

Read the Case   The first step to a successful case solution is to read the case, carefully and with an eye for detail—more than once. Personality theorists tell us that some people are eager to get to the end of a story quickly. "Don't bother me with details," they say. "Just tell me what happened." Such people, often dependent on *Cliff's Notes* and executive summaries, will bypass the details of a case in order to reach a conclusion about what happened in the story. They are often reluctant to read the case attachments and will frequently avoid tables of numbers altogether. Many arrive at conclusions quickly and begin formulating responses before they have all the facts. The less clever in this crowd see the details of a case as a nuisance; reading the facts will only interfere with their preparation of a response.

After you have read and thought about the issues in a case, if you are uncertain about what to do, read it again. As you mature in the experiences of business school, you will get better at this; but at first, your best defense against being surprised or frustrated by a case is to read it thoroughly.

Take Notes   College students typically want to either underline or highlight much of what is contained in a book chapter, reprint, or essay. Case studies, however, are constructed a bit differently. Textbook chapters are typically organized in a hierarchical fashion, with key points and subpoints listed in order of importance, carefully illustrated and summarized. Not so with case studies, which are often simply arranged in chronological order. Textbooks usually proceed in logical fashion, with one concept building on others that came before it. Case studies, on the other hand, are seemingly chaotic: many events happen at once, order and discipline are sometimes missing, and key issues are not always self-evident.

Case studies may also contain substantial amounts of information in tabular form: annual revenues, product shipment rates, tons of raw materials processed, or cost data organized by business units. To know what such data mean, you will have to read the tables and apply what you have learned about reading a balance sheet, or about activity-based costing. You may find crucial information contained in a sequence of events or a direct quote from a unit manager. Sometimes you will discover that the most important issues are never mentioned by the principals in the case—they are simply ideas or tools that they weren't clever enough to think of or didn't think were important at the time.

Your notes should focus on the details you will need to identify the business problems involved the case, the issues critical to solving those problems, as well as the resources available to the managers in the case. Those notes will be helpful in producing a case solution.

Identify the Business Problem   In each case, at least one fundamental business problem is present. It may be a small, tactical issue, such as how this company will collect money from a delinquent customer. But the issue may be broader in nature: "How can they reduce accounts receivable aging to 30 days or less?" Larger, more strategic problems might involve the company's chronic, critical cash-flow difficulties. "If this company were no longer cash-starved, what longer-term opportunities might open up?"

You may identify more than one problem in a case. Complex cases often involve several such problems simultaneously. They may be technical in nature and involve accounting or cost-control systems. They may involve the use of technology. You might see supply-chain problems in the business you are studying. You may identify marketing deficiencies. Or, you might see human problems that involve supervision, communication, motivation, or training.

Specify an Objective for the Managers Involved   Once you have identified one or more business problems present in the case, think about the outcome(s) you would most hope to see for the company and people you have read about. If you were asked to consult on this company's problems—and that is the role most business students are playing as they read a case study—what results would you hope for? Don't limit your thinking to what the company should *do,* but what the most *successful outcome* would look like. Be specific about how the company will know if they have succeeded. Quantify the desired results whenever you can.

Identify and Rank Order the Critical Issues   These issues are at the heart of the case. If you miss a critical issue, you may not be able to solve the case to the satisfaction of your professor.

- *Some issues are interdependent.* That is, a solution to one issue might necessarily precede or depend on another. In a product-contamination case, for example, a media relations team can't draft a press release until the production or packaging team knows what's wrong with the product. The team responsible for a new product launch can't make final advertising and promotion decisions until issues related to packaging, transportation, and distribution have been solved.
- *Some issues are more important than others.* A company may have a great opportunity to launch a product line extension, but not have sufficient market research data to support the idea. More to the point, they may not have the talent on staff to understand and properly use such data. Thus, hiring a market research chief might be more

important than simply contracting with an outside firm to find the data.

- *Each issue has a time dimension.* While two problems may be equally important to the success of a company, one may be near-term in nature while the other is long-term. Setting up a corporate Web site may be important, but it won't solve the longer-term issue of marketing strategy: should we sell direct over the Web or use retail part-ners to market our products? Specify which problems must be addressed first; but think, as well, about the duration of the solutions—how long will it take to fix this?

- *Some issues are merely symptoms of larger or deeper problems.* Two managers in open warfare with each other about budget or resource issues may be symptomatic of more serious, long-term budget problems, inadequate communication among the management team, or perhaps a corporate culture that encourages confrontation over minor issues. When Sears Roebuck & Co. discovered that auto service managers in California were charging customers to replace parts that were not yet worn out, the problem was deeper than a few overzealous managers. After analyzing the complaints brought by the California Attorney General, Sears realized that their compensation system rewarded managers for selling more parts and not for simply servicing customers' vehicles.

Consider Relevant Information and Underlying Assumptions Accept the fact that much of the information contained in the case will not be useful to your analysis. You should also accept the fact that you will never know all that you would like in order to produce a solution. Life is like that. So are case studies. Identify the relevant facts contained in the case and think carefully about them. Identify addi-tional information you might like to have—that might be part of your solution—but don't dwell on it.

Separate facts from assumptions. Recognize that there are some things you will know for sure and others that you will not. Recognize further that you may be required to subjectively inter-pret some evidence and to assume other evi-dence not directly stated in the case. The more suppositions you make, however, the weaker your analysis becomes.

List Possible Solutions to the Problem Every problem lends itself to more than one solution. Keep looking for good ideas, even when you have already thought of one that will solve the problem. Listing possible solutions is a form of brainstorming that will later permit you to assign values or weights to those ideas: is one solution less expensive than another? Will one be more effective than another? Will one idea work more quickly? Will one of these ideas have a more enduring effect?

Select a Solution After assigning weights and values to the various solutions you have thought about, select the one you like best and prepare to defend it. Show why the ideas you have thought about are superior and how they will work. If you have rejected other, more obvi-ous ideas, you may want to explain why.

Decide How to Implement the Best Solution Having good ideas is insufficient. You must be able to put them to work. Graduate students of business are often praised by executives for being theoretically well-grounded, but criticized for lacking practical application. "A team of young MBAs told me that we needed to sell this division of my com-pany," said an executive in the chemical indus-try. "But they couldn't tell me what to do or how to go about it. All they knew was that we should try to find a buyer. Interesting," he con-cluded, "but not very helpful."

Explain How to Communicate the Solution In a management communication case study, you will be asked to identify key audi-ences for your message. That means identifying which groups you want to communicate with and the means you will use to reach them. Think carefully about the broad range of stakeholders in the case: employees, customers, shareholders, business partners, suppliers, regulators, and the marketplace at large. Identify exactly how you would plan to transmit your message, assure that it has been received and understood, and how you would analyze feedback from those audi-ences. You should think, as well, about timing and sequencing of messages. Who should you speak with first? Who should send the message? How should this particular audience hear about this particular message?

Write It Up   Different professors will have different expectations about what they want from you in a written case solution. They will probably not provide you with specific, detailed instructions regarding their expectations, but they will certainly tell you if you've missed the boat or have produced a solid response. Some will ask for wide-ranging responses that cover many issues, while others will expect a more focused response. Just provide your professor with your best thinking and be as detailed as you think you can within the page limits you have been given.

WHAT YOU SHOULD EXPECT

If you have read the case thoroughly, identified the business problems, rank-ordered the critical issues, proposed various solutions, and then identified how you will implement and communicate them, you can expect to be more-or-less as well prepared for classroom case discussion as your classmates. Here's what else you should expect.

- *An occasional cold call.* Be prepared for your professor to ask you to provide key details from the case, sometimes referred to as a *shred*. Simply explain what happened in the case, identifying the business and its principals, and give your best thinking on critical issues in two minutes or less. Don't worry about providing a solution just yet. Your professor is likely to want a more thorough discussion of the issues first. If you are feeling especially confident, you may wish to volunteer.
- *A logical, step-by-step approach.* If classmates offer information that is useful but not relevant or in line with the question the professor asks, expect the discussion to return to the issues the professor thinks are most important before you move on.
- *Different approaches from different professors.* No two professors are exactly the same in their approach or preferences. Virtually all of them, however, appreciate a

bold, "do something" approach over hedging, caution, and a reluctance to act.

WHAT YOU SHOULD NOT EXPECT

- *More information.* From time-to-time, your professor will present you with a "B" case that offers new or subsequent information. Such cases represent an extension of the facts in the "A" case and usually provide another managerial decision opportunity. For the most part, though, the information given in the "A" case is all you will have and you must make do with that.
- *A "right answer."* Because case studies are most often based on real events, no one can say for certain what would have happened if your ideas or other "better" ideas had been implemented. Some solutions are clearly better than others, but many ideas will work. Some of the very best ideas may not yet have been thought of or spoken aloud.
- *An explanation of what "actually happened."* Many professors either don't know what happened to the managers and the businesses described in your case studies, or they don't think that your having that information will be useful or productive in the learning process. Your own thinking may be limited or skewed if you focus on actual outcomes.
- *A single discipline focus to each case.* While some cases are principally about accounting, they may contain issues related to finance, operations management, human resources, or communication. Authentic business problems are rarely, if ever, unidimensional. The more you are willing to think about other dimensions of business and their interdependency, the more you will learn about how real businesses work.
- *That your response will solve all of the problems in the case.* Focus on the most important, most urgent, and most relevant problems first. You may wish to identify issues for further thought or investigation by the management team described in the case, but you cannot and should not try to solve all the problems in the case.

In summary, your task is to read, identify, and understand the business problems in the case. By identifying, rank ordering, and exploring the critical issues it contains, you should be able to propose a workable solution, identifying how to implement and communicate it. From that point forward, you must explain your choices in writing and be ready to defend them in the classroom.

For Further Reading

Barnes, L. B., C. R. Christensen, and A. J. Hansen. *Teaching and the Case Method,* 3rd ed. Boston, MA: Harvard Business School Press, 1994.

Bouton, C. and R. Garth, (eds.). *Learning in Groups.* San Francisco, CA: Jossey-Bass, 1983.

Corey, R. "The Use of Cases in Management Education." Harvard Business School Case No. 376-240.

Erskine, J., M. R. Leenders, and L. A. Mauffette-Leenders. *Teaching with Cases.* London, Ontario: School of Business, University of Western Ontario, 1981.

Gragg, C. J. "Because Wisdom Can't Be Told." *The Case Method at the Harvard Business School.* New York, NY: McGraw-Hill, 1954, p. 6.

McNair, M. P. "The Genesis of the Case Method in Business Administration." *The Case Method at the Harvard Business School.* New York, NY: McGraw-Hill, 1954, pp. 25–33.

Penrose, J. M., R. W. Raspberry, and R. J. Myers. "Analyzing and Writing a Case Report," in *Advanced Business Communication,* 3rd ed. Cincinnati, OH: South-Western College Publishing, 1997.

Wasserman, S. *Put Some Thinking in Your Classroom.* Chicago, IL: Benefic Press, 1978.

SAMPLE BUSINESS LETTER

B I G D O G S O F T W A R E
Innovative Applications • *Enterprise Software* • *Business Control Systems*

August 1, 2001

Mr. Ryan P. McCarthy
786 Elliott Street
Seattle, WA 91277-3022

Dear Mr. McCarthy:

This is an example of the Full Block Letter style, one of the most popular styles in business use today. The primary reason the Full Block style is so popular is its clean, efficient look. Typists favor this style, too, because it's easy to prepare and simple to compose.

Each element in this letter style begins at the left-hand margin. That includes the date, the inside address, the salutation, each body paragraph, the complimentary close, and the signature block. There is no need to use additional keystrokes to center the date or to move the complimentary close and signature block to the other side of the page.

Please note that this letter style uses full punctuation, including the colon following the salutation, and the comma following the complimentary close. The open, or ragged, right-hand margin gives the letter a slightly informal appearance, yet requires no additional work on the typist's part.

This is the most common variation of business letter format in use today. Some writers prefer other styles, especially if the letter extends beyond one page, because it's easy to tell where a paragraph begins if it's indented. In the Full Block Letter style, none of the paragraphs is indented. The letter is composed with a single space between lines within each paragraph, and two spaces between paragraphs.

The vast majority of business correspondence in North America features the one-page letter. There are two reasons for this: first, most business letters are focused on just one subject, and most writers can say what they must in three or four paragraphs. Second, the Full Block Letter style doesn't waste style with indented paragraphs.

P.O. Box 1743 • LaJolla, California 92037 • 858-555-4321
www.bigdogsoftware.com

Mr. Ryan P. McCarthy
August 1, 2001
Page 2

There is another reason for the popularity of the one-page letter, and it's cultural. Most North American business writers come directly to the point in the first—or at the very least—second paragraph. While European, Asian, and Latin American business writers will spend more time developing personal relationships, inquiring about the health and well-being of the readers, most U.S. and Canadian writers prefer to put their main point up front and say what they mean, using fewer words.

If you choose to write a multipage letter, the Full Block Letter style can easily accommodate that. You must simply be sure to enter a page heading in the upper left-hand corner of each succeeding page. That page heading should contain the name of the letter recipient, the page number, and the date of the letter.

Remember, if you write a two-page letter, the second page must contain at least two lines of text. Most writers prefer to include at least a full paragraph. The final paragraph of the letter is followed by a complimentary close, a signature block, and—if circumstances require—a copy line or an enclosure line, indicating either that others have received a copy of the letter or that the envelope contains other documents.

Sincerely,

Mallala Fadul
General Manager

Enclosures

cc: Doug Hemphill

APPENDIX C

SAMPLE BUSINESS MEMO

THE EUGENE D. FANNING CENTER

DATE: August 16, 2001

TO: Management Communication Students

FROM: J.S. O'Rourke (234 College of Business / 555-8397)
            Director, Fanning Center for Business Communication

SUBJECT: Customary Memo Formats

FACTS. A number of different memo formats are available to the business writer. In general, though, most memos are characterized by three qualities in particular.

    1. *Brief.* Most memos are just one or two pages in length. Occasionally, a writer may need to include information that would create a three-page (or longer) memo. Extensive, detailed data should be displayed in appendices or attachments.
    2. *Direct.* Most memos specify exactly who should receive the information and are narrow, specific, and to the point. In addition, most memos are concerned with just one subject: the issue described in the "subject" line.
    3. *Informal.* Most memos use spoken language, including contractions, personal pronouns, and easy-to-understand words and phrases to reach the reader. They are, on the whole, considerably less formal than most business letters.

DISCUSSION. After presenting the basic facts, most memo writers discuss their implications for the reader. You must not only tell the reader what he or she needs to know, but tell them what it means and why it matters. The discussion section explains the meaning, implications, and circumstances that may affect a manager's decision.

RECOMMENDATION. Finally, after the reader has all of the facts (and, perhaps, a few of your assumptions), and after you have discussed the importance or relevance of what you know, you should present your proposed recommendations.

    1. Put your most important or most immediate recommendation first. Say in very specific terms what you want to do, how you want to do it, and when it should happen.
    2. Put your next most important recommendation here. On occasion, you may wish to include obvious possibilities for action that you have chosen *not* to recommend, and then—very briefly— explain why you have rejected them.
    3. Most memos don't have more than three recommendations. A longer recommendation section is fine, as long as it tells the reader what he or she needs to know (or do). Don't raise more questions than you answer. Keep the issue simple, lead with verbs, and use the memo format to document action, solve problems, and implement decisions.

COMMUNICATION STRATEGY MEMO

THE EUGENE D. FANNING CENTER
University of Notre Dame • College of Business

DATE: February 1, 2000

ACTION: Management Communication Students

INFO: Interested People with a Need to Know but No Responsibility for Action

FROM: J.S. O'Rourke (234 College of Business; Phone 555-8397)
Fanning Center for Business Communication

SUBJECT: **COMMUNICATION STRATEGY MEMO: FORMAT AND CONTENTS**

This memo format recommends a communication plan in response to a specific event or circumstance facing a company or organization. It will briefly summarize the details of the event/circumstance; discuss their implications, importance, or probable outcome; and provide a specific list of actions taken and actions recommended.

BACKGROUND

In this portion of the memo, the writer briefly but completely reviews the *facts* of the case. This paragraph will contain historical data, information that is a matter of public record, and facts that are relevant to the recommended communication strategy.

- Crisp, tightly expressed sentences set apart from the main paragraph by bullet points are often useful in highlighting factual information.
- This paragraph *does not* include assumptions, suppositions, or speculative information. Nor does it include gratuitous references in the first personal singular, such as "I think . . . ," "In my opinion . . . ," or "I feel . . ."
- If a specific source is available for each piece of information in this paragraph, the writer should consider embedding it directly in a sentence, that is, "1990 Census figures reveal that . . ." Another approach is to list a source in parentheses following the information you provide, that is, "Mead Corporation's Stevenson, Alabama, mill has an annual production capacity of 400,000 tons of corrugated containerboard. (Source: *Mead Financial Fact Book,* Mead Corp., 1999, p. 5).

DISCUSSION

In this portion of the memo, the writer expands on the implications of the facts cited above. This is where the writer explains to the reader what those facts mean and why they matter. The discussion paragraph often becomes the basis for the recommendations that follow. If the discussion is extended or complex, writers often use separate paragraphs, subheadings, and bullet-points to highlight various issues.

COMMUNICATION STRATEGY MEMO: FORMAT AND CONTENTS
February 1, 2000
Page 2 of 2

RECOMMENDATIONS

In this paragraph, the writer lays out each recommendation in specific terms. Where possible, recommendations lead with a verb, are separated from one another with white space, are underlined or printed in boldface type for emphasis, and are either numbered (if the writer recommends more than three actions) or bullet-pointed. For example:

1. **Sign the attached letter of apology to the customer.** The letter not only apologizes for the flaw discovered in our shipment of July 1st, but offers a 2% discount on the shipment and a full replacement of all defective parts. (Action: President)

2. **Forward the defective parts to Quality Control for examination.** When the QC report is complete, copies of their findings should be shared with Sales & Marketing, Customer Service, and members of the Senior Management Team. (Action: Customer Service)

3. **Contact the retailer who sold the equipment to review return/refund procedures.** We must make certain that each retailer handling our products fully understands his/her obligation to accept customer returns and to provide full refunds, if appropriate. (Action: Sales Manager)

4. **Follow-up with the customer to make sure he is satisfied with our actions on his behalf.** This is a particularly large account and, while each customer is important to this company, some customers are more important than others. Direct, personal contact to ensure customer satisfaction, followed by an after-action report for company files is essential. (Action: Customer Service)

OTHER ISSUES

On occasion, the paragraph above will be labeled "Actions Recommended" and would be preceded by a paragraph labeled "Actions Taken." The difference is a matter of authority in the organization. The memo writer clearly has authority to take certain actions on his or her own and to *backbrief* the supervisor or manager by means of this memo. That same writer might propose actions for his superiors or for other divisions/agencies in the company that the reader is asked to agree to. It's always useful for the reader to know what tasks have already been done, and what tasks he or she is being asked to approve.

Most memoranda *do not* include a signature block, nor do they feature salutation lines ("Dear . . .") or complimentary closing lines ("Sincerely yours,"). Rather than a full signature, most memos will include the initials of the writer next to the "**FROM:**" line above.

Please note that this two-page memo requires a "second page header" which includes the subject line (exactly as written on page one), a date line, and a page number.

To conclude, most memos will feature some distinctive typographical mark just beneath the last line of type. Some authors will use their initials, other will simply use the pound sign or other mark of their choice.

# # #

APPENDIX E

PREPARING FOR A TELEVISION
INTERVIEW

INTRODUCTION

During the course of your career in business, it will be virtually impossible for you to avoid meeting and dealing with the news media. Inevitably, the media will want access to you as a functional expert when you are least prepared and willing to deal with them—often during a crisis of some sort.

While they are not a surrogate for dealing with the public directly, and while their influence on public opinion formation is indirect and somewhat limited, the news media can provide a useful service and valuable opportunity to reach large numbers of people with a carefully prepared message. Those people who have been most successful in dealing with the news media have discovered that such encounters require careful preparation and some understanding of how media representatives operate.

DISCUSSION

Have you ever done a media interview before? How did it go? What was your impression of the reporter? Did you have an opportunity to see the broadcast or read the interview after it was completed? Did the reporter treat you fairly in the interview and in the story to which it contributed?

A separate series of questions concerns the news media in general. What's your impression of the media? Of reporters in general? Do you think it's a good idea to cooperate when reporters or editors ask for your reaction to something?

Regardless of your initial experience, are you ready to do it again?

In general, most businesses and profit-making organizations have taken a very positive stance regarding press interviews and public appearances by company officials, particularly those in positions of senior responsibility. Most not-for-profit institutions have a policy that requires that you work with and through your public relations office to arrange and prepare for such interviews, but contact with reporters is not limited, by any means, simply to the public relations office. In fact, most news organizations would rather speak with a "newsmaker" or responsible official than an "official spokesperson."

If you are asked to do an interview, look on it as a positive experience, an opportunity to tell your company's story, a chance to get your point-of-view across to the public. It is, at the very least, an

2

inexpensive means of communicating your message to a very large audience. It's an opportunity to show the flag and to talk about your agenda—regardless of why the interview was called for—with the public at large.

If you agree to an interview, though, remember that it's not without risk. You can fail—it's not common, but it can happen if you're unprepared for the occasion. Preparing yourself is not difficult if you keep a few basic suggestions in mind.

ONE WEEK BEFORE THE INTERVIEW

Several things you may wish to consider at least a week before you're to be interviewed:

• Consult with your public relations director on his or her plan for the interview. When and where will it take place? What's the subject? Will we plan to limit the questions to a particular subject or will the reporter want to talk about many subjects? Remember, it's best to focus or limit the interview and prepare yourself well to answer a narrow range of questions than it is to let a reporter "go fishing." If your business does not have a public relations officer, prepare yourself by speaking with a knowledgeable, senior colleague whom you trust. Think about the questions you're most like to be asked, and think about those you would most like to answer. Think, as well, about those you really hope you don't have to answer. After a thorough review session with a trusted colleague, if you still aren't confident, consider asking a professional media relations consultant for help. The time and money spent on such help will pay huge dividends down the road—in protecting your company's reputation, share price, market share, and public image.

• Read some of the reporter's work, or watch a videotaped copy of the show you're to appear on. Get some idea of how the interviewer or reporter works, what his style may be, how she works.

• Begin to assemble information for and to define your agenda. What's on your mind? What's your message? What three or four key issues do you want to talk about? Get the most current facts and figures together and focus your mind on how best to package that information. Practice expressing your point of view in 15- to 20-second segments that could stand alone if they were edited out of a longer interview. Say your message aloud until you are thoroughly familiar with the words, numbers, and phrases you will use. Practice until you are confident, self-assured, and professional in your approach to the subject.

• Prepare a pocket or purse card. Be sure to include the time, place of the interview, name of the interviewer, and his or her media outlet. Include other key details, as well, such as how you will get there, who will accompany you, phone numbers, and names. On the other side, write down your three or four key points, along with supporting detail, numbers, or facts you want to talk about.

ONE DAY BEFORE THE INTERVIEW

The day before you do the interview, check on a few final details.

• Have your public relations director confirm the time and place of the interview with the reporter or host. Who will you follow on the show? Who else is being interviewed? Who will ask the questions? You don't need any surprises at this point.

3

- Check your card to make sure it's complete and accurate and fully reflects your position on the issues to be discussed. Make sure that position also reflects institutional policy and current administration views. Remember, you represent not only the university, but its employees, students, and alumni, as well.

- Check on transportation, parking, and other elements in your schedule for tomorrow. How will you get there? Where will you park? How long will it take to get there? Will traffic or weather be a problem?

- Make sure your clothing is among the best you own. Dress conservatively so that your attire doesn't detract from your message. Consider getting a haircut.

THE DAY OF THE INTERVIEW

On the day you are to be interviewed, you'll have a few, final details to attend to.

- Watch the news that morning; read the papers. Check the local news and have a look at the morning's latest stories. Is there anything late-breaking that could serve as a springboard for a reporter's question? Even though the issues in the morning's news may be well beyond your expertise or influence, they could still become part of a reporter's question. Prepare yourself to respond.

- If the interview is scheduled for late afternoon or later in the day, men may want to shave again, particularly if you have a heavier beard. Check your shirt, suit coat, and shoes. You want to make the best impression possible.

- Plan to arrive early. Give yourself a few minutes to calm down, examine your surroundings, and review your notes before you go on the air.

- Unbutton your suit jacket if it's a sit-down interview. To remove wrinkles and "collar creep," pull the jacket down from the rear. Button your jacket if it's a stand-up interview.

- Men: Wear over-the-calf socks. Choose complementary colors and plain patterns. Women: wear plain, unpatterned hosiery. Keep jewelry simple. Those diamonds may look terrific at a dinner party, but on television, they'll catch the light and distract the audience.

- Wear your glasses if you need them to see. They will make you more comfortable and, often, people will develop facial marks if they wear glasses all the time. You don't want those to show.

- Don't wear sunglasses, either indoors or outdoors if at all possible, or tinted photochromatic lenses while you are on camera. Studio lights will turn those lenses very dark, and you don't want to hide your eyes from the audience.

- Men: Don't wear vests, wide stripes, or checks. Solid colors, pinstripes, or narrow chalkstripes are best.

- Women: Don't wear extremely light or exceptionally dark dresses. Extremely short skirts can be difficult during a sit-down interview, as well.

4

BEFORE YOU GO ON CAMERA

As you arrive at the studio, there are a few things to think about.

• Look at the studio and set. Observe the cameras, mikes, lighting equipment, and positions of the crew members. Talk with crew members if you have the opportunity—it will make you seem more human to them, and it will dispel any nervousness you may be experiencing.

• Men: If they offer make-up, swallow your pride and take it. You will look better on camera, and it's easy to remove once you're done. Women: Don't do anything different or unusual about your make-up. If it's suitable for a business meeting, it's suitable for television.

• Check out the position of the studio floor monitor, then ignore it while you're on the air. Focus only on your host.

• Introduce yourself to people. The act of reaching out to someone, psychologically, will help you to feel friendly, generous, and relaxed.

• Tell the program staff if you have a genuine physical reason for preferring one profile or side (for example, a hearing disability).

• Sit on the front of the chair, turning your body 45 degrees to the camera lens, facing the interviewer. Hands on your knees or in your lap; don't slouch and sit up straight.

• Gestures are constructive communication. Hold your hands lightly, loosely on your legs so they're free to gesture when you need to. Gestures will also help dispel nervous energy.

• Plan to look at the person conducting the interview about 90 percent of the time. Look away infrequently, only to focus your thoughts as necessary. Try as best you can to maintain eye contact to heighten sincerity.

• About 7 percent of the meaning in our statements comes through in our words; some 38 percent is delivered in our voice and vocal quality, while about 55 percent of our total meaning is communicated in other, purely nonverbal ways, including muscle tone, facial expression, body posture, body movement, and hand gestures. Some of this happens at the conscious level, but much of it goes on with little or no awareness on our part. Your goal is to project a relaxed, confident, professional image. People will listen to what you say, but they will take their measure of you by watching how you behave.

• Try to remember that your audience will remember less of what you say than they will of the way in which you've said it. How your message is packaged and delivered is important. That's unfortunate, but it's true—they'll come away with few facts from a television interview, but many impressions and images.

• Use the audio-level check, or "mike check" to identify yourself and make a positive point about your organization or your cause.

• Don't ever say anything into or near a microphone that you wouldn't want broadcast to the rest of the world. Assume that all cameras are on and all microphones are live. Remember, you're always on the record and if you say or do something dumb, they will save the tape.

5

GETTING YOUR CONVICTIONS ACROSS

• Your presentation must contain not only your thoughts, but your feelings. Your emotions, energy, and enthusiasm will account for much of your success in this interview—stress the affective more than the cognitive.

• You need to get your points across through your voice, your gestures, proxemics and body motion, as well as your words. Those words won't stand alone; they're accompanied by facial expressions, vocal tone, and a host of other nonverbal mannerisms.

The Kinds of Questions You Are Likely to Face

In most interviews, you will find a number of different question types. Your success in handling those questions depends, in part, on your being able to identify what sort of question is being asked.

• *Focus Questions.* Those that give you an opportunity to expand on a point by going into further detail or by giving an illustration.

• *Avoidance Questions.* Those that you would just as soon not have to answer, probably because they put you or your school in a bad light. Acknowledge the question by repeating the key part in a positive way and then bridge to the point you want to make.

• *Control Questions.* Those that seem relatively simple, but which you would like to pass back to the interviewer. You should respond to these questions by making a positive point about the thrust of the question, not by dealing with the question itself. You may even consider restating the question in a way you'd like to have it asked.

• *Factual Questions.* Those that seem very direct or straight-forward. They ask for factual data. Don't stop with the facts or the numbers, though. Show how they are related to a positive point you want to make.

• *Hypothetical Questions.* Those that require you to speculate about the future or provide a response to a set of assumptions that may never prove to be true. Don't be drawn into speculation, assumptions, or guessing. Deflect a hypothetical question by answering one you wish the interviewer had asked.

• *Forced Choice Questions.* Those that require you to adopt either of two unacceptable viewpoints put forward by the interviewer. Don't be drawn into accepting a reporter's terminology, choices, analyses, or alternatives. Use your own words and avoid the trap of selecting one or another of the extremes presented in a question. Most issues are rarely black and white, this choice or that; most issues are sufficiently complex to have several points of view.

• *False Facts or False Assumption Questions.* Those that begin with an error in fact by the reporter or host, leading to a mistaken impression in the audience. Set the record straight directly and politely, but don't ever let a mistaken or erroneous statement of any significance go unchallenged in the course of answering a question.

• *Leading or Loaded Questions.* Those that are clearly headed in the direction of a predetermined conclusion on the part of the questioner. Don't be led down the garden path by a reporter who is looking for evidence to support a conclusion he or she has already reached; take control of the interview by raising the more important issue or by refocusing the discussion on the one point you think the audience most needs to understand.

6

MAINTAINING CONTROL OF THE INTERVIEW

A few simple techniques will help you to control the interview, rather than the reporter or host. If you're in control, you get to focus on your agenda, say what you want, and put your point of view forward. If you don't maintain control, the reporter or host takes the interview in whatever direction he or she wants, and it's a lost opportunity for you, your company, and your people.

* *Gaining Time to Think.* You can create a few moments of thinking or organizing time for yourself by asking the reporter to repeat the question or by asking for the question to be restated in another way. Don't overuse this technique, but once or twice in a long interview, it may buy you some time.

* *Set the Pace Yourself.* Don't let a reporter rush or badger you by picking up the pace of the interview. Just because a questioner jumps in at the end of a response with another question or interrupts you is no reason to change your pacing, timing, or frame of mind. Stay cool, slow down, and stay in charge.

* *Bridging.* If you're faced with a tough question that you simply can't duck, go ahead and acknowledge it. After acknowledging the factual aspect of what's been asked, bridge to a point you want to make.

* *Flagging.* In a long interview that may be subject to editing, you can help yourself, the interviewer, and the editor by identifying the key points, the one thing to remember, the principal issue at hand.

* *Hooking.* You can draw the interviewer into asking a question that might not otherwise have occurred to him or her by addressing an issue at the end of a response to another question that leaves the area open for questioning.

* *Stay Positive.* Don't repeat negative words or phrases. Don't let the reporter put words in your mouth; don't use any emotionally loaded words or phrases just because that's the way the interviewer chose to describe things.

* *Don't Say More than You Intend.* Once you have answered a reporter or talk-show host's question fully and accurately, once you have said all you need to say on a given subject, it's perfectly alright to remain silent. After all, it is not your responsibility to "feed the microphone"—it is the host or reporter's responsibility. If the adrenaline rush produced by standing or sitting before the camera and microphone leads you to talk more than you usually might, protect yourself by preparing and offering responses that are complete, accurate, and thoughtful, but which don't lead you to continuous, nonstop talking. Don't ramble on and say things you might later wish you hadn't.

OTHER THINGS TO KEEP IN MIND

* *Know your interviewer and your audience.* Who are you talking to? Who is watching, listening, or tuning in?

* *Tell the truth.* Answer honestly. If you don't know the answer, say so, but don't ever say "no comment." That simply sounds like you are guilty and are afraid to talk about it.

- ***Avoid an argument.*** You can't win when you grow antagonistic with a professional journalist or talk-show host. They've been doing this sort of thing much longer than you have.

- ***Protect the record.*** You are *never* off the record.

- ***Use your experience, ethos, authority, and expertise.*** You, after all, are the one they want to see, hear, and talk to.

IN CONCLUSION

An interview with a reporter or talk-show host can be a win-win situation for you both: he or she gets an interview, fills airtime or column inches, and you get an opportunity to get your agenda or point of view across. You must prepare yourself, though, stay confident, and maintain control. If you do, your company, coworkers, shareholders, and customers will be better for it.

APPENDIX F

SAMPLE PRESS RELEASE

NEWS RELEASE   *RELEASE # 2001-03*

CONTACT: Prof. J.S. O'Rourke
             Phone: 219/555-8397
             Fax: 219/555-5255
             E-mail: James.S.ORourke.2@nd.edu

FOR IMMEDIATE RELEASE

FORMAT SUGGESTIONS FOR PREPARING A NEWS RELEASE

NOTRE DAME, INDIANA (July 25, 2001)—This is a sample of what a typical press release might look like. According to Scott M. Cutlip and Allen H. Center, authors of *Effective Public Relations,* 6th edition, news releases should be typed, printed, or reproduced cleanly on standard 8-1/2″ by 11″ paper and transmitted or mailed to all media whose audiences would have an interest in the subject matter. As press and airtime deadlines approach, it is often a good practice to hand-deliver releases to local media outlets.

IDENTIFICATION: The name, address, and telephone number of the source should appear at the upper left. The release should also include the name and number of the person to contact for more information.

RELEASE DATE: Most releases should be *immediate.* Stipulate a HOLD FOR RELEASE time and date only when circumstances warrant holding until a certain hour.

MARGINS: Use wide margins. Double space copy for print media, triple space copy for broadcasters.

HEADLINES: Many news/press releases do not indicate a heading; others, such as this one, include a brief, descriptive headline. If you choose not to include a headline, leave two inches between the release line and the body of copy so the editor or rewrite desk can insert one that they compose.

LENGTH: Never make a release two pages if one will do. Edit your material tightly. Make certain it's accurate, timely, free of puffery. Don't split a paragraph from first to second page. Put the word *more* at the bottom of the first page to indicate that another page follows.

SLUGLINE: Journalists include a traditional "slugline" at the upper left of a second page, much as you might in a memorandum.

STYLE: Use a summary lead (who, what, when, where, why) most of the time. Double space. Editors prefer short, punchy sentences with active verbs. Make sure spelling and grammar are 100 percent correct.

CHECK: Never trust your typist or keyboard operator. Proofread every original. Get the highest-level supervisor or manager you can to initial a file copy of each release. Don't hesitate to check your copy with your sources.

FOOTER: Conclude your release with the mark "30" at the foot of the last page.

INDEX